The Business of Culture

Strategic Perspectives on Entertainment and Media

Edited by

Joseph Lampel
City University, London

Jamal Shamsie
Michigan State University

Theresa K. Lant
New York University

LEA
LAWRENCE ERLBAUM ASSOCIATES, PUBLISHERS
2006 Mahwah, New Jersey London

Lawrence Erlbaum Associates, Inc., Publishers
10 Industrial Avenue
Mahwah, New Jersey 07430
www.erlbaum.com

Cover design by Kathryn Houghtaling Lacey

Library of Congress Cataloging-in-Publication Data

The business of culture : strategic perspectives on entertainment and media / edited by Joseph Lampel, Jamal Shamsie, Theresa K. Lant.
p. cm.
Includes bibliographical references and index.
ISBN 0-8058-5105-4 (cloth : alk. paper)
ISBN 0-8058-5582-3 (pbk. : alk. Paper)
1. Culture—Economic Aspects—Congresses. 2. Cultural industries—Congresses. 3. Popular culture–Economic aspects—Congresses. 4. Industries—Social aspects—Congresses. I. Lampel, Joseph. II. Shamsie, Jamal. III. Lant, Theresa K.

HM621.B85 2005
306.4'8—dc22 2004063591

Books published by Lawrence Erlbaum Associates are printed on acid-free paper, and their bindings are chosen for strength and durability.

Printed in the United States of America
10 9 8 7 6 5 4 3 2 1

Contents

Foreword — ix
Arthur P. Brief and James P. Walsh

Preface — xiii

Introduction — 1

1 **Toward a Deeper Understanding of Cultural Industries** — 3
Joseph Lampel, Jamal Shamsie, and Theresa K. Lant

2 **Observations on Research on Cultural Industries** — 15
W. Richard Scott

Part I: The Process of Value Creation — 23

3 **Conflicts Over Creative Control: Power Struggle on Prime Time Television** — 27
Joann Keyton and faye l. smith

4 The Genius Behind the System: The Emergence of the Central Producer System in the Hollywood Motion Picture Industry 41
Joseph Lampel

5 Maestro or Manager? Examining the Role of the Music Director in a Symphony Orchestra 57
Mary Ann Glynn

Part II: The Challenge of Positioning 71

6 Game Not Over: Competitive Dynamics in the Video Game Industry 75
Melissa A. Schilling

7 Playing to Their Strengths: Strategies of Incumbent and Start-Up Firms in Web-Based Periodicals 105
Alan B. Eisner, Quintus R. Jett, and Helaine J. Korn

8 A Question of Timing: Strategies for Scheduling Television Shows 119
Jamal Shamsie, Danny Miller, and William Greene

Part III: The Nature of Markets 135

9 Charting the Music Business: *Billboard* Magazine and the Development of the Commercial Music Field 139
N. Anand

10 Are They Playing Our Song? Programming Strategies on Commercial Music Radio 155
Jarl A. Ahlkvist and Robert Faulkner

11 **Skating on Thin Ice: Confronting Knowledge Ambiguity in the U. S. Motion Picture Industry** 177
Jamal Shamsie

Part IV: The Role of Technology 191

12 **From Technology to Content: The Shift in Dominant Logic in the Early American Film Industry** 195
Candace Jones

13 **From 78s to MP3s: The Embedded Impact of Technology in the Market for Prerecorded Music** 205
Timothy Dowd

14 **Silicon Alley.com: Struggling for Legitimacy in New Media** 227
Theresa K. Lant and Patricia F. Hewlin

Part V: The Impact of Globalization 239

15 **Let the Children Play: Muppets in the Middle of the Middle East** 243
Joseph Lampel and Benson Honig

16 **Surviving in the Shadow of Hollywood: A Study of the Australian Film Industry** 263
Wendy L. Guild and Mary L. Joyce

17 **Uncertain Globalization: Evolutionary Scenarios for the Future Development of Cultural Industries** 275
Joseph Lampel and Jamal Shamsie

Conclusions 287

18 Untangling the Complexities of Cultural Industries: Directions for Future Research 289
Joseph Lampel, Jamal Shamsie, and Theresa K. Lant

19 Promising and Neglected Types of Studies on Cultural Industries 305
W. Richard Scott

Author Index 311

Subject Index 319

Foreword

Culture defines us. Although we inherit our culture from years past, we also recreate and create it everyday. A hallmark of contemporary life is that culture does more than define us—it sells. Fortunes are made and lost in the worlds of music, art, film, television, magazines, games, and more. This commingling of the sacred and secular poses all kinds of interesting questions for management scholars. Just what is value in this world? How do you create it? How do you beat your rivals and sell cultural products at a handsome profit? These business-oriented questions are really interesting. Their answers not only inform those working in these industries but also those who do other kinds of knowledge intensive work. And yet, we know that there is more to the story. Because culture is so essential to our identity as human beings, the question of limits naturally arises. Should we sell our culture? Are we ennobled or debased by the practice? Who are "we?" Seeking new markets, cultural products move across borders. Do we welcome or object to one culture selling its cultural products to another? These broader contextual questions are just as interesting as the other more business-centric questions.

Read this wonderful collection of work and enter this world. Lampel, Shamsie, Lant, and their colleagues wrap their minds around all of these kinds of questions. At the end of the day, you will come away with a set of wonderful insights about how cultural industries operate…and how they affect our lives. Our guess is that you may also come away intrigued by their questions as much as by their answers. This book is important not only for what it accomplishes but for what it calls us to accomplish. Much work remains to be done. Their work informs and inspires. That's an unbeatable combination! Enjoy.

—Arthur P. Brief
Tulane University
—James P. Walsh
University of Michigan

LEA'S ORGANIZATION AND MANAGEMENT SERIES

Series Editors

Arthur P. Brief

Tulane University

James P. Walsh

University of Michigan

Associate Series Editor

Sara L. Rynes

University of Iowa

Ashforth (Au.): *Role Transitions in Organizational Life: An Identity-Based Perspective*

Bartunek (Au): *Organizational and Educational Change: The Life and Role of a Change Agent Group*

Beach (Ed.): *Image Theory: Theoretical and Empirical Foundations*

Brett/Drasgow (Eds.): *The Psychology of Work: Theoretically Based Empirical Research*

Darley/Messick/Tyler (Eds.): *Social Influences on Ethical Behavior in Organizations*

Denison (Ed.): *Managing Organizational Change in Transition Economies*

Elsbach (Au): *Organizational Perception Management*

Earley/Gibson (Aus.): *Multinational Work Teams: A New Perspective*

Garud/Karnoe (Eds.): *Path Dependence and Creation*

Jacoby (Au.): *Employing Bureaucracy: Managers, Unions, and the Transformation of Work in the 20th Century, Revised Edition*

Kossek/Lambert (Eds.): *Work and Life Integration: Organizational, Cultural and Individual Perspectives*

Lampel/Shamsie/Lant (Eds.): *The Business of Culture: Strategic Perspectives on Entertainment and Media*

Lant/Shapira (Eds.): *Organizational Cognition: Computation and Interpretation*

Lord/Brown (Aus.): *Leadership Processes and Follower Self-Identity*

Margolis/Walsh (Aus.): *People and Profits? The Search Between a Company's Social and Financial Performance*

Messick/Kramer (Eds.): *The Psychology of Leadership: Some New Approaches*

Pearce (Au.): *Organization and Management in the Embrace of the Government*

Peterson/Mannix (Eds.): *Leading and Managing People in the Dynamic Organization*

Rafaeli/Pratt (Eds.): *Artifacts and Organizations: Beyond Mere Symbolism.*

Riggio/Murphy/Pirozzolo (Eds.): *Multiple Intelligences and Leadership*

Schneider/Smith (Eds.): *Personality and Organizations*

Thompson/Choi (Eds.): *Creativity and Innovation in Organizational Teams.*

Thompson/Levine/Messick (Eds.): *Shared Cognition in Organizations: The Management of Knowledge*

Preface

At the dawn of the digital age, Marshall McLuhan keenly described the transformation shaping the relationship between culture and business in the following words: "We are swiftly moving at present from an era when business was our culture into an era where culture will be our business." Propelled by the development of radio, records, films, and television, business gradually moved into the cultural arena, and then began to change culture from a local and small-time activity into industries with global reach.

New technology, combined with the expansion of leisure activity, created and established markets for cultural products. And, as in other areas in modern business, the entrepreneurs who brought to mass markets recorded music, motion pictures, and paperback books eventually ceded their place to large corporations run by professional managers who produced, packaged, distributed, and promoted cultural products the world over. These large enterprises did not initially seem to differ in methods and philosophy from their counterparts in the banking, fast food, or steel industries. But as they evolved and spread across the globe, their strategies and organizational methods could no longer be reconciled with traditional views of management.

The business of culture demanded and developed new methods and new thinking. It also called for systematic study and scholarly reflection by researchers who have both the knowledge of modern management and the sensitivity to the uniqueness of cultural products. This book has its origins in the conviction that management scholars must turn their attention to an intensive study and analysis of cultural industries. Such a conviction is founded in large part on the belief that these industries have become too important to be relegated to the periphery of management research. Furthermore, it is quite likely that the lessons that will be gained from the study of these industries will transform our understanding and practice of management in other industries as well.

The book that you hold in your hand represents the collective efforts by scholars committed to both propositions. The journey that produced this book began with a conference that was organized at the Stern School of Business of New York University in May 1997 by the editors of this book. At the time we were uncertain as to how many researchers and scholars were sufficiently interested to attend, let alone contribute original research. We were therefore amazed and gratified by the volume and quality of submissions and the enthusiasm of the participants. Whatever doubts we had about the appeal of the topic to scholars and researchers around the world were laid to rest. Almost half of the submissions came from outside the United States, most from various European countries, but some from as far afield as China.

As we geared up for the conference, Arie Lewin, the editor of *Organization Science,* gave us the go-ahead to develop a special issue on cultural industries, which eventually appeared in May 2000. The announcement attracted many outstanding submissions that could not be accommodated in a single issue. Given the abundance of work on cultural industries, we started to plan to follow up with a book. But we preferred to wait for a few years until we felt sufficiently confident that we had just the right mix of material for a collection that would do justice to the topic.

We made two resolutions along the way: first, that the book should cover as many cultural industries as possible, and as many perspectives as possible, and second, that the material should be original and intended for this book, rather than previously published. With these resolutions in mind we made use of the best material submitted to, but not published in, the special issue of *Organization Science.* We solicited pieces from scholars whose work we respected. And we kept an eye out for work in progress presented in conferences and workshops.

We hope that we lived up to our aspirations, but we will let the readers judge the results. The gamut of cultural industries that we cover is extensive, but by no means exhaustive. The book contains chapters on motion pictures, television, music, radio, video games, and multimedia. The perspectives that inform the discussion and analysis are as varied as our contributors, who come from business fields such as strategy, organization theory, and marketing as well as from the related fields of economics, sociology, and communication studies.

Although our primary objective was to pull together in one volume some of the best as well as the most current research on the management of cultural industries, as we noted earlier, we, the editors, had another objective. We believe that within these industries lie some of the most interesting examples of managing businesses under the increasingly high levels of uncertainty and ambiguity that confront businesses in the 21st century. This book will surely provide a variety of frameworks for researchers, practitioners, and students trying to gain a better understanding of firms and industries in the "culture" business, but at the same time it should also be useful to individuals who are not involved with industries that fall into this narrow definition. It is our belief that the dilemmas faced by cultural industries are becoming increasingly relevant to a broad cross-section of managers across a wide range of industry contexts.

We, as editors, also hope that this book will prove to be a useful primer on cultural industries for students and scholars who are engaging in the study and research of this area for the first time. We believe this book will serve to fill a void by offering much needed managerial and organizational perspectives of such industries.

We would like to conclude with an appreciation for the considerable help that we had along the way. We are grateful for the support that we received from New York University for the conference and to *Organization Science* for a special issue that led to the development of this book. We are especially indebted to the authors for the splendid effort they put into developing the articles that appear here.

We would also like to thank a few people who have helped us to pull together this book. To begin with, we appreciate the faith that Anne Duffy at Lawrence Erlbaum Associates placed in us and in our book. Next, we would like to thank Anne Downey at Michigan State University for her invaluable help in preparing the manuscript. Finally, we express our gratitude to Kristin Duch at Lawrence Erlbaum Associates for her administrative support.

—Joseph Lampel
—Jamal Shamsie
—Theresa K. Lant

Introduction

CHAPTER

1

Toward a Deeper Understanding of Cultural Industries

Joseph Lampel
City University, London

Jamal Shamsie
Michigan State University

Theresa K. Lant
New York University

In 1940, while German bombs were being dropped on London, an eccentric Oxford professor by the name of J. R. R. Tolkien was pouring his vivid imagination and his extensive knowledge of Celtic and Norse mythology into a series of novels that later came to be known as *The Lord of the Rings.* When it was first published in 1954, the work attracted mixed reviews and generated tepid sales. The books failed to receive much attention in spite of the decision by the BBC in 1956 to dramatize the novel in 12 parts.

However, demand for the series finally began to take off in 1965, when a pirated paperback edition made an appearance in the United States. The ensuing copyright dispute alerted the public to this unusual book, and the cultural climate of the

1960s did the rest. The book became massively popular, first as a cult classic, and then as a standard title in the literary collection of young people all over the world.

Years later, a director of animated films by the name of Ralph Bakshi adapted the first book of *The Lord of the Rings* for the screen. The movie was released in 1978, but it failed to generate much enthusiasm. Given the relatively moderate box office returns, Bakshi decided against making any films from the following two books in the trilogy. The failure of the animated version also deterred the movie studios from attempting any other feature-length adaptation of the book.

In time, a relatively new Australian director became interested in developing a series of films based on the three books. Peter Jackson worked hard to find a studio that would be willing to support the production, marketing, and distribution of these movies. With the support of New Line studio, Jackson shot the entire trilogy together, with plans to release the three different parts separately. Between 2001 and 2003, all three films based on the trilogy were released, raking in considerable commercial and critical success.

As has become typical with many films, a large amount of additional revenue was raised through the development, marketing, and distribution of many types of products tied to the film. Crowds flocked to purchase the captivating soundtrack of the movie, various forms of attractive merchandise, and some hot-selling computer games. There was also a considerable amount of renewed interest in the books, resulting in the introduction of Tolkien's legendary characters to a new generation of readers.

What began as a private work of imagination eventually led to a tidal wave of movies, music, toys, and games. What seemed at one point a modest publishing venture was gradually transformed into a lucrative franchise whose commercial potential encouraged movie directors, music composers, and video game developers, among others, to borrow and emulate themes from Tolkien's world. The words of Tolkien are likely to live on for a long time as they are reintroduced to the world in various forms.

The story, however, does not stop there. Shortly after J. R. R. Tolkien's master work reached the Soviet Union in the late 1980s, thousands of young people began to dress as hobbits and reenact scenes from the book. In most of the disintegrating Soviet Union these so-called "Tolkienists" were tolerated as harmless eccentrics. However, in the newly established central Asian republic of Kazakhstan they have attracted the hostility of the authorities, and are regularly arrested and thrown into jail for "bohemian" tendencies. "The police may not like it," protested one of the Tolkienists, "but we are not going to stop. It's our entire life."

The circuitous route that turned the fertile ideas of an Oxford philologist into a life-transforming experience for young people in central Asia serves to remind us of much that is unique about the world of entertainment and media: a world that management scholars have traditionally referred to as "cultural industries." In this world, an idea begins life in the heart and mind of an artist and then journeys through various translations and mutations into different media over time. The same idea is experienced by different people, over and over again, in different cultural and historic contexts. The idea's path through history is not orderly or predetermined. A seemingly chance confluence of events and individuals gives new life and new expression to a cultural product over time and in different contexts.

Although entertainment and media products inundate our lives, the business of culture can never be simply a business. Bjorkegren (1996), among others, emphasized that cultural products are as much about identity, imagination, and creativity as they are about sales, employment, and profits. It is a business that is as old as human society, and as new as the latest technology. It brings us intensely private experiences, and delivers collectively exhilarating events. It produces perishable commodities, and creates works that are truly immortal. It may be a business, but it is no ordinary business.

In many ways, the business of culture does not fit easily into our conventional perceptions of business. Automobiles, semiconductors, and banking may challenge our understanding, but they rarely push us to move beyond our established models or frameworks. The dizzying kaleidoscope of cultural industries, by contrast, seems to challenge the very models or frameworks that we have constructed to guide our thinking about business. How can we make sense of bureaucracies that make music, entrepreneurs that sell fun, and multinationals that merchandise dreams? Is the business of culture too different for business scholarship, or can we bring theories and tools that have been developed in other industries to bear on these industries as well? Does the examination of these industries inform our existing management theories?

For the most part, attempts to analyze and explain cultural industries have been stymied by unorthodox business and organizational practices. Individuals who work in the cultural industries are generally accustomed to these practices and thus take them for granted. Researchers, however, have tended to classify these practices as anomalies that fall outside current understanding of how industries normally function. This outlook, however, is changing. As innovation and creativity become increasingly central to competitive advantage, and as the entertainment and media sectors become too large to ignore, practices in the cultural industries are no longer seen as anomalies, but as the result of business conditions that confront many other industries at present.

The shift reflects an intellectual development that is often observed in other fields of research. As Kuhn (1970) perceptively observed, anomalies are often initially set aside as curiosities, then seen as interesting but unimportant, and finally, when researchers note not only their unique properties, but also their relevance to wider problems, they emerge as an important subject of study in their own right. This is indeed the story of cultural industries in recent times. Treated first as interesting but peripheral to our understanding of business, cultural industries are receiving increasing attention as the challenge they pose to conventional theories of management becomes too strong to ignore and too intriguing to set aside.

DEFINING CULTURAL INDUSTRIES

The first step in considering cultural studies as a proper subject for research and study is to provide a workable definition of what is meant by the term *cultural industries*. The simplest definition is denotative, consisting of examples of what most people would agree are part of the entertainment and media sector. In this respect, cultural industries constitute an important part of, but do not represent, entertainment and media in their entirety. When cultural industries are mentioned, most people would associate them with such areas of creative expression as movies, television, video games, music and theater. However, although a definition that relies on examples may be sufficient for informal discussion, it clearly falls short of what is needed for research. To move beyond the denotative, we need a definition that captures key general features of what is meant by cultural industries.

Defining cultural industries must begin with the recognition that the term brings together two domains: culture and industry. Culture is the product of ongoing symbolic human activity that is as old and as pervasive as human society itself. Culture is intrinsic to what makes us human. It is manifested in activities as simple as a mother's lullaby or as complex as a Kabuki play. Industry, by contrast, is a system of production, distribution, and marketing that delivers products to consumers. The system is created by specialist organizations and sustained by consumer demand. Bringing culture and industry together therefore gives rise to cultural industries: systems of production, distribution, and marketing that deliver symbolic products to consumers, where each cultural industry is made up of firms that specialize in the production, distribution, and marketing of specific cultural products, and is sustained by consumer demand for these products.

Definitions of cultural industries often emphasize the unique aspects of cultural goods that constitute the main outputs of these industries. Adorno (1991), who was the first to reflect systematically on the relationship between culture and commerce in the capitalist economy, defined culture industry as the complex economic and social processes that transform culture into marketable goods. For Hirsch (1972), the definition of cultural industries began with defining of cultural products as "non-material goods directed at a public of consumers for whom they generally serve as an aesthetic or expressive, rather than clearly utilitarian function" (p. 44).

The emphasis on cultural products as defining cultural industries was shared by Lawrence and Phillips (2002, p. 431), who also saw cultural goods as "products that are consumed in an act of interpretation rather than being used in some practical way to solve some practical problem," but they opened the definition further by arguing that cultural products are "goods and services that are valued for their 'meaning.'" Power (2002) saw cultural products as a good point of departure, but expanded Hirsch's (1972) definition even further. Power argued that cultural industries consist of "economic actors involved in the production of goods and services whose value is primarily or largely determined by virtue of their aesthetic, semiotic, sensory, or experiential content" (p. 106).]

The difficulty of defining cultural industries exclusively from the perspective of cultural products is that it promotes the perspective of the consumer over that of the producers who create new products, entrepreneurs who invest in them, and managers who oversee them. Although the subjective experience of consumers is of considerable importance for understanding cultural industries, the perspective that drives this book is that of the individuals and organizations that make up these industries, rather than the individuals and organizations that consume their products. This shift in perspective means that cultural industries are not only defined by the nature of cultural products, but also by the industry system in which they are produced and consumed. In this respect, Towse's (2003) definition of cultural industries provides a useful counterbalance to excessive reliance on the intrinsic nature of cultural products as the defining characteristic of cultural industries. As Towse put it:

> Cultural industries mass-produce goods and services with sufficient artistic content to be considered creative and culturally significant. The essential features are industrial-scale production combined with cultural content.... The possibility of mass production is due to the development of technologies—printing, sound recording, photography, film, video, internet, digitilization—and the growth of the cultural industries accordingly gathered force during the twentieth century. (p. 170)

To gain insight into how cultural industries operate as industry systems, it is useful to recapitulate what gives rise to cultural industries. Cultural industries emerge as the result of the industrialization of cultural activities that in the past were undertaken for expressive or communicative purpose without an explicit economic motive, or if undertaken for economic purpose took place in craft production, often at the behest of affluent patrons. The industrialization of cultural activity gave rise to the production of cultural goods with the intent of reaching a mass audience. This has a number of consequences that transform the processes of producing and consuming culture.

The rise of cultural industries goes hand in hand with the emergence of new technologies such as printing, sound recording, photography, film, video, and the Internet. These new technologies give advantage to economies of scale in production, distribution, and marketing. As in other sectors, this leads to large corporate entities whose main business is to create, market, and distribute cultural goods. It also produces new occupations and new skills, and ecology of large and small firms that specialize in creating content and assisting delivery. Cultural industries are in effect the complex interconnections of organizations, individuals, activities, and knowledge that make up industry systems. But as we argue later, these industry systems deserve to be studied in their own right, for what they reveal about cultural industries, and for what they reveal about industries in general.

RELEVANCE AND RATIONALE FOR STUDYING CULTURAL INDUSTRIES

The research and study of cultural industries falls into a middle ground between the analysis of individual cultural industries such as motion pictures, recorded music, or video games, and the broader study of all of them in general. The emergence of cultural industries as a complex of intertwined industries, which share many common characteristics and are joined by a web of collaboration and corporate ownership, create an object that is worthy of study for a number of reasons.

The first and most obvious reason is the impact of cultural industries on society (Bell, 1996; Wolf, 2003). Cultural industries do not simply represent a significant set of economic activities, they are also of enormous social importance. By design and accident, they exert an extraordinary influence on our values, our attitudes, and our lifestyles. Prior to the emergence of cultural industries these were largely driven by parental upbringing, communal contact, and religious congregation. Cultural industries do not supplant these institutions, but they have reduced their influence considerably.

Indeed, as far as most observers are concerned, cultural industries have taken the place of home and community as the dominant source of values and beliefs (Seabrook, 2000). This momentous shift has elicited fear and antagonism from many who distrust the economic and business imperatives that shape most cultural industries (Bryman, 2004). Prejudice and hostility, however, are a poor basis from which to explore the cultural industries. Research that yields deeper understanding of the practices and dilemmas that face the organizations in these industries would clearly be of substantial value to practitioners as well as to researchers.

The second reason for studying cultural industries, and one that flows directly from the first, is our intrinsic fascination with these industries. Cultural industries have long been the topic of intense public fascination, a fascination that has been nurtured and reinforced by extensive media coverage. There are surely many who reach for the remote control when news about cultural industries appears on their screen, but there are probably many more who willingly or unwillingly participate in the narratives and dramas of these industries (Lewis, 1992). These industries, far more than most others, are more amenable to narrative escape and dramatic enactment. Beyond the immediate engagement, however, the extensive media coverage of cultural industries is now an industry in its own right—it has its own specialist organizations, channels of distribution, and established practices (Hills, 2002).

At the heart of this industry is the cult of the celebrity (Ponce, 2002). This cult did not come into being with the emergence of cultural industries, but there is little doubt that it operates alongside and in conjunction with cultural industries (Schickel, 2000). That we know star performers and celebrated talent not only for what they do on the screen or on the stage, but also for how they live, is not unusual (Barbas, 2001). What is unusual is the degree to which the lives of celebrities contribute to the development and distribution of cultural products.

The third reason for studying cultural industries must surely reside in what other industries can learn from these industries. Many industries are struggling with the problem of integrating business and creative knowledge, a struggle that is central to the very nature of cultural industries (Brown & Duguid, 2001). Though cultural industries are diverse in many respects, they do have strong common features as far as each industry's value chain is concerned. An overview of the value chains in cultural industries reveals the following common features from upstream to downstream activities.

To begin with, cultural content is created through the application of knowledge and insight of how to embed ideas in a particular medium, be it film, television, books, magazines, or the Internet. Second, the content is distributed to consumers via different means such as broadcasting, cable, satellite, video, DVD, print, and the Internet. Distribution requires the knowledge to combine the creative resources with the technological resources. Third, a cultural product is experienced rather than consumed in the conventional sense of the term. Consumers interact with a cultural product and derive some meaning or entertainment from it (Avrich, 2002).

The integration of business and creative knowledge runs through value chains in cultural industries. This integration is also becoming crucial in industries as different as automobiles, computers, and apparel. The lessons of cultural industries are increasingly relevant as these industries recognize that competitive advantage depends on rapid integration of creative and business activities. The transfer of lessons from cultural industries to other industries, however, depends on attaining a better understanding of how this integration is achieved in cultural industries in the first place. Hence research on cultural industries ought to be of considerable interest to organizations that are engaged in breaking down the barriers that currently exist between business and creative thinking in their own industries.

Finally, the fourth reason for studying cultural industries emerges from a blurring of the boundaries between industries that are clearly in the business of culture, and industries that are not, and yet are increasingly incorporating features of cultural industries into their design, marketing, and distribution. Pine and Gilmore (1999) referred to this as the rise of the "experience economy." The essence of the experience economy is the increasing centrality of experience to consumption in almost every industry. In an experience economy, products are purchased not only for their utility, but also for the associated intangible experiences that emerge during consumption, a process that is enriched by the subjective involvement of the consumer with the product. In an interview, Pine cited an example to illustrate this new concept:

> An example of this [experience economy] is the Forum Shops in Las Vegas, where all of the stores are laid out on streets that look like an old Roman marketplace. Every hour there is a five- or 10-minute staged production—like a re-creation of the drowning of Atlantis or a parade of Roman centurion guards—to captivate the audience of

> shoppers. Despite the fact that five or 10 minutes of every hour are basically lost, with no shopping done, the Forum Shops earn by far the highest dollar amount per square foot, three or four times that of the typical mall. (Levinson, 1999, p. 72)

The blurring of boundaries is also leading to wholesale organizational experimentation in industries as far afield as automobiles. Almost all the major car companies, domestic as well as foreign, have design studios in California. Although the design studios are formally owned and funded by the car companies, they are managed separately, often by a charismatic designer-manager, in much the same way that the so called independents are run by the major Hollywood studios, or recording labels are set up by large music groups for highly imaginative record producers. The task of these studios is to promote original design thinking, and their organizational methods resemble more closely the practices of cultural industries than what one encounters in the traditional corporation.

Jerry Hirshberg, who pioneered the first California design studio on behalf of Nissan, described the approach practiced in his studio:

> Here we have thrown multiple disciplines into the same geographic and organizational pot and we deliberately fuzz the borders between them. And if an engineer says, "You know I think your design sucks. I think that's fat and stupid looking and inappropriate," in most places he'd be fired for that or at least reprimanded or at the very least ignored. Here none of that will occur. Here, it's expected, hoped for. We encourage the folks to find somebody who's not humming their tune and ask that person for their thoughts. Likewise, designers are expected to input into the engineering process. And to think about the planning process. And to think about marketing problems. And to think about sales issues. And as a result, I think, we still work with our intuitions but we're working with very richly informed intuitions. (Cato, 2000, p. 46)

If an industry as emblematic of the industrial age as automobiles adopts organizational methods and work practices that are current in cultural industries, than the promise of these approaches to the economy at large could indeed be considered to be significant. However, a proper appreciation of how to make the most of these practices calls for an understanding of how they emerge and operate in cultural industries as well as how they must be adapted to the constraints and conditions of other industries. This appreciation will no doubt come about from direct contact and internal analysis, but some will need the work of researchers who have a wide understanding of the organizational and strategic implications of how business and creative knowledge are integrated in different settings.

ORGANIZATION OF THE BOOK

The objective of this book is to pull together in one volume original research on cultural industries that reflect both the diversity of the spectrum of cultural industries, while at the same time exploring the thematic commonalities that are shared by all of these industries. With this in mind, the book is organized into five parts, each of which focuses on a key concept or issue surrounding cultural industries, with some degree of emphasis on both research and managerial perspectives. We have also made a serious effort to cover a relatively broad range of cultural industries in the examination of each of these concepts or issues.

Part I explores the process of creating value in cultural industries. Our use of the term *value* is intentionally vague. Value can mean several things in the context of cultural industries, depending on the metric one uses to measure value. The term can imply artistic or aesthetic value. It can imply commercial value. It can also refer to cultural, professional, political, moral, or ethical values. The search for value in cultural products creates numerous tensions and conflicts among those engaged in cultural production. The artistic value of a cultural product can vary depending on one's cultural, professional, or political perspective. Cultural products are often attempting to satisfy multiple definitions of value, such as being simultaneously culturally and commercially valuable. These tensions, which produce thorny managerial issues, and the means to balance them, are explored in this section.

Part II examines the varieties of strategies that organizations in cultural industries use to translate successful products into well-established positions. Developing and executing such strategies, however, confronts cultural industries with a number of dilemmas. To begin with, although successful products in the cultural industries are often the result of originality and fresh insight, using these successful products to build a powerful position relies on a process of duplication and replication. There is a contradiction here between the first and the second that bedevils organizations in cultural industries: The freshness and originality that is often necessary for creating hits and blockbusters runs contrary to the conservatism and formulaic thinking of repeating success.

Should organizations therefore focus their resources on a search for highly unconventional artists and ideas, or should they concentrate on making the most of the successful products that they chance to own? In addition to this difficult contradiction, organizations in cultural industries are also fully aware that there are no strategies that can reliably deliver highly successful products, and none that can ensure the replication of success. Notwithstanding these difficulties, organizations dedicate considerable efforts to building capabilities and developing strategies that can improve the odds on creating successful products and then repeating this success as often as possible. But to tackle this task effectively they must address the issue of risk: Should they stake their resources on a few highly risky projects, or spread their risks across many more less risky bets?

Part III turns its attention to how cultural industries make sense and understand their own markets. The struggle to make sense and understand why consumers prefer one product over another, or why products that have enjoyed enduring popularity fall out of favor, is not unique to cultural industries, but it is made singularly difficult in cultural industries by the complex relationship that exists between market demand and human psychology. The inherent ambiguity of the relationship between consumer motivation and observed behavior in cultural industries creates two fundamental challenges for managers. First, how can markets for cultural products be created and demand manipulated? Second, how should information about such markets be interpreted and used to guide action?

Collecting information is a first step to tackling this problem, but even more crucial is the ability to interpret the information. The chapters in this section explore the practices and institutions that collect and make sense of information, as well as the reasons why these practices and institutions are of limited value. These limits increase the value and power of experienced individuals with deep insight into consumer and market psychology in cultural industries. Because these individuals occupy strategic positions in these industries, their decision-making processes form an important theme in this section.

Part IV examines the role of technology in the evolution of cultural industries. Cultural industries owe their existence to a series of technical innovations such as electrical sound recording, motion picture photography, television broadcasting, and the Internet. These technologies opened new frontiers that grew into great industries. The expansion phase, however, was championed not by the technologically knowledgeable, but by creative and business talent.

Technology in creative industries has always been an enabler, rather than an end in itself. It is an enabler for the creation of content, but it is also a force that threatens the control and exploitation of content. The chapters in this section explore the duality of technology as an enabler and a threat. The duality poses questions that managers and creative talent continue to face today: What is the best use of a new technology? How should managers react to new technologies that potentially threaten their intellectual property rights? What should organizations do when new technologies shift the very foundations of their industry?

Part V examines the contentious subject of globalization in cultural industries. The process of globalization in cultural industries shares many of the characteristics of globalization generally: Organizations that build a national base use global communication and transportation systems to extend their reach across the world. But producers of cultural products encounter far more virulent opposition than manufacturers of shoes and automobiles. Culture is central to community and identity. Cultural goods may be bought and sold like any other goods, but their social and psychological impact transcends their economic significance.

Large organizations that produce and market cultural products exert a powerful influence on the lives of their customers. This influence may be positive insofar as it enriches people's lives by introducing them to the imagination and creativity of other lands, but it may be negative insofar as it challenges the values and received wisdom of long-established traditions. For this reason, the expansion of cultural industries is often feared and frequently resisted. And it is especially feared and resisted when the organizations that profit from cultural products are based in distant countries and thus are not accountable for their actions to the individuals or communities that consume their products.

sisted when the organizations that profit from cultural products are based in distant countries and thus are not accountable for their actions to the individuals or communities that consume their products.

The chapters in this section explore the contradictions and ambiguities of globalization in cultural industries. They highlight the positive as well as the negative aspects of globalization, and they raise questions about where cultural industries are headed in an era dominated by the forces of globalization. Will globalization give rise to a world dominated by large organizations or many small organizations? Will globalization produce much-feared homogenization of products and tastes, or will the mingling of cultures produce a profusion of ideas and experiences? And finally, does globalization in cultural industries bring people closer together and thus improve peaceful coexistence, or does it aggravate existing political and social tensions?

These questions, and the questions that are raised elsewhere in this book, have at best tentative answers. Any book on cultural industries is merely a snapshot in a rapidly evolving picture. A perceptive snapshot, however, often reveals enduring truths that lurk below the surface of a changing reality. The present book, however, is not a single snapshot, but a series of snapshots, each with its own perspective. On the whole these perspectives are complementary, and together they point to issues that we believe to be of enduring relevance to cultural industries. The organization of this book reflects our own sense of how these issues group together, but ultimately we hope that readers will make their own discovery of how the various aspects of cultural industries are connected.

REFERENCES

Adorno, T. W. (1991). *The culture industry: Selected essays on mass culture.* London: Routledge.

Avrich, B. (2002). *Selling the sizzle: The magic and logic of entertainment marketing.* Toronto: Maxworks.

Barbas, S. (2001). *Movie crazy : Fans, stars, and the cult of celebrity.* New York: Palgrave Macmillan.

Bell, D. (1996). *The cultural contradictions of capitalism.* New York: Harper Collins.

Bjorkegren, D. (1996). *The culture business.* London: Routledge.

Brown, J. S., & Duguid, P. (2001). Creativity versus structure: A useful tension. *Sloan Management Review, 42*(4), 93–94.

Bryman, A. (2004). *The Disneyization of society.* London: Sage.

Cato, J. (2000, July 14). Legendary designer who dismissed boundaries calls it quits: Hirshberg felt artistic freedom helps create better cars. *Edmonton Journal,* p. H6.

Hills, M. (2002). *Fan cultures.* London: Routledge.

Hirsch, P. (1972). Processing fads and fashions: An organization-set analysis of cultural industry system. *American Journal of Sociology, 77,* 639–659.

Kuhn, T. (1970). *The structure of scientific revolutions* (2nd ed.). Chicago: University of Chicago Press.

Levinson, M. (1999, November 15). Experienced required: An interview with Joseph B. Pine. *CIO Magazine, 13,* 70–73.
Pine, J. B., & Gilmore, J. H. (1999). *The experience economy.* Boston, MA: Harvard Business School Press.
Ponce, C. L. (2002). *Self-exposure: Human-interest journalism and the emergence of celebrity in America, 1890–1940.* Chapel Hill: University of North Carolina Press.
Power, D. (2002). Cultural industries in Sweden: An assessment of their place in the Swedish economy. *Economic Geography, 78,* 103–128.
Towse, R. M. (2003). Cultural industries. In R. M. Towse (Ed.), *A handbook of cultural economics* (pp. 170–176). Cheltenham, UK: Edward Elgar Publishing.
Schickel, R. (2000). *Intimate strangers.* Chicago: Dee.
Seabrook, J. (2000). *Nobrow: The culture of marketing-The marketing of culture.* New York: Knopf.
Wolf, M. (2003). *The entertainment economy.* New York, NY: Three Rivers Press.

CHAPTER

2

Observations on Research on Cultural Industries[1]

W. Richard Scott
Stanford University

In my view, the bulk of the quite considerable volume of work that has recently appeared on cultural industries represents a confluence of two trends in the social sciences. The first of these trends, principally affecting work on organizational studies, was a shift from more micro to more macro levels of analysis. The second, associated with the resurgence of interest in cultural studies, involved a change from more subjective to more objective conceptions of culture. Each development can be briefly described.

FROM MICRO TO MACRO ANALYSES OF ORGANIZATIONS

The introduction of more macro levels of analysis in organizational studies commenced with the emergence of open systems models in the 1960s (Buckley, 1967; Katz & Kahn, 1966) . These ideas directed attention to all the ways in which organizations are dependent on, penetrated by, and constituted by a wider variety of environmental forces and agents, both near and far. They also focused interest on

[1]An earlier version of these ideas was presented at a conference on Research Perspectives on the Management of Cultural Industries held at New York University's Stern School of Business in May 1997.

interorganizational systems existing above and beyond the structures of individual agencies and firms. In rapid succession, researchers expanded their conceptual frameworks to encompass organization sets—a focal organization and its immediate exchange partners (Blau & Scott, 1962; Evan, 1966); organization populations—collections of organizations with similar structural features making similar demands on their environments (Aldrich, 1979; Hannan & Freeman, 1977); and organization fields or industries—a diverse set of organizations, including exchange partners, competitors, and regulators, operating in a recognized area of institutional life (DiMaggio & Powell, 1983; Scott & Meyer, 1983).

These levels were employed, variously, as more elaborated models of the environmental structures confronting particular organizations and as models of more complex organizational systems of interest in their own right (Scott, 2003). As Hirsch (2000) pointed out, the broader models enabled us to better examine those increasingly frequent situations in which products and services are constructed, reproduced, and distributed by systems of interdependent organizations rather than by single firms. More generally, the models shifted attention from the environment of organizations to the organization of environments.

FROM SUBJECTIVE TO OBJECTIVE CONCEPTIONS OF CULTURE

While these developments were underway in the organizations arena, equally significant efforts were breathing new life into cultural studies. Foundational contributions came from anthropology (e.g., Douglas, 1975; Geertz, 1973), from sociology (e.g., Berger & Luckmann, 1967; Bourdieu, 1977), and from the humanities (e.g., Barthes, 1977; Rorty, 1967). I have found the analysis provided by Robert Wuthnow to be most informative in sorting out this work, and I rely on his interpretation in this review. (See, especially, Wuthnow, 1987; see also Wuthnow, Hunter, Bergesen, & Kurzweil, 1984, and Wuthnow & Witten, 1988).

Wuthnow (1987) proposed that conceptions or approaches to culture can be classified into two general categories: those that emphasize the subjective meanings of cultural objects and those that emphasize objective features, the characteristics or functions of the objects themselves. Subjective approaches were the earliest and remain the most common approaches to culture. They focus on beliefs, attitudes, opinions, orientations, and values of individuals. Culture is conceived as the subjective states of individuals. The methodology employed is survey research, participant observation, and the in-depth interview. Representative theorists include Parsons (1951) and Lenski (1963).

Objective approaches, as noted, attend to the characteristics of cultural objects. They are differentiated into three subtypes: the structuralist, the dramaturgic, and the institutional approaches. The structuralist approach, exemplified in the work of Levi-Strauss (1963) and Douglas (1966), attempts to identify the general patterns or rules that are implicit in the relationships among cultural elements. Culture is analytically separated from the internal subjective states of the individual participant, and is instead viewed as external elements: as texts, gestures, and discourse that can be heard or read, as acts and events that can be seen, recorded, and classified. The appropriate methodology involves various forms of content analysis.

In the dramaturgical approach, which focuses on the expressive or communicative properties of culture, culture is approached as it interacts with social structure. Emphasis is placed on the examination of rituals, ideologies, and other acts that symbolize and dramatize the nature of social relations. Ranging widely from analysts such as Durkheim (1915/1965) to Goffman (1974), researchers in this tradition rely on descriptive, ethnomethodological, and participant-observation techniques. Meyer and Rowan (1977) employed and extended this approach by examining the symbolic meanings conveyed by formal organization structure.

Institutionalist approaches have arisen that embrace and extend the structuralist and dramaturgic models to emphasize the roles played by occupations and organizations in producing and disseminating cultural objects. Pioneering work in this tradition was carried out by Becker (1973, 1982), DiMaggio (1977), Hirsch (1972), and Peterson (1976). As Peterson (1979, p. 153) commented, this "production of culture" perspective employs "the insights and methods of industrial, economic, organizational, and occupational sociology" to examine "how the milieux in which culture is produced influences its form and content." (See also Peterson & Anand, 2004.)

The resurgence of interest in studying culture as an objective phenomena has given rise to new methodologies that have been termed the *new archival tradition,* which systematically examines documents and textual materials, analyzing the "shared forms of meaning that underlie social organizational processes" attempting to "understand the configurational logics that tie these various elements together" (Ventresca & Mohr, 2002, p. 810).

What distinguishes the current sizable volume of work on cultural industries—including that contained in the present book—is the convergence of more macro research models and more objective conceptions of culture. In particular, organizational set and field models are being combined with institutionalist approaches, emphasizing the varying combinations of people, processes, resources, strategies, and structures that come together in the production of symbolic materials.

DEFINING AND DIFFERENTIATING CULTURAL INDUSTRIES

There remains some disagreement regarding how the term *cultural,* as used in cultural industries, is to be defined. An associated issue concerns whether and how, if at all, cultural industries differ from other industries. Lampel, Lant, and Shamsie (2000, p. 263) adopted Hirsch's (1972, pp. 641–642) definition of cultural goods as "non-material goods directed at a public of consumers for whom they generally serve an esthetic or expressive, rather than clearly utilitarian function." This view pushes toward the more normative and ritualistic aspects of culture and away from their cognitive, instrumental uses.

This definitional choice is somewhat surprising given that the direction of development in cultural studies—and in related work in institutional analysis as well—has moved from an emphasis on the normative to the cognitive features of symbolic systems (DiMaggio & Powell, 1991; Scott, 2001). It arbitrarily directs interest to the production of cultural materials for entertainment or to reinforce mores or religious beliefs while defocusing cultural materials intended to inform and educate. Music and art would be included but only certain forms of writing and other media products. Fiction but not nonfiction? Movie musicals but not documentaries? *People* but not *Time*? Religion but not science? It seems preferable to me to define cultural industries as those concerned with the production, reproduction, and dissemination of symbolic materials and services of all types. Armed with this broad conception, scholars can then examine important differences in these activities along a number of dimensions, including the nature of the production and dissemination process, media employed, size and nature of audience, expressive versus instrumental value of the symbolic materials, and whether production and distribution is by profit or nonprofit forms.

What, if any, are the distinctive attributes of cultural industries, considered as one among many arenas of production and consumption? Scholars have suggested a number of possibilities, including the nature of the work, the characteristics of organizational forms, and the kinds of problems or issues they pose for managers. With respect to distinctive features of work, because cultural industries deal primarily with symbolic products, the subjective response of their consumers or audience is an integral part of the process. As Bourdieu (1977) emphasized, consumers are coproducers of the products. However, how generously defined the relevant audience is varies across different arenas of culture. As Crane (1976) and others suggested, science has attained a greater degree of autonomy and exerts more control over the criteria governing its field than other cultural enterprises such as art or religion. The critical audience for a scientist is other scientists (Latour & Woolgar, 1979).

Many observers of cultural industries point out that work activities require a high level of creativity. Novel and innovative products are in demand. But this observation is more true for some phases of the process (e.g., creation of a new song or novel) than for others (e.g., marketing or distribution) and it is more true for some types of cultural production (e.g., popular music) than for others (e.g., news media). Others suggest that the industry faces a high level of uncertainty—both on the supply side, because of the difficulties in routinizing innovation, and on the demand side, because of the unpredictability and volatility of audience tastes. But again, these descriptions seem more appropriate for some than other industry branches, applying more aptly, for example, to contemporary art than to mainstream religions.

It is often claimed that different types of organization and modes of organizing are more often found in cultural than in other industries. Cultural products are often produced by creative individuals employing craft-type processes and structures. Even though individual artists may loom large and receive the credit, Becker

(1973, 1982) demonstrated that multiple, diverse parties are typically involved in the production of artistic products. Creative processes are more likely to be informal and highly variable, but they must often be connected to more bureaucratic production and distribution systems. The connections are made by yet another class of actors: various boundary spanners, including agents, editors, and brokers. These arrangements help to protect and support the more individualistic values of artists while at the same time working to buffer more conventional, formalized organizations from high levels of uncertainty (Hirsch, 1972). Such complex systems, including independent, diverse units linked by informal understandings, contracts, or other flexible connections are argued to be particularly characteristic of organizations in cultural industries.

Scholars observing cultural industries also suggest that they are characterized by distinctive managerial problems. Among these are the art-versus-commerce dilemma (see Glynn, 2000; Mouritsen & Skærbæk, 1995), and the need to balance innovation and recognizability or familiarity (see Mezias & Mezias, 2000; see also Blau, 1988; Lampel et al., 2000).

Although there is utility in recognizing and studying all of these dimensions and distinctions regarding work, organization, and managerial problems, I have difficulty in viewing them as either characteristic of or distinctive to cultural industries. Because I prefer a broadened definition as noted earlier, I perceive great diversity across organizational structures and processes in cultural industries that undermines the validity of these generalizations. If we attend to the full range of cultural organizations, great variation can be found along all of the dimensions identified.

Furthermore, in my view, the characteristics that in the past made cultural industries more distinctive are rapidly being swept away by a wide array of new industries—as well as some reinvented old ones—that are strongly based on knowledge creation and exploitation. On every side, we confront flexible forms, loose and shifting connections (contracts, alliances, networks) among diverse structures and participants, segmented and rapidly changing markets, and a heightened reliance on innovation (Powell, 2001). And the contemporary literature is laden with discourse on the multiple managerial dilemmas posed by these developments. But note: To the extent that emerging industries begin to acquire many of the distinctive features of cultural industries, it renders even more valuable the study of cultural industries. They represent early and continuing instances of a complex of work patterns, organizational forms, and management issues that characterize an ever-expanding set of new and reinvented industries.

REFERENCES

Aldrich, H. (1979). *Organizations and environments.* Englewood Cliffs, NJ: Prentice-Hall.
Barthes, R. (1977). *Image, music, text.* London: Fontana.
Becker, H. S. (1973). Art as collective action. *American Sociological Review, 39,* 767–776.
Becker, H. S. (1982). *Art worlds.* Berkeley: University of California Press.

Berger, P. L., & Luckmann, T. (1967). *The social construction of reality.* New York: Doubleday Anchor.
Blau, J. (1988). Study of the arts: A reappraisal. *Annual Review of Sociology, 14,* 269–292.
Blau, P. M., & Scott, W. R. (1962). *Formal organizations: A comparative approach.* San Francisco: Chandler.
Bourdieu, P. (1977). *Outline of a theory of practice.* Cambridge, UK: Cambridge University Press.
Buckley, W. (1967). *Sociology and modern systems theory.* Englewood Cliffs, NJ: Prentice-Hall.
Crane, D. (1976). Reward systems in art, science, and religion. *American Behavioral Science, 19,* 719–734.
DiMaggio, P. J. (1977). Market structure, the creative process, and popular culture. *Journal of Popular Culture, 11,* 436–452.
DiMaggio, P. J., & Powell, W. W. (1983). The iron cage revisited: Institutional isomorphism and collective rationality in organizational fields. *American Sociological Review, 48,* 147–160.
DiMaggio, P. J., & Powell, W. W. (1991). Introduction. In W. W. Powell & P. J. DiMaggio (Eds.), *The new institutionalism in organizational analysis* (pp. 1–38). Chicago: University of Chicago Press.
Douglas, M. (1966). *Purity and danger: An analysis of concepts of pollution and taboo.* London: Penguin.
Douglas, M. (1975). *Implicit meanings: Essays in anthropology.* London: Routledge & Kegan Paul.
Durkheim, E. (1965). *The elementary forms of religious life.* (J. W. Swain, trans.). New York: Free Press. (original work published 1915)
Evan, W. M. (1966). The organization set: Toward a theory of interorganizational relations. In J. D. Thompson (Ed.), *Approaches to organizational design* (pp. 173–188). Pittsburgh: University of Pittsburgh Press.
Geertz, C. (1973). *The interpretation of cultures.* New York: Basic Books.
Glynn, M. A. (2000). When cymbals become symbols: Conflict over organizational identity within a symphony orchestra. *Organization Science, 22,* 285–298.
Goffman, E. (1974). *Frame analysis: An essay on the organization of experience.* New York: Harper & Row.
Hannan, M. T., & Freeman, J. (1977). The population ecology of organizations. *American Journal of Sociology, 82,* 929–964.
Hirsch, P. M. (1972). Processing fads and fashions: An organization-set analysis of cultural industry systems. *American Journal of Sociology, 77,* 639–659.
Hirsch, P. M. (2000). Cultural industries revisited. *Organization Science, 11,* 356–361.
Katz, D., & Kahn, R. L. (1966). *The social psychology of organizations.* New York: Wiley.
Lampel, J., Lant, T., & Shamsie, J. (2000). Balancing act: Learning from organizing practices in cultural industries. *Organization Science, 11,* 263–269.
Latour, B., & Woolgar, S. (1979). *Laboratory life: The construction of scientific facts.* Beverly Hills, CA: Sage.
Lenski, G. (1963). *The religious factor.* Garden City, NY: Anchor.
Levi-Strauss, C. (1963). *Structural anthropology.* New York: Basic Books.
Meyer, J. W., & Rowan, B. (1977). Institutionalized organizations: Formal structure as myth and ceremony. *American Journal of Sociology, 83,* 340–363.
Mezias, J. M., & Mezias, S. J. (2000). Resource partitioning, the founding of specialist firms, and innovation: The American feature film industry, 1912–1929. *Organization Science, 11,* 306–322.
Mouritsen, J., & Skærbæk, P. (1995). Civilization, art, and accounting: The royal Danish theater–an enterprise straddling two institutions. In W. R. Scott & S. Christensen (Eds.),

The institutional construction of organizations: International and longitudinal studies (pp. 91–112). Thousand Oaks, CA: Sage.
Parsons, T. (1951). *The social system.* Glencoe, IL: Free Press.
Peterson, R. A. (Ed.). (1976). *The production of culture.* Beverly Hills, CA: Sage.
Peterson, R. A. (1979). Revitalizing the culture concept. *Annual Review of Sociology, 5,* 137–166.
Peterson, R. A., & Anand, N. (2004). The production of culture perspective. *Annual Review of Sociology, 30,* 311–334.
Powell, W. W. (2001). The capitalist firm in the twenty-first century: Emerging patterns in western enterprise. In P. DiMaggio (Ed.), *The twenty-first-century firm* (pp. 33–68). Princeton, NJ: Princeton University Press.
Rorty, R. (Ed.). (1967). *The linguistic turn: Recent essays in philosophical method.* Chicago: University of Chicago Press.
Scott, W. R. (2001). *Institutions and organizations* (2nd ed.). Thousand Oaks, CA: Sage.
Scott, W. R. (2003). *Organizations: Rational, natural and open systems* (5th ed.). Upper Saddle River, NJ: Prentice-Hall.
Scott, W. R., & Meyer, J. W. (Eds.). (1983). The organization of societal sectors. In J. W. Meyer & W. R. Scott (Eds.), *Organizational environments: Ritual and rationality* (pp. 129–154). Beverly Hills, CA: Sage.
Ventresca, M. J., & Mohr, J. W. (2002). Archival research methods. In J. A. C. Baum (Ed.), *The Blackwell companion to organizations* (pp. 805–828). Oxford, UK: Blackwell.
Wuthnow, R. (1987). *Meaning and moral order: Explorations in cultural analysis.* Berkeley: University of California Press.
Wuthnow, R., Hunter, J. D., Bergesen, A., & Kurzweil, E. (1984). *Cultural analysis: The work of Peter L. Berger, Mary Douglas, Michel Foucault, and Jürgen Haberman.* Boston: Routledge & Kegan Paul.
Wuthnow, R., & Witten, M. (1988). New directions in the study of culture. *Annual Review of Sociology, 14,* 49–67.

1

The Process of Value Creation

The enjoyment and appreciation of plays, films, music, or books rarely demands a deep understanding of how these works are created. The value of cultural products seems to depend less on how they are created, and more on how they are experienced. We, as consumers, rarely mediate on the struggles behind the mounting of a first-rate musical, wish to delve into the messy details of the production of a great film, or want to probe into the obstacles that had to be overcome to create a best-selling book. We want our cultural products to be delivered to us as polished and as complete as possible, without knowledge of the turbulence and difficulties that marked the process for those who were directly involved.

What may be of marginal importance to consumers is of paramount importance to the organizations and individuals that create cultural products. If you could move behind the scene in any cultural industry, you would find a perennial debate, at times friendly and at others acerbic, about how credit should be shared. The debate is often framed as a struggle between commercial and creative imperatives, more pejoratively between the so-called "suits" and the "creatives." The passion and polemics that usually mark this debate suggest that this is not an academic exercise. What we have here are fundamental disagreements over power, ideology, and the processes that shape the way that cultural industries are structured and managed.

In this section we see three contributions to this debate. In chapter 3, Keyton and smith go behind the scenes of a successful network television series to uncover a struggle between Linda Bloodworth-Thomason, its executive producer, and Delta Burke, one of its stars. As the executive producer, Linda Bloodworth-Thomason straddled the divide between the creative and commercial domains of a major television series. In addition to being the person responsible for the basic concept of the series, she also wrote scripts for each of the shows and made key decisions about character development.

As often happens when television programs gain plaudits and audience, one or more of the actors rise to prominence, often embodying to the audience the very spirit of the program. When this happens, the actor or actors become stakeholders in the program, not only with an interest in the program's success, but also because they are concerned about the creative direction of the series. This is what happened to Delta Burke in *Designing Women.* Her portrayal of Suzanne Sugarbaker, a self-centered ex-beauty queen with several wealthy ex-husbands, captured the imagination of the American audience, and catapulted her to star status. As Delta Burke rose to the status of a star on the show, she began to develop a proprietary attitude toward the character of Suzanne. She clearly derived some degree of power because her portrayal of Suzanne was central to the success of the series. But Delta Burke also viewed her close identification with the character as an asset that she could continue to exploit for many years afterward.

Because the character of Suzanne Sugarbaker was conceived and developed by Linda Bloodworth-Thomason, the issue of who controlled the development of this character that was so crucial to the success of the series became a bone of contention. Although Linda Bloodworth-Thomason was not closed to ideas and suggestions from her actors, in principle she believed that as the executive producer she was responsible for and had the right to make final decisions about scripts and roles. This strong stand set the stage for a confrontation between herself and Delta Burke.

Seen from afar, the confrontation appears to be one between commercial and artistic sensibilities, between the part of the organization that is concerned about costs and audience ratings and another that is exclusively focused on imagination and narrative. A closer examination, however, suggests that a line cannot be so sharply drawn. The script that brought Linda Bloodworth-Thomason into confrontation with Delta Burke reflects the executive producer's deep artistic beliefs, whereas Delta Burke's position was as much a reflection of her concern about her image and career as it was about her sense that her emerging power was being challenged.

When asking the question of who creates value in the cultural industries, it is often tempting to select the individuals who appear on the cover of the book or CD album, on the marquis or during the opening credits: in other words, the actors, directors, composers, and authors, rather than the individuals who work behind the scenes, the producers, editors, financiers, and marketers. This tendency to privilege the highly visible and frequently more glamorous unintentionally results in attributing clear demarcation between artistic and commercial spheres, with the first often seen as the main source of value, and the second as primarily responsible for exploitation of value. In practice, as we can see in *Designing Women*, the boundary between commercial and creative areas can be ambiguous. Individuals who are closely identified with commercial interests may be motivated by creative ideas, whereas individuals who embody the creative spirit may be motivated by commercial factors.

The ambiguity of this division between commercial and creative spheres is explored in chapter 4 by Lampel, who uses the career of Irving Thalberg to track the emergence of the crucial role of the Hollywood producer as the individual who makes the links between creative and commercial decisions. In the early days of the cinema, the boundary between creative and commercial decisions was well demarcated: Directors made most of the creative decisions and producers took care of such issues as budgets and marketing. Thalberg, who gained control of production at MGM in 1925, was one of the first to perceive the demarcation between creative and commercial decisions as a product of politics and ideology, rather than a reflection of the actual process of film making. In response to the question "Who creates value?," Thalberg decisively answered: What matters is not who creates value, but how value is created. For Thalberg the process of creating value called for a system: not a system of the type observed in the manufacturing sector, but a team-based system that brought together individuals with the requisite competencies, without adopting a rigid divide between the creative and commercial spheres.

Thalberg saw the demarcation between the creative and commercial as primarily temporal. The issue was not who has the right to make certain kinds of decisions, but when creative considerations should be allowed to take precedence over commercial considerations, and when commercial considerations should be given primacy over purely artistic concerns. His system was based on deep involvement in the early phase of value creation, a stage during which commercial and creative issues were explored and debated in the now legendary "script conferences." This was followed by a relaxation of control as production teams headed by directors translated meticulously prepared scripts into film. At this point Thalberg and his team reasserted control, editing, reshooting, and testing the film until they believed it blended perfectly both creative intent and commercial viability.

The extraordinary track record of Thalberg and MGM in terms of both critical and commercial success speaks to the power of the system he created. The producer system that he created has been subjected to much criticism over the years. His approach and philosophy, however, points to an important truth that is often lost in the bitter debates about whether value comes from the artist or from the persons who create the resources and conditions necessary for culture to flourish. First, every successful cultural industry evolves roles that combine creative insight with commercial instincts. Second, the quality and caliber of the individuals who occupy these roles evolve. Having the roles alone does not suffice: It is also important to have the right people in these roles.

The relationship between role and individual is extensively explored by Glynn in chapter 5. The modern symphony orchestras date back to the middle of the 19th century. A product of the willingness of civic authorities to fund culture, and the increased availability of professional musicians, the symphony orchestras catered to the burgeoning urban middle classes. At the heart of the symphony orchestra as a cultural product system stand the music directors. They must combine deep knowledge of classical music tradition with shrewd appreciation of popular tastes. They should use this to mediate between the management committees that oversee budgets and schedules, and the musicians who jealously guard their economic and professional prerogatives.

Glynn's chapter focuses on one individual: Yoel Levi, the musical director of the Atlanta Symphony Orchestra. She explores Levi's position and actions during a pivotal moment in the life of the Atlanta Symphony. In 1996, following a pressing need for financial retrenchment, the board decided to lay off six musicians. The decision exacerbated long-standing conflicts between the musicians and the management of the Atlanta Symphony, leading to a strike. As a musical director, Levi was caught in the middle, in sympathy with the strikers, while fully aware of the financial difficulties that forced the decision in the first place.

The crisis reveals as much about what Glynn calls the "hybridized organizational identity" embodied in the role of musical director, as it does about Yoel Levi as a person. As the tensions implicit in this role come to the surface, we can clearly see the multiple strands that make up the job of music director. At the same time, we are made to appreciate the humor and ingenuity that Levi employed to manage a situation that could have easily descended into acrimony, bitterness, and failure. At one point he tendered his resignation, only to withdraw it in response to popular support. Though his role put him in a difficult position, he used his multiple allegiances to explore ways out of the stalemate between the management and the musicians.

Put together, these three chapters suggest that value in cultural industries is the product of intersections and evolutions: the intersection between creative and commercial domains, and the evolution of systems and roles. Debating who gets the credit for creating the successful film, musical, or book may be a favorite pastime in restaurants and boardrooms, but ultimately the credit belongs to too many people and is driven by too many factors for the answer to be constant or straightforward.

CHAPTER

3

Conflicts Over Creative Control: Power Struggle on Prime Time Television

Joann Keyton
University of Kansas

faye l. smith
Emporia State University

A forum for creativity and creative control consists of necessary, central, and sometimes opposing, components in cultural industries. Without creativity, a cultural product cannot be produced because the product is dependent on a creative vision. Many individuals may contribute to the creative process, but in scripted cultural products the primary source of the creativity is the writer who develops the characters and places them within a story narrative. Another source of creativity is the person who plays the character and acts out the story. The mass production feature of cultural industries requires that creativity be viewed as potentially residing within individuals, and resulting from the interactions among them. As a result, the locus of creative control can become the site of power and power struggles in cultural industry organizations.

In this chapter we describe the power shifts related to character control in producing a television series. The process of developing and producing the series, and each episode, relies on the relationships among a set of principals and agents who are both loosely coupled and contractually bound. The regular and repeated process of producing episodes provides a static framework of organizational relationships. Yet, each episode is unique, requiring the creativity of the cast and crew most directly involved in producing the cultural product. As such, the tension between creativity and creative control surfaces and illustrates some of the unique features associated with creating cultural products (Lampel, Lant, & Shamsie, 2000; Shamsie, 1997).

Because the creative and production processes of cultural industry products are completed behind the scenes, consumers or viewers of these products are likely not able to associate the product with those who produce it. A television series is most often associated with the actors and actresses who portray the series' characters; yet, other individuals sustain the product and contribute to the creative processes required to produce the episodes. For example, the producers and writers of a television series are instrumental in designing and maintaining the focus of the story line of the series, yet often are relatively unknown to the primary consumer—the viewing public.

For an organization to produce the episodes of a television series, it must allocate power to the various individuals who work on the show. Despite the specification of formal power in written, transactional contracts, informal power also exists among these organizational members. Thus, both formal and informal power are properties of the relationships between parties, or part of their relational contracts (Emerson, 1962; MacNeil, 1985; McLean Parks & smith, 1998; Mechanic, 1962; Rousseau & McLean Parks, 1993).

Power is relationship specific rather than person specific, and is a function of the reliance or dependency of one of the parties on the other (McLean Parks & smith, 1998). If dependence is symmetric, then power is balanced; if it is asymmetric, then power is out of balance and the least powerful party will be motivated to restore balance (McLean Parks & smith). Over the life cycle of producing a cultural product, parties may evolve through zones of power balance (or imbalance) based on emerging dependencies.

In this chapter we examine a network of principals and agents comprised of Columbia Broadcasting System (CBS), Mozark Productions, its executive producer, Linda Bloodworth-Thomason, the television show *Designing Women*, and the show's four lead actresses. Archival analyses and analyses of the scripts were used to supplement direct observation of the filming of one episode that was part of an initial study of the character roles as representations of Southern women (Keyton, 1994). The evidence of power shifts and creative conflicts among the show's producers and actresses were a serendipitous finding and reported in smith and Keyton (2001).

THE ORIGINS OF *DESIGNING WOMEN*

Linda Bloodworth-Thomason and her husband Harry Thomason founded Mozark Productions to produce the television series *Designing Women*. Produced for CBS beginning with the 1986–1987 season, a minicrisis occurred early in the show's first season. However, letters from viewers convinced CBS to keep the show. By the 1989–1990 season the series was a part of popular culture because it addressed controversial social issues of particular importance to women (e.g., AIDS, breast cancer, breast implants, women in the church hierarchy, domestic abuse; Dow, 1992; Keyton, 1994; smith & Keyton, 2001). The setting of *Designing Women* was an Atlanta interior design firm, Sugarbaker's. Julia (Dixie Carter), Suzanne (Delta Burke), Mary Jo (Annie Potts), and Charlene (Jean Smart) were partners in the design firm, which was located in Julia's home.

As a situation comedy, Bloodworth-Thomason wrote ensemble scripts in which the characters resolved personal and professional problems, made decisions, managed conflict with outsiders, and discussed societal problems. At that time, television critics applauded Bloodworth-Thomason's efforts for developing these characters "as women with a degree of depth, competence, wit, and texture undreamed of by their sisters in the early days of television" (Schrag, 1991, p. 112). After just three seasons, Bloodworth-Thomason was honored by the Museum of Broadcasting as "a leader in writing and producing programs that feature intelligent female characters who don't shrink from verbal expression" (Museum of Broadcasting, 1990, p. 11A).

Whereas a creative team more typically writes situation comedies, Bloodworth-Thomason was the primary author of the *Designing Women* scripts. Combining this instrumental role with her roles as series creator and producer gave her substantial power and creative control over the television series. The weekly schedule used to produce situation comedies requires a tight turnaround and intense focus on the organizational product. The regularity of these scripts from Bloodworth-Thomason acted as a communication vehicle for discussing organizational tasks and issues, much in the way written procedures communicate to employees. Production employees reported that "they relied on the script for directions about their tasks without receiving (or expecting) direct communication from Bloodworth-Thomason" (smith & Keyton, 2001, p. 156).

Scripts were viable downward communication devices because cast and crew were relatively stable both within and throughout seasons. Moreover, episodes were produced weekly creating a repeatable cycle of task work (i.e., table reading of script, blocking rehearsals to set lighting, and filming) even though the content of the creative output changed. Thus, Bloodworth-Thomason's scripts were a channel of organizational communication that controlled organizational processes and the task work of cast and crew.

Other evidence supports Bloodworth-Thomason's use of scripts as an organizational communication device (smith & Keyton, 2001). Bloodworth-Thomason publicly acknowledged that the four characters represented different aspects of her personality. Indeed, her close association with the characters was analyzed and reported on in the popular press (Davis, 1988). As such, Bloodworth-Thomason's characters became vehicles to comment on her Southern roots and to liberate what she perceived to be the trapped Southern female stereotype (Keyton, 1994).

In particular, Bloodworth-Thomason acknowledged that the character of Julia was most closely aligned with her style and viewpoint. Julia's diatribes about social injustices were a hallmark of the series. With this acknowledged autobiographical characteristic of both the characters and their commentary, it is easy to see how Bloodworth-Thomason's identity was encapsulated in the scripts and how the scripts spoke for her as a communicative device. In her role as creator, producer, and writer, Bloodworth-Thomason had the opportunity and apparent motive to create scripts that controlled the organizational interaction environment, the organizational agenda, and the roles of cast and crew.

Bloodworth-Thomason's work on *Designing Women* has been described as providing a distinctly feminist and liberal sensibility at a time when few television shows presented women in this way. As a result, her scripts helped to recast conventional images of women and of the South (Graham, 1993). Thus, she was the source of knowledge that provided the story lines for the scripts, not only from the technical perspective as writer, but also from the perspective of understanding this tacit knowledge. The relationship between the tacit knowledge and the writer's identity seems to have overlapped substantially, suggesting that any challenge to the ownership of the characters' identities would be parallel to a challenge to Bloodworth-Thomason's individual identity. The functions of the scripts and the tacit knowledge gave Bloodworth-Thomason real and symbolic control of the identity of the show as well as its characters.

Common to television series, the coupling of characters to continuous story lines required that Bloodworth-Thomason invest in the actresses as the voices and personae of characters. Despite the close identity of Bloodworth-Thomason to the characters and the story lines of the scripts, she had to rely on them to enact her characters and stories, as well as provide consistency for the viewing audience. Although this is a common strategy necessary for the constraints of television, it creates absolute dependencies (smith & Keyton, 2001) that can become the source of conflict. The potential for tension was heightened as Bloodworth-Thomason specifically wrote the roles of Julia and Suzanne for Dixie Carter and Delta Burke, with whom she had developed friendships when the actresses were hired for roles on Bloodworth-Thomason's first television series, *Filthy Rich*.

GROWING CONFLICTS OVER CREATIVE CONTROL

Conflict over creative control is a frequent tension when an actor or actress wants to contribute to a character's voice or portray a character differently from the scriptwriter's intension. This is most likely to happen when an actress becomes so identified with a character that viewers have difficulty separating the fictional character from the actress portraying the character. This was the case with Delta Burke's portrayal of Suzanne. Conflict emerged between Burke and Bloodworth-Thomason because Bloodworth-Thomason controlled the identity of the Suzanne character and the character's voice through writing the scripts, whereas Burke's popularity with viewers empowered her to challenge Bloodworth-Thomason's creative control. Writers have legal ownership of characters they create (Norwick & Chasen, 1992), even though viewers may associate specific actresses with those characters. In this case, the actress used her substantial power base to defend her claim of ownership of the character voice.

The power conflict between Burke and Bloodworth-Thomason reached a confrontation stage when Burke refused to do a scene in a mud bath for the last episode ("La Place Sans Souci") of the 1989–1990 season. Burke's refusal resulted in contract negotiations that included the potential for her to be written out of this script and out of the series. The conflict was so acute that rehearsals were delayed 2 days for this episode. Using the script to deliver metaphorical messages about the power struggle, Bloodworth-Thomason signaled to Burke and the other employees that she remained in control of the characters, and that the future of the series and its identity hinged on how this power conflict was resolved (smith & Keyton, 2001).

Although Burke's formal contract controlled the explicit and objective nature of the professional relationship such as how, when, and where she would deliver the script that was written, the informal and personal relationship between Burke and Bloodworth-Thomason also contributed to the tension. Bloodworth-Thomason and Burke had a long working history together. Burke first appeared as an ex-beauty queen in Bloodworth-Thomason's first television series, *Filthy Rich*. Although not a popular success, the series reinforced Bloodworth-Thomason's creative talent (earlier recognized with two Emmy nominations for *M*A*S*H*), and her ability to connect with a female audience, and also validated her ability to produce a television series. This was significant given that Bloodworth-Thomason was one of the first female television producers—a field still largely dominated by men.

The tension between Bloodworth-Thomason and Burke was exacerbated by two influences. First, Burke and Bloodworth-Thomason were (or had been) friends. Just prior to this conflict, Bloodworth-Thomason had written a script for Burke dealing with Burke's weight gain, which had garnered considerable scrutiny from both trade and popular press. Literally weeks before this power struggle, Bloodworth-Thomason had empathized with Burke and wrote a script denouncing that "thin is everything" even for ex-beauty queens, and had appeared in pictures with Burke in the trade press supporting the actress and explaining why she wrote this episode for Burke. Later, Burke would claim that it was a lie to pretend that "everything was hunky-dory" as Bloodworth-Thomason and her husband hassled her about her weight, even from the beginning of the series (Park, 1991).

Second, Bloodworth-Thomason viewed Mozark Productions and *Designing Women* as establishing her independence from other industry influences. Graham (1993) reported her as "no longer allow(ing) any fundamental aspect of her work to be outside her own control" (p. 66). Personally, this series represented her Southern upbringing and her view of contemporary values and issues. Professionally, this series marked her independence and recognition as a producer and writer. Based on the top-10 success of *Designing Women*, CBS offered Bloodworth-Thomason and Mozark Productions a $45-million contract and free rein to produce other shows, at that time the biggest production deal the network had ever made (Graham, 1993).

To resolve the tension, Bloodworth-Thomason could have rewritten the script to remove the tangible point of conflict (the mud bath scene) from the "La Place Sans Souci" episode. Rather, she chose to assert her professional and formal power by insisting that the mud bath remain, thus humiliating Burke's character, Suzanne, and communicating to Burke that Bloodworth-Thomason controlled the script. During the filming of the episode, multiple power-laden messages were conveyed that indicated that Burke was threatening the success of the series as an ensemble story line, that Bloodworth Thomason was tired of Burke's grandstanding, and that Burke was not playing by the rules (smith & Keyton, 2001). For example, Julia admonishes Suzanne after she rants about the small portions of food and the exercise she's expected to do in their trip to the health spa:

Julia: And now, all of a sudden, just because this place is not exactly what you envisioned and only you alone know what that was–but my guess is you pictured yourself floating on some big barge while a bunch of slaves fed you grapes, anyway, just because it is less than your expectations, you now want to spoil it for the rest of us!

Later in the spa's restaurant, Julia scolds Suzanne about her disruptive dining behavior:

Julia: Oh, Suzanne, for crying out loud. Just because you're not having a good time, you are absolutely hell-bent on trying to start something. Well, I have had just about enough for one day. Until you get over your obnoxious disposition, Mary Jo and I will just take our dinner and go back to the room.

In the middle of the episode, the four women play a marathon of Trivial Pursuit™. The next day in the mud bath, Julia and Mary Jo find out that Charlene and Suzanne cheated. Julia spouts, "What gets me, Suzanne, is that you thought you could get away with it." Now with Charlene and Suzanne in a mud fight against Julia and Mary Jo, Julia continues, "You've been begging for it right between the eyes, Suzanne, and now you're gonna get it!" Fighting and arguing continues. Julia ends the scene with "You are a dead woman!"

The production of this episode, then, revealed the power struggle between the parties, in both its formal and informal forms, with Bloodworth-Thomason retaining the upper hand through her control of the script and story line. Though largely invisible to the viewing audience when the episode aired, months later Burke made the power struggle public in media interviews. Whereas Bloodworth-Thomason won creative control in this instance, Burke eventually sued Bloodworth-Thomason and Thomason for breach of contract. Months later, both parties were still regularly and publicly airing their contempt for one another.

THE ROLE OF CONTRACTS IN CREATIVE CONFLICTS

The nature of a cultural product such as a television series provides a rich source of information that illustrates the power dependencies among the formal organizations (CBS, Mozark Productions), the formal contracts (legal documents), relational contracts between parties (Bloodworth-Thomason, actresses), and power asymmetries and symmetries over time. Organizational contracts embody both economic and social features, and may be viewed on a transactional-relational continuum of psychological contracts that incorporates power differences between parties (McLean Parks & smith, 1998). Transactional contracts are more likely to have terms of the contract expressed explicitly, such as in employment contracts that legally govern the actresses for the series.

When the power distribution is symmetric between parties, each party can rely on the terms of the formal contract to enact the behaviors specified in the contract and to resolve disputes according to those terms. When power distribution is asymmetric, however, the more powerful party becomes a "contract maker" and the less powerful party is a "contract taker" (McLean Parks & smith, 1998). It is expected that the contract maker will be in a better position to influence the terms of the contract and to be able to exit the relationship at will (McLean Parks & smith).

The norm in television series production is that actresses and producers are bound by legal, transactional contracts for a specified number of episodes or seasons. Within this contract, the producer maintains a contract-maker role. The conceptual distance between producers as contract makers and actresses as contract takers, however, may become altered over multiple seasons if the series, characters, and actresses playing specific characters gain popularity with the viewing audience. When such popularity occurs, dependencies among them increase as the original power distance shrinks, so that the power between parties becomes more symmetric over time.

Producers are more likely to befriend actors and actresses who contribute to their series' success, just as actors and actresses are likely to befriend producers who provide a vehicle for their popularity. Even if the affection is not genuine, both parties contribute to the illusion that it is, as fans expect relative harmony among parties. When a crisis for a television series occurs (in this case, the disharmony between Bloodworth-Thomason and Burke over Burke's weight gain, and Burke's refusal to do the mud bath scene), this state of presumed friendly power symmetry may once again become asymmetric as fans can easily (and will) take sides when a popular actress or character is perceived to be under attack.

In the case of *Designing Women*, fans took the side of Burke. After all, she was more visible to fans, and she played a character with a common problem (weight gain). Moreover, fans were aware that Burke was a former beauty queen and was gaining weight, and they were aware of Bloodworth-Thomason's supposed support of Burke in the form of an episode ("They Shoot Fat Women, Don't They") dealing with the problem. The viewer-presumed message of that episode was that it was okay to be the person that you are regardless of weight (a message likely construed as positive and self-referential by many fans). Thus fans were on Burke's side when the power struggle became public.

This case illustrates how power is relative, emergent, and likely to be affected by a multitude of factors. The increasing popularity of a television series enhances the power of the executive producer and writer, who is creating the product. Likewise, it enhances the power of the actresses because they are instrumental in delivering that creative product. Similarly, when the actresses become so popular that their identity is intertwined with the characters, their relative power is enhanced through external sources such as the viewers. Burke, through her popularity as Suzanne on *Designing Women*, had become a star of the show in the viewers' perceptions even though Bloodworth-Thomason's intent was that each of the four actresses would share an equal, but different, voice as a member of an ensemble. Even Burke referred to the ensemble "like a band, everyone playing their own instrument to make beautiful music" (E! Entertainment Television, May 31, 2000)

The type of resource that is exchanged is more particularistic in relational contracts, in contrast with transactional contracts, because the actual identity of the individual(s) is important (Foa & Foa, 1975; McLean Parks & smith, 1998). In addition, there is a willingness to honor the intent of the contract because the terms are mutually understood (McLean Parks 1990, 1992; McLean Parks & smith; Rousseau & McLean Parks, 1993). The codependency characteristics of relational contracts are illustrated clearly in the relationships between Bloodworth-Thomason and the four actresses.

Without Bloodworth-Thomason to write the scripts for the series, it lost its identity, as was evidenced by the 1990–1991 season when Bloodworth-Thomason did not author the scripts, and she turned her attention to other series (e.g., *Evening Shade*). Although the same four actresses remained during this season, the conflict between Burke and Mozark Productions became public fodder in the media, and the ratings for the series slipped even though Burke, the series, and Bloodworth-Thomason were nominated for Emmy Awards for work in the previous seasons.

By the 1991–1992 seasons, the characters and actresses changed, which further eroded the success of the series. The synergy among the writer, the actresses, the story lines, and the characters was based on relational types of contracts that evolved (and dissolved) over time among these five people. Even though legal contract commitments between Burke and Bloodworth-Thomason (transactional contracts) remained for two seasons after the marker event (the episode "La Place Sans Souci"), the interpersonal relationship between them, as well as the relationships between Carter and Burke, and Carter and Bloodworth-Thomason, were forced to change as these friends chose sides, and the perfect *Designing Women* family came apart (E! Entertainment Television, May 31, 2000). Hence, the relational contracts had been destroyed, causing the quality of the series to diminish and eventually fold (smith & Keyton, 2001).

STRUGGLES FOR BALANCE OF POWER

Given that power is relationship specific rather than person specific (Emerson, 1962; McLean Parks & smith, 1998), over time, the symmetry of power between parties in either transactional or relational contracts is likely to evolve through zones of power balance or imbalance. A factor that contributes to this evolution is the source of power. In *Designing Women*, we can trace the evolution through zones of power balance based on the sources of power exerted by the two primary parties engaged in the conflict, Burke and Bloodworth-Thomason, as well as the power evolution between organizations.

After Bloodworth-Thomason convinced CBS to shoot the pilot in 1986, CBS contracted with Mozark Productions to regularly produce *Designing Women*. The ratings for the series, however, were lackluster and CBS planned to cancel the show after changing its timeslot nine times and briefly putting the show on hiatus. In an attempt to save the show, Harry Thomason contacted Viewers for Quality Television, who had named *Designing Women* as the Best Quality Comedy Series that year, and asked their viewer members to initiate a letter-writing campaign.

The viewing audience had connected already with the show's identity as one that was written by women, about women, and for women. When they learned that the series was going to be canceled, their write-in campaign saved the show. Although power in the transactional contract between CBS and Mozark was asymmetric in that CBS had greater power to cancel the show, Mozark and the televisions series were able to benefit from the power gained from external constituents, the viewers, to adjust the power asymmetry and change it to power symmetry. The television series was not cancelled, and during the next three seasons, the show achieved top-10 status on a regular basis.

Near the end of the filming for the 1989-1990 season, the conflict between Burke and Bloodworth-Thomason became acute, however, and power asymmetries were evident within the boundaries that created, acted, and produced the show. In March 1990, the last episode of the season, "La Place Sans Souci," was being filmed. (The dynamics of the script story, the rehearsals, and the filming of this last episode are reported in smith & Keyton, 2001.) Comparing the story line of the script to the underlying conflict, there is a noticeable parallelism. In the episode, the character played by Burke receives multiple power-laden messages about her behavior relative to the other characters. It appears that Bloodworth-Thomason used this control mechanism to reinforce her insistence that the identity of the series remain centered on an ensemble portrayal of issues that had made it successful and that had triggered the viewers' write-in campaign (smith & Keyton).

This apparent parallelism is further reinforced by the media reports of the "feud" between Bloodworth-Thomason and Burke. Burke first discussed the feud on a *Barbara Walters Special* and then on *The Arsenio Hall Show*. As a result, the tabloid media picked up the story, most often with a viewpoint that supported Burke, not Bloodworth-Thomason. Years later Carter and Burke talked about the feud on Lifetime's *Intimate Portrait* and E!'s *Celebrity Profiles*. The feud remains a topic of interest to viewers who continue to follow the show in reruns on Lifetime Television, as demonstrated on the message boards on Lifetime's web site. Even though Bloodworth-Thomason, Burke, and the other actresses have moved on to other professional endeavors, the show's identity and the loss experienced by the viewers after its contractual demise cast a long shadow.

The evolution through the zones of power balance between Bloodworth-Thomason and Burke illustrates relative power shifts based on multiple sources of power. For example, initially it appears that the power balance between these two parties took the form of an "ordinary" exchange between a producer–writer and an actress. Despite Bloodworth-Thomason's efforts to sustain the ensemble presentation of the show, viewers began to indicate a preference for Burke's character (and by definition, Burke), and she gained power through her popularity with viewers. Bloodworth-Thomason, on the other hand, was gaining power through her professional recognition as a producer–writer, and her additional contracts to produce other television series (e.g., *Evening Shade*).

In other words, both parties were gaining power based on their professional success, but the actress gained it through a solid, yet diffuse, set of external viewers, whereas the producer–writer gained it through additional formal contracts for her services. Bloodworth-Thomason gained industry attention, which she apparently hoped would translate into economic gains; Burke gained viewer attention that gave her substantial economic leverage. One of the interesting power issues illustrated by this case, and left silent in the McLean Parks and smith (1998) treatment of power distributions in contractual exchanges, is that there is a theoretical assumption that both parties in a dyad agree about who has more, less, or equal power.

As Mechanic (1962) suggested, less powerful parties may not be powerless. In the dyad of Bloodworth-Thomason and Burke, it appears that Bloodworth-Thomason perceived herself as the principal with the most power, and Burke as the agent with less power. However, Burke appears to have perceived herself as the contract maker because of her fan loyalty, which enhanced her power via an external coalition (Pfeffer, 1981; Salancik & Pfeffer, 1974). Whereas the formal contract power favored Bloodworth-Thomason, the informal public power favored Burke.

Within a few months of the initial event, the behind-the-scenes power struggles between Bloodworth-Thomason and Burke became visible to fans as both parties aired their grievances in public. Both parties entered into contract renegotiations while Burke continued to play Suzanne. Bloodworth-Thomason withdrew from the show, conceding creative control to other writers. Thus, whereas Bloodworth-Thomason became invisible to viewers, Burke was still portraying Suzanne in story lines of diminished quality. Essentially, Burke continued to command public sympathy for her plight—both contractually and creatively—at the hands of Bloodworth-Thomason. Although Bloodworth-Thomason and her husband may have won the contractual and legal struggles, Burke's popularity was not eroded. To date, Burke's fans demonstrate their support for Burke and their displeasure about the power struggle on the web site that supports Lifetime Television's syndication of the series.

CONCLUSION

Throughout the evolution of the life cycle of the *Designing Women* television series, one factor that appears to have been a competitive advantage for it compared to other series was its identity. Bloodworth-Thomason's identity with the characters propelled viewers' identity with the show. We propose that for many artistic and cultural products, the creator, as founder, embodies and articulates the identity of the product without substantive consideration for commercial success. The identity is embedded in the creator's conception of what that product is, whether it is a television series, a painting, or a piece of music. Creating the product is an expression of the artists, themselves, suggesting that there is a significant merging of the artist's and the product's identity.

Thus, the concept of organizational identity is extended to less tangible forms of organizing. In other studies of organizational identity that have examined noncultural types of organizations (e.g., Dutton & Dukerich, 1991; Dutton, Dukerich, & Harquail, 1994; Elsbach & Kramer, 1996; Gioia & Thomas, 1996), the observation was made that at least some aspects of the organization's identity changed when its original identity was challenged. In each of these studies, the organizational identity became less central, distinctive, or durable across time when challenged.

In the case of the *Designing Women* television series, the factors that were central, distinctive, and durable (Albert & Whetten, 1985) initially remained intact even when challenged significantly. We suggest that its ability to remain intact may be a characteristic of the cultural product industries, because there would be a close association between the creator's identity and the product's identity in most cultural industry organizations. In this television series, this identity was challenged, first, when CBS indicated it would cancel the series because it was not capturing a sufficient number of viewers. Even in that short period of time, the viewers identified with the messages communicated in the series about women's issues, and campaigned successfully to keep the show.

Whereas CBS was measuring performance based on the quantity of viewers, the true performance measure of the show's success was the depth of identification the viewers had with the show. This depth of identification appears to have been the result of congruence of values (McLean Parks & smith, 2000) between the creator's stories, the ensemble acting, and the creator's ability to capture experiences that many women had faced and felt strongly about but were unable to voice. When the value of this identity was challenged by traditional performance measures, the identity remained intact.

The second challenge to the identity of *Designing Women* was Burke's defiance of the ensemble presentation of the scripts. Burke's challenge appears to have been driven by the viewers' identification with her character, which was one of limited critical inquiry about the women's issues. Apparently many in the viewing audience felt closer to Suzanne, Burke's character, because Suzanne bridged between being a victim of issues and wanting to change those issues like her sister, Julia, Carter's character. The creator's conception of the show's identity, however, was that to allow one character voice to dominate the ensemble would be to lose the message that was central and distinctive about this television series in the first place. If the character voice that was less critical thinking were to emerge as the dominant voice, then the momentum of women's voices as they transitioned from traditional voices to emerging voices would be endangered.

From Bloodworth-Thomason's perspective, it appears that destroying the ensemble voice for the show would destroy the show's identity to which she was so deeply rooted. It was this central and distinctive value that had to remain durable in order for the show to remain socially or commercially successful, and it was Bloodworth-Thomason who appeared to acknowledge that connection. Had she not been the creator of the scripts and story lines, and had she not used her own Southern background as a source of ideas (Keyton, 1994), then she may have become a victim of the viewing audience's (and Burke's) majority opinion about how the show's identity should evolve. Instead, through the script, rehearsals, and filming of the "La Place Sans Souci" episode, she communicated how important it was to retain the identity as she had crafted it (smith & Keyton, 2001). The parallelism between this script and the events surrounding the production of this episode were irrelevant to viewers, as production took place in March, the episode aired in May, and the feud became public in August.

Subsequent to the end of the 1989–1990 season when the "La Place Sans Souci" episode was aired, additional challenges to *Designing Women*'s identity occurred. First, Bloodworth-Thomason diminished her writing and creative activities significantly, as she did not write any of the scripts in the 1990–1991 season. Second, two characters were changed in the 1991–1992 season, including Burke's character, Suzanne. Characters changed again in the 1992–1993 season, which was the final season of the series, except for syndication.

It appears that once Bloodworth-Thomason left the series by turning over her writing duties to others, the core identity of the series was dismantled. Even in the 1990-1991 season when the characters and actresses remained the same, it began to lose appeal with the viewing audience, and ratings began to slip. By then, however, Bloodworth-Thomason was no longer protecting her identity with the show, and it was allowed, more or less, to dissolve on its own. No one else was able to retain the identity of the show, or those factors that were central, distinctive, and enduring.

The power struggles that can develop over the life of a television series raise some interesting questions. Can interpersonal influences ever be separated from formal, contractual relationships? The interdependence required between contract maker and contract taker, and the intertwined identities of producer–writer and actress–character suggest that power struggles in cultural industries will be difficult to resolve because the tension is as public as it is private. By viewing this television series through the lenses of creative control and power asymmetries, and as challenges to identity, we have been able to articulate some of the creative tensions and unravel some of the social fabric embedded in the life cycle of a cultural product.

REFERENCES

Albert, S., & Whetten, D. (1985). Organizational identity. In L. L. Cummings & B. M. Staw (Eds.), *Research in organizational behavior* (Vol. 7, pp. 263–295). Greenwich, CT: JAI Press.

Davis, R. (1988, November 15). Sassy insouciance. *American Way,* pp. 86–89, 91–93.

Dow, B. J. (1992). Performance of feminine discourse in *Designing Women. Text and Performance Quarterly, 12,* 125–145.

Dutton, J., & Dukerich, J. (1991). Keeping an eye on the mirror: Image and identity in organizational adaptation. *Academy of Management Journal, 34,* 517–554.

Dutton, J., Dukerich, J., & Harquail, C. V. (1994). Organizational images and membership commitment. *Administrative Science Quarterly, 39,* 239–263.

E! Entertainment Television (2000, May 31). *E! Celebrity profile: Dixie Carter* [Television broadcast]. Los Angeles: E! Entertainment Television.

Elsbach, K. D., & Kramer, R. M. (1996). Members' responses to organizational identity threats: Encountering and countering the *Business Week* rankings. *Administrative Science Quarterly, 41,* 442–476.

Emerson, R. (1962). Power-dependence relations. *American Sociological Review, 27,* 31–41.

Foa, U., & Foa, E. (1975). *Resource theory of social exchange.* Morristown, NJ: General Learning Press.

Gioia, D. A., & Thomas, J. B. (1996). Identity, image and issue interpretation: Sensemaking during strategic change in academia. *Administrative Science Quarterly, 41,* 370–403.

Graham, J. (Ed.). (1993). *Bloodworth-Thomason, Linda: Current biography yearbook* (pp. 64–67). New York: Wilson.

Keyton, J. (1994). Designing a look at women. *The Mid-Atlantic Almanack, 3,* 126–141.

Lampel, J., Lant, T., & Shamsie, J., (2000). Balancing act: Learning from organizing practices in cultural industries. *Organization Science, 11,* 263–269.

MacNeil, I. R. (1985). Relational contracts: What we do and do not know. *Wisconsin Law Review, X,* 483–525.

McLean Parks, J. (1990). *Organizational contracts: The effects of contractual specificity and social distance.* Unpublished doctoral dissertation, University of Iowa, Iowa City, IA.

McLean Parks, J. (1992, May). *The role of incomplete contracts and their governance in delinquency, in-role, and extra-role behaviors.* Paper presented at SIOP meetings, Montreal, Canada.

McLean Parks, J., & smith, f. l. (1998). Organizational contracting: A "rational" exchange? In J. Halpern & R. Stern (Eds.), *Debating rationality: Non-rational elements of organizational decision making: An interdisciplinary exploration* (pp. 125–154). Ithaca, NY: ILR.

McLean Parks, J., & smith, f. l. (2000, August). *Organizational identity: The ongoing puzzle of definition and redefinition.* Paper presented at Management and Organizational Cognition Track, Academy of Management Meetings, Toronto, Canada.

Mechanic, D. (1962). Sources of power of lower participants in complex organizations. *Administrative Science Quarterly, 7,* 349–364.

Museum of Broadcasting. (1990). *The Museum of Broadcasting's 7th Annual Television Festival in Los Angeles.*

Norwick, K. P., & Chasen, J. S. (1992). *An American Civil Liberties Union handbook: The rights of authors, artists, and other creative people.* Carbondale, IL: Southern Illinois University Press.

Park, J. (1991, January 28). When not battling Delta Burke, Linda Bloodworth-Thomason and Harry Thomason are redesigning CBS. *People Weekly, 35,* 49–51.
Pfeffer, J. (1981). *Power in organizations.* New York: Harper Business.
Rousseau, D. M., & McLean Parks, J. (1993). The contracts of individuals and organizations. *Research in Organizational Behavior, 15,* 1–43.
Schrag, R. L. (1991). From yesterday to today: A case study of M*A*S*H*'s Margaret Houlihan. *Communication Education, 40,* 112–115.
Salancik, G. R., & Pfeffer, J. (1974). The bases and use of power in organizational decision making: The case of a university. *Administrative Science Quarterly, 19,* 453–473.
Shamsie, J. (1997, May). *Introductory remarks.* Paper presented at the Conference on Research Perspectives on the Management of Cultural Industries, New York.
smith, f. l., & Keyton, J. (2001). Organizational storytelling: Metaphors for relational power and identity struggles. *Management Communication Quarterly, 15,* 149–182.

CHAPTER

4

The Genius Behind the System: The Emergence of the Central Producer System in the Hollywood Motion Picture Industry

Joseph Lampel
City University, London

> Its trade, which is in dreams and at so many dollars a thousand feet, is managed by businessmen pretending to be artists and by artists pretending to be businessmen. In this queer atmosphere, nobody stays as he was; the artist begins to lose his art, and the businessman becomes temperamental and unbalanced.
>
> —J. B. Priestley in *Midnight on the Desert* (cited in MacGowan, 1965, p. 305)

Film buffs are familiar with the phenomenon of the *director's cut*: famed directors restoring the prerelease version of a movie that had been distributed years, if not decades, earlier. The term evokes a fight to preserve the integrity of an original vision. It suggests precious footage on the cutting room floor, victim to studio insistence that exhibition constraints should take precedence over directorial intentions. It is "time is money" in the crudest sense of the phrase: Money buys talent, and talent must obey the dictates of money. There is nothing new about the struggle between creative artists and their backers. Creative artists always want the freedom to create without financial or market constraints, whereas their backers want to maximize returns on their investment. One side appeals to artistic freedom, the other points to financial risk (Glynn, 2000).

The rise of the cultural industries has exacerbated the conflict. Prior to the 20th century, artists tended to be entrepreneurs or contractors. Their autonomy was circumscribed by the dictates of the market or by the expectations of their employers, but their ability to pursue their artistic vision within these constraints remained relatively intact (Wijnberg & Gemser, 2000). In the corporate hierarchies that characterize the new cultural industries, individual autonomy must often give way to supervised team production, but it must do so without fundamentally subverting the organization's creative capabilities (Seely Brown & Duguid, 2001).

In this chapter, I argue that the corporate management of cultural production often deals with the inherent tension between artistic and commercial imperatives by creating new forms of strategic organization (Lampel, Lant, & Shamsie, 2000). My case study is the Hollywood motion picture industry in the period before and after the formation of the studio system. It was during this period that the American motion picture industry was transformed into a vertically integrated oligopoly based in Hollywood, California (Puttnam, 1997). It was also during this period that the Hollywood studios developed the central producer system, a set of practices that combine team production and individual artistic effort (Mezias & Kuperman, 2000).

The principal protagonist in my story is Irving Thalberg, chief of production at Universal Pictures from 1923 until 1925, and subsequently chief of production at MGM until his death in 1936. Thalberg is the main innovator behind the central producer system. He did not invent most of the practices that make up the system, but he brought them together into a cohesive system that successfully balanced artistic quality with the commercial imperative of the movie business. For this reason focusing on Thalberg not only provides a window into the motion picture industry at a crucial phase in its development, but also gives us a clearer idea of how crucial actors responded to the forces shaping the industry.

In the first part of this chapter, I describe and analyze the central producer system. My purpose here is to explain how the system as a whole addresses some of the key technical and artistic problems facing motion picture production. In the second part of the chapter, I turn my attention to the role of Irving Thalberg in the evolution of the central producer system. I track the work of Thalberg beginning with his arrival at Universal Pictures, and subsequently his reshaping of film making at MGM between 1925 and 1933. In the third part, I seek to place the central producer system in the context of cultural industries in general. I suggest that the nascent period in the formation of cultural industries is fraught with conflict over identity and control. In particular, I argue that corporate control of cultural industries is not ultimately viable without organizational innovation that balances artistic imperatives with the need to ensure commercial success.

CENTRAL PRODUCER SYSTEM DEFINED

Much has been written about the Hollywood motion picture studios as vertically integrated firms (Caves, 2000). Outwardly, the studios resembled the vertically integrated firms that dominated American business in such areas as steel, automobiles, and petroleum. Inwardly, however, the studios were essentially project-based organizations, and their strategies were therefore shaped by the problems that arise from the planning and execution of projects (Staiger, 1985a, 1985b; Turner, Keegan, & Crawford, 2000).

Generically, project-based organizing is divided into two principal phases: The first involves design, planning, and gathering of resources, and the second involves committing these resources to full production (Cleland, 1995). The constraints of design irreversibility shape the relationship between the first and the second phase. In manufacturing design irreversibility is high: It is difficult to modify basic design following production (Sanchez, 2000). In the motion picture industry, on the other hand, lower design irreversibility makes it possible to make major changes in the product prior to market launch. This characteristic is key to understanding how the central producer system works.

The flow of studio operations is divided into preproduction, production, and postproduction work. Preproduction consists of three distinct but related sets of activities. First, it involves coordinating the activities of departments such as story reading and writing, background research, set design, costumes, makeup, and cinematography. Second, preproduction involves the integration of creative, technical, and marketing knowledge into a coherent and detailed shooting script. Third, director, cast, and key members of the production team are selected.

Production consists of principal photography on location or studio backlot. Rushes—each day's worth of film shooting—are normally developed for viewing on the same day (hence the term). Key members of the team, including the producer, view the rushes to check for quality of photography and performance.

Postproduction consists of editing, additional photography (retakes), and soundtrack. Postproduction also includes previewing the rough cut to a select audience, gauging their reaction, and making further changes if they are deemed necessary. These changes may run the gamut from minor editing to extensive reshooting of major scenes in the film.

The focal point in the central producer system is the team of producers headed by the studio head of production. The team has two roles. The first role focuses on controlling the process of movie making, from scripts to final editing. The second role constitutes direct involvement in shaping the content of the film itself. What

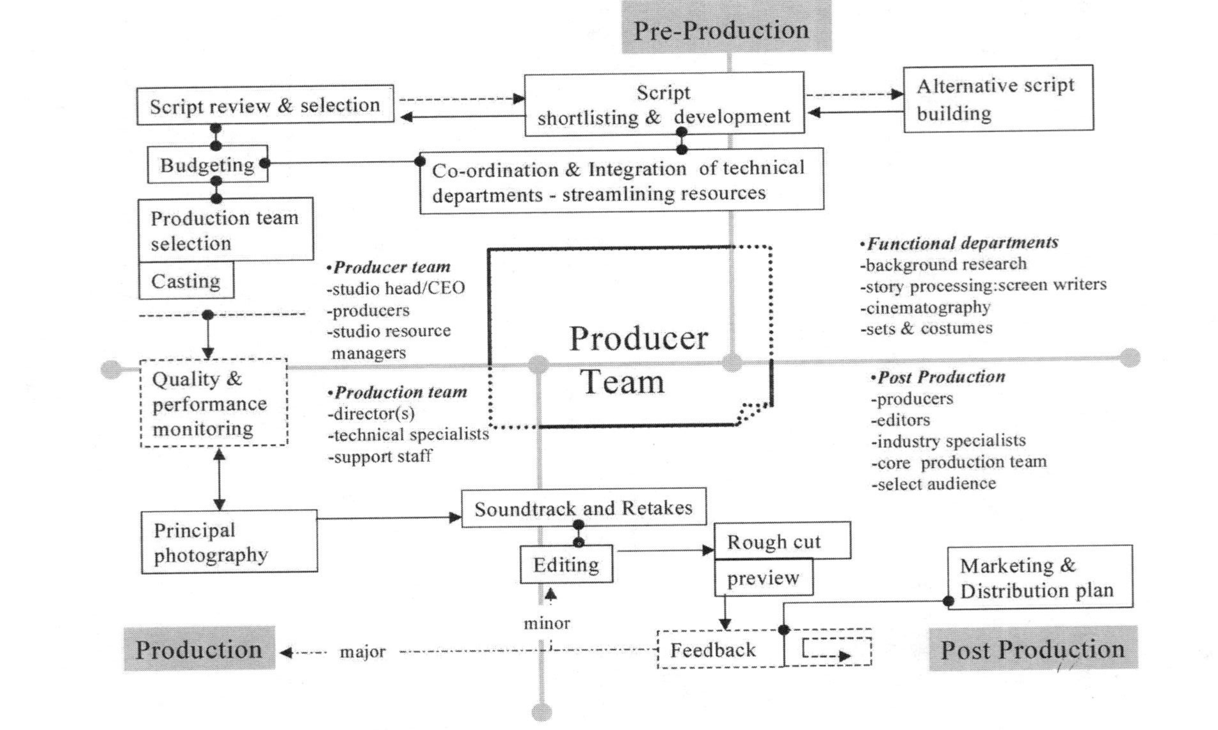

FIG. 4.1. The Central Producer System during the Studio Era.

made the central producer system so effective was the way in which process and content were balanced and closely integrated.

The producer team exerted its influence in critical transitions in the development of movie projects. Early script development was generally left to a group of writers that worked in specially designated departments. Scripts that were seen as promising were selected for further development by the team. This development consisted of intense analysis and discussion of every aspect of the script. The team brought to bear its collective experience. The script was examined from the perspective of narrative logic, motivation, and appeal to audience. At the end of the process a detailed script was prepared, a director assigned, and casting decided.

During principal photography the producer team reduced its involvement, but maintained close monitoring of the production. Their role was primarily one of knowledgeable observers, occasionally pointing to problems or suggesting improvements. Exception to this hands-off supervision would be a major crisis that required additional allocation of resources or forceful intervention to deal with key personnel such as stars or directors.

The first complete version of the film—the rough cut—was generally handled by specialists under the guidance of the director. Upon completion the rough cut was submitted to the producer team for analysis and opinion. In effect, the producer team took possession of the film and laid out a series of recommendations of what the finished version should look like. Under the studio system it was not uncommon for a completely different director to take over the finishing process. In effect, the central producer system was based on the assumption that the director did not have the necessary perspective to ensure the full integrity of the film as an artistic and commercial product.

Previewing the film with select audiences allowed the producer team a last opportunity to reshape the film, but this time with marketability as the key consideration. Enthusiastic audience response fed directly into release and marketing decisions. Ambiguous or negative audience response required rethinking. Individual and collective experiences were mobilized to decide exactly what is wrong with the movie and how it should be corrected.

Surveying the Hollywood studios in the first half of the 20th century, Schatz (1996) spoke of the "genius of the system," the heart of which was the central producer system. But what exactly made it so uniquely capable of balancing artistic and market demands?

There is a fundamental tension between the dynamics of departmental specialization that underpins modern corporations and the imperatives of project management. The first imperative pulls toward dividing the project into distinct tasks that are controlled by departments (Wheelwright & Clark, 1992). The second imperative pulls toward concentrating control within the project team. The role of managerial hierarchies is to balance this tension according to the strategic needs of the firm. This usually means overseeing the project-planning process, but not being intensely involved in the detail. And it also means stepping away from the process once a project leader has been appointed and his or her authority has been defined (Greiner & Schien, 1981).

The central producer system, with a managerial hierarchy in the form of the top producer team, deviates from the common practice described earlier in several ways. First, the top producer team is often deeply involved in the conceptualization and detail of the project. Second, and more importantly, it does not resolve the tension between functional specialization and project leaders in favor of one or the other. Rather, the perennial struggle between functional departments and project managers is resolved by bringing top management downward into the process. This is not a solution that is frequently adopted in most project-based organizations, but one that seemed to work well during the studio era (Lampel, 2001; Turner et al., 2000).

THE EVOLUTION OF THE CENTRAL PRODUCER SYSTEM

The evolution of the motion picture industry can be divided into roughly four phases. The technological phase, in which key film making technologies were introduced, began around 1891 and ended at 1903 with the first narrative film, *The Great Train Robbery* (1903). The prestudio era, characterized by standardization of film content into specified length and set of conventions lasted from about 1903 to 1915 with the first feature film, *Birth of a Nation* (MacGowan, 1965). During this era the director-unit system, which I discuss later, came to dominate.

The studio era of vertically integrated firms commenced around 1915 and entered decline in 1948 with the U.S. Supreme Court decision that forced the Hollywood studios to exit the exhibition business. It was here that the central producer system evolved and became dominant. And finally, the poststudio era began in the mid 1950s and is still with us today. The industry structure and business strategies that dominate each of these phases were crafted and negotiated during the transition periods from one phase to the next.

The studio system emerged as a result of distinct strategic developments that coalesced into a strong configuration. The first development was the emergence of vertical integration (Gomery, 1986). Most studios (though not all) saw the joint ownership of production, distribution, and exhibition as creating synergies that are essential for competitive advantage. Control of exhibition allowed the studios to offset the risks of production, and control over distribution permitted coordinated release that is essential for national marketing.

Second, after a period of resistance, primarily due to fear of excessive salary demands, all the studios acquiesced to the "star system," a human resource strategy based on the premise that feature films will depend heavily for their commercial success on popular actors. The star system was strongly coupled with the third element of the studio system, exclusive contracts binding key personnel, such as stars, to the studios.

As the studio system emerged, the so-called moguls, the entrepreneurs who created the vertically integrated system, faced a dilemma: How will this system be managed in such a way as to deliver a stream of quality feature films at predictable intervals at the lowest cost possible?

The central producer system was the answer that the studios developed to deal with this dilemma. It is not, however, an answer that emerged as a result of deliberate analysis and conscious design. Rather, it evolved as a series of experiments that eventually culminated in the central producer system. The driving force behind many of these experiments was Irving Thalberg, production chief at Universal under Carl Laemmle, and subsequently at MGM under Louis B. Mayer.

Although Thalberg was the primary innovator behind the central producer system, there is no evidence that he thought through his actions with a view to designing such a system. Instead, what we see are discrete actions in the face of problems that are the product of tensions in an industry in transition. To understand these actions it is necessary to examine the problems Thalberg faced in the context in which he was operating.

Thalberg was barely 20 years old when he accompanied Carl Laemmle on an inspection tour of Universal's studio operations in Hollywood. At the end of the visit, Laemmle went back to New York, but instructed Thalberg to remain behind as an observer (Thomas, 2000). Thalberg observed but did not interfere. What he saw could be charitably described as organized chaos. Much of the chaos could be attributed to the director unit system (Staiger, 1985b). The system, which dates back to the prestudio era, developed at the same time as the feature film was emerging as a standardized design. In an industry where the quality of the finished product was highly inconsistent, the success or failure of the film was generally attributed to the director. The trade press closely analyzed notable productions for innovations in technique and narrative (Bowser, 1990). Directors such as D. W. Griffith and Cecil B. de Mille became sufficiently well known to be a marketing force in their own right.

Inevitably, these attributions translated into power for the directors. Successful directors were accustomed to setting terms. They demanded autonomy and control. When Biograph Company contracted with exhibitors in 1913 to produce two feature films a week, D. W. Griffith, Biograph's leading director, decided to leave. Aside from being angry at not having been consulted about the move, Griffith was not inclined to set aside his projects and direct feature films based on plays favored by the exhibitors (Bowser, 1990, p. 219). This should not have come as a complete surprise to Biograph. He had, after all produced a four-reel spectacle, *Judith of Bethulia* (1914), in early 1913 without bothering to ask permission from Biograph's executives (Bowser, p. 204).

The power of the directors was first challenged when they failed to stop the emergence of the star system. Both directors and moguls opposed the emergence of film stars. Moguls were concerned that naming actors in the credits would encourage them to demand higher salaries. At the same time, however, the moguls were quick to capitalize on the box office pull of stars. Directors, on the other hand, opposed the rise of the star system for two important reasons. First, stars represented a direct threat to their almost total control of production. Second, prior to the contract system that bound stars to the studio, stars had contracted with the highest bidder. Directors, accustomed to seeing the popularity of stars as merely the reflective glory of the picture they directed, were naturally resentful when stars used this popularity to negotiate better terms elsewhere (Bowser, 1990, pp. 103–119).

The entrepreneurs who dominated the prestudio era sought to reduce the autonomy of directors, but prior to the studio era these efforts seemed to falter. (Although some of these entrepreneurs would go on to restructure the industry and become the moguls of the studio system, most would not survive the transition.) In 1913, the Lubin Company announced the creation of a script department with the intent of confining directors to executing detailed script prepared by "experts" (Staiger, 1985b, p. 137). In practice, the cost advantages of this move were often undermined by the difficulty of ensuring box office success. The industry entrepreneurs still believed that directors knew best how to transform a film scenario into successful box office product. In 1917, for example, Jesse L. Lasky Feature Film Company revealed that it was abandoning the attempt to limit the autonomy of directors. From now on, the company announced:

> Each director in our four studios will be absolutely independent to produce to the best of his efficiency and ability. With the discontinuance of the central scenario bureau each director will have his own writing staff and the author will continue active work on every production until its conclusion, staying by the side of the director even when the film is cut and assembled. (Staiger, p. 137)

Under the director unit system, directors were in full control of producing, rewriting, directing, and editing functions. They had to report at regular intervals to top management, but the supervision was light. H. M. Horkeimer, general manager and president of Balboa in 1915, was not atypical:

> I have a fixed time each day for meeting directors. We go over the work in hand. I have confidence in them, hence I never ask them why they are doing a thing while they are at work. I wait until the production is finished and then pass [a decision] on it. (cited in Staiger, 1985a, p. 123)

As a rule, directors and their teams stayed together from picture to picture. Inevitably, they focused on maximizing the resources that could be made available for their projects. This struggle for resources led to the chaos that Thalberg observed. Each director was a center of power in his own right. Their power waxed and waned with the performance of their pictures in the box office. At Universal the situation was exacerbated by the lack of an effective and unified managerial control system. Local managers were so weak that directors often invented orders from head office in New York to justify their actions.

When Laemmle returned to Universal City, Thalberg had a simple recommendation: "The first thing you should do is establish a new job of studio manager and give him the responsibility of watching day-to-day operations" (Thomas, 2000, p.

27). Laemmle's response was to give to Thalberg the very responsibility he suggested. At the age of 20 Irving Thalberg became the youngest person to head a Hollywood major studio.

Thalberg's first challenge was to bring the studio's costs under control. This meant confronting the excesses of the director unit system, something that could not be accomplished without coming into direct conflict with some of the more powerful directors in Universal.

The battle was joined when Thalberg took on the extravagant expenditures of Erich Von Stroheim, one of Universal's leading directors. Von Stroheim had insisted that the studio build a life-size replica of Monte Carlo, complete with casino and Hotel de Paris for his film *Foolish Wives* (1922). Unfortunately, the landlocked Universal could not replicate the Riviera, so Von Stroheim therefore insisted that another set be constructed by the ocean on the Monterey peninsula, some 350 miles north of Los Angeles.

A year into the shooting, and a million dollars into budget, Thalberg went to Monterey, and overriding Von Stroheim's strenuous objections insisted that the shooting should end. The film was a critical success, but barely broke even. Nevertheless, Thalberg was willing to give Von Stroheim's next project, *Merry-Go-Round* (1923), the green light. Five weeks into the shooting Thalberg began to realize that Von Stroheim had no intention of abiding by the budget or schedule constraints. He had spent $210,000 and had produced only a few hundred feet of film. Von Stroheim was invited to appear in front of Thalberg. According to Thomas (2000, p. 31), Thalberg informed Von Stroheim that he was off the picture. Von Stroheim was indignant. "That is impossible. *Merry-Go-Around* is *my* picture. I conceived it, and I will see it through to the end. No one can take Von Stroheim off a Von Stroheim picture" (emphasis in original).

In 1923 Thalberg left Universal and moved to the Mayer Company, which became Metro Goldwyn Mayer (MGM) in 1924. It did not take long before he had to confront Von Stroheim again. Von Stroheim had embarked on a major project for MGM that eventually became *Greed* (1924). Von Stroheim eschewed the studio lot, preferring to shoot in the all too realistic setting of Death Valley. After months of shooting, and close to half a million dollars spent, Von Stroheim had amassed 42 reels of film, enough for four long feature films. Thalberg asked Von Stroheim to cut the movie to a manageable length. Von Stroheim refused. It was left to Thalberg and an editor to cut the film. Von Stroheim's career at MGM however was not yet over. Thalberg gave Von Stroheim another chance with *The Merry Widow* (1925), a popular stage operetta. As always, Von Stroheim ran over budget, abused his actors, and eventually got into a violent altercation with Louis B. Mayer himself. He was shown the door, but in true Hollywood fashion made a comeback as an actor in MGM's *As You Desire Me* which was released in 1932.

Von Stroheim's conflict with Thalberg was remarkable only because the talented Austrian director refused to read the writing on the wall. Most directors fell into line. Soon after he took over, Thalberg asserted his authority by taking over the production of *Ben Hur* (1925), another Goldwyn project that had run into trouble.

The film was being shot in Rome. Watching the rushes in Los Angeles, Thalberg concluded that the film would not live up to the bestselling novel on which it was based. His next move showed how the central producer system would differ from the director unit system that had dominated the industry.

At Universal, Thalberg's main focus had been efficiency. With *Ben Hur* he showed that he was willing to focus on quality as well. Thalberg took decisive action. He replaced the original director and the star, incurring an upfront loss of a half-million dollars. The shooting recommenced in Rome with Fred Niblo as director and Ramon Navarro in the role of Ben Hur. Thalberg was still dissatisfied with the quality of the rushes. He ordered the film back to Culver City. The film had so far cost 2 million dollars, and was only one third finished. For Thalberg, the film's salvation lay in the famous chariot race. He allocated $300,000 for construction of the Antioch Coliseum on a field near the studio. No expense was spared in filming the chariot race. Thalberg edited the film himself, and it was a phenomenal box office success.

Ben Hur had cost 4 million dollars, twice the amount of any previous production. It made only a modest profit for MGM when it was released in 1925. It was, however, an important learning experience for Thalberg, and a powerful demonstration, if such was needed, that the director unit system was being replaced by the central producer system.

The transition from the director unit system to the central producer system was partly hastened by major changes in script-writing practices. In the early days of the motion picture industry, directors worked from outlines that they developed as the shooting progressed. The director unit system saw the emergence of scripts. Most scripts contained a title, a short synopsis, and a shot-by-shot account of the action (Staiger, 1985a, p. 126). However, as films became longer and narratives more complex, it became increasingly important to produce what came to be known as "continuity scripts"—scripts that carefully detailed every shot in the film.

Preparing an effective continuity script required special skills that most directors lacked. Scenarists were often employed for the task of translating a loose script into a proper continuity script. Inevitably this reduced the freedom of directors to introduce changes during production. When Thalberg was at Universal he took advantage of continuity scripts to control costs and enforce schedules. At MGM he shifted the center of gravity in film making further toward story development and script analysis.

Thalberg was unusual in Hollywood in that he did not rely on summaries prepared by readers to identify promising novels or plays. He read the original material himself, and if he liked it, it was assigned to one of his deputies, the so-called supervisors. The assigned supervisor worked with writers and so-called story constructionist to produce the initial script (Schatz, 1996, p. 105). The team met regularly with Thalberg to go over the progress of the script. In lengthy meetings they thrashed out the detail of the script. Thalberg was obsessive when it came to ensuring the narrative integrity of the film. Full story and script development took anywhere from 6 months to a year, but he believed that not only should each scene and sequence be well scripted, but that the entire film should be seamless.

A meticulously prepared script allowed Thalberg to relax control during shooting. As long as the director stayed faithful to the script, and as long as no major problems emerged, Thalberg confined his involvement to periodically viewing the rushes. When shooting and first editing was complete, however, he personally took control of the film.

Thalberg was fond of saying that "movies aren't made, they're remade" (Thomas, 2000, p. 117). He was not the first to use previews to test audience reaction, but he developed the practice into a finely tuned craft. For Thalberg, the preview was not simply an opportunity to gauge potential box office performance, it was also a crucial opportunity to experience the movie in its totality. Thalberg previews evolved into a ritual that all the supervisors were required to attend. If the preview was unsatisfactory the entire team swung into action, bringing their collective experience to bear on how the movie could be improved.

This often involved major reshooting. Thalberg did not shy away from the expense involved. He believed that reshooting could transform a bad movie into a good one. And for those who criticized what seemed like throwing good money after bad, he responded posing the following question:

> Take a man in the oil business. Supposing he drills a thousand feet and he starts producing four hundred barrels a day. But the experts tell him if he drills another thousand feed he might well get a thousand barrels a day. Would he be wise man to be satisfied with four hundred barrels? (Thomas, 2000, p. 118)

Thalberg was the undisputed chief of production until 1932 when he and Louis B. Mayer had a falling out. Though they papered over their differences, the confrontation prompted Mayer and Nick Schenck, MGM's top executive, to reorganize production in 1933. The restructuring involved giving more autonomy to Thalberg's immediate subordinates, his so-called supervisors. Thalberg accepted the change. The success of the central producer system he helped to develop created a scope of operations that were greater than he alone could oversee.

The new structure at MGM severed the strong relationship between the studio head of production and the central production system. The central producer system was pushed downward. Supervisors became associate producers, each with responsibility for a small portfolio of films—usually within a genre. Thalberg continued to be highly influential, attending story conferences and often giving informal advice to his former subordinates. Now that his power was diminished, it became even more evident the extent to which the central producer system had become deeply embedded in MGM, and beyond. The central producer system was being widely emulated beyond MGM, in part due to the migration of talented MGM producers such as David Selznick, and in part because MGM was the dominant studio in Hollywood with profits that were greater than all the other major studios combined.

When Thalberg died in 1936, Hollywood shut down for his funeral. Though his name never appeared in the credits of any of the films that he made during his lifetime, he was widely viewed as the embodiment of the studio's managerial system. As Schatz (1996, p. 174) put it, when Thalberg died, Hollywood "lost the man who first learned to calculate the whole equation of pictures, who understood the delicate balance of art and commerce in moviemaking. Thalberg developed a management style that was efficient without being inflexible, disciplined without being inhumane, extravagant without being wasteful."

CONTROL VERSUS AUTONOMY IN CULTURAL INDUSTRIES

When new industries evolve beyond the nascent phase of their development, established firms, key providers of resources, and actors with investments in the industry must negotiate anew the distribution of power and the exercise of influence (Wiesenfeld, Raghuram, & Garud, 2001). The early phase of industries is one of exploration, invention, and financial risk taking (Mezias & Mezias, 2000). Power and influence in this phase often goes to capital providers, entrepreneurs, and owners of intellectual property (Jones, 2001). As consumer tastes are revealed, technologies become well defined, and the value chain coalesces around distinct activities, the power relations that were established during the emergence of the industry are often challenged (Aldrich & Fiol, 1994). The challenge usually comes from individuals and organizations with an interest in establishing a dominant position in the industry, either by controlling crucial resources and key areas, or by imposing unified governance structures on separate activities (Freeland, 2000).

As may be expected, resistance to this effort inevitably comes from individuals and organizations that have the most to lose from industry restructuring (Starkey, Barnatt, & Tempest, 2000). Resistance, however, tends to be even more tenacious when the attack is experienced at the level of identity and ideology. Individuals and organizations that closely link their identity with their autonomy often see efforts to transform the industry not merely as economic action but as an existential threat (Quinn, Andrews, & Finkelstein, 1996). At a minimum they passively resist the industry transformation, mostly by attempting to preserve their roles in the new order. If they can, however, they openly fight to have it stopped (Raelin, 1991).

Such open resistance is most often the case when human resources are central to the product's creation, as in the case of cultural industries. Cultural industries attract individuals with a strong sense of vocation, a passion for autonomy, and powerful ideologies that are legitimized by wider cultural traditions (Wijnberg & Gemser, 2000). New cultural industries provide an opportunity for creative individuals to acquire resources and forge new roles in an emerging economic space (Faulkner, 1987). New cultural industries also promote collective action (Friedrich, 1997). Creative individuals network for a variety of reasons: to exchange employment information, to share craft experience, and to sense future developments. Networks evolve into communities as common knowledge and shared consciousness are transformed into structured interaction and articulated ideologies (Abrahamson & Fombrun, 1992).

Communities of artistic practice generally enjoy a high degree of autonomy during the nascent phase of industry formation and are able to control resources by virtue of their catalytic role in the creation of the industry (Huberman & Hogg, 1995). Their relationship to the commercial realities of the industry, however, is ambiguous. On the one hand, they actively seek the rents that derive from market and product development, but at the same time they resist the economic forces that push for incorporating creative activities within a managerial and organizational logic (Glynn, 2000).

If power alone was the key factor in the clash between communities of creative practice and economic actors seeking to reorganize the industry, then the outcome would be almost inevitable. Creative communities of practice seldom have the structure and resources needed to resist incorporation into corporate hierarchies (Noble, 1979). (Mobilizing state support for the arts or migration to the nonprofit sector are usually the only viable alternatives.) The conflict, however, rarely comes down to a pure power play. As Seely Brown and Duguid (2001) pointed out, attempts to impose managerial and organizational discipline on creative processes tend to backfire. Creative work cannot be systemized into set processes. Attempts to reengineer the creative process in much the same manner as other production or organization processes are doomed to failure. Beyond a certain point, gains in efficiency come at the expense of the creative process. In all too many cases, imposing a neo-Taylorist managerial process on creative practice ends up killing the goose that lays the golden eggs.

The key challenge facing those who wish to transform a nascent cultural industry into a mature oligopoly is how to strike a balance between efficient processes and creative capabilities. Seely Brown and Duguid (2001) outlined the magnitude of the challenge:

> That balance is not easy to achieve. Process emphasizes the hierarchical, explicit command-and-control side of organization the structure that gets things done. By contrast, practice emphasizes the implicit coordination and exploration that produces things to do. Practice without process tends to become unmanageable; process without practice results in the loss of creativity needed for sustained innovation. (p. 93)

In some cultural industries (e.g., recorded music) balance is struck by allowing islands of creative practice to evolve within the corporate structure (Huygens, Baden-Fuller, Van den Bosch, & Volberda, 2001). The corporation monitors financial and market performance, but otherwise allows these creative islands a high degree of autonomy. The strategy that tends to emerge is one of portfolio management. Corporate management spends much of its energy identifying promising individuals and projects, providing the required resources, and then hoping that commercially successful products will emerge (Faulkner & Anderson, 1987; Peterson & Berger, 1971).

Thalberg could have developed this structure for MGM. This strategy also emerged in the poststudio era of the film industry (Robins, 1993; Storper, 1989). Thalberg, however, developed a managerial system that took more complete advantage of the creative and commercial resources of MGM by cross-leveraging these resources across multiple projects. He did this by creating a producer team and a set of practices that melded managerial processes with creative input. Key to the success of the system was an understanding of creative abrasion: deliberately bringing into conflict divergent and opposing perspectives as a way of unleashing design ideas that satisfy opposing imperatives (Hirshberg, 1999).

For Thalberg, the opposing imperatives were box office success on the one hand, and delivering movies with high-quality on-screen performance and coherent film narrative on the other. The central producer system allowed Thalberg and MGM to satisfy both of these imperatives by creating a virtuous circle between project experience and producer team expertise. Each project generated lessons that made their way via the producer team into the planning and execution of the next project. The concentration of general project experience in the producer team both counteracted and complemented the tendency of specialized areas to focus on their territory at the expense of wider issues. It promoted commercial appeal at the very earliest stages of planning without sacrificing artistic integrity, and it ensured artistic integrity at the very end of the process by institutionalizing a search for solutions that were artistically as well as commercially creative.

CONCLUSION

In 1916 Charlie Chaplin sought a court injunction preventing Essanay Production and V-LS-E from releasing the film *Charlie Chaplin's Burlesque on "Carmen"* (1916). Chaplin had been an employee of the company, but after his departure the company added another 4,000 feed of film, which, Chaplin charged, was of such low quality that it injured his reputation (Staiger, 1985b, p. 140).

Chaplin lost the case. The courts ruled that the rights of ownership took precedence over the rights of authorship. The ruling had important ramifications to the emerging motion picture industry, and beyond (Vaidhyanathan, 2001). It put managers in control of the final product, and sent a clear warning to creative artists who, by tradition and inclination, had always equated the integrity of cultural products with the identity of individual artists.

The struggle, however, was not over. It had simply been transformed into a clash between commercial risk and artistic risk. Firms in the cultural industries are sensitive to the financial risks that are normally attached to the production and distribution of cultural goods. Artists, on the other hand, are sensitive to the risks to their reputation that come with market rejection and critical failure. Cultural industries have evolved mechanisms to balance these risks. Sometime these mechanisms work badly, and at other times they work well. The challenge, as this chapter suggests, is not simply to balance risks, but to develop organizations that can creatively fulfill both commercial imperatives and artistic aspirations.

REFERENCES

Abrahamson, E., & Fombrun, C. J. (1992). Forging the iron cage: Interorganizational networks and the production of macro-culture. *Journal of Management Studies, 29,* 175–194.

Aldrich, H. E., & Fiol, C. M. (1994). Fools rush in? The institutional context of industry creation. *Academy of Management Review, 19,* 645–670.

Bowser, E. (1990). *The transformation of cinema 1907–1915.* Berkeley, CA: University of California Press.

Caves, R. (2000). *Creative industries: Contracts between art and commerce.* Cambridge, MA: Harvard University Press.

Cleland, D. I. (1995). *Project management: Strategic design and implementation* (2nd ed.). New York: McGraw-Hill.

Faulkner, R. R. (1987). *Music on demand: Composers and careers in the Hollywood film industry.* New Brunswick, NJ: Transaction Books.

Faulkner, R. R., & Anderson, A. B. (1987). Short-term projects and emergent careers: Evidence from Hollywood. *American Journal of Sociology, 92,* 879–909.

Freeland, R. F. (2000). Creating hold-up through vertical integration: Fisher Body revisited. *Journal of Law and Economics, 43,* 33–66.

Friedrich, O. (1997). *City of nets: A portrait of hollywood in the 1940's.* Berkeley and Los Angeles, CA: University of California Press.

Glynn, M. A. (2000). When cymbals become symbols: Conflict over organizational identity within a symphony orchestra. *Organization Science, 11,* 285–298.

Gomery, D. (1986). *The Hollywood studio system.* Oxford, UK: Palgrave, Macmillan.

Greiner, L. E., & Schein, V. E. (1981). The paradox of managing a project-oriented matrix: Establishing coherence within chaos. *Sloan Management Review, 22,* 17–22.

Hirshberg, J. (1999). *The creative priority: Putting innovation to work in your business.* New York: Harper Business.

Huberman, B. A., & Hogg, T. (1995). Communities of practice: Performance and evolution. *Computational and Mathematical Organization Theory, 1,* 73–92.

Huygens, M., Baden-Fuller, C., Van den Bosch, F. A. J., & Volberda, H. (2001). Coevolution of firm capabilities and industry. *Organization Studies, 22,* 971–1012.

Jones, C. (2001). Co-evolution of entrepreneurial careers, institutional rules and competitive dynamics in the American film, 1895-1920. *Organization Studies, 22,* 911–944.

Lampel, J. (2001). The core competencies of effective project execution: The challenge of diversity. *International Journal of Project Management, 19,* 471–483.

Lampel, J., Lant, T., & Shamsie, J. (2000). Balancing act: Learning from organizing practices in cultural industries. *Organization Science, 11,* 263–269.

Macgowan, K. (1965). *Behind the screen: The history and techniques of the motion picture.* New York: Delacorte Press.

Mezias, S. J., & Kuperman, J. (2000). The community dynamics of entrepreneurship: The birth of the American film industry, 1895–1929. *Journal of Business Venturing, 16,* 209–233.

Mezias, J. M., & Mezias, S. J. (2000). Resource partitioning, the founding of specialist firms, and innovation: The American feature film industry, 1912–1929. *Organization Science, 11,* 306–322.

Noble, D. (1979). *America by design: Technology and the rise of corporate capitalism.* Oxford, UK: Oxford University Press.

Peterson, R. A., & Berger, D. G. (1971). Entrepreneurship in organizations: Evidence from the popular music industry. *Administrative Science Quarterly, 16,* 97–106.

Puttnam, D. (1997). *Movies and money.* New York: Vintage Books.
Quinn, J. B., Andrews, P., & Finkelstein, S. (1996). Managing expertise. *Academy of Management Executive, 10,* 7–27.
Raelin, J. A. (1991). *The clash of cultures: Managers managing professionals.* Boston: Harvard Business School Press.
Robins, J. (1993). Organization as strategy: Restructuring production in the film industry. *Strategic Management Journal, 14,* 103–118.
Sanchez, R. (2000). Modular architectures, knowledge assets and organizational learning: New management processes for product creation. *International Journal of Technology Management, 19,* 610–629.
Schatz, T. (1996). *The genius of the system: Hollywood filmmaking in the studio era.* New York: Holt.
Seely Brown, J., & Duguid, P. (2001). Creativity versus structure: A useful tension. *Sloan Management Review, 42,* 93–94.
Staiger, J. (1985a). The Hollywood mode of production, 1930–1960. In D. Bordwell, J. Staiger, & K. Thompson (Eds.), *The classical Hollywood cinema: Film style and mode of production to 1960* (pp. 309–337). London: Routledge.
Staiger, J. (1985b). The Hollywood mode of production to 1930. In D. Bordwell, J. Staiger, & K. Thompson (Eds.), *The classical Hollywood cinema: Film style and mode of production to 1960* (pp. 85–95). London: Routledge.
Starkey, K., Barnatt, C., & Tempest, S. (2000). Beyond networks and hierarchies: Latent organizations in the U.K. television industry. *Organization Science, 11,* 299–305.
Storper, M. (1989). The transition to flexible specialization in the US film industry: External economies, the division of labor, and the crossing of industrial divides. *Cambridge Journal of Economics, 13,* 273–305.
Thomas, B. (2000). *Thalberg: Life and legend.* Beverly Hills, CA: New Millennium Press.
Turner, J. R., Keegan, A., & Crawford, X. (2000). Learning by experience in the project-based organization. In J. R. Turner, A. Keegan, & X. Crawford (Eds.), *Proceedings of Project Management Institute (PMI) conference* (pp. 445–456). Place: Publisher still needed.
Vaidhyanathan, S. (2001). *Copyrights and copywrongs: The rise of intellectual property and how it threatens creativity.* New York: New York University Press.
Wheelwright, S. C., & Clark, K. B. (1992). *Revolutionizing product development: Quantum leaps in speed, efficiency, and quality.* New York: Free Press.
Wiesenfeld, B., Raghuram, S., & Garud, R. (2001). Organizational identification among virtual workers: The role of need for affiliation and perceived work-based social support. *Journal of Management, 27,* 213–229.
Wijnberg, N. M., & Gemser, G. (2000). Adding value to innovation: Impressionism and the transformation of the selection system in visual arts. *Organization Science, 11,* 323–329.

CHAPTER

5

Maestro or Manager? Examining the Role of the Music Director in a Symphony Orchestra

Mary Ann Glynn
Emory University

The question of identity is paramount for cultural institutions. Most organizations involved in the production of culture have identities that are hybrid (Albert & Whetten, 1985), consisting of elements—artistic and utilitarian—that are potentially conflictual. The artistry defines the cultural institution, as for example, a museum of modern art, a cutting-edge theater company, or a popular music studio, but the utilitarian aspects of managing the cultural institution as a business build generative capabilities that enable strategic adaptation to changing economic conditions. And although these two identity elements can be in conflict, it is by managing a healthy balance between the dual aspects of identity that cultural institutions create and maximize value.

Managing the fragile balance between potentially conflictual identity elements is consequential for organizations, as it affects not only how an organization defines itself, as, for instance, a world-class symphony or as a fiscally responsible one, but also how strategic concerns, as well as organizational capabilities and resources, are understood and managed (Dutton, 1997; Dutton & Dukerich, 1991; Dutton, Dukerich, & Harquail, 1994), and to what effect. However, in spite of its consequential impact, organizational scholars still know little about managing hybrid identities. Some researchers have begun to uncover how the strains between hybrid identity elements operate within organizations (e.g., Glynn, 2000; Golden-Biddle & Rao, 1997), but little is known about the role organizational structures play in managing hybrid organizational identities.

Cultural institutions are opportune sites for examining the structural dynamics of hybridized organizational identities. Within cultural institutions, different actors in different organizational roles—managers who balance budgets and artisans who produce culture—typify the dual identity elements. Moreover, the roles are characterized by very different professional ideologies, each associated with different agendas and interests (Glynn, 2000). Thus, different actors, in their different organizational roles, can emphasize and advance different aspects of the organization's identity (Albert & Whetten, 1985; Golden-Biddle & Rao, 1997), either exacerbating latent tensions between artistic and utilitarian elements or dampening them to achieve synthesis and organizational synergy.

In this chapter, I investigate the role of the music director, a pivotal structural role in the symphony orchestra that incorporates, and bridges, artistry and administration. I examine changes in the role and its occupant during a time of particularly high conflict and contestation between the organization's hybrid identity elements—a musician's strike at the Atlanta Symphony Orchestra (ASO) in 1996. Drawing from a larger study reported elsewhere (Glynn, 2000), and incorporating new data from interviews and press accounts, I examine the impact of identity claims made by, and made on, the ASO music director during this time of heightened and public organizational strife.

My research site is the ASO, where latent conflict between musicians and administrators culminated in the 1996 musicians' strike. Strikes administer organizational jolts and render transparent issues that may have been hidden during more routine periods (Meyer, 1982). The chapter is organized as follows. I begin by theorizing how elements of hybrid organizational identities map on to features of organizational structure. In particular, I focus on how the role of the music director (also called the orchestra conductor) both embodies and demarcates the potentially discordant elements of the orchestra identity. Next, I examine how this role serves to compartmentalize and contain these latent conflicts, by focusing on the identity claims made by, and made on, the music director, both internally and externally, by employees of the symphony (administrators and musicians), as well as music critics and journalists who cover the symphony in the local Atlanta newspaper. I expose how structural roles in organizations carry critical identity elements as well as manage the boundaries between them. Finally, I draw out broader implications for managing structural and identity dynamics that underlie the business of culture.

HYBRID IDENTITIES AND ORGANIZATIONAL STRUCTURE

In their influential article on organizational identity, Albert and Whetten (1985) defined hybrid identities as those that contain two different identity elements that are not typically found together. The archetypical hybrid is one that conjoins a normative (or ideological) element to a utilitarian (or economic) element. Interestingly, this particular combination of identity elements seems to describe cultural institutions, where, increasingly, the production of culture yokes artistry to economics.

Under girding normative-utilitarian hybrids are "two logical systems of management": "In a normative organization, the principle for determining what ought to be retained is tradition. In a utilitarian organization, the principle is cost-effectiveness" (Albert & Whetten, 1985, p. 287). Moreover, the "loosely coupled ... ideographic structure [acts] as a set of boundaries, keeping apart what might be conflicting points of view, philosophies of education, rules of procedure, and priorities" (Albert & Whetten, p. 286). In the parlance of institutional theorists, such identity elements are bounded by different systems of meaning, cultural values, and institutional logics, all of which lend meaning and thus legitimacy to the collective (Suchman, 1995), but function to separate different aspects so that one does not contaminate another.

Hybridized organizational identities come in two different forms, each with a corresponding organizational structure that has differential capabilities to resolve and integrate identity elements. One form of hybrid identity is holographic, in which each organizational unit mirrors the complex, multifaceted nature of the organization's identity. Each structural unit contains both identity elements, leaving individual organizational members to manage any strains emerging from the conflict between the identity elements. Thus, the hybrid identity is diffuse, and the different identity elements are not restricted to particular structural units or organizational roles; any organizational member conceivably has the capability to enact, perform, or manage the institutional identity. In a study of a holographic, nonprofit organization, Golden-Biddle and Rao (1997) demonstrated that such Janus-headed, hybrid identities create dilemmas for their members to manage. Thus, in holographic organizations, conflicts are resolved within structural units, with each member potentially integrating (or compartmentalizing) the latent conflict implied by the disparate identity elements.

The second form of hybrid identity is ideographic; this form is more characteristic of cultural institutions. Cultural organizations have hybrid identities that are typically specialized or ideographic, for example, artists perform the ideology (music, dance, painting) and administrators manage the business. Thus, incongruous identity elements—normative artistry and utilitarian economics—exist side by side and are claimed by different structural units within the organization (Albert & Whetten, 1985, p. 271). Thus, ideographic organizations have specialized roles that enact and professionalize different elements. For example, in Hollywood movie studios, there is a clear separation of roles and identities between the actors who star in films and the producers who finance and underwrite them. Similarly, in the recording industry, we see specialized roles and identities for the recording artists who make the music and the marketing management who packages and promotes it's cultural products.

In ideographic cultural institutions like these, the organization seeks to sustain and uphold the different identity elements but not necessarily realize synergy between them (Pratt & Foreman, 2000). Clearly, there is little to be gained by having theater actors do organizational accounting or arts administrators perform on stage. Each organizational unit is specialized in its identity, with an attendant set of capabilities, expertise, and professionalism. In my earlier study of a musicians' strike at a symphony orchestra (Glynn, 2000), I found that claims on the orchestra's identity were voiced and championed by the different identity groups—artists and administrators—in ways that were consistent with the legitimating values of their profession: Musicians advanced norms of artistic excellence while administrators espoused fiscal guardianship. Given these specialized roles, the organizational dilemma in ideographic identities when fissures erupt is one of integration, of bringing the two disparate identity elements, with their attendant employees, together to produce the culture that is the hallmark of the institution.

In the remainder of this chapter, I examine such identity and structuration dynamics in one organization: the symphony orchestra during a period of retrenchment and strife. I focus on a highly visible and critical organizational role that reflects and spans the structural boundaries between the two identity elements embedded in the symphony, that of the conductor or music director.

THE MUSIC DIRECTOR AT THE SYMPHONY ORCHESTRA

Allmendinger and Hackman (1996, p. 340) described symphony orchestras as "ensembles whose primary mission is public performance of those orchestral works generally considered to fall within the standard symphonic repertoire and whose members are compensated nontrivially for their services." Symphony orchestras were one of the first institutions to produce and deliver art (*Americanizing the American Orchestra*, 1993, p. 2) and thus they have special standing as a cultural institution.

In the symphony orchestra, musicians playing the symphonic canon enact the normative identity, whereas administrators (managers and board members) enact the utilitarian identity, "governed by values of economic rationality, the maximization of profit, and the minimization of cost" (Albert & Whetten, 1985, pp. 281–282). The structure of the symphony mirrors its hybrid and ideographic identity: Musicians, in their role as orchestra members, enact the ideological (normative) identity that is predicated on artistry, aesthetics, and the music canon; orchestra executives, in their role as managers and board members, emphasize the economics of the symphony, focusing on business acumen and fiscal responsibility.

The specialization of identities in the symphony has yielded a structural design that has been described as somewhat rigid and isolationist, compartmentalizing both the roles and their incumbents (musicians, administrators), as well as their associated identities and logics (*Americanizing the American Orchestra*, 1993, p. 177). The organization of the symphony has been compared to a three-legged stool, consisting of three administrative roles: executive director, chair of the board of directors, and music director (or conductor). Thus, the music director is formally part of the symphony's administrative structure and yet has explicit responsibility for the normative elements of identity and the musical performance of the symphony. In this configuration, the role of music director is unique, in that it reflects, and incorporates, both of the dual identity elements in the orchestra; it is the only role having explicit responsibility in the realm of the aesthetic with a direct line to the symphony's board of directors. The musicians have no formal role in the leadership structure, but instead voice their concerns through the music director or alternative structures, such as the union (i.e., the American Federation of Musicians).

In an interview I conducted with one ASO musician, the role of the music director was described as that of an intermediary, linking the musicians to the symphony's board of directors, bridging, as it were, the normative identity (represented by the musicians) and the utilitarian identity (represented by the administration). It is depicted in Fig. 5.1. As shown, the role of the music director is a structural component that can potentially integrate or mediate conflict arising from the two disparate elements of artistry and administration, or potentially exac-

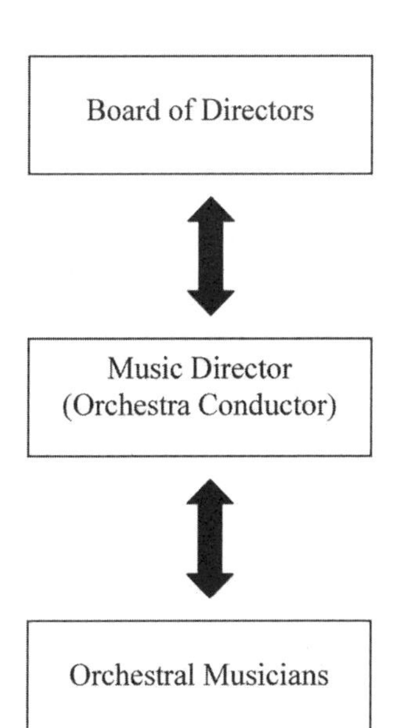

FIG. 5.1. Structure of the symphony orchestra.

erbate such conflict by inflaming and politicizing both sides. Thus, this role is central both to maintaining the hybrid identity of the symphony, because it encapsulates both identity elements (artistic and utilitarian), and to demarcating the boundary between them. Moreover, the role can also be thought of as a strategic resource that can amplify or temper tensions arising from conflicts between these two identity elements, as, for instance, when financial issues threaten to diminish the aesthetic capabilities of the orchestra.

I focus on an overlooked aspect of managing hybrid identities, that of the structural dynamics of organizational roles that speak to both of the key elements of cultural institutions. The hybrid orchestral identity has a parallel in the ways that resources are emphasized and the ways in which the definition of core capabilities is contested. Professional, occupational, and public groups—artists, administrators, and audience—constitute separate identity fields (Hunt, Benford, & Snow, 1994) within the symphony orchestra and, filtered through their particular identity lens, emphasize differential sets of resources and define different institutional capabilities. Their divergent interests, strained by competing claims to a fixed set of resources, can erupt into conflict. At the ASO, this initially occurred over the board's denial of tenure to six probationary musicians for purely financial reasons. Ultimately, this decision not to tenure was reversed and the musicians tenured; however, the initial decision exacerbated the latent rift between musicians and managers and precipitated a musicians' strike in 1996.

Throughout the strike period, the music director was associated at different times with one or the other identity elements, in various accounts, both public and private. In music reviews of the orchestra, published in the local paper (*The Altanta Journal-Constitution*), the music director is always associated with the orchestra but also recognized as an entity apart from it. A sample of several representative descriptions from the published reviews follows. Note how the conjunction *and* routinely joins but separates the conductor from the musicians:

"Even though the music is a briar patch waiting to ensnare a conductor and orchestra, Levi and the ASO are probably the Brer Rabbit of symphonic partnerships ..." (Schwartz, 1997b, p. 23).

"Beethoven, Levi and the ASO used to be two hours of root canal. This is two hours of music" (Schwartz, 1997a, p. 23).

"Yoel Levi's conception of the symphony and his beautifully wrought direction of the orchestra was a wonder" (Schwartz, 1998e, p. 6H).

When the music director and the orchestra are conjoined, at their best they are described as a "penetrating partnership" (Henry, 1995a, p. 4H) or "masterly collaboration" (Henry, 1996c, p. 3D). And, at his best in this relationship, the music director "crafted a virtuoso instrument in the ASO" (Schwartz, 1995, p. 4H). But, even in their partnership, they are recognized as distinctive. For instance, in this passage from a critic's review, the artistic maturity of the music director and the symphony are judged to be different: "[The music director's] bold, dramatic interpretation [of Dvorak] has matured considerably, taking on more subtlety and individuality. The ASO has matured too, projecting a richer, more resplendent sound" (Henry, 1996c, p. 3D). During the crisis precipitated by the musicians' strike, the music director seemed to take an empathetic stance. The newspaper reported his emotional reaction to the decision that triggered the musicians' strike:

> Atlanta Symphony Orchestra music director Yoel Levi expressed hope ... that there's still time to save the jobs of the six musicians whose contracts won't be renewed next season. He even offered to bring out his violin for the first time in 20 years to give a benefit concert. "I want to believe that we can find a way to reverse the situation," said Levi.... Levi was not involved in the decision, made by the board of directors.... Levi refused to comment directly about the artistic consequences of eliminating the six positions, although in the past he has called such downsizing "basically a death sentence." (Henry, 1996b, p. D7)

Levi was not only aligning with the musicians—he was offering to be a musician! Thus, beyond claim making, the music director was embracing one of his roles, that of musician rather than conductor. And, when an anonymous donor came forward, to reduce the deficit and alleviate the financial stress that was bearing down on the artistry, "ASO Music Director Yoel Levi called the grant 'a big miracle; I had tears in my eyes.'" (Henry, 1996a, p. D1). Moreover, in a 1996 leaflet announcing that the ASO would not renew six, nontenure musicians for the 1996–1997 season, Music Director Yoel Levi was quoted as saying:

> This has been a most difficult decision to make. I want to assure the Orchestra and the community that we are committed to maintaining the high level of musical excellence that we have achieved in Atlanta ... but the ultimate success of our Orchestra will depend on the support of this Community, and now is the time for our supporters to come forward and be counted. (ASO Leaflet, 1996)

Thus, as much as the music director is involved in the musical performance, and in planning, interpreting, and conducting the orchestral program, he is still recognized as somewhat apart and distinct from the orchestra and its musicians. Yoel Levi claims the normative identity of the orchestra in his concerns about musical excellence. More than that, he compartmentalizes and safeguards it; the success of the orchestra, it seems, does not lie in its artistry but in its economic support (from the community). In a newspaper article on the strike, the music director was quoted as saying, "The deficit 'definitely puts every artistic aspect of this organization in a question mark'" (Henry, 1995b, p. L8). Thus, he seems to serve in a boundary role, buffering the ideological core—the symphonic artistry—from the demands of marketplace economics. The question then becomes: Does claiming an ideological identity by the music director preclude any additional claims on the utilitarian elements of the symphony identity?

Metaphorically, the music director was described as one of the three legs of the structural stool; it is that configuration that is invoked in aligning him with the administration in other public accounts. For instance, in a leaflet distributed to ASO subscribers and audiences, dated March 15, 1996, and entitled (and capitalized) "AN IMPORTANT MESSAGE," he seems to be on management's side:

> In recent weeks you have seen or heard numerous and serious messages about the Atlanta Symphony Orchestra. This message is coming to you from the Music Director and representatives of the Atlanta Symphony Orchestra's board of directors, staff, and volunteers. While we do not agree on every course of action, we are resolute in our shared commitment to the Orchestra.

However, the same pamphlet continues on, explaining what this administrative group sees as both "The Problem" and its solution ("The Answer"). The effect is to align the music director with very basic utilitarian (economic) concerns, and further cleave him from more normative issues:

> Like each of America's top ten orchestras, the ASO consists of musicians professionally employed under a collective bargaining agreement. Under our agreement, after a two-year probationary period, each musician is tenured ... provided that the organization is financially viable and that the musician continues to meet artistic standards.... "The Problem" [is that] basically the rate of growth of expenses has consistently exceeded the rate of growth of income. [This is due to] the stagnant ticket sales, an inadequate endowment, and debt and operating losses. "The Answers" [are found in] more ticket sales; a generous community of individuals and businesses and reduction of expenses.

Both in claims made by the music director and in those made by music experts and authorities in the press, it is evident that this institutional role carries the dual identity elements that characterize the orchestra: normative ideology (musical artistry) and utilitarian economics (financial concerns). And, by viewing the prominence of this role during an organizational crisis, it becomes evident how one identity element hems in the other. It also reveals the difficult tension between the two, something that this music director was unable to resolve, either for the organization or himself.

Subsequent to the 1996 strike, ASO Music Director Yoel Levi submitted his resignation, effective in 2000. Press accounts made the attribution that this was a response to pressure from the administration; however, both the musicians and the audience made their support clear. Lamented the ASO concertmaster: "It's devastating news. I came here because he had a vision for this orchestra. If we lose him, we lose that vision" (Henry, 1997, p. F1). Stated an ASO board member ("one of the few ASO board members who is a trained musician"): "I think Levi is one of the major talents of this generation and has [built] one of the finest orchestras in the world.... We need to do whatever it takes to [get him to] change his mind and stay here" (Henry, 1997, p. F1).

The ASO Board accepted Levi's resignation; however, subsequent reports claimed that the music director attempted to retract his resignation (Schwartz, 1998a, p. E1):

> In a move almost without precedent in the history of American orchestras, Yoel Levi has asked to withdraw his resignation as music director of the ASO and stay on beyond the expiration of his contract in the summer of 2000.... Levi submitted his letter of resignation last April 23 during negotiations for a new three-year contract.... It was widely believed at the time that Levi's resignation was not submitted voluntarily, but rather was required as a condition of being given his current three-year extension.... It is acknowledged by both Levi's supporters and detractors, however, that his support among the orchestra musicians has eroded in recent years on each annual survey. (Schwartz, 1998b, pp. E1, E2)

After 10 years of conducting orchestral performances, Yoel Levi was popular with the audiences, with most supporting him in his fight with the board: "[Audience] support was unstinting and nearly universal" (Schwartz, 1998c, p. B2). A grassroots organization, "Atlanta for Levi," formed and ran newspaper ads seeking support for the music director:

> An unprecedented event has occurred. 15,247 people have signed a petition in support of Yoel Levi that he continue as Music Director & Artistic Leader of the Atlanta Symphony Orchestra. We know of no other time when there has been a similar expression of support for a Music Director of a symphony orchestra. We know that there are more of you out there who are our perspective. Please join our efforts to keep Yoel Levi! We want Yoel! (Advertisement in *The Atlanta Journal Constitution*, September 26, 1998, p. C7)

However, the board had a different opinion and voted "to thank Yoel Levi for his 10 years of service as the orchestra's music director, but reiterated that he will not stay past the expiration of his contract in the summer of 2000" (Schwartz, 1998a, p. E1). Today, Yoel Levi is Music Director Emeritus of the ASO. His biography states:

While he was ASO Music Director from 1988 to 2000, Mr. Levi's impact on the orchestra was summed up by *Gramophone* magazine, which said, "Yoel Levi has built a reputation for himself and his orchestra that is increasingly the envy of his Big Five American counterparts in New York, Philadelphia, Cleveland, Boston, and Chicago." Among his many ASO milestones are a highly successful performance of Mahler's Symphony No. 2 ("Resurrection") featuring the award-winning ASO Chorus in New York's Avery Fisher Hall, a featured role at the Opening Ceremony of the Centennial Olympic Games in 1996, an extensive and critically acclaimed European tour in 1991, and nomination of the ASO as Best Orchestra of the Year for 1991–1992 by the first annual International Classical Music Awards. He was applauded in a review for his professionalism:

> After this most fractious year in the life of the Atlanta Symphony Orchestra, it's of the highest importance to be reminded that even on an average night the Atlanta

> Symphony Orchestra is a remarkable ensemble and that Yoel Levi, whatever faults are being ascribed to him, will never deliver a less than professional performance. (Schwartz, 1998d, p. 10H)

DISCUSSION AND CONCLUSION

In this chapter, I examined the structural dynamics attending the role of the music director in a symphony orchestra during a period of crisis. I sought to illuminate some of the organizational issues underlying the creation of cultural products, particularly in light of the hybridized identity that typifies these institutions. And, more generally, I sought to show how the tension between the two hybrid identity elements—the aesthetic elements that craft cultural products and the economic elements that characterize their production—create strains for the occupants of organizational roles that embody aspects of both of these elements, particularly in times of organizational crisis and contestation.

This examination of the symphony orchestra revealed how its dual identity elements—artistic and utilitarian—mapped onto one key structural role, that of the music director or conductor. In stable times, this role was pivotal in articulating the dual identity of this cultural institution and creating a boundary that served to compartmentalize and contain the two essential—but potentially conflictual—elements. The role also bridged the divide occasionally, serving as a conduit for ideas, influence, and information (see Fig. 5.1). By incorporating elements of both the normative and utilitarian identities of the orchestra, the role of music director straddles both elements. However, it was in times of organizational strife, retrenchment, and heightened tensions between the identity elements that the role was under the greatest strain, becoming perhaps untenable for the role and its occupant.

At the ASO, the musicians' strike brought out the latent tensions between the two identity groups: musicians and administrators (Glynn, 2000). With declining attendance, graying audiences, and decreased opportunities for touring and recording, orchestras everywhere are facing something of an identity crisis as the aesthetic comes under the assault of market forces that push for greater commercialism and economic savvy (e.g., Glynn, 2002). As orchestras, and other cultural institutions, experience the struggle between defining themselves as artistic endeavors but surviving in the market (e.g., Glynn & Lounsbury, in press), the organizational structure bends—and occasionally breaks—the tenure of its occupant under the weight of such pressures.

The case of the ASO, and its music director Yoel Levi, is not an isolated one. Orchestra conductors are finding that their role is "controversial" (Medrek, 1999, p. A1), both in the United States and in Europe (Loomis, 2004). The reason for this is related to the changing nature of the symphony, as orchestral programs increasingly try to update and change, in an attempt to bring in larger and younger audiences. In response to market and economic pressures, orchestras have begun to draw on more popular interpretations of the musical canon (Glynn, 2002), sometimes blending the "highbrow" art of the classics with more "lowbrow" forms from popular culture (Dowd, Liddle, Lupo, & Borden, 2002). This creates a blurring of the symphony's identity, as the long-dominant aesthetic identity yields to a more commercialized market logic; the result is to challenge the very identity of the symphony. The strain creates pressures for an orchestral role that straddles the two elements, that of the music director, who now has to respond to challenges arising from the demands of both identity elements, and their associated groups: "The challenge music directors everywhere will soon face— indeed are already facing in some cities—is to justify the continued existence of the symphony orchestra, period, an institution already considered by many in the general public to be a relic of the past" (Medrek, 1999, p. A1).

Thus, a structural role that, in stable terms, offers the promise of building these aspects of the art world, ironically, is challenged in both times of organizational strife and retrenchment, when the tension between the identity elements was brought to the fore. The role of music director seemed to be a pivotal one, claimed by identity groups (musicians and administrators) contesting the role and its implications for the organizational identity, but ultimately, at the symphony I studied, abandoned by both, as neither musicians nor administrators rose to support the incumbent.

More generally, this chapter illustrates the challenges of managing the business of culture. The hybridized identity of cultural institutions carries latent and competing tensions that can pit the aesthetics of cultural products against a more commercial market orientation. At the ASO, the duality of these identity elements became salient in the wake of an organizational crisis, the 1996 musicians' strike, and had important implications for structural changes within the organization, particularly that of the Music Director. This role, served to partition and bridge the identity elements, in stable times, by carrying the conflict that the orchestra faced, and in strident times, by managing both the artistry and the economics of cultural production. The contribution to our understanding of the business of culture offered by this perspective is to underline the unique structures and roles that are implied in the notion of cultural production. Hopefully, this chapter will also contribute to emerging literature on organizational identity by illustrating how structural roles can carry and bridge hybrid identity elements.

REFERENCES

Albert, S., & Whetten, D. A. (1985). Organizational identity. In B. M. Staw & L. L. Cummings (Eds.), *Research in organizational behavior* (pp. 263–295). Greenwich, CT: JAI Press.

Allmendinger, J., & Hackman, J. R. (1996). Organizations in changing environments: The case of East German symphony orchestras. *Administrative Science Quarterly, 41,* 337–389.

Americanizing the American orchestra: Report of the National Task Force for the American Orchestra: An initiative for change. (1993, June). Washington, DC: American Symphony Orchestra League.

Dowd, T. J., Liddle, K., Lupo, K., & Borden, A. (2002). Organizing the musical canon: The repertoires of major U.S. symphony orchestras, 1842 to 1969. *Poetics: Journal of Empirical Research on Culture, Media, and the Arts, 30,* 35–61.

Dutton, J. E. (1997). Strategic agenda building in organizations. In Z. Shapira (Ed.), *Organizational Decision Making* (pp. 81–107).Cambridge, UK: Cambridge University Press.

Dutton, J. E., & Dukerich, J. M. (1991). Keeping an eye on the mirror: Image and identity in organizational adaptation. *Academy of Management Journal, 34,* 517–554.

Dutton, J. E., Dukerich, J. M., & Harquail, C. V. (1994). Organizational images and member identification. *Administrative Science Quarterly, 39,* 239–263.

Glynn, M. A. (2000). When cymbals become symbols: Conflict over organizational identity within a symphony orchestra. *Organization Science, 11,* 285–298.

Glynn, M. A. (2002). Chord and discord: Organizational crisis, institutional shifts, and the musical canon of the symphony. *Poetics: International Journal of Empirical Research on Art, Media, and Literature, 30,* 63–85.

Glynn, M. A., & Lounsbury, M. (in press). From the critics' corner: Logic blending, discursive change and authenticity in a cultural production system. *Journal of Management Studies.*

Golden-Biddle, K. H., & Rao, H. (1997). Breaches in the boardroom: Organizational identity and conflicts of commitment in a nonprofit organization. *Organization Science, 8,* 593–611.

Henry, D. (1995a, September 8). A dramatic ASO season opening, inside and out. *The Atlanta Journal Constitution,* p. 4H.

Henry, D. (1995b, August 13). Midlife crisis at the ASO? *The Atlanta Journal Constitution,* p. L8.

Henry, D. (1996a, March 2). ASO given $4 million anonymously. *The Atlanta Journal Constitution,* p. D1.

Henry, D. (1996b, February 2). Levi offers to play benefit to save jobs. *The Atlanta Journal Constitution,* p. D7.

Henry, D. (1996c, April 18). Verdict Safe program, mostly satisfying performances. *The Atlanta Journal Constitution,* p. 3D.

Henry, D. (1997, April 25). Levi's decision gives ASO 3 years to find new conductor. *The Atlanta Journal Constitution,* p. F1.

Hunt, S. A., Benford, R. D., & Snow, D. A. (1994). Identity fields: Framing processes and the social construction of movement identities. In E. Larene, J. Johnston, & R. Gurfield (Eds.), *New social movements: From ideology to identity* (pp. 185–207). Philadelphia: Temple University Press.

Loomis, G. (2004, April 22). A conductor woos the provinces. *International Herald Tribune,* p. 9.

Medrek, T. J. (1999, June 23). Controversy colored maestro's Boston Symphony Orchestra career. *Boston Herald,* p. A1.

Meyer, A. (1982). Adapting to environmental jolts. *Administrative Science Quarterly, 27,* 515–537.

Pratt, M. G., & Foreman, P. O. (2000). Classifying managerial responses to multiple organizational identities. *Academy of Management Review, 25,* 18–44.

Schwartz, J. (1995, September 15). One moment of passionate music-making in an otherwise professional but lusterless evening. *The Atlanta Journal Constitution,* p. 4H.

Schwartz, J. (1997a, September 26). Better Beethoven from Yoel Levi and the ASO. *The Atlanta Journal Constitution,* p. 23P.

Schwartz, J. (1997b, September 19). Spectacular music, spectacularly performed: Mahler soars in skilled hands of Levi. *The Atlanta Journal Constitution,* p. 23P.

Schwartz, J. (1998a, March 11). ASO board confirms Levi leaves in 2000. *The Atlanta Journal Constitution,* p. E1.
Schwartz, J. (1998b, February 27). ASO's Levi asks to stay. *The Atlanta Journal Constitution,* pp. E1, E2.
Schwartz, J. (1998c, March 2). Most in symphony audience back Levi in fight with board. *The Atlanta Journal Constitution,* p. B2.
Schwartz, J. (1998d, May 22). Season finale for ASO ends serenely, eloquently. *The Atlanta Journal Constitution,* p. 10H.
Schwartz, J. (1998e, February 6). Splendid performance of Mahler's last: Demanding Mahler score brings out the best of ASO. *The Atlanta Journal Constitution,* p. 6H.
Suchman, M. (1995). Managing legitimacy: Strategic and institutional approaches. *Academy of Management Review, 20,* 571–610.

II

The Challenge of Positioning

Two strategic achievements capture the imagination of individuals and organizations in cultural industries. The first achievement is that of first-time success: the bestselling book, the hit song, and the blockbuster movie that generates enormous sales and gains wide critical acclaim. The second achievement comes from using the first to generate more success: Using a loveable character from a highly rated program to launch a popular series, taking a proven plot line from a movie and adapting to another, or building on the notoriety of an author or a performer to launch more books and publicize forthcoming rock concerts. The two strategic achievements are not of course separate. Get the first one right, and you stand a better chance at the second. Get the second right, and you are well on the way to establishing a powerful position in your particular corner of the cultural industries.

The perennial search for strategies that can transform past success into a strong position is the main theme that runs through this section. Cultural industries are by no means unique in this respect. In most industries, managers regularly attempt to use past success as a foundation for future success. But cultural industries suffer more than most others from the problem of making sense of the past and then reliably transforming this knowledge into building and sustainable a formidable position. A film that takes an audience by storm is often regarded as a good bet for other similar films, but many a producer has lost a fortune attempting to do just that. Spinning a television series into a new one by taking a much loved character from the first into the second may seem like a sure thing, but there are few network executives who cannot tell stories of disasters that began with just such an idea.

It is this difficulty that can be translated into opportunity. An ability to repeat success has often represented the high road to career success in cultural industries. This is true for individuals who struggle to maintain their fame by following their first hit with subsequent ones, as it is for organizations that base their livelihood on using their past successes into developing new ones. In view of the gains, it is not surprising that there is intense interest in individuals and organizations that successfully carry out these strategies. The interest, however, is accompanied by much debate as to whether this success is the product of knowledge and skill, or the result of accident and luck. The added complication in these discussions is the surprising success of many novices in cultural industries, and the frequent failure of established players to make the best of position and experience.

In chapter 6, Melissa Schilling uses the video game industry to demonstrate the frequency with which industry leaders lose their dominance in spite of technological and market factors that should ensure their ability to link past success to future performance. As is often the case in cultural industries, the main cause of instability can be found in the relationship between technology and content. At first sight, technology should be the main driving force in the video game industry. The dominant firm ensures its dominance by virtue of network externalities: The more consumers adopt a particular console, the more incentive there is for other consumers to buy the system, and for game developers to produce games for this system.

Although this strategy has served firms in several other technology-driven industries, it has not worked as well in the video game industry. Technological discontinuities, more specifically, the introduction of new and more powerful microchips, have created opportunities for competitive entry by more creative rivals. Although consumers may have some desire for continuity and predictability, they are more interested in new and exciting games that are able to make the most of the new technology. This is equally true of a wide range of cultural industries.

Schelling shows how the role of content often trumps the power of technology. Atari had built up a dominant position within the industry by 1983 with $5 billion of sales, only to be displaced by Coleco within a year of the latter's entry. The lack of new and exciting games, however, eventually led to a collapse in sales for both firms, so much so that many observers declared the video game industry to be dead.

The successful entry of Nintendo and Sega swept aside these gloomy predictions. It also established a pattern that still prevails: New and more powerful technology opens the way to establishing a strong position, but a strong position can only be sustained by delivering new and more exciting games. The technical challenge calls for managing anticipated discontinuities: New generations of consoles are planned and developed on the back of relatively predictable progress in semiconductor technology. The success of new generations of games, however, often builds on the unanticipated: on breaking with past conventions and past game concepts.

The relationship between the past experience and future success is further explored in chapter 7 by Eisner, Jett, and Korn. They look at the emergence of web-based magazines, or webzines, as a distinct magazine publishing category. The crucial contrast is between webzines that are launched by existing print-based magazines and new entrants with no previous print-based operations.

For print-based magazines, the web represents a discontinuity that runs through their operations and culture. They have built effective competencies in the process of mastering the challenges of managing a print-based magazine. Should they transfer these competencies to webzines? Purely economic logic points to the cost advantages of repackaging existing material for the web, but the interfacing potential of web-based access points to the attractiveness of creating new material. What works in one medium will only work in another up to a point, and what is possible in a new medium often calls for a break with the habits and ways of thinking developed in the past.

Webzines that have no print-based counterpart have more freedom to explore the technological and creative possibilities of the web. But this freedom is purchased at a disadvantage: Webzines without print-based counterparts cannot rely on revenues from traditional publishing to fund their initial content creation. Faced with this problem, Eisner et al. suggest that they affiliate their web pages with other successful sites via hyperlinks. The use of this strategy allows them to multiply content availability many times more than is ordinarily possible in traditional publishing. Internet users with maximum need for information and with limited time at their disposal will therefore consult more regularly and hence become more loyal to sites that are widely linked, and hence information rich, than sites that are constrained by the conventions and competencies of traditional print-based publishing.

Finally, Shamsie, Miller, and Greene focus in chapter 8 on the attempt by the traditional television broadcast networks to use scheduling strategies in order to translate success from one of their shows to another one. In particular, their study shows that these networks have been trying to use their successful shows to draw audiences to their other shows that are still struggling in the ratings. This practice has gained in importance as the advent of cable has led to a proliferation of channels, providing an abundance of choices to television viewers.

In this tougher competitive environment, networks are abandoning some of the traditional strategies of maintaining a stable timeslot for each of their shows and matching shows of similar content. Instead, the networks are starting to move around their successful shows much more than they have in the past. They may move shows to match up a show that is still struggling with one that has already established a sizeable audience, regardless of the similarity of their content. In other words, the networks are beginning to couple a popular comedy show with a drama that needs to build an audience.

These findings suggest that the networks face a greater challenge in transferring their success with a show into higher ratings for other shows. They are responding to this challenge through the use of a much more dynamic approach to scheduling. In the process, they are focusing much more on using a show that has already become a hit in order to develop others.

Business strategies that focus on building on past success have been a key issue in many cultural industries. In most cases, this is achieved by using the success of one product to promote the prospect of another. The potential to create such linkages, however, has been constrained by the lack of systematic knowledge. Most of what is known about how to create complementary linkages is based on accumulated industry know-how, on trial and error, rather than systematic analysis. The chapters in this section make a contribution in this direction, but they also indicate that much more remains to be done.

CHAPTER

6

Game Not Over: Competitive Dynamics in the Video Game Industry

Melissa A. Schilling
New York University

According to *NPD Funworld*, sales in the U.S. video game industry reached $11.4 billion in 2003, just under the $11.7 billion high attained in 2002. The industry has experienced a remarkable degree of growth and turbulence over the last three decades, making it a popular subject for speculation and analysis. The video game industry provides an exceptional context for studying competition in culturally based industries for a number of reasons. First, it is a highly visible industry that has been well documented over the past two decades. Second, the industry has undergone several distinct generations of competition, permitting us to examine how different battles played out over time and to attempt to identify the critical factors influencing the success and failure of competitors.

Finally, the video game industry is characterized by a moderate degree of network externalities, meaning that the value a game system offers to customers is to some degree a function of how many other users there are of the same game system due to such factors as compatibility and games availability (Choi, 1994; Katz & Shapiro, 1986, 1992). In such industries, there is strong pressure to select one or a few dominant platforms rather than allowing many different incompatible platforms to coexist (Schilling, 1998, 2002). This leads to unambiguous winners and losers in the video game industry, and permits us to compare their strengths, weaknesses, and strategic choices.

In this chapter, I first provide a brief review of the history of the U.S. video game industry, beginning with the introduction of the Magnavox Odyssey and Atari's Pong, and ending with the 128-bit generation. Next, the generations of competition are analyzed with respect to three competitive dimensions: the ability to provide advanced technology consoles, the ability to ensure that games of high quality and rich content are widely available, and the ability to manage network externalities to the firm's favor.

This analysis reveals that providing a technologically advanced console is necessary for competition, but typically has not proven to be a limiting factor for most competitors. The more difficult competitive dimensions have been to provide popular games and manage network externalities. Comparing firms' strategies of relying on internal versus external developers, number of game titles at launch, and the top-selling games of each year reveals a number of critical factors for succeeding in the video game industry.

First, console makers must be able to produce games in house in addition to attracting third-party developers. Console makers that have relied solely on third-party developers have typically failed. This is likely due to the need for a console to launch with games, and the inability of console makers to attract third-party developers until they have proven some measure of success. Second, producing games with rich content has proven more difficult for firms than might be initially expected. Sony and Microsoft have had difficulty matching Nintendo's success at developing the rich story lines and appealing characters necessary to penetrate the action and role-playing games that dominate the top-selling games lists. Competencies for developing popular character-based games are very different from those required for designing, producing, and distributing an advanced console, leading Sony and Microsoft to rely more heavily on third-party game developers.

This leads to a final observation about the third competitive dimension: Although firms can use market relationships to some degree to bolster their ability to provide advanced technology consoles and to provide popular games, the ability to understand and manage network externalities to the firm's favor is a difficult competency to obtain on the market. It requires a combination of strategic acumen and a harmonized set of resources that include reputation, distribution leverage, and capital.

THE U.S. VIDEO GAME INDUSTRY

The very first home video game system was the Odyssey, introduced in 1972 (, 1977). The product was commercially produced and sold by Magnavox, but it was based on technology developed in 1966 for military simulations by Ralph Baer and Sanders Associates, a military electronics consulting firm. At a price of $100, over 100,000 units of the game system were sold (Schilling, Kittner, & Karl, 2003). However, the Odyssey came to an end rather quickly with the rise of a game system that would prove to be much more successful and establish home video game systems as an important and viable industry: Atari's Pong.

Pong, the Beginning of an Era

In 1972, Nolan Bushnell founded Atari and introduced Pong, a ping-pong-like game that was played on a user's television set with the aid of the Atari console. In its first year, Pong earned over $1 million in revenues. Pong, and over 60 similar knockoffs, soon flooded the market. The creation of large-scale integrated circuits enabled the systems to be fast and yet produced inexpensively. Pong dominated the market until Atari's 1977 introduction of the Atari Video Computer System (VCS), later renamed the 2600, which would lead the second generation of video games (Polssen, 1977). The VCS/2600 utilized a microprocessor, and could play multiple games. The console sold for $200, with games selling for between $20 and $40. Atari had sold over $5 billion worth of 2600 systems and products by 1983.

The height of this generation saw yearly sales of $3 billion in the United States alone (Cohen, 1984). However, the 1976 acquisition of Atari by Warner Communications had also turned the company's focus more to developing personal computers. The next few years saw a variety of Atari computer introductions, but none would prove to be big money makers for Atari. While Atari's attention was diverted toward computers, Coleco entered the market and introduced the Coleco Vision video game system in 1982. The Coleco Vision was very successful, and in 1983 Coleco Vision games actually managed to outsell Atari games.

In the mid 1980s profits for video game makers began to decline; many feared that video games had reached market saturation. Compounding this, the rapid proliferation of unauthorized games (games produced for a console without authorization of that console's producer) led to a market glut of games of dubious quality, and many unhappy retailers with video game inventories they were unable to move. By 1985, many industry observers were declaring the video game industry dead.

Much to everyone's surprise, however, two new entrants from Japan entered the U.S. video game market: Nintendo, with its 8-bit Nintendo Entertainment System (NES) introduced in 1985, and Sega, which launched its 8-bit Master System in the United States in 1986 (Sega had previously introduced an 8-bit system dubbed SG-1000 in Japan in 1983; Polsson, 1997). Though Sega's Master System appeared to be technologically superior, Nintendo spent much more on advertising and development of quality games and characters, and had more game titles available than Sega. The Master System went on to sell 2 million units and at times held an 11% market share. The NES sold over 1 million units in the first year, sold 19 million units by 1990, and could be found in more than a third of the households in America and Japan (Sheff, 1993). Nintendo's Super Mario Brothers 3 grossed over $500 million in America in 1989, selling 7 million copies in the United States and 4 million in Japan (Kittner, Schilling, & Karl, 2001).

In 1987 Atari released its last 8-bit system, the Atari XE Game System, but the product was unable to compete with the power and graphics in the systems made by Nintendo and Sega. Furthermore, Atari only spent roughly $300,000 promoting its system, whereas Sega and Nintendo each spent $15 million promoting their systems. Finding itself unable to compete, Atari sued Nintendo in 1988 for monopolistic practices (the court sided with Nintendo; "Cheap didn't sell," 1992). In the same year, Coleco filed Chapter 11.

Thus from 1985 to 1989, Nintendo held a near monopoly of the U.S. video game industry. The company sold its consoles for a price very close to production costs, while earning the bulk of its profits from games. Nintendo made games for its system in house, and licensed third-party developers to produce games through very strict licensing policies that: (a) limited the number of titles a developer could produce each year, (b) required the developer to preorder a minimum number of cartridges from Nintendo (which had its own contract manufacturers produce the games), and (c) restricted the developers from making similar games for other consoles. Nintendo also restricted the volume and pricing of consoles sold through distributors, ensuring that no single distributor acquired significant bargaining power (Brandenburger, 1995a). Nintendo's restrictive policies were very profitable, but they also caused the company to be sanctioned by the Federal Trade Commission, and alienated distributors and developers, potentially leaving the company more vulnerable to a competitor.

The 16-Bit Video Game Industry

In September of 1989, Sega introduced the 16-bit Genesis to the U.S. video game market. The Genesis offered dramatic performance enhancement over 8-bit systems. Furthermore, Sega leveraged its popular arcade games to the Genesis, and made it backward compatible with its 8-bit Master System games. There were 20 Genesis game titles on offer by December 1989. NEC also introduced a 16-bit system, the TurboGrafx-16, in the fall of 1989, and had 12 game titles on offer by December 1989. Though Nintendo had its own 16-bit system in the works, it delayed introducing it to the United States fearing cannibalizing its 8-bit system sales.

By the end of 1989, Sega had already sold 600,000 consoles in the United States, and NEC had sold 200,000. In 1990 and 1991 both Sega and NEC added game titles to their lists, bringing their totals to 130 and 80 respectively. By the end of 1991, Sega had sold 2 million consoles in the United States, and NEC had sold 1 million. Unlike Sega, which produced a major portion of its games in house, NEC relied completely on external game developers, who found the system to have only a small technological advantage over 8-bit systems (Brandenburger, 1995b). Developers began to abandon the NEC platform, and NEC exited the market in 1991. Nintendo finally introduced its own 16-bit Super Nintendo Entertainment System (SNES) in 1991, but it was too late to quell Sega's momentum. In 1992, Nintendo controlled 80% of the video game market based on combined 8-bit and 16-bit sales, but in 1994 and 1995, Sega was the market leader.

Like Nintendo, Sega made little profit on the consoles, and focused instead on increasing unit sales to drive game sales and software developer royalties. Sega, however, used less restrictive licensing arrangements than Nintendo, and consequently was able to rapidly lure a large number of developers to make Sega game titles. Furthermore, though Nintendo could have chosen to make its 16-bit system backward compatible, thus linking the value consumers possessed in their 8-bit game libraries to the new system, Nintendo chose to make the system incompatible with the 8-bit games. By the end of 1991, the SNES had 25 game titles compared to the 130 available for Genesis. Nintendo had given Sega 2 years of installed base lead on a system that offered a significant technological advantage, and then entered the market at a ground-zero position with respect to the availability of complementary goods.

The consequence of Nintendo's late move is aptly captured in the following quote from a review of video game players published in *Fortune* (Hadju, 1993, p. 1): "To tell the truth, Nintendo just isn't cool anymore. This one is 16 bits, so it's better than the original Nintendo. But the company only made it to compete with Sega, and most kids already have that. So they don't need Super Nintendo, unless they're jerks and have to have everything. That's just idiotic." Over time sales of the Nintendo SNES accelerated, and it would ultimately prove to be one of the more successful game systems ever introduced, but Nintendo's near-monopoly position had been broken; Sega had successfully technologically leapfrogged Nintendo (see Fig. 6.1; Schilling, 2003).

32/64-Bit Systems

The late 1980s and early 1990s also attracted a number of other competitors to the video game market. In 1989, Philips announced its 32-bit Compact Disc Interactive (CD-I), an interactive multimedia compact disc system that would serve as a game player, teaching tool, and music system. But the CD-I was very complex, requiring a 30-minute demonstration. Furthermore, it was expensive—initially introduced at $799 and later reduced to a below-cost $500, more than twice the cost of Nintendo or Sega systems (Turner, 1996, p. A6). Its role was very unclear to American consumers. Although the product was actually much more than a video game machine, customers compared the product to the popular Nintendo and Sega systems, and were dismayed by its price and complexity. Making matters worse, Philips was reluctant to disclose the technical specifications of the machine, greatly limiting the software development for the system. In 1996, Philips CD-I was still around, but had less than a 2% market share (Trachtenberg, 1996). Philips soon indicated that it would no longer push the CD-I in the United States.

Other companies also introduced 32-bit systems, including Turbo Technologies' Duo, and 3DO's Interactive Multiplayer, but the cost of the systems ($600-700) was prohibitive. Turbo Tech's Duo was very short-lived and received little attention. 3DO's system, on the other hand, received considerable attention. 3DO was founded in October 1993 by Trip Hawkins, formerly of Electronic Arts,

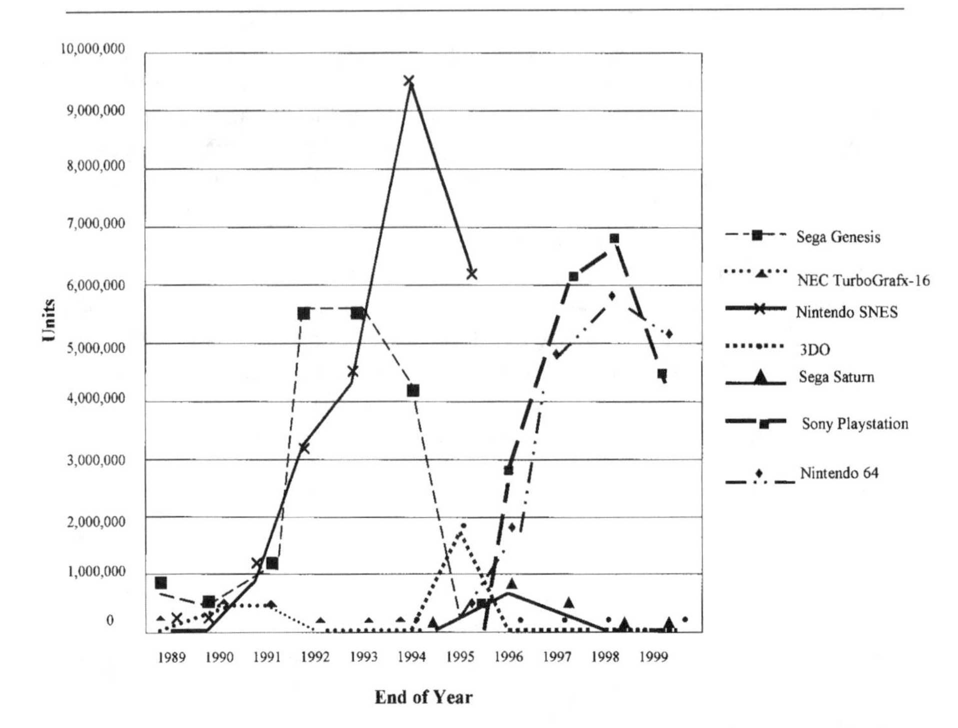

FIG. 6.1. U.S. sales of 16-bit and 32/64-bit video game consoles. Data compiled from Scally (1997), Rigdon (1996), Kasten (1997), company press releases, company annual reports, Brandenberger (1995a, 1995b, 1995c), Gallagher (2001), *Market Share Reporter* (years 1990 to 2000), and from http://www.videogames.com.

who made a number of games for the Sega Genesis console. Though 3DO had signed agreements with an extremely large number of developers (750 by July 1994), most of those development agreements did not result in actual game titles. The system had five game titles at launch, and 40 by July 1994. Furthermore, 3DO's unique strategy of licensing out all game and hardware production made it next to impossible to achieve the low console prices of Sega and Nintendo by subsidizing console production with game royalties. 3DO's hardware producers (Matsushita and Panasonic) did not sell games, and were consequently unwilling to sell the consoles without a margin. 3DO tried to rectify this problem by establishing a "Market Development Fund" whereby a portion of the game royalties would be used to subsidize hardware production. However, ultimately sales of the machine never took off, and 3DO exited the market in 1996.

Atari had also made a surprising reentrance to the video game market in 1993 with the technologically advanced Jaguar. Though promoted as a 64-bit system, it had a 13.3 MHZ clock speed and was technically equivalent to a 32-bit system.[1] However, Atari's long struggle had not inspired great confidence in either developers or distributors, and several of the large retail chains (e.g., Toys R Us) chose not to carry the product (Sinakin, 1996). At this point in time 16-bit systems still dominated the market, and Sega and Nintendo both had very large installed bases, a large number of available games, and considerable brand recognition for many of their game characters (e.g., Super Mario, Sonic the Hedgehog). The companies had also expanded their game distribution channels to include video rental outlets. It would not be until 1995 that the 16-bit video game systems would be displaced by technologically superior consoles.

In May 1995, Sega introduced its 32-bit Saturn system and in September 1995, Sony introduced its 32-bit Playstation. Both the Sony and Sega platforms were based on compact discs, and offered a tremendous performance advantage over 16-bit systems. Both systems were introduced with great fanfare, and considerable developer support. Although of the two only Sega had experience and brand image in the video game market, Sony entered with tremendous brand image in consumer electronics, access to (and leverage in) very extensive distribution channels in electronics and media, and captive content providers in the form of Tri Star and Columbia.[2]

To rapidly gain insight into the toy industry, Sony hired experienced toy executive Bruce Stein to head the video game unit (Stein had formerly served as president of Hasbro's Kenner products division, and as chief operating officer at Marvel Entertainment Group; Trachtenberg, 1995). Its size and previous success in several electronics markets (including the development and control of the compact disc format) could not go unnoticed by software developers. It signed a sweetheart deal with Electronic Arts, then one of the largest game software developers in the United States, and convinced several other developers to produce only Playstation titles for the first 6 months after its introduction. There were 50 Playstation titles by the end of 1995, and this number had grown to 800 by the end of 2000.

Though Sega's Saturn had beaten Sony's Playstation to market, it was shipped to only four retailers due to limited supply: Toys R Us, Babbage's, Software Etc., and Electronics Boutique. This aggravated retailers such as Best Buy and Walmart, who had long supported Sega (Hisey, 1995). Developers also felt that it was easier to program for the Playstation than the Saturn, causing it to lose crucial

---

[1]It is interesting to note that Atari's 1993 introduction of the 64-bit Jaguar with performance comparable to the other 32-bit systems is probably a significant reason for the blurring of the distinction between 32-bit and 64-bit systems. It may thus have contributed to the erosion of any perceived technological advantage Nintendo's 64-bit system had over the 32-bit systems.

[2]The electronics and toy supply chains share some notable similarities. Both require fast speed to market, are characterized by short life cycles and quickly eroding margins, and demonstrate high rates of cannibalization (Johnson, 2001).

developer support (Lefton, 1998). By the end of 1996, the installed base of Sony Playstation in the United States (2.9 million units) was more than double the Sega Saturn installed base (1.2 million units).

In 1996, after more than 2 years of preannouncements, Nintendo introduced its 64-bit game system, Nintendo 64. Nintendo stuck with the cartridge format, arguing that it enabled faster access for the graphics desired by hard-core gamers. The system was based on a 64-bit RISC CPU with a clock speed of 93.75 MHZ. Although there were only two software titles available at the console's release (one being Super Mario), the game units were sold out within weeks of their release. Though Nintendo's 64-bit system gained rapid consumer acceptance, neither Nintendo nor Sega was able to reclaim dominance over the video game industry. Though several new entrants (and one returning entrant, Atari) had tried to break into the video game industry through technological leapfrogging, only Sony had the successful combination of a product with a technological advantage, strategies and resources that enabled it to rapidly build installed base and availability of complementary goods, and a reputation that signaled the market that this was a fight it could win.

An Unfolding Battle: 128-Bit Systems

In September of 1999, Sega launched its 128-bit Dreamcast console, a $199 gaming system that enabled narrow-band (56 Kbps) access to the Internet. Prior to Dreamcast's release, Sega was suffering from its lowest market share in years at 12%. The Dreamcast was the first 128-bit system to market, and 514,000 units were sold in the first 2 weeks, achieving an installed base of 5 million by October of 2000. Sega's success turned out to be short-lived, however. In March of 2000, Sony launched its 128-bit Playstation 2 (PS2) in Japan, and introduced the system to the United States in October of the same year. Despite price cuts on the Dreamcast, and a promotion rebate that would make the console essentially free (in exchange for a 2-year contract for Sega's SegaNet Internet service) the Dreamcast was crushed in the holiday sales season.

In early 2001, Sega announced that it would cease making consoles and transform itself into a third-party developer of games for other consoles. Developer support for the system had been lackluster, and Sega's losses had been mounting in the battles against Sony's Playstation and PS2, and the Nintendo 64. After having come close to bankruptcy, it was ready to give up the fight for the console market and focus on the more lucrative game production. Notably, it signed a deal to produce games for Microsoft's entry into the video game console business—the Xbox (Sega's Dreamcast system had been based on Microsoft's Windows CE operating system; Kittner et al., 2001).

Sony's PS2 was an unprecedented success. During the opening sales weekend of March 4, 2000, PS2 sales reached about 1 million units, a figure that eclipsed by 10 times the amount of original Playstation units sold during the 3-day release period in 1994. Demand for the new unit was so high that on the opening day of preorders on Sony's web site, over 100,000 hits in 1 minute were received, and Sony was forced to briefly shut the web site down. The chip used in the system was the result of a $1.2 billion joint venture between Sony and Toshiba, and offered a significant technological advantage over previous systems. Furthermore, the PS2 was backward compatible, enabling gamers to play their Playstation games on the console until they amassed new game libraries (Schilling, Chiu, & Chou, 2003).

At the time of the PS2 release, Nintendo had just postponed the launch of its new 128-bit system, the GameCube (code named Dolphin), to a release date in the first half of 2001. The GameCube was a joint venture with Matsushita, one of Sony's main rivals, and IBM. The console promised a faster processor than that of the PS2, but its graphics capabilities would be similar. Unlike the PS2, however, the GameCube did not offer backward compatibility with N64 games. The GameCube was also targeted toward a younger market (8–18 year olds) than Sony's 16–24-year-old demographic. The real threat to Sony's PS2 came in the form of a new entrant to the video console industry: Microsoft's Xbox.

Microsoft had previously produced PC-based computer games (such as Flight Simulator and the Age of Empires series) and operated an online gaming service (Microsoft Gaming Zone) that enabled multiplayer games, and thus had some familiarity with the industry. It did not have, however, the arcade experience of either Sega or Nintendo, nor the consumer electronics experience of Sony. The Xbox seemed a strange fit with Microsoft's product portfolio and competencies, which had historically focused almost exclusively on packaged and licensed computer software. However, both Sega's Dreamcast and Sony's PS2 had added the ability to access the Internet, making video game consoles increasingly a threat to the PC industry. If video consoles became a primary portal for accessing the Internet, they could undermine the foundation of Microsoft's empire. This possibility was strengthened by the fact that nearly 25% of PC households surveyed indicated that the primary use of the PC was for playing games (Kittner et al., 2001).

Microsoft thus announced that it would enter the video game fray with its own technologically advanced game console, the Xbox (launched in November of 2001). The Xbox targeted the 18- to 34-year-old male, positioning it directly against the PS2 rather than the Nintendo GameCube. By the time the Xbox hit the market, PS2 already had a significant lead in installed base and availability of games (there were more than 300 PS2 game titles available at the end of 2001), but Microsoft was counting on the technological advantages offered by the Xbox to tip consumer preferences.

The Xbox operating system ran on a 733-MHZ microprocessor from Intel, which was more than twice as fast as the processors used in any other game console on the market—including the Toshiba 300-MHZ microprocessor supplied in the PS2. The Xbox had 64 megabytes of memory and a data rate of 400 megabits per second per pin with 6.4 GB per second bandwidth, enabling more information to be processed faster. The Xbox memory chip would give game developers nearly twice the memory offered in other game consoles. The Xbox also offered a 10-gigabyte hard drive, enabling gamers to save a virtually unlimited number of games. Customers also did not have to trade off technological advantages against price: The Xbox launched at a retail price of $299, significantly less than its production costs (it is estimated that Microsoft loses between $100 and $125 per unit; Becker & Wilcox, 2001; Norton, 2001; Wildstrom, 2001).

To rapidly deploy the console and build installed base, it leveraged its existing relationships with distributors that carried its software, though it was now forced to seek much greater penetration into distributors such as Toys R Us, Babbages, and Circuit City. Microsoft also faced the challenge of cultivating a radically different brand image in the game console market than the one it had achieved in the software market, and to make much greater use of marketing channels such as television advertising and gaming magazines. To that end, Microsoft budgeted $500 million to be spent over 18 months to market the Xbox—more than any other marketing campaign in the company's history (Elkin, 2000). Microsoft's biggest brand disadvantage was its lack of a big hit game that carried the sales of the console (e.g., Mario for Nintendo, and Gran Turismo for PS2).

To ensure that there would be wide availability of complementary goods, Microsoft utilized both in-house development, and aggressively pursued licensing arrangements with third-party developers. By 2001, Microsoft was well established as a leader in developing PC games (Age of Empires, for example, was the fourth-bestselling PC game in 2000), and planned to produce 30 to 40% of games in house (similar to Sony's percentages). To attract developers, Microsoft gave away $10,000 in game development kits and funded focus research groups for games (Clash of the Titans, 2001). Furthermore, because Microsoft used its DirectX technology in the Xbox, it would be very easy for existing PC game developers to transition to the console.

Both the and Nintendo's GameCube were launched in November of 2001 (in time for the extremely important Christmas season) and sold briskly. By the year's end, it was estimated that 1.3 million GameCube units had been sold, and 1.5 million Xbox units had been sold (Frankel, 2001). However, both of the new consoles were outrun by PS2, of which approximately 2 million units were sold during the month of December, bringing its worldwide installed base to over 20 million units (Clash of the Titans, 2001). PS One (a modified version of the original Playstation) was also selling well at its $99 price tag.[3] The PS2 continued to outsell the Xbox and GameCube in 2002.

By September 30, 2002, estimates put both Xbox and GameCube sales at just under 7 million units worldwide, and PS2 unit sales at over 40 million worldwide (Pham, 2002). Furthermore, the number-one bestselling video games in 2001 and 2002, Grand Theft Auto III, and its sequel, Grand Theft Auto: Vice City, were available only on the PS2 platform (Snider, 2002). By the end of 2003, Sony reported that over 70 million units of the PS2 had been sold worldwide (29.3 mil-

[3]It is worth noting that all of the game consoles were outsold by Nintendo's Gameboy Advance handheld game machine over the Christmas 2001 selling season. Its price point and small size made it a popular choice for gift giving.

lion in North America alone), whereas Microsoft's Xbox and Nintendo's GameCube were believed to have sold just over 10 million units each (Technology Briefing, 2004; Peterson, 2004).

COMPETITIVE DIMENSIONS OF THE U.S. VIDEO GAME INDUSTRY

Analysis of the history of the video game industry suggests that at least three primary dimensions have sharply influenced the success and failure of competitors: technological functionality, availability and quality of game titles, and the ability to manage network externalities. Firms have been required not only to introduce technologically advanced consoles, but also to produce content with captivating story lines and appealing characters, while simultaneously ensuring that they maximize their installed base through penetration pricing, backward compatibility, leveraging distribution agreements, managing customer switching costs, and using advertising, reputation, and credible commitments to shape the industry's expectations for the future.

Technological Functionality

For new entrants to take market share away from incumbents in the video game industry, they have had to offer a significant technological advantage in their consoles. In each generation, successful competitors have offered at least three times the clock speed of the fastest system in the previous generation (see Table 6.1). An incumbent's best defensive strategy, in turn, is to invest in continuous innovation in the standard, thus making it difficult for a potential entrant to create a significant technological gap. This means the incumbent must often willingly embrace cannibalization of its current product platform, and provide incentives for customers to upgrade to more advanced models to gain a foothold in the market (Schilling, 2003).

Each generation of the video game industry illustrates this aptly. Despite Nintendo's near-monopoly position in the video game market throughout much of the 1980s, its enormous brand equity, and relationships with suppliers and distributors, Sega was able to successfully enter the market in the fall of 1989 by offering a 16-bit system. Though Nintendo had a 16-bit system in the works, it was initially intent on continuing to sell 8-bit systems, believing the systems had not yet maximized their potential. Nintendo thus helped create the window of opportunity for Sega. The value of the increased processing power of the Sega machines was readily apparent to most customers. Customers could readily appreciate that a 16-bit system would be faster than an 8-bit system, and offer a significant advantage in graphics-processing capability resulting in more exciting and lifelike play. NEC also had a 16-bit system on the market, but with much slower clock speed (3.6 MHZ compared to Sega's 7.6 MHZ) and no prior arcade games or experience to leverage.

TABLE 6.1
Technological Advances in Each Generation of Consoles

	Introduction	Clock Speed	RAM	Format
16-bit systems				
Sega Genesis	September 1989	7.6 MHZ	128K	Cartridge based, CD add-on
NEC Turbo	Fall 1989	3.6 MHZ	8K	Cartridge based, CD add-on
Nintendo SNES	September 1991	3.6 MHZ	128K	Cartridge based
32/64-bit systems				
Philips CD-I (32)	October 1991	16–26 MHZ	NA	CD-ROM based
3DO (32)	October 1993	12.5 MHZ	3MB	CD-ROM based
Atari Jaguar	Fall 1993	13.3 MHZ	2MB	Cartridge based, CD-ROM
Sega Saturn (32)	May 1995	28.6 MHZ	2MB	CD-ROM based
Sony Playstation	September 1995	34 MHZ	16MB	CD-ROM based
Nintendo 64 (64)	September 1996	93.75 MHZ	36MB	Cartridge based
128-bit systems				
Sony Playstation2	March 2000	300MHz	38MB	CD/DVD based
Microsoft Xbox	November 2001	733 MHZ	64MB	CD/DVD based
Nintendo	November 2001	485 MHZ	40MB	CD/DVD based

By the time Nintendo introduced its own 16-bit system, it had already lost its dominant position. Furthermore, Nintendo did not offer any upgrade incentive to lure its existing 8-bit users to the 16-bit platform. Consequently, when 8-bit users were ready to buy a 16-bit system, there was little reason for them to stay with Nintendo (this was exacerbated by Nintendo's decision to not make its 16-bit systems compatible with its 8-bit games as further discussed later in the chapter). Nintendo spent heavily in advertising, and fought fiercely to regain market share, and by 1994 it appeared that the tide was again tipping towards Nintendo's favor, but by this point Sega was already transitioning to its new 32-bit system, the Sega Saturn (see Fig. 6.1).

Similarly, both Sony and Microsoft entered the market with products that offered dramatic technological advantages. When Sony first introduced its 32-bit Playstation, Sega already had its own 32-bit system, and several other competitors (e.g., Atari, 3DO, and Philips) had beaten both Sega and Sony to market with 32-bit systems. The Playstation, however, had a much faster clock speed (34 MHZ to Sega's 28.6 MHZ, Jaguar's 13.3 MHZ, and 3DO's 12.5 MHZ) and more than five times the RAM of any other existing 32-bit competitor. Furthermore, unlike the other new entrants, only Sony combined the technological advantage of its system with a set of complementary strategies and resources that enabled it to wrest control of the video game industry from Sega and Nintendo. Similarly, Microsoft's Xbox would be relatively late to the 128-bit generation, but it would arrive with a clock speed of 733 MHZ (more than twice that of PS2), and 64 MB of RAM (compared to 38 MB in the PS2).

Availability and Quality of Game Titles

One of the most crucial drivers of success of a video game console is the availability of popular games. Not only do games shape the consumer decision about which console to purchase, but they also provide the majority of the console producer's revenues (in the form of license fees) due to the strategy of selling consoles at or near cost.

In-House Games Development. Although a console producer could theoretically rely solely on third-party developers for games, this strategy has not proven to be particularly successful. Third-party developers may be unwilling to bear the risk of supporting a platform that is not already widely popular, and it is impossible for a console to be widely popular without games. This Catch-22 is why the most successful video game console producers have had to produce game in house (to ensure that high-quality games would be available at launch) in addition to offering aggressive licensing policies to attract third-party developers. Table 6.2 demonstrates this vividly: Every successful console producer in any generation (Nintendo, Sega, Sony, and Microsoft) had in-house games production in addition to aggressive licensing policies. NEC, 3DO, and Philips, by contrast, had no in-house games production, and the strict reliance on external developer support proved dire.

Third-Party Games Development. Console producers must also go to great lengths to forge and retain relationships with third-party games developers, and provide attractive licensing and pricing policies. This translates into charging more reasonable prices from licensors than their relative bargaining power demands. The U.S. video game industry provides several examples of the importance of this strategy. When Nintendo controlled approximately 85% of the 8-bit video game market, its licensing policies with games producers ensured that Nintendo reaped most of the profits while the games producers bore most of the risk. Games producers were permitted to produce a maximum of five titles for Nintendo, encouraging them to sink heavy research and development funds and market research into only a few titles.

Once titles were approved by Nintendo, the games producers were required to give the design to Nintendo, who would have its own contract manufacturers produce the game cartridges. The games producers were then required to purchase a minimum order of 10,000 of the cartridges from Nintendo, thus ensuring that the

TABLE 6.2
Game Development Strategies and Number of Titles

	Game Development	Titles
16-bit systems		
Sega Genesis	Internal and external: 200 in-house developers; 1500 freelance developers by 1993	20 by December, 1989; 130 by September, 1991; 320 by January, 1993
NEC Turbo Grafx-16	External only	12 by December, 1989; 80 by end of 1991
Nintendo SNES	Internal and external: 65 licensees by end of 1991	25 by end of 1991; 130 by January, 1993
32/64-bit systems		
Philips CD-I (32)	External only	Emphasized educational and reference
3DO (32)	External only: 300 external developers by March 1994; 750 by July 1994	5 at launch; 40 by July 1994; 220 by October 1995
Atari Jaguar	Internal and external	5 by May 1994; 30 by October 1995
Sega Saturn (32)	Internal and external	4 to 8 at launch
Sony Playstation	Internal and external	50 by end of 1995; 800 by end of 2000
Nintendo 64 (64)	Internal and external	2 at launch; 6 by end of 1996
128-bit systems		
Sony Playstation2	Internal and external; 40% of games produced in house	About 300 by December 2001; 483 by March 2002; 1,582 by December 2002 (334 specific to PS2, 1248 for PS1 but playable on PS2)
Microsoft Xbox	Internal and external; 40% of games produced in house	About 40 by December 2001; 205 in March 2002; 215 by December 2002
Nintendo GameCube	Internal and external; 80% of games produced in house	About 20 by December 2001; 117 by March 2002; 306 by December 2002

games producers bore all the investment risk for the games. On top of the payment for the minimum order of cartridges, games producers were also required to pay royalties to Nintendo for each game copy actually sold. Thus, Nintendo's policies ensured that it received the lion's share of the profits of third-party games while bearing almost none of the risk. Games producers continued to make games for the Nintendo system while Nintendo held a near-monopoly position, but on Sega's introduction of its 16-bit Genesis with more attractive licensing policies, many developers flocked to the new system. Nintendo was subsequently forced to loosen its licensing restrictions in order to compete for third-party developer support.

Compelling Creative Content. Producing top-selling video games is not an easy feat. It requires not only technological skills, but also an in-depth understanding of customer preferences and strong competencies in developing rich creative content. The importance of content (and the difficulty firms have had in mastering its development) is revealed through an examination of the type and popularity of the games produced by console makers and third-party developers. Tables 6.3 through 6.6 list the top 20 video games in 2000, 2001, 2002, and 2003 based on

TABLE 6.3
Top Selling Video Games, 2000

Rank	Title	Publisher	Platform	Price	Type
1	Pokemon Silver	Nintendo	GBC	$27	Role playing, general
2	Pokemon Gold	Nintendo	GBC	$27	Role playing, general
3	Pokemon Stadium	Nintendo	N64	$59	Role playing, general
4	Pokemon Yellow: Pikachu Edition	Nintendo	GBC	$27	Role playing, general
5	Tony Hawk's Pro Skater 2	Activision	PSX	$40	Sports
6	Legend of Zelda: Majora's Mask	Nintendo	N64	$50	Action, general
7	Gran Turismo 2	Sony	PSX	$40	Driving, racing
8	Tony Hawk's Pro Skater	Activision	PSX	$40	Sports
9	Pokemon Blue	Nintendo	GB	$25	Role playing, general
10	Pokemon Red	Nintendo	GB	$25	Role playing, general
11	WWF Smackdown	THQ	PSX	$40	Sports
12	Tony Hawk's Pro Skater	Activision	N64	$49	Sports
13	Pokemon Trading Card	Nintendo	GB	$25	Strategy, general
14	Super Mario Brothers BLX	Nintendo	GB	$28	Action, general
15	Madden NFL 2001	Electronic Arts	PSX	$41	Sports
16	Mario Party 2	Nintendo	N64	$50	Action, general
17	Perfect Dark	Nintendo	N64	$58	Action, general
18	WWF Smackdown 2	THQ	PSX	$41	Sports
19	Final Fantasy IX	Square EA	PSX	$40	Role playing, general
20	WWF No Mercy	THQ	N64	$60	Sports

Note. GBC-Gameboy, Color; GB-Gameboy; N64-Nintendo 64; PSX-Playstation.

TABLE 6.4
Tope Selling Video Games, 2001

Rank	Title	Publisher	Platform	Price	Type
1	Grand Theft Auto 3	Rockstar Games	PS2	$50	Action, modern
2	Madden NFL 2002	Electronic Arts	PS2	$50	Sports
3	Pokemon Crystal	Nintendo	GBC	$29	Role playing, general
4	Metal Gear Solid 2	Konami	PS2	$49	Action, shooter
5	Super Mario Advance	Nintendo	GBA	$30	Action, general
6	Gran Turismo 3:A, Spec	Sony	PS2	$50	Driving, racing
7	Tony Hawk's Pro Skater 3	Activision	PS2	$48	Sports
8	Tony Hawk's Pro Skater 2	Activision	PSX	$29	Sports
9	Pokemon Silver	Nintendo	GBC	$29	Role playing, general
10	DRIVER 2	Infogrames	PSX	$30	Driving, mission based
11	Pokemon Gold	Nintendo	GBC	$29	Role playing, general
12	Pokemon Stadium 2	Nintendo	N64	$60	Role playing, general
13	Gran Turismo 2	Sony	PSX	$20	Driving, racing
14	Halo	Microsoft	XBX	$49	Action, shooter
15	Harry Potter: Sorcerer	Electronic Arts	PSX	$40	Action, book
16	Final Fantasy X	Square EA	PS2	$51	Role playing, general
17	Mario Kart: Circuit	Nintendo	GBA	$30	Action, general
18	Tony Hawk's Pro Skater 3	Activision	PSX	$39	Sports
19	Super Smash Bro Melee	Nintendo	GCN	$50	Action, general
20	Zelda: Oracle Ages	Nintendo	GBC	$31	Action, general

Note. PS2-Playstation 2; GBC-Gameboy Color; GBA-Gameboy Advance; PSX-Playstation; N64-Nintendo 64; XBX-Xbox; GCN-Gamecube.

TABLE 6.5
Top Selling Video Games, 2002

Rank	Title	Publisher	Platform	Price	Type
1	Grand Theft Auto: Vice	Rockstar Games	PS2	$49	Action, modern
2	Grand Theft Auto 3	Rockstar Games	PS2	$50	Action, modern
3	Madden NFL 2003	Electronic Arts	PS2	$49	Sports
4	Super Mario Advance 2	Nintendo	GBA	$29	Action, general
5	Gran Turismo 3:A, Spec	Sony	PS2	$24	Driving, racing
6	Medal of Honor Frontline	Electronic Arts	PS2	$50	Action, historic
7	Spiderman: The Movie	Activision	PS2	$45	Action, movie
8	Kingdom Hearts	Square EA	PS2	$49	Role playing, action
9	Halo	Microsoft	XBX	$48	Action, shooter
10	Super Mario Sunshine	Nintendo	GCN	$49	Action, general
11	Tony Hawk's Pro Skater 4	Activision	PS2	$48	Sports
12	Yu-Gi-Oh! Eternal	Konami	GBA	$29	Strategy, fantasy
13	Dragonball Z: Goku	Infogrames	GBA	$31	Role playing, TV
14	Lord of the Rings: Towers	Electronic Arts	PS2	$50	Action, book or movie
15	Yu-Gi-Oh! Dark Duel	Konami	GBC	$29	Strategy, fantasy
16	Yu-Gi-Oh! Forbidden	Konami	PSX	$30	Strategy, fantasy
17	NCAA Football 2003	Electronic Arts	PS2	$50	Sports
18	Sonic Advance	THQ	GBA	$36	Action, general
19	T. Clancy's Splinter	Ubi Soft	XBX	$48	Action, book
20	Socom: U.S. Navy Seals	Sony	PS2	$60	Action, shooter

Note. PS2-Playstation 2; GBC-Gameboy Color; GBA-Gameboy Advance; PSX-Playstation; N64-Nintendo 64; XBX-Xbox; GCN-Gamecube.

TABLE 6.6
Top Selling Video Games, 2003

Rank	Title	Publisher	Platform	Price	Type
1	Madden NFL 2004	Electronic Arts	PS2	$49	Sports
2	Pokemon Ruby	Nintendo	GBA	$31	Role playing, general
3	Pokemon Sapphire	Nintendo	GBA	$31	Role playing, general
4	Need for Speed: Underground	Electronic Arts	PS2	$49	Driving, racing
5	Legend of Zelda: The Wind Walker	Nintendo	GCN	$47	Action, general
6	Grand Theft Auto: Vice City	Rockstar	PS2	$41	Action, modern
7	Mario Kart: Double Dash	Nintendo	GCN	$49	Action, general
8	Tony Hawk's Underground	Activision	PS2	$47	Sports
9	Enter the Matrix	Atari	PS2	$46	Action, science fiction
10	Medal Honor Rising	Electronic Arts	PS2	$49	Action, historic
11	NCAA Football 2004	Electronic Arts	PS2	$49	Sports
12	Halo	Microsoft	XBX	$38	Action, shooter
13	True Crime: Streets of LA	Activision	PS2	$48	Action adventure, modern
14	Final Fantasy X-2	Square Enix	PS2	$50	Role playing, general
15	NBA Live 2004	Electronic Arts	PS2	$49	Sports
16	Socom II: Navy Seals	Sony	PS2	$49	Action, shooter
17	Grand Theft Auto 3	Rockstar	PS2	$21	Action, modern
18	NBA Street Vol.2	Electronic Arts	PS2	$48	Sports
19	The Getaway	Sony	PS2	$40	Action adventure, modern
20	Mario Brothers 3: Mario 4	Nintendo	GBA	$29	Action, general

Note. PS2-Playstation 2; GBC-Gameboy Color; GBA-Gameboy Advance; PSX-Playstation; N64-Nintendo 64; XBX-Xbox; GCN-Gamecube.

total U.S. sales (data are from *NPD Funworld*). Information is also provided on the game publisher, the platform the game is for,[4] the asking price of the game, and the game type as designated by GameSpot, a popular game review web site.

In 2000, 11 of the top 20 games sold in the U.S. were produced by Nintendo. Nintendo dominated the role-playing and action-general categories. Only 1 of the top 20 games is produced by Sony, a driving based game called Gran Turismo 2. A total of 8 of the top 20 games were produced by third-party developers, and of those, 7 were based on sports. Sports games are notable in that they typically do not require extensive story-line or character development. As the top 20 list demonstrates here, sports-based video games often rely on existing brands and celebrities. Games based on popular movies or books also reduce both the burden of story line development and the risk of a game.

In 2000, 13 of the top 20 games were for the Nintendo 64 or Gameboy platforms, and 7 were for the Playstation platform. It is interesting to note that the games for the Nintendo 64 platform sold for an average of $14 more than games for the Playstation platform. Overall, it appears in 2000 that Nintendo's competencies in character and story line development for video games were stronger than its competitors, but Sony was pretty successful at attracting third-party developers to develop sports games for the console.

By 2001, it is starting to look like the tables are turning in Sony's favor. As shown in Table 6.4, in 2001, 8 of the top 20 games were produced by Nintendo (down from 11), and 2 of the top 20 games were produced by Sony (though both are versions of Gran Turismo). Nintendo still dominated the role-playing and action-general categories. More importantly perhaps, one game produced by Microsoft (Halo, an action-shooter game) broke into the top 20. Nine out of the top 20 games were produced by third-party developers, and notably only four of the nine were sports based, whereas the others indicate that third-party developers were penetrating the top-20 list in the action, role-playing, and driving-based categories.

Across all developers, only 1 of the top 20 games was for the Nintendo 64 platform, and one was for the GameCube (though 6 of the top 20 were for the Gameboy platform), 11 of the 20 games were for the Playstation and PS2 platforms (6 are for PS2), and only 1 of the 20 was produced for the Xbox (the game Microsoft produced itself). It is important to note that several of the third-party games were produced for multiple consoles, thus the success of a third-party game for one console but not for another may be due to differences in console sales.

By 2002, only 2 of the top 20 games were produced by Nintendo. Sony produced 2 of the 20, and Microsoft produced only 1 of the 20. Intriguingly, Nintendo's loss appears to have been the gain of third-party developers. Although Sony and Microsoft outmaneuvered Nintendo in their console launches, neither

---

[4]Several of the games are produced for multiple consoles, but the sales data are based on a console-specific version of the game. For example, a version of Final Fantasy designed for Sony PS2 may make the top-selling list whereas a version for Final Fantasy designed for Xbox does not.

company filled the top slots in video game sales that Nintendo vacated. Instead those positions were filled by Rockstar Games, Electronic Arts, Square EA, Activision, and Konami. Third-party developers produced 15 of the top 20 games in 2002, and now they were showing success in a wider range of game types, including action, strategy, role playing, and sports.

Several of these games (including Grand Theft Auto) were available exclusively for the Playstation and PS2 platforms. In 2002, a total of 12 of the top 20 games were produced for the Playstation and PS2 consoles (10 were for PS2). Five of the top 20 games were produced for the Gameboy platform and one was produced for the new GameCube. Only 1 of the 20 top-selling games was produced for the Xbox, and again it was Halo, produced by Microsoft.

In 2003, 5 out of the top 20 games were published by Nintendo, 2 by Sony, and 1 by Microsoft. Twelve of the top 20 games were produced by third-party developers. Of the 20 top-selling video games sold in 2003, a staggering 14 were for the PS2 platform. Of the remaining 6, 5 were for Nintendo's Gameboy and GameCube, and 1 was for the Xbox.

The preceding suggests that of the console makers, Nintendo has the strongest ability to develop compelling game content in house (third-party developers, however, may be beginning to match or exceed this competency). Although Sony and Microsoft were well positioned to produce technologically outstanding consoles, it has been harder for them to develop strong competencies in developing compelling game content. This has led both of them to rely much more heavily on third-party developers. Furthermore, to the extent that Sony and Microsoft rely on third-party developers, the battle tips in Sony's favor due to its advantage in installed base. First, third-party developers are more likely to design games for the platform with the largest installed base, giving Sony an advantage in attracting developers. Second, even when third-party developers design a game for both platforms, the relative sizes of the PS2 and Xbox installed bases ensures that the Sony version of the games are more likely to make the top-selling list. As a result, despite a massive amount of investment over 2 years, an Xbox game has only ever claimed one spot on the top-selling games list.

Managing Network Externalities

Successful competitors in the video game industry have not only competed on the quality of their consoles and games, but also used network externalities to their advantage by rapidly building installed base and manipulating customer perceptions. There are a number of strategies a new entrant in the video game industry can employ to rapidly build its installed base. One of the most obvious is to offer the product at an aggressive discount to encourage adoption. It can also work to reduce customer resistance to adopting a new console by lowering customer switching costs. Incumbents, in turn, have a number of strategies they can use to protect their installed base advantage. First, the incumbent can use attractive or powerful distribution policies to tie existing distributors closely to its console, and create switching costs for customers. The incumbent can also make new generations of its platform backward compatible. Backward compatibility allows the incumbent to leverage its advantage in installed base and complementary goods across generations (Schilling, 2003).

Aggressive Discounting. In network externality industries firms may initially offer products at or below cost to rapidly deploy the product, with the hope of recouping profits through later sales on either the core technology or complementary goods once the standard is established (Hill, 1997). In the video game industry this has proven to be a very important strategy. Nintendo, Sega, Sony, and Microsoft have each employed a strategy of selling consoles at a price very close to (or below) production costs while profiting from subsequent game sales and licensing royalties (see Table 6.7). The systems offered by Philips and 3DO, by contrast, were both introduced at price points that were more than triple the price of 16-bit systems, and twice the price of the launch prices of 32-bit systems ultimately introduced by Sega and Sony.

Backward Compatibility. A particularly powerful defensive strategy on the part of the incumbent is to combine continuous innovation with backward

TABLE 6.7
Pricing and Backward Compatibility

	Price	Backward Compatibility
16-bit systems		
Sega Genesis	Initially $190, reduced to $150	Yes, with 8-bit master system
NEC Turbo Grafx-16	Initially $200, reduced to $99	Not applicable
Nintendo SNES	Initially $200, reduced to $150	No
32/64-bit systems		
Philips CD-I (32)	Initially $1000, reduced to $499	Not applicable
3DO (32)	Initially $700, reduced to $500, reduced to $299	Not applicable
Atari Jaguar (64/32)	Initially $249	Unknown
Sega Saturn (32)	Initially $399, reduced to $199	No
Sony Playstation (32)	Initially $299, reduced to $199	Not applicable
Nintendo 64 (64)	Initially $199	No
128-bit systems		
Sony Playstation2	Initially $299, reduced to $179	Yes
Microsoft Xbox	Initially $299, reduced to $179	Not applicable
Nintendo GameCube	Initially $199, reduced to $149 in 2002, then $99 in 2003	No

compatibility. The incumbent that both innovates to prevent a competitor from creating technological gap and utilizes backward compatibility so that its new platform or models are compatible with previous generations of complementary goods can leverage the existing value yielded by a large range of complementary goods to its new platforms. Although such a strategy may cause the firm to forfeit some of the sales of complementary goods for the new platform (at least initially) it can also effectively link the generations through time, and can be a very successful way of transitioning customers through product generations while preventing competitors from having a window to enter the market.

Microsoft has utilized this strategy deftly with Windows—though the operating system is regularly updated, each successive generation provides backward compatibility with most of the major software applications developed for previous generations. Thus customers can upgrade without having to replace their entire libraries of software applications. By contrast, when Nintendo introduced its 16-bit system (and later its 64-bit system) it prevented the system from being compatible with 8-bit Nintendo games (which existed in tremendous range), believing that it would be more profitable to require customers to purchase new games. This is understandable given that the consoles were sold at cost and profits were made through game sales, but it also meant that Nintendo forfeited a significant potential source of advantage over Sega.

In contrast, Sega made its 16-bit Genesis compatible with its 8-bit Master System games, though this may not have proven terribly persuasive to customers given the limited success of the Master System. More significantly, Sony made its PS2 console backward compatible with Playstation games, thereby not only ensuring that there was a tremendous existing library of compatible games at its launch, but also providing a significant incentive to Playstation owners who were considering upgrading to a 128-bit system to choose the PS2 instead of Sega's Dreamcast, or waiting for the Xbox or GameCube.

Relationships With Distributors. Successful video game console producers have also paid careful attention to their relationships with distributors to ensure that a wide range of distributors would carry and promote the consoles. Whereas good distribution cannot ensure a console's success, bad distribution can ensure a console's failure. Lack of distribution may have contributed significantly to the failure of the Sega Saturn to gain installed base. Sega had limited distribution for its Saturn launch, which may have slowed the building of its installed base both directly (because customers had limited access to the product) and indirectly (because distributors that were initially denied product may have been reluctant to promote the product after the limitations were lifted). Nintendo, by contrast, had unlimited distribution for its Nintendo 64 launch, and Sony not only had unlimited distribution, but had extensive experience with negotiating with retailing giants such as Walmart for its consumer electronics products. Consequently, Sony Playstation had better distribution on its first day of business than the Sega Saturn, despite Sega's decade of experience in the market (Machan, 1996).

Reducing Resistance. The new entrant can reduce both the real and perceived risk of adopting the system by offering guarantees. When there is uncertainty about whether a new console will succeed in penetrating the market, customers, distributors, and third-party developers face great risk in supporting the new console. Should the console fail to gather the necessary momentum, customers may find that they have born switching costs only to end up with a console with few games available. Similarly, distributors might end up with inventories of product that cannot be sold, and that have a rapidly eroding value. Games developers may find that they have forfeited both their production cost investment and the value of their time and effort devoted to developing games for a console with little future.

By offering full money-back guarantees to customers (or distributors), the firm creates an option for customers to reverse their switching costs (at least that portion accounted for by the purchase price of the console) should the console not be successful. Thus, although the customer still faces switching costs to adopt the new console, their risk of loss of the switching cost investment is reduced. Console producers can also create guarantees for third-party developers: The firm can guarantee particular quantities of games to be purchased, or provide the capital for production itself, thus bearing the bulk of the risk of producing complementary games for the console.

The third-party developers may still have forfeited time or effort in producing games that may not have a long-term market, but the direct costs will be less at risk. An excellent example of this was the original Nintendo NES system. After the crash of the video game industry in 1984 and 1985, distributors were understandably reluctant to stock new consoles and games. Therefore, Nintendo introduced its 8-bit system to the United States by selling it on a consignment basis. Retailers bore little risk in distributing the goods because unsold units could be returned to Nintendo, and the video game industry was reborn.

By contrast, once a firm's console is entrenched as the dominant system, it is in its best interest to build customer switching costs. As already mentioned, the incumbent can encourage upgrading to the incumbent's newest platform, both increasing switching costs and reducing the likelihood of a new entrant achieving a significant technological gap. However, another more subtle way of increasing customer switching costs is through the provision of peripheral add-on devices specific to the platform. For instance, a competitor that can induce video game customers to buy additional joysticks, 3D headsets, or other accessories can ratchet customers investment in the platform to higher levels, and increase their resistance to an incompatible system offered by a potential competitor. This indicates that peripheral devices play more strategic importance than simply providing additional revenue streams—they are ties that further bind the customer to the platform. This, in turn, implies that the incumbent may wish to invest more in development of such accessories than standard NPV analysis of the projected revenue streams from the devices would indicate.

Advertising And Vaporware. A firm that aggressively promotes its products can increase both its actual installed base and its perceived installed base. Even products that have relatively small installed bases can obtain relatively large "mind shares" through heavy advertising (thus Microsoft's $500-million marketing budget for the Xbox). Because perceived installed base may drive subsequent adoptions, a large perceived installed base can lead to a large actual installed base. Such a tactic underlies the use of *vaporware*—preadvertising products that are not actually on the market yet, and may not even exist—by many software vendors. By building the impression among customers that a product is ubiquitous, firms can prompt rapid adoption of the product when it actually is available.[5] Vaporware may also buy a firm valuable time in bringing its product to market. If other vendors beat the firm to market and the firm fears that customers may select a dominant design before its offering is introduced, it can use vaporware to attempt to persuade customers to delay purchase until the firm's product is on offer.

The Nintendo 64 provides an excellent example. In an effort to forestall consumer purchases of 32-bit systems, Nintendo began aggressively promoting its development of a 64-bit system (originally named Project Reality) in 1994, though the product would not actually reach the market until September 1996. The project underwent so many delays that some industry observers dubbed it "Project Unreality" (Brandenburger, 1995c). Another interesting vaporware example was Nintendo's rewriteable 64M disk drive. Though the product was much hyped, it was never actually introduced.

The major video game producers also go to great lengths to manage impressions of their installed base and market share, often to the point of exaggeration or deception. For example, at the end of 1991, Nintendo claimed it had sold 2 million units of the SNES to the U.S. market, whereas Sega disagreed, arguing that Nintendo had sold 1 million units at most. Nintendo also forecast that it would sell an additional 6 million units by the end of 1992 (actual installed base of SNES systems in the United States reached just over 4 million units in 1992). By May of 1992, Nintendo was claiming a 60% share of the 16-bit market, and Sega was claiming a 63% share (Brandenburger, 1995b). Similar tactics were deployed in the battle for the 32/64-bit market. For example, in October 1995, Sony announced

[5]There are risks, however, to creating demand for products that are not yet available. A firm the preadvertises its next generation of products may find that it prematurely dampens sales of its existing products as customers hold off purchases in anticipation of the next generation (Billington, Lee, & Tang, 1998). Furthermore, advertising products that do not yet exist can create the impression of shortages, which can spur customers to inflate their expected purchases. Volatility and uncertainty in demand are amplified as they travel up the supply chain, resulting in a bullwhip effect that can cause severe inventory and cash flow problems for a producer (Lee, Padmanabhan, & Whang, 1997).

to the press that it already had presold 100,000 consoles in the United States, to which Mike Ribero, Sega's executive vice president for marketing and sales, countered that Sony's figures were deceptive, arguing that many preorders would never materialize into actual purchases (McGann, 1995).

Reputation. When a new entrant is posed to challenge an entrenched dominant design, its reputation for both technological and commercial competence will critically influence the market's expectation about its likelihood of success. Customers, distributors, and complementary goods producers will use the firm's track record for technological innovation as an indicator of the new product's functionality and value. The firm's degree of prior commercial success acts as an indicator of the firm's ability to build and manage the necessary support network around the new technology (distribution, advertising, alliances) to create the necessary momentum in the installed base-complementary goods cycle.

When Sega originally entered the market, it had the benefit of having several highly successful arcade games to its credit (both Atari and Nintendo had also been arcade game producers prior to developing home video games). The company thus entered with a reputation for developing exciting games, and this reputation may have facilitated customer acceptance of its 16-bit challenge to Nintendo's 8-bit dominance. By contrast, when Sony entered the video game market, it did not have the arcade background that underscored the other primary competitors. However, it did have a wealth of technological expertise as a consumer electronics manufacturer, and exceptional brand equity in electronic products. Furthermore, Sony had demonstrated its ability to win a format war through its successful introduction of the CD format (with Philips) that supplanted vinyl records and analog cassettes.[6]

Similarly, reputation is probably Microsoft's greatest strength in the battle for dominance over 128-bit video game systems. Microsoft's near monopoly in the PC operating system market was achieved through its unrivaled skill in using network externalities to its advantage. Microsoft had skillfully leveraged its controlling share in the PC operating systems into domination over many categories of the software market, obliterating many would-be competitors in the process. Microsoft's reputation thus sent a strong signal to distributors, developers, and customers that would shape their expectations for its future installed base and availability of complementary goods. Its success was not assured, but it was a powerful force to be reckoned with.

Credible Commitments. A firm can also signal a market its commitment to winning its fight to enter an industry by making substantial investments that would be difficult to reverse. For example, it was well publicized that Sony spent over

[6]It is interesting to note that Philips should have also benefited from such reputation effects; however, its product was considerably more expensive and not targeted directly at the games market. Philips also did not have the extensive relationships with software developers and other content providers that Sony had.

$500 million developing the Playstation. It would also manufacture the system itself, as well as establish an in-house games development unit. By contrast, 3DO's cumulative research and development costs at the time of the launch of its multiplayer were less than $37 million, and the company utilized a strategy whereby all console and game production was performed by third parties. Thus, 3DO may not have signaled the market that it had enough confidence in the platform to bear the brunt of the capital risk.

Although both incumbents and potential entrants may benefit from shaping perceptions or expectations about installed base and availability of complementary goods through aggressive advertising, reputation, and credible commitments, it is worth noting that the incumbent is typically at a significant advantage in actual installed base and availability of complementary goods. Thus, the incumbent may leverage this by aggressively advertising comparative figures based on actual data, thereby defusing any inflated perceptions the potential entrant may have been able to achieve.

DISCUSSION

Analysis of the video game industry suggests that firms require three primary competencies to be successful in the home video game console industry: an ability to provide advanced technology consoles, an ability to provide compelling content and ensure that high-quality games are widely available, and an ability to strategically manipulate network externalities. Arguably, the first two competencies could be obtained on the market through licensing and joint ventures, however, as the analysis of games strategies in the video game industry demonstrated, successful firms must typically also have strong games development capabilities in house. Furthermore, to effectively manipulate network externalities typically requires a set of closely integrated abilities (including strategic acumen and market leverage) that are difficult to obtain on the market.

In 2003, only Sony possessed all three competencies internally. Sony's background in consumer electronics made it relatively simple for the company to produce an advanced technology console. Sony's resources in film and music production should have given it an edge over other new entrants in developing compelling game content. However, the independence of the game business division from the entertainment business division may have slowed the realization of this potential. Furthermore, Sony's brand equity, capital resources, distribution leverage, and prior experience with markets driven by network externalities put Sony in a strong position to manage network externalities to its favor.

Microsoft proved that the technological hurdle was the easiest to surmount, and was exquisitely skilled in manipulating network externalities, but was still struggling to create (through both internal development and third-party agreements) a strong armory of content. Nintendo's great strength was content, and it also proved repeatedly that technology would not prove to be an obstacle. However, the company consistently made decisions that demonstrated a poor understanding of the network externalities of its industry. Given this analysis, it is easy to see why in 2003 PS2's market share of the U.S. video game console market was approximately 50%, whereas Xbox and GameCube split the rest of the market. The question remains, however, whether (and how fast) Microsoft and Nintendo can build competencies in developing content and managing network externalities respectively.

IMPLICATIONS FOR OTHER CULTURAL INDUSTRIES

One of the unique advantages of examining the video game industry is that its history is characterized by distinct generations of competition, enabling us to observe a series of battles and to identify the drivers of success and failure. Such a systematic analysis is crucial; consider what the implications would have been of examining only a single generation of the video game industry. A cursory examination of the industry in the mid-1980s (after the fall of Atari) would have suggested that the most important dimension of success was controlling game quality.

Examining only the 16-bit generation would have suggested that introducing a technologically powerful console early was the most important determinant of success. However, an examination of the 32/64-bit generation might have suggested that technological power was not nearly so important as price. Finally, if one only had examined the 128-bit generation, one would have been tempted to conclude that success was all about timing. Through comparing a series of generations, it becomes clear that multiple dimensions determined the outcomes of each of these battles. Inadequacy in any dimension can result in failure—only firms that effectively manage all of the dimensions are likely to be successful. The 128-bit generation is particularly apt in demonstrating this point; neither Nintendo's exceptional skill in content nor Microsoft's exceptional skill in managing network externalities is sufficient to guarantee their success.

One of the primary implications of this analysis for other culturally based industries is the need to identify the critical dimensions of competition in the industry and to assess each organization's ability to manage all of them. It is tempting to assume that organizations need only focus on the most salient dimension—such as musical talent in an orchestra, or choosing exceptional screenplays in movie production—however, such an approach is likely to fail. In fact, it is when most organizations focus on the most salient dimensions than an unconventional competitor has the most opportunity to penetrate the market by excelling in those dimensions that have been overlooked.

REFERENCES

Becker, D., & Wilcox, J. (2001, March 6). Will Xbox drain Microsoft? *CNET News.com*. Retrieved July 9, 2001 from http://news.com.com

Billington, C., Lee, H., & Tang, C. (1998). Successful strategies for product rollovers. *Sloan Management Review, 39*, 23–30.

Brandenberger, A. (1995a). Power play (A): Nintendo in 8-bit video games. *Harvard Business School* Case #9-795-167.
Brandenberger, A. (1995b). Power play (B): Sega in 16-bit video games. *Harvard Business School* Case #9-795-103.
Brandenberger, A. (1995c). Power play (C): 3DO in 32-bit video games. *Harvard Business School* Case #9-795-104.
"Cheap didn't sell." (1992, August 3). *Forbes,* 52–55.
Choi, J. (1994). Network externalities, compatibility choice, and planned obsolescence, *Journal of Industrial Economics, 42,* 167–182.
Clash of the titans. (2001, December 27). *Accountancy,* 30.
Cohen, S. (1984). *Zap! The rise and fall of Atari.* New York: McGraw-Hill.
Elkin, T. (2000). Gearing up for Xbox launch. *Advertising Age, 71,* 16.
Frankel, D. (2001, December 31). Video game business boffo on big launches. *Video Business, 21*(52), 38.
Gallagher, S. (2001). Innovation and competition in standard-based industries: A historical analysis of the U.S. home video game market. *IEEE Transactions on Engineering Management, 49,* 67–82.
Hadju, J. (1993, December 27). Rating the hot boxes. *Fortune, 128,* 112–113.
Hill, C. W. L. (1997). Establishing a standard: Competitive strategy and technological standards in winner-take-all industries. *Academy of Management Executive, 11*(2), 7–26.
Hisey, P. (1995). Saturn lands first at Toys 'R' Us. *Discount Store News, 34*(11), 6–8.
Johnson, M. E. (2001). Learning from toys: Lessons in managing supply chain risk from the toy industry. *California Management Review, 43*(3), 106–124.
Kasten, A. (1997). Off-computer: CD-ROM and the game machines. *E Media Professional, 10*(3), 66–73.
Katz, M., & Shapiro, C. (1986). Technology adoption in the presence of network externalities. *Journal of Political Economy, 94,* 822–841.
Katz, M., & Shapiro, C. (1992). Product introduction with network externalities. *Journal of Industrial Economics, 40,* 55–83.
Kittner, J., Schilling, M. A., & Karl, S. (2001). Microsoft's Xbox. *Boston University Teaching Case.*
Lee, H. L., Padmanabhan, V., & Whang, S. (1997). The bullwhip effect in supply chains. *Sloan Management Review, 38*(3), 93–102.
Lefton, T. (1998, March 2). Looking for a sonic boom. *Brandweek, 39,* 26–30.
Machan, D. (1996, September 23). Great job–you're fired. *Forbes, 158,* 145–147.
McGann, M. E. (1995, October). Crossing swords. *Dealerscope Consumer Electronics Marketplace, 37,* 63–65.
Norton, L. P. (2001, May 14). Toy soldiers. *Barrons, 81,* 25–30.
Peterson, K. (2004, February 16). Proven titles are biggest sellers in video game business. *Knight Ridder Tribune Business News,* p. 1.
Pham, A. (2002, November 22). Nintendo's first-half profit drops by 45%. *The Los Angeles Times,* p. C3.
Polsson, K. (1997). *Chronology of events in the history of microcomputers.* Retrieved July 7, 2001 from http://www.islandnet.com
Rigdon, J. (1996, September 17). Game over: 3DO intends to exit hardware business. *The Wall Street Journal Europe, 14,* p. 4.
Scally, R. (1997, April 1). Next generation platforms engage in shelf-war games. *Discount Store News, 36,* 45.
Schilling, M. (1998). Technological lock out: An integrative model of the economic and strategic factors driving technology success and failure. *Academy of Management Review, 23,* 267–284.

Schilling, M. A. (2002). Technology success and failure in winner-take-all markets: Testing a model of technological lock out. *Academy of Management Journal, 45,* 387–398.

Schilling, M. A. (2003). Technological leapfrogging: Lessons from the U.S. video game console industry. *California Management Review, 45*(3), 6–32.

Schilling, M. A., Chiu, R., & Chou, C. (2003). Sony Playstation2: Just another competitor? In M. Hitt, D. Ireland, & B. Hoskisson (Eds.), *Strategic management: competitiveness and globalization* (5th ed., pp. C459–C471). St. Paul, MN: West.

Schilling, M. A., Kittner, J., & Karl, S. (2003). Microsoft's Xbox. In A. Thompson & A. Strickland (Eds.), *Strategic Management* (13th ed.). New York: McGraw-Hill.

Shcff, D. (1993). *Game over: How Nintendo zapped an American industry, captured your dollars and enslaved your children.* New York: Random House.

Sinakin, Y. D. (1996, February 19). Players take bold step to keep up with new rules. *Electronic Buyers' News,* p. 50.

Snider, M. (2002, November 18). "Vice City" shakes up video game industry. *USA Today,* p. D3.

Trachtenberg, J. (1995, October 23). Sony interactive gets Bruce Stein as president, CEO. *The Wall Street Journal,* p. B5.

Trachtenberg, J. (1996, June 28). Short circuit: How Philips flubbed its US introduction of electronic product. *The Wall Street Journal,* p. A1.

Turner, N. (1996, January 24). For giants of video games it's an all-new competition. *Investor's Business Daily,* p. A6.

Wildstrom, S. H. (2001, December 24). It's all about the games. *Business Week, 3763,* 22.

CHAPTER

7

Playing to Their Strengths: Strategies of Incumbent and Start-Up Firms in Web-Based Periodicals[1]

Alan B. Eisner
Pace University

Quintus R. Jett
Dartmouth College

Helaine J. Korn
Baruch College, CUNY

Emerging industry segments can be useful to study because they represent a setting that tends to exhibit considerable ambiguity and uncertainty (Aldrich & Fiol, 1994; Budros, 1993; Nelson & Winter, 1982). These conditions can be attributed to the early stages of the development of these segments, where much of the future

[1]Earlier drafts of these ideas were presented at the New York University Cultural Industries Conference, the 1997 Academy of Management Annual Meeting, and the 1997 Seybold Seminar, New York. We are grateful to Nigel Minors, Robert Panco, Jr., and Megumi Shimbaya for their assistance with data collection and coding.

course of evolution can be relatively hard to predict. As such, emerging industry segments can provide a significant opportunity for entrants to try to find their own ways to exploit the potential of the growing product and market. At the same time, the entrants may be able to exert some form of influence on the subsequent course of the development of the new industry segment.

Various researchers have focused on the types of moves that are made and the degree of success that is achieved by firms that make an entry into emerging industry segments (Baum, Korn, & Kotha, 1995; Budros, 1993; Mitchell, 1989, 1991). Studies have concentrated on the time at which firms have entered, the strategies that they have attempted to use, and the type of organization that they have tried to create. Success has been measured either through the ability of a firm to survive or through the share of market that a firm has been able to capture.

In this chapter, we focus on the emergence of web-based periodicals, or *webzines*, as a new segment within the traditional publishing industry. The development of the Internet during the 1990s created an opportunity for firms to enter into a new segment where content that was previously limited to print form could now be distributed in electronic form. By the late 1990s, a large number of firms had entered into this emerging industry segment. They exhibited a range of strategies to try to create a viable market for the new product.

We compare and contrast the strategies of firms based on their prior experience within the established publishing industry. Several researchers have predicted that incumbent firms will respond differently to the opportunities created by emerging industry segments compared to new entrants (Eisner, Jett, & Korn, 2001; Mezias & Eisner, 1997; Mitchell, 1991; Tushman & Anderson, 1986). However, most of these studies have focused on the timing of entry of each of these types of firms into the emerging segment and on the types of innovation that each of them is likely to undertake.

In this chapter, we build on this research by examining the innovativeness of the strategies with which incumbents and start-ups may choose to enter. We suggest that incumbent firms are likely to enter with strategies that allow them to exploit their existing competencies. In other words, they are more likely to try to pursue strategies that draw upon their already developed competencies, allowing them to find ways to extend these to the emerging segment (Tushman & Anderson, 1986). In this way, they increase the likelihood that the pattern of subsequent development of the new industry segment will be pushed in the direction of competencies in which they are best positioned to compete.

In the next part of the chapter, we provide some background on the emergence of web-based periodicals or webzines. Following this, we propose and test some hypotheses that contrast the entry strategies of incumbent entrants with those of start-up firms. We also carry out a more detailed qualitative comparison on a small subset of our sample. Our results suggest that incumbent firms do enter emerging segments within their industries with strategies that are designed to build on their established strengths. As such, they do try to exploit the new opportunities that these segments may uncover, but in ways that allow them to reduce their exposure to ambiguity and uncertainty.

WEB-BASED PERIODICALS AS AN EMERGING CULTURAL FORM

Web-based periodicals represent a new form of a traditional cultural good (Bjorkegren, 1996; Hirsch, 1972). Their emergence is a consequence of the World Wide Web, a global computer network that has attracted significant attention and use since 1994. By 1996, the World Wide Web (or more simply, the web) had more than 35 million regular users (CyberAtlas, 1996), a number that has been increasing at an exponential rate, and many forms of web-based usage have emerged in recent years.

One form is the web-based periodical, or webzine, a cultural form that resembles a print magazine but uses an electronic media and delivery system. As interest in the web has expanded, hundreds of these webzines were launched by incumbents as well as by start-up firms. By 1997, a weekly search of related terms on the web produced an over 50% increase in usage throughout the year. Within a 3-year time span, webzines had already emerged as a new cultural form, offering new possibilities to producers and consumers of newspapers and magazines.

Although webzines are similar in some ways to traditional magazines and newspapers, they have distinguishable features that set them apart as a new cultural form. They are like traditional magazines in that they deliver text, photographs, and illustrations oriented around a particular specialty or interest. Webzines have publishers, editorial staff, and other traditional staff roles. Their content includes feature articles, essays, advertising, photographs, graphics, news briefs, opinion essays, and letters to the editor. Many webzines follow traditional publication schedules (e.g., daily, weekly, monthly) and conform to standard print layouts and organizational conventions (e.g., table of contents, masthead).

What distinguishes web-based periodicals from print periodicals is how readers retrieve them, how readers access their content, and what is required to launch them and keep them in publication. To retrieve a webzine, a reader needs a computer, a direct-wired or telephone-line dial-up Internet connection, and web-viewing software (e.g., Netscape's Navigator or Microsoft's Internet Explorer packages). Unlike traditional print periodicals, a web-based periodical is neither delivered nor picked off the shelf at the local newsstand. Readers must access the web through their computer and their Internet connection, using the browsing software to find and view the webzine.

Readers access webzine content differently from magazine and newspaper content because webzines are an electronic rather than a paper media. Readers can interact more with the published content, using provided hyperlinks to travel to other websites and participating in online chat with writers, editors, and other readers. In addition to reading, webzine consumers may also listen to audio samples or watch live pictures and video. Although they are unable to carry a webzine around with them, readers can print (or download) selected webzine articles and text from their computer. Though similar to paper magazines and newspapers, webzines deliver a different experience to readers.

Relative to newspapers and magazines, which have large capital requirements, webzines are particularly easy to launch and operate. Once an intended publisher has access to a computer, a webzine can be created on a commercial online service or Internet Services Provider (ISP; e.g., Compuserve, or America Online) for as little as $20 to $40 per month. In contrast, paper publishers often need advertising commitments in order to launch. Once launched, webzines exist electronically and, consequently, they tend to have lower overhead. Updating published content on the web via computer is relatively cheap and quick compared to the cost and lead time of using the printing press. Moreover, it is easy to publicize the presence of a new webzine. Publishers may register for free with dozens of search engines (e.g., Yahoo, Altavista, Webcrawler), the most common method to find information about topics of interest on the Internet.

All these factors constitute low barriers to creating new webzines. Relative to the traditional print media, it is easier for a would-be publisher to launch a web-based periodical. One of the ways in which webzines inspire interest is in the change in the economics of cultural goods. Within the emerging web-based publishing arena, both hobbyists and commercial ventures seeking to create cultural goods are on a much more equal footing. Because the printing and production costs of a webzine are very small relative to paper publication, a whole new means and distribution of cultural expression has become available to those with significantly fewer resources.

Web-based periodicals have a complex relationship with print periodicals. The traditional periodical publishing industry is established and mature. The market consolidation and decline of specific segments, like newspapers, predates the emergence of web-based periodicals, but it is due in part to the increasing pervasiveness of alternative media (e.g., television). The emergence of web-based periodicals does not necessarily mean the demise of those who produce traditional (print) periodicals. In fact, incumbent publishers of print newspapers and magazines are developing webzines that mirror their paper editions, in order to extend their reach to more readers. Among emerging web-based periodicals, incumbent producers are therefore operating simultaneously with newcomer producers in experimenting with this new cultural form.

STRATEGIES OF INCUMBENTS AND NEWCOMERS

The emergence of web-based periodicals clearly had significant implications for the established publishing industry (Mossberg, 1996). To begin with, they provided a new channel for the dissemination of traditional content to a broader audience. At the same time, they reduced the reliance on other traditional capabilities for printing and physical distribution. Finally, they also created the need to develop some new competencies for the creation of webpages, such as the ability to program in the hypertext languages and to benefit from the advanced multimedia technologies.

For entrepreneurial start-up firms, webzines provided a relatively easy and inexpensive method of delivering their content in a new form to a wide audience. Many would be unable to publish as broadly, or with the same quality, under the traditional publishing paradigm. For conventional incumbent publishers, however, webzines provided an additional channel that could increase the value of the content that they already had become skilled at either acquiring or developing. At the same time, they could diminish the value of their print production and distribution capabilities or cannibalize their existing advertising and sales revenue through their traditional print media.

In order to minimize the threat posed by webzines, incumbent firms were more likely to push hard to maintain the value of competencies that they already had established in their print operations. Foremost among these is the ability to generate sufficient amount of content that may be of sufficient interest to readers. In order to generate this content, established magazines and newspapers have well-developed sources and methods for obtaining content articles from their pools of staff and freelance writers. These organizations can also generate interissue continuity because of their well-articulated publication mission and their well-developed editorial policies. By contrast, newcomers will need to develop the capabilities to create or obtain content that they can use in their webzines. They therefore may not rely as heavily on different forms of content, trying instead to supplement their more limited content with features that the new technology has made possible.

Hypothesis 1: Incumbents will exploit their content generating capabilities more than newcomers.

Incumbents are also more likely to have relationships that they have created over time with others within their industry. For example, they will be able to share information or refer to each other in their publications. Existing publishers therefore will be more likely to exploit these linkages with other individuals or organizations in their newly launched webzines. On the other hand, newcomers may not have any significant links with others within the established publishing industry because of their recent entry. They are less likely therefore to be able to exploit such links in the development of their webzines.

Hypothesis 2: Incumbents will exploit their ties to existing organizations within their industry more than newcomers.

Incumbent producers will also have the relationships, reputation, and credibility with potential advertisers to secure advertising for their publications. They have connections with media purchasing firms and agents, as well as a track record of editorial stability that sponsors may be concerned about. Newcomer producers will have more difficulty convincing potential advertisers and sponsors about the strength and desirability of their readership. Consequently, these firms will rely less on the established revenue generating mechanisms than incumbents.

Hypothesis 3: Incumbent producers will rely more heavily on generating revenues from advertisers than newcomers.

Last, incumbent producers may be locked into the methods and technologies of print production. This is likely to make it difficult for them to fully exploit the new multimedia, electronic technologies. These new technologies are not bound by the two-dimensional page, but allow design personnel the capabilities to creatively express their concepts with motion, sound, and interactive dialogue. Newcomer producers have the advantage of not having an investment in existing publishing technologies and a clean cognitive slate to embrace new multimedia technology.

Hypothesis 4: Incumbent producers will be slower to adopt new process technologies than newcomer producers.

METHODS

Sample Selection

Our sample consists of 114 randomly selected, web-based periodicals. We used the Yahoo search engine to construct our sample, because it was considered the most widely known engine and returned the most useful search results (Flynn, 1997; Haring, 1997). We began by searching for the following seven terms: webzine, ezine, magazine, journal, newspaper, publication, and periodical. These keywords were individually pretested to determine that they would return links to electronic publications. The search yielded 13,968 uniform resource locators (URLs). URLs refer to hypertext links used to identify specific locations on the Internet.

The results of an Internet search engine often produce a considerable amount of irrelevant information and noise (Manes, 1997). Every URL result does not yield a unique website, and a website may easily have hundreds of URLs associated with it. We screened our initial search results and eliminated many URLs. Many were simply web pages that made brief reference to webzines. Once we had identified 300 candidate websites, we began evaluating their suitability for the study. A site was considered suitable (i.e., classified as a web-based periodical) if it: (a) was periodically published, (b) had multiple authors, (c) had articles or stories, and (d) specified a topic or domain of interest. After this final screen, we had a sample of 114 suitable, web-based periodicals.

Although there is heterogeneity on many dimensions within the sample, we distinguished between incumbents and newcomers. Previous research has demonstrated the validity of these categories, and no other factor had emerged as more significant in distinguishing the various types of this new cultural form. Within our randomly selected sample, 67 are web-based complements to an existing paper periodical (incumbent), and 47 are exclusively web-based periodicals (newcomer producers).

Data and Analysis

We focused on the second half of 1997, tracking on a weekly basis a number of variables associated with the 114 web-based periodicals that made up our sample. Table 7.1 lists our variables and their measures.

Content-generating capabilities were measured in two different ways. The first was a count of the number of articles per issue. The second was a dummy variable that took the value of 1 if the webzine used illustrations and 0 otherwise. Next, the ties to existing organizations were measured by the number of links that each webzine offered to other publications or content providers.

We used two measures of reliance on advertising revenue. We collected data on: (a) whether producers had an advertising policy statement on their website and (b) how many advertisers or sponsors they displayed advertisements for on their website. Finally, use of new process technologies was measured through three separate dummy variables. These took on a value of 1 if the webzine used online video, online audio, or online forums or chatrooms.

In order to test our hypotheses regarding the differences in characteristics of the newcomer and incumbent webzines, we performed comparison of means between incumbent and newcomer periodicals. We performed standard *t* tests to check for statistically significant differences in the means for the period that we studied.

RESULTS

The results of our comparisons of means between newcomer and incumbent producers are presented in Table 7.2.

We found partial support for Hypothesis 1, which stated that incumbent producers would try to exploit their content-producing capabilities more heavily than start-ups. This was not supported by the number of articles per issue, but it was supported by the use of illustrations. Whereas the mean number of articles per issue was greater for incumbents, the difference was not statistically significant. However, the mean usage of illustrations was at 0.60 for incumbents and at 0.41 for start-ups, yielding a significant difference in means in the hypothesized direction ($t = -1.80, p < .01$).

TABLE 7.1
Variable Descriptions and Coding Information

Newcomer or incumbent webzine
1. Type of webzine (Newcomer = 1, Incumbent = 2)

Public ties to other organizations
2. Number of links to other publications, providers, or other organizations (Count)

Revenue-generating mechanisms
3. Is there an advertising or sponsorship policy or price list online? (Yes = 1, No = 0)
4. Number of advertisers or sponsors (Count)

New process technologies
5. Use of online audio (Yes = 1, No = 0)
6. Use of online forums or chatrooms (Yes = 1, No = 0)
7. Use of online video (Yes = 1, No = 0)

Existing process technologies
8. Number of articles per issue (Count)
9. Use of illustrations (Yes = 1, No = 0)

There is considerable support for Hypothesis 2, which indicated that incumbent producers would exploit their ties to other organizations within the industry. Incumbents had a greater mean number of hyperlinks (25.73 mean links) than start-ups (15.00 mean links), yielding a significant difference in means in the hypothesized direction ($t = -1.88, p < .01$).

We also found support for Hypothesis 3, which proposed that the incumbent producers would be more likely to rely on advertising revenue than start-ups. For the advertising policy measure we found incumbents more likely to have an advertising policy. For the advertiser count measure, we found a greater mean number of advertisers for incumbents. The difference from start-ups was statistically significant.

Finally, we did not find support for Hypothesis 4, that incumbents would be less likely to adopt new process technologies than newcomers. In fact, neither incumbents nor newcomers were making any significant use of any of the three technologies that we had chosen to investigate. By the end of the year, however, some of the start-ups and incumbents were starting to use chatroom technology and a few of these firms were also experimenting with audio-streaming technology.

TABLE 7.2
Comparison of Means

	Period 1 (beginning of year)			Period 2 (end of year)		
Variable	Newcomers	Incumbents		Newcomers	Incumbents	
	Mean	Mean	t Value	Mean	Mean	t Value
Hyperlinks to other sites	4.69 (42)	3.81(52)	0.28	15.00 (43)	25.73 (64)	–1.88**
Advertising policy	0.20 (46)	0.39 (62)	–2.23**	0.20 (46)	0.40 (62)	–2.41**
Advertisers	0.49 (45)	0.64 (47)	–0.25	0.95 (46)	1.60 (55)	–1.85*
Multimedia						
Online chat	0.00 (46)	0.00 (63)	—	0.13 (45)	0.13 (60)	0.00
Online video	0.00 (46)	0.00 (63)	—	0.00 (46)	0.00 (63)	—
Online audio	0.00 (46)	0.00 (63)	—	0.02 (46)	0.01 (61)	0.196
Print media						
Articles	4.15 (33)	5.75 (24)	–1.13	3.49 (39)	4.24 (49)	–0.79
Illustrations	0.31 (45)	0.35 (57)	–0.42	0.41 (39)	0.60 (57)	–1.80**
Staff members	10.85 (20)	30.23 (22)	–2.87**	8.56 (25)	25.58 (33)	–2.91**

Note. Values enclosed in parentheses represent number counted.
$*p < .05$. $**p < .01$.

STRUCTURED COMPARISONS

In order to develop further insight, we performed a structured comparison between newcomer and incumbent periodicals, based on methods for developing constructs from qualitative data (Eisenhardt, 1989; Glaser & Strauss, 1966; Strauss & Corbin, 1990). We followed three critical standards. To begin with, we attempted to get as close to the data as possible by launching an in-depth investigation of particular webzines. Next, we tried to compare and contrast the cases by focusing on selected pairs of webzines in order to capture their common and distinct qualities. Finally, we iterated among data and constructs, that is, we developed abstract categories from comparing particular cases, and then iterated those categories back onto the data.

We began with a random draw of six webzines from our sample, where three webzines each came from the categories of newcomer and incumbent producers. Then each of the researchers was asked to make an in-depth study of two start-up and two incumbent producer webzines. The researchers, operating independently, visited their assigned webzines and collected data on each webzine's content and layout. After completing data collection on their four assigned webzines, each researcher performed a pairwise comparison among these cases, producing within- and across-category comparisons for newcomer and incumbent producers. Subsequently, the researchers brought together the results of their comparisons across particular webzines to develop more general constructs. Although our analysis involved a systematic comparison of pairs among all six webzines, we provide specific comparisons to illustrate the more general differences we found between incumbent and newcomer webzines.

Whereas newcomer producers of web-based periodicals emphasize original content, periodicals managed by incumbent producers often repackage existing content from their paper editions. The *Charleston Regional Business Journal Online*, an incumbent webzine, is like many incumbent entrants in that it focuses on articles and news that have already appeared in print, with some additional services and features offered (e.g., directory of local businesses, regional information, and resources). This particular webzine from the traditional media is a repackaged edition with a sample of older articles addressing commerce interests in Charleston, North Carolina.

In contrast, newcomer *Praise Bob* is a webzine that makes "a call to move forward and extend yourself, beyond the every day constraints that too easily restrict the imagination." Like many web-only periodicals, it aspires to be original in either layout or design. This specific webzine illustrates its originality both ways: an all-black Web homepage with a luminescent painting of a kneeling man (Bob?) and a prominent hyperlink that transports the reader to the homepage of the Naked Dancing Llama (a fictional, hip, and humorous talking animal who is running for president in the year 2000). Perhaps because of their new content and attempts to be original and groundbreaking, the publication frequency of these entrepreneurial, newcomer ventures can sometimes be more sporadic.

Essex County Newspapers, like many other webzines from incumbent producers, tends to push for conventional profit-seeking business models. The *Essex County Newspapers* webzine simply provides an online site for a group of regional newspapers serving Essex County in the United Kingdom. The grouping of newspapers is designed to create a large enough market for the webzine in order to increase its chances of profitability. Furthermore, *Essex County Newspapers* does not appear to use the new medium to push for different types of content. Instead, it tries to reduce its costs by relying on the more conventional articles that have already appeared in the newspapers that it represents. Finally, it tries to derive revenue from sponsors that it tries to attract and from advertisers, by offering both classified and display forms of advertising.

Meanwhile, *Radio Control Soaring* is representative of newcomer webzines in its tendencies to experiment with existing business models. To begin with, it is much more willing to focus on a fairly narrow niche of readers. Based in the United Kingdom, *Radio Control Soaring* presents itself as "the premier source for radio control soaring nuts the world over." The website includes original articles, reviews, software, and cartoons devoted to the interests of radio-control airplane aficionados. Furthermore, *Radio Control Soaring* does not rely as heavily on conventional forms of revenue from either sponsors or advertisers.

Incumbent producers tend to make more limited use of the new technology relative to start-ups. This is evident in comparing webzines such as *Florida Care Giver* and *FEED*. With its masthead reference as a consumer magazine for "caregivers of all ages," *Florida Care Giver* provides material in rather conventional form on its web page. Like several other webzines from incumbents, it typically uses traditional tools such as a table of contents. Furthermore, it strives for a consistent color scheme and layout throughout its online, electronic edition. With such conservative applications of the new technology, *Florida Care Giver* especially has the look of a paper publication on a computer screen.

Conversely, the webzine *FEED* lists its awards for innovative web-page design. Like most other start-ups, *FEED* is technologically sophisticated—using the latest Internet technology for innovative user interfaces and web-page navigation systems. On the whole, start-up producers of webzines are more creative and innovative with graphics, multimedia, and Internet technologies than the ventures of incumbent producers. *FEED* is currently attempting to translate this advantage into a more traditional publishing advantage. Its web page of public announcements mentions a collaboration with *The New York Times* to exchange its expertise in innovative web-page layouts for the journalistic and market expertise of the paper publisher.

DISCUSSION AND CONCLUSION

Schumpeter (1939, 1950) referred to innovation as a principle source of "creative destruction." The emergence of a new industry segment, such as webzines, represents such a form of innovation. However, our study illustrates that such opportunities can still allow existing firms to try to expand their existing competencies by developing strategies to exploit them within the emerging context.

The purpose of this research was to investigate the characteristics of incumbent and newcomer producers within the emerging industry segment of web-based periodicals. We attempted to show that incumbent firms are more likely to deploy strategies that build on their existing competencies when they enter into the new industry segments. In general, our hypotheses about the differences between incumbents and newcomers into the segment were supported by our quantitative and qualitative data. We did not, however, find support for the slower adoption of new process technologies by incumbent entrants.

We believe that we did not find support for the predicted difference because hardly any of the web-based periodicals were using the new process technologies that were available. An interview we had with an editor of an online journal indicated that it may be an issue of technological maturity and sophistication among mainstream customers. In other words, although it was possible in theory to implement online chat, online video, and online audio, most customers were not prepared to use these technologies at the time of our study.

The implementation of these technologies was itself immature. At the time of our study (1997), the network requirements to run the new media features we measured were beyond that of most users. Because the ability to use these features was beyond that of mainstream customers, it would be in poor judgment for producers to limit their pool of customers by relying only on the technologically sophisticated users.

This research has implications beyond emerging cultural forms, expanding to the early stages of the creation of new industry segments. Although organization and management scholars have long directed their efforts toward understanding the evolution of industries, a fundamental but less understood aspect is the emergence of new industry segments. One reason there are more unknowns about the creation of new industry segments is the left censoring of data, that is, the lack of data available during the fledgling years of new segments. This suggests a survivor bias in analyses of evolving industries: Unsuccessful firms that were founded early on may have disappeared from the industry by the time any systematic observation is conducted. The real-time approach of the current research addresses this issue, performing data collection and analysis while an industry segment is emerging. This provides more detailed information about and insight into a number of issues, such as what various groups within the new population do, which factors or attributes are most important to watch, and what kinds of change and experimentation take place in business models over time.

REFERENCES

Aldrich, H. E., & Fiol, C. M. (1994). Fools rush in? The institutional context of industry creation. *Academy of Management Review, 19,* 645–670.

Baum, J. A. C., Korn, H. J., & Kotha, S. (1995). Dominant designs and population dynamics in telecommunications services: Founding and failure of facsimile transmission service organizations, 1965-1992. *Social Science Research, 24,* 97–135.

Bjorkegren, D. (1996). *The culture business: Management strategies for the arts-related business.* New York: Routledge.

Budros, A. (1993). An analysis of organizational birth types: Organizational startup and entry in the nineteenth-century life insurance industry. *Social Forces, 70,* 1013–1030.

CyberAtlas. (1996). *Market size information.* Retrieved November 30, 1996 from http://cyberatlas.com/market.html

Eisner, A. B., Jett Q. R., & Korn, H. J. (2001). Web-based periodicals as emerging cultural forms: Incumbent and newcomer producers in the early stages of industry evolution. *International Journal of Electronic Commerce, 5*(2), 75–93.

Eisenhardt, K. M. (1989). Building theories from case study research. *Academy of Management Review, 14,* 532–550.

Flynn, L. (1997, February 11). Are Internet search engine companies still hit or miss? *The New York Times,* p. D8.

Glaser, B. G., & Strauss, A. L. (1966). *The purpose and credibility of qualitative research.* San Francisco: University of California Press.

Haring, B. (1997, January 13). The best ways to navigate the Net. *USA Today,* p. 3.

Hirsch, P. M. (1972). Processing fads and fashions: An organization-set analysis of cultural industry systems. *American Journal of Sociology, 77,* 639–659.
Manes, S. (1997, February 11). Why Web search engines may speed past missing links. *The New York Times,* p. C3.
Mezias, S. J., & Eisner, A. B. (1997). Competition, imitation, and innovation: An organizational learning approach. *Advances in Strategic Management, 14,* 261–294.
Mitchell, W. (1989). Whether and when? Probability and timing of incumbents entry into emerging industrial subfields. *Administrative Science Quarterly, 34,* 208–230.
Mitchell, W. (1991). Dual clocks: Entry order influences on incumbent and newcomer market share and survival when specialized assets retain their value. *Administrative Science Quarterly, 34,* 208–230.
Mossberg, G. (1996, June 6). One Web magazine avoids mediocrity of the usual on-line fare. *Wall Street Journal,* p. B1.
Nelson, R. R., & Winter, S. G. (1982). *An evolutionary theory of economic change.* Cambridge, MA: Belknap Press.
Schumpeter, J. A. (1939). *Business cycles: A theoretical, historical, and statistical analysis of the capitalist process.* New York: McGraw-Hill.
Schumpeter, J. A. (1950). *Capitalism, socialism, and democracy.* New York: Harper & Row.
Strauss, A. L., & Corbin, J. (1990). *Basics of qualitative research: Grounded theory procedures and techniques.* San Francisco: Sage.
Tushman, M. L., & Anderson, P. (1986). Technological discontinuities and organizational environments. *Administrative Science Quarterly, 31,* 439–465.

CHAPTER
8

A Question of Timing: Strategies for Scheduling Television Shows

Jamal Shamsie
Michigan State University

Danny Miller
HEC and University of Alberta

William Greene
New York University

Over the last 20 years, NBC has worked hard to maintain its dominance on Thursday evenings with a series of programs that it promoted heavily as "Must See TV." Individual programs changed over the years from *The Cosby Show, Cheers,* and *L.A. Law* to *Seinfeld, Friends,* and *E.R.*. However, the network ensured that it drew enough viewers by maintaining some of its hit shows as anchors for Thursday evenings. It placed new shows, often of a similar type, to follow ones that had already become established hits. The powerful block of programming also discouraged the rest of the networks from placing shows of a similar type to those offered by NBC on this evening because of worries that they might not do well.

Such cases are quite common in a wide range of industries that produce cultural goods. Firms clearly understand that the success of their motion pictures, television shows, recorded music, or popular books can depend on the critical issue of timing. Most cultural products have a short window to demonstrate their market potential before they are replaced by newer offerings (De Vany, 2003; Lampel & Shamsie, 2000). They must therefore be launched or offered at a time when they are most likely to be successful. A cultural product can do well if it is made available at a time when it can count on getting a sufficient audience. The potential audience that such a product can draw will depend, in large part, on its timing relative to other products that are also being offered. In spite of its obvious importance, this concept of time has received little attention as an aspect of positioning in studies of cultural industries.

In this chapter, we expand on the concept of positioning that has dominated a large part of the strategy field (Porter, 1980, 1985). More specifically, we examine timing as a critical dimension of positioning within the television broadcasting industry. Like many other cultural industries, the television broadcasting industry is becoming hypercompetitive, with the growth in the number of choices that are becoming available to viewers. Under these conditions, it is becoming more important for the broadcast networks to look at factors other than the types of shows that they want to offer. Each show has to be placed in the timeslot where it is most likely to either become or stay successful.

Given the importance of scheduling, a few basic rules have become widely accepted among television executives. Many of these have been used by researchers to suggest optimal scheduling of a slate of shows that are offered by a network during any given season. But few of these rules have been rigorously tested for their ability to increase viewers for a television show. We could therefore learn more about the strategic use of time by examining the effect of the use of these scheduling strategies, particularly within the context of growing competition as a result of the proliferation of broadcast and cable channels.

In the next section, we present a framework for positioning based on the dimension of time. We review the literature on the use of models to develop optimal schedules for the shows that are offered by a television network. Based on these models, we develop a few hypotheses about the effect of specific scheduling strategies on the audience for a television show. Next, we randomly select 25 television shows from the 1999–2000 television season. We then use the data from the airing of all of the original episodes of these selected shows in order to test our hypothesis.

Our findings suggest that conventional scheduling practices may have to be reassessed in part because of the marked increase in the number of competing broadcast networks. In fact, the number of viewers that were drawn to a particular television show was clearly tied to the number and type of shows that were available during the same timeslot on competing networks. Within such a competitive environment, many of the accepted scheduling strategies did not seem to produce any significant effect on the audience for a television show.

More specifically, there do not seem to be any observable benefits from the maintenance of a stable timeslot or from the pairing of similar shows with each other. Instead, the networks have been able to derive benefits from a more dynamic pairing of their stronger shows with their various weaker ones throughout their schedule. Weaker shows are moved around to follow stronger ones in order to improve their ratings and stronger shows are moved around to improve the ratings of other shows that follow them. We use these findings to offer some observations about the importance of timing as a dimension of positioning in a wide variety of cultural industries.

POSITIONING OF CULTURAL PRODUCTS

Over the past 20 years, there has been a considerable emphasis within the strategy literature on the concept of positioning. Ever since it was first outlined by Porter (1980, 1985), researchers have been exploring the advantages and disadvantages of various positions that a firm can strive for in the market. In spite of the level of interest in the positioning concept, there has been a relative lack of clarity in its definition and use.

In basic terms, positioning is concerned with where, when, and how a firm chooses to compete. The roots of the concept can be traced back to the model of spatial competition introduced many years ago by Hotelling (1929). Various aspects of the positioning of a firm's offerings in the market have been subsequently explored by various economists (Bonanno, 1987; Dorward, 1982; Eaton & Lipsey, 1975; Hay, 1976; Prescott & Visscher, 1977; Shaw, 1982; Swann, 1985). For the most part, however, these studies have tended to focus primarily on the distinctive characteristics of the products and markets that each firm may be trying to develop.

At the same time, the issues attached to positioning can encompass more than just the selection of products and markets. As Porter (1996) suggested recently, the concern with where and how a firm chooses to compete can involve many dimensions of a firm's strategy. In this chapter, we focus on timing as a critical aspect of the positioning concept. In a growing number of industries, timing can play an important role in the eventual success of a firm's products and in its ability to develop the markets that it is pursuing. For example, a firm may have to make key strategic decisions about when to introduce a new offering based on the timing of its own earlier offerings and the anticipated timing of new product launches from its competitors.

The issue of timing is of particular significance in a wide variety of cultural industries. Most cultural products, such as motion pictures, television shows, popular books, or recorded music must compete for valuable space in limited distribution channels (De Vany, 2003; Lampel & Shamsie, 2000). They tend to get pushed out by newer offerings as soon as their sales begin to drop. A motion picture begins to lose screens as attendance begins to drop. It is quite common for a motion picture to completely drop out of exhibition within a few weeks after its release. Similarly, television shows get dropped from a network's schedule, in some cases after just a couple of airings, if they fail to draw sufficient viewers.

Cultural products must therefore be launched or offered at a time when their chances of success are likely to be higher. In part, this timing must be based on complementary factors. Film studios tend to release many of their action-adventure and science-fiction movies during the summer season. The success of each of these films is presumed to help create a higher level of demand for the similar films that follow. Television networks try to create blocks of similar programming such as the TGIF concept that ABC successfully executed on Friday evenings for many years.

However, cultural products must also be offered at a time when they could be expected to encounter the lowest level of competition from rival firms. Major film studios have generally tried to avoid opening a film during a week when it may go up against a similar film from another studio. For the most part, studios try to ensure that each of their films will have as much time as possible on the screens before they face competition from other films of the same genre. Similarly, television networks have followed a practice of counterprogramming. Each network tries to avoid as much as possible offering programs of the same type that are being offered on competing channels at the same time. NBC may offer dramas to go up against comedies that are being offered on ABC on Friday nights.

In the following section, we focus on such timing issues as they apply specifically to television shows on the major broadcast networks. We draw on the literature on television programming to develop a set of hypotheses about the effect of scheduling on the number of viewers that are drawn by particular shows. Our exploration of the scheduling of television shows allows us to investigate the important but neglected issue of timing as an element of positioning.

SCHEDULING OF TELEVISION SHOWS

Most network television executives are well aware of the headaches that arise out of their annual ritual of scheduling their shows for each new television season. An article that appeared a few years ago in *The New York Times* described the "stunting, shuffling, substituting, and scheming" that must go into the complex task of scheduling television programs. It will be difficult to find many other industries where timing is as critical an aspect of a firm's attempts to position its products in order to reach the targeted markets. The success of a program, particularly one that is just being introduced, is heavily dependent on the timeslot in which it is placed.

A stream of research across various disciplines has attempted to examine the significance of the scheduling decisions that are regularly made by broadcast television executives (Danaher & Mawhinney, 1995; Gantz & Zohoori, 1982; Gensch & Shaman, 1980; Head, 1985; Henry & Rinne, 1984; Horen, 1980; Reddy, Aronson, & Stam, 1998; Rust & Eechambadi, 1989). However, these studies have generally attempted to propose optimal timeslots for a particular slate of programs that are offered by the major broadcast networks for a specific season with the use of various forecasting models. In most cases, this research has attempted to predict how the audience is likely to be split up between the three major networks based on the scheduling decisions that each of them will make for their individual shows.

More specifically, because of the focus on prediction, these studies have made a limited contribution toward a deeper understanding of the use of timing by a network as a strategy for increasing the audience for their shows. In order to develop their models, researchers have relied heavily on broadly based historical patterns of audience viewing behavior. The predictions have been drawn largely from assessments of viewer preferences for particular shows, timeslots, and networks.

There have been few attempts to pay much attention to the specific impact of particular scheduling practices. A couple of studies (Henry & Rinne, 1984; Tiedge & Ksobiech, 1986) did attempt to measure the effect of certain scheduling strategies, but each of these was limited in the range of strategies that they covered. Furthermore, they also examined the relative share of the total audience rather than the actual size of the total audience that viewed each show. Based on this measure, a show could increase its audience, but drop in share if the other networks also drew more viewers.

In this chapter, we focus more specifically on the scheduling strategies that any network could use to increase the audience for its shows. Although many of the prior studies did not specifically test for the effectiveness of specific scheduling practices, they did suggest some of the principles on which their optimal schedules may have been based. We raise each of these in what follows as a separate aspect of positioning.

Stable Positioning

To begin with, viewers are likely to be drawn to a show increasingly over time. Shows usually find their audience only after they have been on the air for a year or two. Several of the shows, such as *Seinfeld* and *Everybody Loves Raymond*, which eventually became very popular, did not attract many viewers during their first year. Various researchers have shown that the audience for a television show is tied to the number of years that it has been shown (Henry & Rinne, 1984; Tiedge & Ksobiech, 1986; Wakshlag & Greenberg, 1979). Thus older shows usually return each year because they have already established a core set of viewers.

Most audiences are also more likely to continue to watch a television show when it occupies a stable timeslot on the schedule. Several studies have shown that television viewing tends to become routinized (Gantz & Zohoori, 1982; Gensch & Shaman, 1980; Henry & Rinne, 1984; Rust & Eechambadi, 1989). Audiences typically develop a habit of watching a particular show at a specific time every week. Even in the early years of television, shows like *The Ed Sullivan Show* were a staple of a specific evening during the week. Consequently, there is a risk that viewers may not follow the show into a different time period. In order to continue to watch a show in a new time period, they must bc willing to adjust their own schedules in order to accommodate the new time for the show.

Taken together, ratings for a television show are likely to be higher if the show has been on the air for some time, especially if it occupies a stable position during a television season. Research on viewing habits suggests that these tend to get stronger over time. Once audiences have become accustomed to viewing a show at a specific time on a particular day of the week, they may be more reluctant to follow it to another spot on the schedule. We formulate the following hypotheses:

Hypothesis 1a: Ratings for a television show will be higher when it has been on the air for a few years.

Hypothesis 1b: Ratings for a television show will be higher when it occupies a stable timeslot over the television season.

Hypothesis 1c: Ratings for a television show will be higher when it has been on the air for a few years and it occupies a stable timeslot over the television season.

Complementary Positioning

The draw of a television show is likely to be influenced by various attributes of the show that precedes it on the same network. Several studies have shown that programs may be able to draw more viewers if the preceding show was of the same type (Henry & Rinne, 1984; Horen, 1980; Wakshlag & Greenberg, 1979). It has generally been assumed that audiences show their preference for a particular type of show by their decision to watch it on a particular channel. They are therefore more likely to watch the next show on a network if it is similar in content to the one that they have just finished watching. Networks have created comedy blocks, such as CBS on Monday around *The King of Queens* and *Everybody Loves Raymond.* NBC has similarly ended up pairing two legal dramas by scheduling *Law & Order: Criminal Intent* with *Crossing Jordan.*

At the same time, audiences are also more likely to watch a television show if it is scheduled by the network to follow a show that has already attracted a large audience. Although most viewers are now able to change channels through the use of a remote control, they may be curious to see what may follow the program they have just finished watching. Various researchers have emphasized the importance of this "lead-in" effect (Henry & Rinne, 1984; Horen, 1980; Reddy et al., 1998; Tiedge & Ksobiech, 1986; Wakshlag & Greenberg, 1979; Webster, 1985). Most of these studies have shown that a television show is likely to inherit a part of the audience from the show that immediately precedes it on the same network.

Taken together, a television show is likely to draw more viewers if it follows another show of the same type, especially if this earlier show had attracted a large audience. Clearly, a substantial part of the large audience that tuned in to watch a popular comedy or drama is more likely to watch the next show on the same channel if it is similar to the one that they just finished watching. Based on this, we formulate this second set of hypotheses:

Hypothesis 2a: Ratings for a television show will be higher when it follows a show of a similar type.

Hypothesis 2b: Ratings for a television show will be higher when it follows a show that has a large audience.

Hypothesis 2c: Ratings for a television show will be higher when it follows a show that was similar in type of content, especially if this previous show had a large audience.

Competitive Positioning

Finally, audiences are more likely to watch a television show on a particular network when they have few alternative programs available on the competing networks. Various researchers have suggested that the audience that a network will be able to develop for each of its shows will depend on the number of choices that are available to potential television viewers (Gensch & Shaman, 1980; Horen, 1980; Tiedge & Ksobiech, 1986; Webster, 1985). Audience levels for any program are therefore likely to be lowest in those periods of prime time when the greatest number of networks are offering shows to a national audience.

Furthermore, the audience for a show is likely to be higher if it is not scheduled against other similar shows on the competing networks. If a network chooses to schedule a comedy in a timeslot where other networks are also offering the same type of show, it will end up splitting the audience that may be interested in viewing a comedy show. Various researchers have stressed the benefits of a "counter-programming" strategy (Gensch & Shaman, 1980; Horen, 1980; Reddy et al., 1998; Rust & Eechambadi, 1989; Wakshlag & Greenberg, 1979). CBS was able to draw higher ratings on Thursday evenings by scheduling the reality show *Survivor* and drama *CSI* to run against NBC's highly rated comedies.

Taken together, more viewers are likely to be drawn to a television show when there are fewer competing channels, especially if none of those channels are offering programs that are similar in content. Viewer numbers for a show are likely to be higher when there are fewer available competing shows and those that are available are not of a similar type. We thus formulate a third set of hypotheses:

Hypothesis 3a: Ratings for a television show will be higher if it is aired at a time when it faces less competition from other channels.

Hypothesis 3b: Ratings for a television show will be higher if it is aired at a time when competitive channels are not offering programs that are similar in type of content.

Hypothesis 3c: Ratings for a television show will be higher when it is scheduled in a timeslot where it faces less competition from other channels, especially when they are not offering shows that are similar in type of content.

METHODOLOGY

Sample

A total of 25 programs were randomly selected from television shows that were scheduled for the 1999–2000 television season. All the shows were either a half-hour or a full hour in duration. We restricted our sample to regular scripted television series and did not include any news magazines, reality shows, quiz or game shows, sports programming, or movies. We eliminated these categories because many of these did not have a sustained or continuous story line and were often offered as specials. Because we did consider all of the possible formats in looking at the shows that competed with those that were included in our sample, we do not believe that our focus on scripted shows would have biased our results.

We also restricted our sample to shows that were scheduled on the four major television broadcast networks. These consisted of ABC, CBS, Fox, and NBC. The smaller broadcast networks and the cable channels do not reach as many households and generally have much lower audience levels.

The 25 shows were relatively evenly distributed in terms of their tenure. Eight of the shows were in their first year, nine had been on air between 2 and 4 years, and eight had been on the air for 5 years or longer. The longest-running show in our sample was in its 11th year. Of the 25 shows, 6 were dropped from the schedule midway through the season. The average tenure of the shows in our sample was 3.72 years.

Data

For all 25 shows, we obtained measures of the audience for each of the original episodes that were aired over the season. We excluded reruns because their ratings tend to be lower, depending on the type of show. Our study was also significant in one other important respect. Other studies have typically relied on mean values for the audience and considered the popularity and format of the shows that preceded them or competed against them for most of the period that was studied. This did not allow them to observe the effect of any possible changes in scheduling that may have occurred from week to week.

We obtained separate measures for each original episode of each of the series in our sample because its audience level tended to vary considerably. In part, this variance could be attributed to weekly changes in its timeslot, in the shows that preceded it on the same network, and in the shows that competed against it on the other networks.

The number of observations for each of the shows was therefore determined by the number of original episodes that were aired. *Touched by an Angel* had the largest number of observations because as many as 26 different episodes were shown by the network during the season that lasted from September 1999 to May 2000. The lowest number of observations were for *Mike O'Malley*, which was only aired twice before being removed from the schedule.

Dependent Variable

The dependent variable in the study was a measure of the audience for each of the shows. The Neilson rating has been well accepted as a measure of the audience for each episode of a television show (Gensch & Shaman, 1980; Reddy et al., 1998; Rust & Eechambadi, 1989; Webster & Lichty, 1991). This measure provides a comparative measure of the number of households that are watching each of the shows when it is aired. The measures for each of the episodes of the 25 shows in our sample were obtained from weekly issues of *Variety* news magazine.

Independent Variables

Stable Positioning. The stable positioning of each of the episodes of our shows was measured in two different ways. First, a variable was used to measure the tenure of the show. For new shows, this variable was given a value of 1, indicating that it was in its first year. For returning shows, the number represented its season.

The regularity of the timeslot for each of the shows was measured by a dummy variable. The variable took a value of 0 when the show was aired at the time that was announced at the start of the season. It took a value of 1 for the episodes that were aired at a different time.

Complementary Positioning. The complementary positioning of each of the episodes of our shows was measured in two different ways. To begin with, a lead-in measure was obtained for each of the episodes. This was the Neilson rating for the episode of the show that immediately preceded it on the same network.

Next, a dummy variable was used to indicate whether the show that preceded it was of the same type of content. This was given a value of 1 if the content was similar, and 0 if it was not. Various researchers have developed classifications of television programs that are relatively similar in terms of the specific categories (Henry & Rinne, 1984; Rao, 1975; Tiedge & Ksobiech, 1986). We used a more extensive categorization of programs that was taken out of two well-known sources of television programming (Brooks & Marsh, 1999; Hill, 2001).

Competitive Positioning. Finally, competitive positioning was also assessed through the use of two different measures. The first of these was a measure of the number of competing broadcast networks that offer programs at the same time. This provides an assessment of the number of alternatives that are available to the viewer at the time that the program is being aired.

The second was a measure of the number of broadcast networks that were offering shows with the same type of content. This measure is more focused on the relatively similar alternatives that are available to the program that is being studied. Again, the categorization of shows was based on classifications that were drawn from reliable sources (Brooks & Marsh, 1999; Hill, 2001).

Control Variable

Because of the cross-sectional time series nature of the data, a lagged dependent variable was used. In other words, for each of the observations, a variable was used to measure the Neilson rating of the previous original episode of the show.

Analysis

As mentioned earlier, observations were obtained for each of the original episodes of the 25 shows in our sample that were aired over the season. Because of the cross-sectional time series nature of the data, a GLS regression was used. This procedure compensated for the correlations that were likely to exist between the ratings of each show across its different episodes. Furthermore, a random-effects model was selected because certain variables, such as the tenure, were fixed across all of the observations on a particular show.

RESULTS

The results of the regression are presented in Table 8.1. In terms of stable positioning, the table shows that there was strong support for Hypothesis 1a. The tenure of a show clearly had a significant effect on its ratings. Older shows did tend to get higher audience ratings. However, there was no support for Hypothesis 1b. The dummy variable that was used to indicate a temporary shift in the time for particular episodes of a show was not significant. A shift in the time period for the shows therefore did not appear to have a substantial effect on the total viewing audience. Finally, there was also no support for Hypothesis 1c. The ratings of older shows did not appear to be influenced by shifts in their timeslot.

In terms of complementary positioning, there was no support for Hypothesis 2a. Ratings for our shows were not affected by the type of content of the show that preceded them on the same network. There was strong support, however, for Hypothesis 2b. The ratings for the show that preceded each of the episodes on the same network did have a significant effect. This indicated that there was a clear effect of a strong lead-in. In other words, the shows in our sample did attract bigger audiences when they followed shows with strong ratings. Furthermore, there was strong support for Hypothesis 2c. A lead-in that was similar in type of content did have strong effect on the show that followed it, but only if this preceding show had generated sufficiently high ratings.

TABLE 8.1
GLS Regression Analysis

Variable	Model 1	Model 2
Constant	3.456***	4.285***
	(0.564)	(0.604)
Lagged dependent variable	0.448***	0.403***
	(0.032)	(0.030)
Tenure of show	0.168**	0.206***
	(0.054)	(0.057)
Time slot	–0.112	–0.390
	(0.168)	(0.330)
Similarity of preceding show	0.119	–1.815
	(0.191)	(0.388)
Rating of preceding show	0.239***	0.213***
	(0.017)	(0.017)
Competing networks	–0.341**	–0.464***
	(0.107)	(0.118)
Similarity of competing shows	–0.283**	–1.263*
	(0.103)	(0.506)
Tenure of show x time slot	—	0.067 (0.085)
Similarity of preceding show x rating of preceding show	—	0.292*** (0.052)
Competing networks x similarity of competing shows	—	0.226* (0.106)

*$p < .05$. **$p < .01$. ***$p < .001$.

Finally, in terms of competitive positioning, there was strong support for Hypothesis 3a. The number of competing channels had a significant effect on the audience for the each of the episodes in our sample. In other words, the audience for a given episode of a show was higher if it was aired at a time when there were fewer competing programs on other broadcast networks. There was also substantial support for Hypothesis 3b. More viewers were likely to watch a show when the other networks are offering fewer competing programs of the same type. Additionally, there was considerable support for Hypothesis 3c. Television shows did get higher ratings when they were aired in timeslots where there were fewer competing channels and these channels offered fewer programs that were similar in type of content.

As expected, the lagged dependent variable was highly significant. The rating for the prior episode of a show had a significant relationship with the rating for a subsequent episode of the same show.

DISCUSSION

Like many other cultural products, television shows must attract an audience in order to stay on a network schedule. The number of viewers that a show can attract will clearly depend on several different characteristics, such as the appeal of the story line, the characters, and the stars. However, the results of this study also indicate that the timeslot in which a show is scheduled can also play a significant role in the size of the audience that it can draw. This is an important aspect of strategic positioning that has not received much attention in the literature.

Above all, our results indicate the importance of competing programs during the same timeslot on the audience that can be developed for a show. This is the first study that could assess the effect of number of competing broadcast networks. Most of the earlier studies were carried out during a period when there were only three major networks all of which offered national programming through the same prime-time hours. During the period of our study, the total number of broadcast networks varied from three to six depending on the timeslot. Fox, WB, and UPN all switch to local news programs during the last hour of primetime. Furthermore, WB and UPN had not expanded their programming to all 7 days of the week.

The number of competing networks did have a strong impact on the audience for a television show. There was a significant decline in the ratings for a show with an increase in the total number of competing networks and the number of competing networks that were offering similar types of programs. These results are noteworthy, given that the study did not consider the larger competition that is coming from a wide variety of cable channels. They also indicate that the additional networks appear to be drawing audiences away from each other, at least as much as they may be drawing audiences away from the cable channels.

But the effect of this growing competition is also reflected in other aspects of our findings. The rise in competition has led to a decrease in significance of the stability of a show's time period. Clearly, most shows tend to build an audience over time. But there seems to be little benefit to keeping the show in the same timeslot, regardless of the tenure of the show. In fact, networks may feel pressured to move shows around on their schedule. In some cases, a successful show may be moved by the network to another evening in order to help draw audiences to other shows that are struggling on that evening. In other cases, a show that is still trying to attract viewers may be moved by the network to another evening in order to draw viewers from another more popular show that it offers on that evening.

NBC may occasionally air an episode of *Law & Order* in a different timeslot on a different day during a particular week to try to gain viewers for another weaker show that follows it. In many cases, a successful show is moved to a different day in order to deal with the challenge that is posed by the shows of a competing network.

CBS eventually decided to challenge NBC's dominance on Thursday evenings by moving some of its shows such as *Survivor* and *CSI*. These had already done well in the ratings when they were aired on other evenings. CBS was hoping to draw away some of the viewers from NBC, but CBS might have been surprised to find that their shows actually rose to the top of the ratings after they were moved to Thursday evenings.

Another effect of the growing competition has been the decline in the effect of creating blocks of similar programs. Our results indicate that a show did not draw more viewers simply by following another similar show. However, a show clearly seems to benefit from being paired with a popular show, even if the other show is not of a similar type. Obviously, a show can draw more viewers if it follows a highly rated show that is also of a similar type.

This has led the networks to try to help their weaker shows by simply scheduling them after their more successful shows, with much less concern for their similarity. CBS initially used their more popular reality show *Survivor* as a lead-in to develop a bigger audience for its relatively new detective show *CSI* show on Thursday evenings. More recently, NBC scheduled its new drama *Las Vegas* to follow its established reality hit *Fear Factor.*

Recent trends suggest that growth in competition may even be pushing the networks to abandon their counterprogramming strategy. With the growth in the number of competing networks, it has become harder for each of them to avoid offering programs that may be similar to those that are offered by the others. On the recently announced schedule for the 2004–2005 season, there are relatively few timeslots in which at least two of the networks are not offering shows that are similar to each other.

In fact, some of the networks are deliberately scheduling a show against a similar one from one of its competitors in order to try to steal away some of the other show's audience. Fox has scheduled its reality show *The Benefactor* at the same time NBC has scheduled its reality show *Fear Factor.* What has attracted the most attention is the decision by CBS to offer its latest version of *CSI, CSI:New York*, to go up against NBC's original *Law & Order.*

Although such moves to meet the competition head-on are becoming more common, their impact on the ratings of shows is still unclear. In such a match, it is more likely that the stronger show will win. In the case of CBS, the momentum of the relatively new *CSI* franchise may be sufficient to withstand the competition from NBC's much older *Law &Order* franchise.

Taken together, this study suggests that timing is becoming an even more important aspect of positioning, especially with cultural products such as television shows. A show that may have the characteristics that could appeal to a large audience may fail if it is offered in an unfavorable timeslot. On the other hand, even a marginal show may be able to find sufficient viewers to survive if it is scheduled in a spot where it is helped by shows that aired before it on the same channel and where it is less likely to be hurt by the competition that is faces from shows on competing channels.

CONCLUSION

Although the concept of positioning has attracted a considerable amount of attention in the strategy literature, there has been little effort to explore its various dimensions. In this chapter, we have focused on the concept of timing as an aspect of a firm's positioning. Firms that compete within industries that could be characterized as hypercompetitive must decide not only what products to launch, but also when to offer them. This is certainly true in many cultural industries. They must decide when to release or offer each of their motion pictures, television shows, or recorded music. These must be offered at a time when they are most likely to draw a large enough audience.

In part, cultural products tend to do better when they are offered at a time when demand for them is likely to be strong. To some degree, this demand is likely to be created by the success of other similar products. Most of the movies that are based on action characters such as Spiderman, X-Men, and Batman are released in the summer when they may help to build on each other. All of the broadcast networks have been turning to reality programming in order to benefit from the growing interest among television audiences for these types of shows.

At the same time, this raises questions about the possible effect of competition from other similar products. Clearly, demand for a movie, record, or book will be affected by the number of other similar products that are being offered at the same time. Movie studios are constantly shifting the release dates of each film so as to pick the specific films that they are willing to open against as well to pick those that they want to avoid opening against. Similarly, television networks are continuously wrestling with decisions about where to place their new shows. Several programs have done well when they were launched in favorable timeslots.

Based on the results of this study, timing deserves more attention from strategy researchers. Future research can focus on other types of cultural industries and choose to investigate various components or aspects of timing. As more industries move toward hypercompetition, firms will need to place more emphasis on the decision about when to launch or display their offerings. This could become as important an aspect of their positioning as the characteristics of the content of what they choose to offer.

REFERENCES

Bonanno, G. (1987). Location choice, product proliferation and entry deterrence. *Review of Economic Studies, 54,* 37–45.

Brooks, T., & Marsh, E. (1999). *The complete directory to prime time network and cable TV shows* (20th ed.). New York: Ballantine Books.

Danaher, P. J., & Mawhinney, D. F. (1995). *An application of choice modeling to optimal television program scheduling.* Unpublished manuscript, University of Auckland.

De Vany, A. (2003). *Hollywood economics: How extreme uncertainty shapes the film industry.* New York: Routledge.

Dorward, N. (1982). Recent developments in the analysis of spatial competition and their implications for industrial economics. *Journal of Industrial Economics, 31,* 133–152.

Eaton, B. C., & Lipsey, R. G. (1975). The principle of minimum differentiation reconsidered: Some new developments in the theory of spatial competition. *Review of Economic Studies, 42,* 27–49.

Gantz, W., & Zohoori, A. R. (1982). The impact of television schedule changes on audience viewing behaviors. *Journalism Quarterly, 59,* 265–272.

Gensch, D., & Shaman, P. (1980). Models of competitive television ratings. *Journal of Marketing Research, 17,* 307–315.

Hay, D. A. (1976). Sequential entry and entry-deterring strategies in spatial competition. *Oxford Economic Papers, 28,* 240–257.

Head, S. W. (1985). A framework for programming strategies. In S. T. Eastman, S. W. Head, & L. Klein (Eds.), *Broadcast/Cable programming: Strategies and practices* (pp. 3–38). Belmont, CA: Wadsworth.

Henry, M. D., & Rinne, H. J. (1984). Predicting program shares in new time slots. *Journal of Advertising Research, 24*(2), 9–17.

Hill, T. (2001). *TV Land to go: The big book of TV lists, TV lore and TV bests.* New York: Fireside.

Horen, J. H. (1980). Scheduling of network television programs. *Management Science, 26,* 354–370.

Hotelling, H. (1929). Stability in competition. *Economic Journal, 39,* 41.

Lampel, J., & Shamsie, J. (2000). Critical push: Strategies for creating momentum in the motion picture industry. *Journal of Management, 26,* 233–257.

Porter, M. E. (1996). What is strategy? *Harvard Business Review, 74*(6), 61–78.

Porter, M. E. (1985). *Competitive advantage.* New York: Free Press.

Porter, M. E. (1980). *Competitive strategy.* New York: Free Press.

Prescott, E. C., & Visscher, M. (1977). Sequential location among firms with foresight. *Bell Journal of Economics, 8,* 378–393.

Rao, V. R. (1975). Taxonomy of television programs based on viewing behavior. *Journal of Marketing Research, 12,* 355–358.

Reddy, S. K., Aronson, J. E., & Stam, A. (1998). SPOT: Scheduling programs optimally for television. *Management Science, 44,* 83–102.

Rust, R. T., & Eechambadi, N. V. (1989). Scheduling network television programs: A heuristic audience flow approach to maximizing audience share. *Journal of Advertising, 18*(2), 11–18.

Shaw, R. W. (1982). Product proliferation in characteristics space: The U.K. fertilizer industry. *Journal of Industrial Economics, 31,* 69–92.

Swann, G. M. P. (1985). Product competition in microprocessors. *Journal of Industrial Economics, 34,* 33–54.

Tiedge, J. T., & Ksobiech, K. J. (1986). The "lead-in" strategy for prime-time TV: Does it increase the audience? *Journal of Communication, 36,* 51–63.

Wakshlag, J. J., & Greenberg, B. S. (1979). Programming strategies and the popularity of television programs for children. *Human Communication Research, 6,* 58–68.

Webster, J. G. (1985). Program audience duplication: A study of television inheritance effects. *Journal of Broadcasting and Electronic Media, 29,* 121–133.

Webster, J. G., & Lichty, L. W. (1991). *Ratings analysis: Theory and practice.* Hillsdale, NJ: Lawrence Erlbaum Associates.

III

The Nature of Markets

The no-questions-asked refund policy may be the cornerstone of American retailing, but it is rarely practiced in the cultural industries. Few would be bold enough to demand money back after they have just seen a disappointing movie, and few if any are likely to get it back. Some may try to return a CD, a video, or even a book, but rarely on the basis that it failed to please. This peculiarity of the cultural industries is a reflection of the complex relationship between mass tastes and individual preferences.

Producers in the cultural industries cater to popular tastes, not in the sense of attempting to please everybody, but with the view of pleasing enough people to ensure a good return on their investment. Doing this, however, runs against the immense diversity of individual preferences. Each of us is different, and each of us experiences cultural products in a somewhat unique way. And what is worse for producers of cultural goods, each of us may change our preferences in the process of experiencing cultural products—moving from initial approval to disapproval or vice versa—and then communicate our opinions to others thereby changing the tastes that cultural producers are struggling so hard to understand and meet.

The difficulty of reconciling popular tastes with individual preferences is at the heart of markets in cultural industries. Although it plays a positive role by encouraging creativity and innovation, thus benefiting consumers, it poses a perennial dilemma for producers of cultural goods. Making sense of popular tastes requires aggregating and consolidating individual preferences into usable knowledge. But transforming the vast diversity of individual preferences into knowledge of popular tastes is more art than science, more industry wisdom than systematic analysis. That producers often get it wrong is not surprising. What is surprising is the variety of practices and institutions that have evolved over the years to deal with this problem, and what is even more surprising—notwithstanding the spectacular failures—is how effective these practices and institutions have become at understanding tastes, and then translating this understanding into effective strategic action.

This section explores both the practices and institutions that have emerged in cultural industries to facilitate an understanding of their own markets. Gathering and compiling information is central to this understanding, but the resources needed to adequately address the task are unusually beyond the means of most cultural producers. Trade publications step into the gap and provide just such a service. In performing this function in cultural industries, these publications are not substantially different from those in most other industries. Where they do differ is in the way that they consolidate the information into best-seller lists, and the way in which these lists become part of the competitive dynamics of the cultural industries.

In chapter 9, Anand examines the rise of *Billboard* as the key trade publication in the American music industry, and the subsequent evolution of its all-important music chart into a powerful force in the industry. The *Billboard* chart, according to Anand, can be understood as a "market information regime," a mechanism whereby information is obtained about individual preferences. In this case, data are collected on the number of records that have been sold for each individual album, allowing this album to be rank ordered according to popularity in a given music category.

Although the process of transforming information on market activity into a chart relies on a relatively objective set of technical practices, the consequences for the way the industry understands itself are profound, triggering interpretative processes that motivate competitive behavior. Chart position and chart movement act as important signals about the popularity of musicians. This in turn has influence on the rate at which the music is played in radio stations, the contractual terms artists are offered by record companies, the promotional tactics of record promoters, and beyond that it has a major impact on the growing enthusiasm or fading loyalty of music buyers.

Hit lists in the music industry, bestseller lists in publishing, or lists of top grossers in movies represent a distillation of an extraordinarily rich information landscape. The distillation is intrinsically imperfect. It works because it is embedded in the way that the industry does business, and once it is accepted, it becomes for better or worse a shortcut to making sense of the industry on a day-to-day basis, and hence an indispensable tool for strategic decision making.

Abstract models of strategic decision making usually postulate rational and highly deliberate decision makers. Anand's chapter makes the contrary point, suggesting that decision makers rely on charts without necessarily understanding—or perhaps even caring about—the accuracy or reliability of the information they contain. Decision makers turn to the charts because they take for granted that reading and interpreting the charts are an intrinsic part of the industry's decision-making routines. This may not be rational from the perspective of an abstract model of information gathering, but it is cognitively efficient and strategically effective.

Ahlkvist and Faulkner, go one step further in chapter 10: They suggest that far from being the result of careful analysis of economic and market forces, routines that govern decisions about programs in music radio stations are a product of a complex interaction of values, politics, and market pressures. The key actors in Ahlkvist and Faulkner's chapter are the music programmers. Music programmers mediate between the music industry and radio listeners. Their task is to maximize their station's ratings, while at the same time satisfying the demand of record companies who are intent on exercising influence on the music that gains airtime.

This complex balancing act has no obvious or optimal solution. There is no set of objective decision-making processes that yields the best response to the music market in which a given station operates. Instead, what Ahlkvist and Faulkner show is how music programmers craft repertoires that meet the conflicting demands of record companies, maintain their station's format, keep abreast of emerging trends, and remain faithful to their own values. These repertoires guide the selection of music. They reflect the tastes of their audiences and emerge from objective analysis or intuitive insight. At the same time, they not only reflect tastes, but also end up shaping them. The music chart plays an important role in this process, but not always a dominant role.

In this respect, Ahlkvist and Faulkner's chapter differs from Anand's. They suggest that while music programmers do pay attention to the music chart, they sometimes resist the dictate of the charts, preferring instead to establish their uniqueness and authenticity by playing music that is neither popular nor widely known. The repertoires that music programmers develop represent their individual response to the conflicting demands of record companies and the strategic imperatives of each station. As a form of strategic adaptation, their emergence reflects a process that is fairly common in the cultural industries.

In chapter 11, Shamsie examines the conflicting imperatives confronting decision makers in the motion picture industry. Trying to make sense of success and failure poses a critical challenge for management and creative personnel in an industry where substantial up-front investment must be made in projects before they can move ahead. As in other cultural industries, the motion picture industry has its own trade journals and charts that keep track of top-grossing movies.

Though helpful, the information they provide may exacerbate rather than aid decision making in this industry. The problem in the motion industry, as Shamsie points out, is not the lack of information, but the absence of reliable frameworks for interpreting the information.

The failure of the motion picture industry to evolve such frameworks is to some extent symptomatic of the diversity and instability of tastes in most cultural industries, but in the main, as Shamsie shows, it is also due to different responses to a set of basic polarities in which the industry operates. These polarities constitute assumptions and routines that can push the interpretation in fundamentally different directions, depending on which of these are used for making decisions. As in the case of the repertoires employed by music programmers, there are no best interpretations here, only interpretative routines that may do well under certain circumstances. Indeed, Shamsie argues that a search for best interpretations may not only be misguided, but may have a negative impact when decision makers are forced by superiors and stakeholders to articulate their tacit knowledge to the detriment of their position and legitimacy as managers.

This point is highly pertinent to all cultural industries. Linking popular tastes to individual preferences involves making sense of information and then using this sense making to reach successful decisions. But there is a distance here between the researcher and his or her subject, and this distance can only be bridged by striving to achieve a deeper understanding of how individuals deal with culture. A crucial step is to avoid imposing assumptions on how markets operate in cultural industries. Researchers must proceed carefully, with attention to the peculiar habits, mindsets, and political conflicts of the consumers of cultural products. For as these three chapters show, to gain useful lessons from these industries researchers must ultimately tackle the entire range of aesthetic and emotional experiences that are central to the consumption of cultural products.

CHAPTER
9

Charting the Music Business: *Billboard* Magazine and the Development of the Commercial Music Field[1]

N. Anand
London Business School

In a wide range of cultural industries, information on comparative market performance of their products—be they books, films, or records—is frequently presented in the form of a bestseller chart compiled by a trade publication. This chapter examines the evolution and impact of *Billboard* magazine and the *Billboard* chart that presents information on music industry sales. The influence of this magazine, and more particularly its well-known chart, on the music industry has been profound. Roger Karshner (1971, p. 115), former vice president of Capitol Records, put it best: "Everybody in the record business is constantly lipping chart potential, trade picks, chart positions and chart life. In fact, the entire industry rises and falls upon the waves of this silly numbers game."

Billboard's great innovation, the "Top 100" singles chart, was introduced in 1955. When the format (and, indeed, the name) was widely imitated by its compet-

[1]I thank Richard A. Peterson for his very insightful comments.

itors, *Billboard* chart editor Tom Noonan retitled the chart "Hot 100" in August 1958, and the name has stuck ever since (Bronson, 1994). *Billboard* even copyrighted the name in order to keep it distinctive. Although the chart still endures and provides the pulse of popularity, now the industry is more focused on the albums chart (which originally debuted in March 1945). Recording companies tend to lose money on singles because radio airplay is practically a promotional activity. Profits are made largely on the sales of albums. The albums chart (now labeled the *Billboard 200*) serves as a readily observable measure of a record company's commercial performance.

In this chapter I intend to show how, in a sociological sense, *Billboard* has been crucial to the evolution of the commercial music field. For more than a century, this weekly publication has held up a window into the significant happenings within the field. The news, information, gossip, advertising, opinion, and the music charts occupying its pages help field participants make sense of recent events of import. Equally, *Billboard* has been the harbinger of the shape of things to come by nudging the field toward promising trends. In the process of field evolution, the manner in which certain information and its derived meanings are shared among members is vital (DiMaggio & Powell, 1983). And this vital service to the commercial music field has been supplied continually by *Billboard* magazine.

Billboard magazine shaped the evolution of the commercial music field in two important ways. First, *Billboard* was critical for the coalescence of the commercial music field. The magazine has always served as a medium where field constituents come together and interact frequently and meaningfully. More importantly, *Billboard* holds field participants in thrall by defining its market information regime (Anand & Peterson, 2000). By supplying a web of information about market activity, *Billboard* de facto defines field participants as regular and habitual consumers of its information. *Billboard*'s music charts have shaped the way in which field participants experience, make sense of, and respond to the market for commercial music. In what follows, I shall draw out some implications concerning the influence of trade periodicals in general and *Billboard* in particular in shaping markets in the culture industries.

BILLBOARD'S ROLE IN FIELD COALESCENCE

William H. Donaldson and James H. Hennegan of Cincinnati, Ohio published the first issue of *The Billboard Advertiser* on November 1, 1894 (Schlager, 1994). Donaldson saw the need for a trade publication to address the needs of the fledgling bill-posting industry. Columns included the "The Bill Room Gossip" and "The Indefatigable and Tireless Industry of the Bill Poster," where readers were informed that the bill poster "loves to be out in the street at night, when, should he discover a fire, he can bill the front of a building and then turn in an alarm" (Schlager, 1994, p. 19). The "midsummer special" issue of *The Billboard Advertiser* from 1896 depicts two handsome bill posters with wholesome grins shaking hands on the scaffolding of a building, each clinging to the tools of his trade: a paste brush and a paint palette. Billboards were the prime advertising medium of *fin-de-siècle* urban America. A picture from that time of the Metropole Hotel in New York City shows the building completely covered with bill posters, advertising *inter alia*, products such as C&B corsets and Williams' talcum powder ("makes the skin feel like velvet"), and also, crucially, theater and vaudeville shows such as *Follies of the Day (A Burlesque Show on Broadway), The Beauty Spot*, and *A Gentleman from Mississippi*.

The credo on its very first cover—"devoted to the interests of advertisers, poster printers, advertising agents and secretaries for fairs"—revealed an ambition to be relevant to multiple constituents within the industry. This trait was preserved intact as Donaldson bought out his partner in 1900 and cut loose from the bill-posting trade for a more lucrative arena. He recast *The Billboard* (as the magazine was now known) as "The Official Organ of the Great Out-Door Amusement World." The magazine began a systematic coverage of fairs, carnivals, circuses, game parks, and vaudeville and burlesque shows (Newman, 1994). Prior to the advent of recording technology, these entertainments—among them illustrious operations such as the Ringling Brothers and Barnum & Bailey circuses, Buffalo Bill's Wild West Show, and E. F. Albee's vaudeville shows—served as the springhead of the modern entertainment industry (Sanjek & Sanjek, 1996).

Along with general news of show openings and closures, fortunes made and lost, accidents and robberies, editorials in the magazine railed against the afflictions of censorship, excessive regulation and lack of professionalism within the business. Various features and columns in the magazine addressed specific segments within the field. For example, the "stage gossips" column dished out the dirt on private lives of popular entertainers; the "tent show" feature was devoted to traveling shows; and the classified advertising even had a section titled "Freaks to Order."

As the railroad began making its way across America, early stars of the entertainment firmament took to the road by forming or joining tent shows, midway companies, dramatic groups, musical ensembles, and burlesque acts. If railway tracks served as the skeleton on which the entertainment business was built, then surely information was its flesh and blood. Two features in the magazine, "Routes Ahead" and "Letter-Box," both well established by 1904, provided information that was vital to organizing the field (Schlager, 1994). "Routes Ahead" listed page after page of entertainers' itineraries and mapped the ever-expanding boundary of the market for popular entertainment, thereby conveying the new industry's scope. *Billboard* developed an innovative mail-forwarding service for traveling entertainers. The magazine's staff collected and forwarded mail and published in the "Letter-Box" column names of entertainers who had letters waiting for them in its offices. This dedicated service made *Billboard* the hub of the entertainment community.

In the early decades of the 20th century, *Billboard* reported and commented on various elements that defined the trajectory of the evolving entertainment industry. A dominant coalition of impresarios and agents was emerging. Chief among these were Abraham Erlanger, Mark Klaw, the Forhman brothers, the Shubert brothers, B. F. Keith, E. F. Albee, the Ringling Brothers, P. T. Barnum, and J. A. Bailey. In addition to reporting their various organizing moves in his magazine, *Billboard* publisher William Donaldson also built close personal ties to many of these individuals enabling him to stay close to those defining the agenda of the industry.

Billboard provided prominent coverage of the progress in technology for recording and replaying images and sounds. Along with news of their development, the magazine also featured advertisements for the marvels of modern technology: the phonograph, graphophone, gramaphone, Victrola, grafonala, silent and then sound-enabled film, wireless radio, and record players. In its editorial pages, the magazine kept a wary eye on regulatory forces seeking to rein in the industry. Although standard-setting measures that professionalized entertainment were welcome, matters of censorship and taxing invited protest and disapproval. The magazine tried to balance the interests of its stakeholders without become hostage to any one group.

In 1920, William Donaldson made the bold move of hiring James A. Jackson, an African American journalist, to write about the Black entertainment scene with these words: "A new feature section, written by a Black man and devoted to Black performers, artists, managers, and agents will appear weekly.... We feel that the professional artists and entertainers of the race have fairly won this recognition.... We are according the representation gladly—even enthusiastically" (Hill, 1994, p. 65). It was timely. African American entertainers had retreated from Broadway by 1910 and were busy creating an impressive cultural scene centered in Harlem (Nelson, 1994). Jackson made this scene visible to a national audience, legitimizing the artistic standing of entertainers such as Bessie Smith, W. C. Handy, Fats Waller, and Paul Robeson. Jackson also exposed prejudices against Black performers such as the problem of securing lodgings while traveling. Through Jackson's pages, *Billboard* magazine shaped the field by broadcasting the distinctiveness and fecundity of African American musical tradition to the nation at large.

By the time Donaldson died in 1925, "Billyboy" (as the magazine was affectionately called owing to its telegraphic address) was firmly established as an influential institution in the field. As the various branches of the entertainment industry developed and diverged, the magazine kept its focus on popular music. In 1957, *Funspot* magazine was spun off from Billboard to cover permanent amusement sites. Four years later, *Amusement Business* was carved out to cover outdoor entertainment. On January 9, 1961 the magazine began to call itself *Billboard Music Week*, noting that it would no longer cover show business in general but devote itself to becoming "a weekly business journal for the professional user of music." The decision to specialize in music came more than six decades after it was founded. I suspect it was spurred on by the unique and imaginative method that the magazine had formulated by 1955 to report on the market for commercial music—the *Billboard* chart.

BILLBOARD CHARTS AS THE FIELD'S MARKET INFORMATION REGIME

Billboard's most enduring and influential creation for the field has been its music charts. Participants in the field rely on the charts to become aware of what's "hot" at present, to justify past success, and to plan for the future. Thanks to *Billboard*, anticipating and reacting to chart information is a way of life in the music industry.

The *Billboard* chart is best understood as a "market information regime," defined by Anand and Peterson (2000, p. 271) as "regularly updated information about market activity provided by an independent supplier, presented in a predictable format with consistent frequency, and available to all interested parties at nominal cost." The chart as market information regime is implicated in five cognitive field-forming processes that are described in detail in the remainder of the chapter:

1. Drawing attention to particular market dynamics within the field.
2. Categorizing domains of activity.
3. Normalizing desirable chart position as an aspiration.
4. Facilitating commensuration of seemingly related domains of activity.
5. Valorizing rationality in sense making of market activity.

Drawing Attention to Particular Market Dynamics

Organizations are suspended in a universe of chaotic stimuli, but they cope with multiple, conflicting demands by routinizing and simplifying the types of information that they attend to (Cyert & March, 1963; March & Simon, 1958; Simon, 1947). Consequently, behavior in organizations can be understood as enactment of issues that command the attention of actors within organizations (Ocasio, 1997). When this perspective is extended to a higher level, it is obvious that organizational fields also cohere to a simplified attention focus (Anand & Peterson, 2000; Hoffman & Ocasio, 2001).

In competitive industries, that focus is often news of comparative market performance. In the music industry it is the *Billboard* chart. Although the chart's obvious influence is on fans and radio programmers who try to stay on top of the latest trends, sociologist Philip Ennis (1992, p. 401) contended that its deep influence on the field comes from the power it has over music retailers who are the ultimate shapers of consumption:

> *Billboard*'s charts were rich enough to satisfy every level of sophistication in the music trades. Busy, lazy, or conservative record dealers and jukebox operators could stock their inventories by simply following the best-selling singles chart.... The more adventuresome in the trade could and did use the reviews and the performers' track records to handicap their selections.

Billboard's earliest attempt at making charts dates from 1913. "Popular Songs Heard in Vaudeville Theaters Last Week" reported the top tunes from live venues in Chicago, New York, and San Francisco. It did not survive in a stable format for long. The recognizably modern chart "Jukebox Record Buying Guide" (later "Most Played in Juke Boxes") made its debut in April 1938. "Best Selling Retail Records" was inaugurated in July 1940, and "Disks With Most Radio Plugs" (later "Most Played by Jockeys") got a start in January 1945. When *Billboard* staff integrated the three charts to compile the "Top 100" in 1955, they had a sure-fire hit on their hands. Top 100 was the first chart to systematically direct the attention of the entire industry on the simple dynamic of how single songs were performing in the marketplace. Although the *Billboard* chart has been undoubtedly influential in the music field, I would argue that it has also legitimized a general cognitive model of market dynamics as chart positions.

Categorizing Domains of Activity

Durkheim (1965) recognized classification as a fundamental social impulse. Our attempts to understand ourselves in relation to our community and society rest on our ability to make categories. Negotiating the social world requires individuals to constantly employ and deploy a vast and implicit cognitive infrastructure of categories of various kinds (Bowker & Star, 1999). In many ways, the categorical schemas used in *Billboard* magazine underpin the cognitive structure of the commercial music field (Anand & Peterson, 2000). By representing market activity in various niches in the form of charts, the magazine has helped legitimize and reify the various genre groupings. Table 9.1 shows a list of major *Billboard* charts that were introduced during the first century of the magazine's existence.

Table 9.1 is very telling with respect to the magazine's attempt to grasp the evolving market for commercial music as technology and style changed over the years. Popular or pop songs were formally charted from as early as 1938 to help jukebox stockers. Pop and classical albums followed from 1945 on. Other major genres were introduced subsequently: easy-listening (1961), gospel (1965), jazz (1967), Latin (1985), modern rock (1988), new age (1988), rap (1989), world music (1990), and reggae (1994).

Table 9.1 also illustrates how certain markets wax and wane with time. The "Children's Records" chart made a promising debut in 1948 only to be discontinued in 1955. Likewise, the "Disco Action" chart, introduced with a lot of fanfare in 1974, lasted until 1987. New media for music also make their impact via the *Billboard* charts. "Compact Discs—pop" had a chart of its own from 1985 until 1990 when it became the dominant medium. The "Video Discs" chart debuted in 1983.

Two *Billboard* employees even take credit for labeling two major genres in the field—rhythm and blues and country and western (Bronson, 1994). African American music was initially presented in chart form as the "Harlem Hit Parade" in October 1942. The name changed to "Race Records" in February 1945. Following a *Billboard* staff meeting in which reporter Jerry Wexler suggested "rhythm and

TABLE 9.1
Select List of Billboard Charts with Year of Introduction

Jukebox Record Buying Guide (Singles)	1938
Relaunched as Bestselling Retail Records (Singles)	1940
Disks With Most Radio Plugs (Singles)	1945
Top 100 (Single sales)	1955
Hot 100	1958
Harlem Hit Parade	1942
Relaunched as Race Records (Jukebox chart)	1945
R&B records (Jukebox, Sales, Jockey)	1949
Most Played Jukebox Folk Records	1944
Relaunched as Country and Western Records/Sides	1949
Bestselling Pop Albums	1945
Classical	1945
Children's Records	1948
Easy Listening	1961
Gospel/Spiritual Albums	1965
Jazz Albums	1967
Disco Action	1974
Relaunched as Hot Dance	1987
Video Sales	1979
Video Discs	1983
Latin Albums	1985
Compact Discs, Pop	1985
New Age Albums	1988
Hot Rap Singles	1989
World Music Albums	1990
Top Pop Catalog Albums	1991
Heatseekers	1991
Reggae Albums	1994

blues," the name was adopted in June 1949, and has lasted until today. Editor Tom Ackerman coined the term *country and western* to refer to varieties of music ranging from country gospel to honky tonk, and from western swing to bluegrass.

After World War II, the alternative term *folk* had become associated with *communist* thanks to Senator Joseph R. McCarthy's dislike of politically left-leaning folk groups such as the Weavers (Peterson, 1997). Overnight, the music press, *Bill-*

board included, switched terms from folk to country. *Billboard*'s "Most Played Jukebox Folk Records," which debuted in January 1944, was rechristened "Country and Western Records/Sides" in June 1949. The new label proved to be a more comfortable one than a host of other terms that had fit less well: *folk, rustic, hillbilly*, and *cowboy*. This move was critical to the self-conscious shaping of a cultural identity for the genre (Peterson, 1997). *Billboard* dropped "and western" from its chart in November 1962, now tracking only "Hot Country Singles," and that slightly modified name has proved enduring.

Normalizing Desirable Chart Position as a Taken-for-Granted Aspiration

Ranking charts such as the *Billboard* "Hot 100" or "Top 200" have the virtue of being simple to understand—if you are at the top, you are the best. Simple measures of performance, however, have their drawbacks, because they conveniently hide much complexity that determines performance (Ridgeway, 1956). So for most social actors who are measured on a ranking chart, getting to the top of the chart becomes a powerful and implicit aspiration independent of other, more relevant, performance criteria. Dr. Hook and the Medicine Show might have sung about another aspiration, getting on the "cover of the *Rolling Stone* [magazine]," but for most people in the commercial music world, getting to the top of the charts is a more powerful calling.

One of the limitations of chart position as a measure of performance is that it is a static snapshot. On its own, it provides little indication of the shape of things to come. While inaugurating the "Hot 100" chart in August 1958, *Billboard* introduced a five-pointed star with the designation "star performer" (subsequently referred to as a "bullet" in the industry) that was placed next to a record to indicate upward momentum. The "bullet" was explained in the magazine as showing "outstanding upward changes of position in the Hot 100 since last week's chart. Its purpose is merely to provide quick visual identification of the sides which moved up most dramatically, or to new entries which moved up most dramatically, or to new entries which first entered the chart at an usually high position." For artists and promoters, the aspiration is not merely to get to the number one position, but to get to "No. 1 with a bullet."

This aspiration is best captured by Feiler's (1998) description of the attempt by Debi Flieshman, a Nashville-based radio promoter, to get a single by upcoming country music artist Wade Hayes on the radio chart. The promoter used her network of personal contacts among radio stations to get the single added to playlists all over the United States, working hard until just before the deadline to report to various radio chart compilers. Subsequent events underscore the strength of aspiration within the field to make it on the charts:

> At just after six, a small *ding* emanated from the terminal and the chart numbers materialized on screen.... Wade Hayes, with a heard-earned seventy new [radio station] adds ... debuted in his first week of release at number forty-five, with a bullet nota-

tion indicating upward momentum. Debi spread her hands out and bowed her head. "It's good be queen," she declared. (Feiler, p. 227)

The dysfunctional consequences of chart position as a singular aspiration are best illustrated by the disastrous history of impresario Neil Bogart's Casablanca record label. Bogart kick-started the disco era by releasing Donna Summer's "Love to Love You Baby" as an extended-play dance track. The Village People, another successful disco band, was signed to the Casablanca label as well. Bogart, a former employee of one-time *Billboard* magazine's rival *Cash Box*, understood the merits of chart position and other conspicuous symbols of strong sales performance only too well.

In a symbolic sense, whoever gets to number one on the chart is a winner. The unofficial motto of the Casablanca label was "what ever it takes"—any method that could be used to boost sales was okay, even if it hurt profitability. The label spent huge amounts promoting its artists so that they could get on the charts, but then it lost money eventually because profits from singles and album sales did not cover the expenses. Dannen (1991, p. 161) quoted one associate of Bogart as saying, "If it cost him [Bogart] three dollars to make two dollars, he would do it."

However, because it takes time to reconcile the accounting books, Casablanca's losses were not immediately noticeable. Meanwhile, impressed by the early success of the label, it was acquired by the Dutch music conglomerate Polygram. Within a year, Polygram executives discovered that they had made a poor decision because Casablanca's liabilities were on the order of tens of millions of dollars more than what the label was worth. To "chart well" is a deep-rooted and taken-for-granted aspiration.

Facilitating Commensuration of Seemingly Related Domains of Activity

Market information regimes facilitate commensuration, or the quantitative comparison of dissimilar or seemingly similar objects. It is possible to argue, for example, that Pink Floyd's *Dark Side of the Moon* album is superior to the Beatles' *Sgt. Pepper's Lonely Hearts Club Band* based on the number of weeks each album spent on the *Billboard* chart. Commensuration is formally defined as the transformation of different qualities into a common metric (Espeland & Stevens, 1998). Commensuration as a social process operates in much the same way as categorization: It helps simplify, condense, and reduce disparate types of information in a manner that lends itself to easy apprehension and comparison. Where it differs from categorization is that it is explicitly quantitative.

In his study of the emergence of rock music, Ennis (1992) argued that commensurability of preexisting pop, blues, and country genres was essential. Rock music emerged as a stylistically different genre by incorporating elements of these three older streams. To some extent, alignment between the three streams was facilitated by use of the phonograph record as the medium of choice, development of an interlinked touring circuit, and the presence of overlapping radio markets. *Billboard* magazine, through its charts, provided the definitive symbolic connection among the three streams.

The market for, and hence the number of records flowing through, the pop music charts was about three times that of country or R & B charts. *Billboard* staff altered the number of slots used to depict each of the markets over time so that it would appear that they had roughly the same number of records per slot—between three and six. This symbolic manipulation, which lasted in a stable form for the two decades between 1950 and 1970, left field participants with the view that the three markets were tightly coupled in terms of rates of activity.

A song could enter the R & B or country charts and soon appear in the pop chart or vice versa, giving a sense that the streams were crossing over; this impression was quite essential to the synthesis of rock and roll music. As Ennis (1992, p. 188) observed, *Billboard*'s tactic "allowed industry personnel to make recordings, exposure, and exploitation decisions on all *three* markets as if they were one unfolding hit parade." Had *Billboard* showed all three markets through a 30- or 50-slot chart, the impression as well as the consequential impact of crossovers would have been much diminished.

Valorizing Rationality in Sense Making of Market Activity

Organizational fields are characterized by dominant belief systems and related practices (Scott, 2001) that serve as their organizing principle (Friedland & Alford, 1991). Townley (2002) argued that dominant belief systems consist of a complex of competing rationalities that become apparent only in the context of institutional change within a field. Although the commercial music field revolves around the logic of market performance, there is an underlying tension created by competing approaches to the measurement and compilation of market information regimes. Theoretical rationality advocates the construction of increasingly precise, abstract, and deductive methods of knowing markets and drives the refinement in methodologies to measure markets. In the case of the *Billboard* chart, this dynamic is most clearly seen in the abandonment of *Billboard* magazine's use of survey methodology using SoundScan technology to compile the sales chart.

Whereas *Billboard*'s album charts have nearly always been influential, several other competitors, including *Cash Box*, have featured charts in their coverage of the music industry. However, *Billboard* sought to distinguish itself as the one with a "scientific" or statistically sound chart-compilation methodology. In the late 1950s, charts published in the magazine were accompanied by a seal, intended to convey a veneer of academic respectability: "Sample design, sample size, and all methods used in this continuing study of retail record sales are under the direct and continuing supervision of the School of Retailing of New York University." By implication, the *Billboard* methodology was, technique-wise, better than tips, intuitions, and hunches that its rivals masqueraded as soundly compiled charts.

Framed as a "continuing study," the *Billboard* chart gives all the appearance of a technically neutral, scientifically robust, and otherwise incorruptible bureaucratic reportage. For several decades, *Billboard* compiled the album chart by surveying a representative sample of stores. At a designated time each week stores would be surveyed for the following information collected during the prior week: 30 top-selling albums arranged in rank order, 50 albums with "strong" sales, and another 50 with "good" sales. The magazine's research department weighted each store based on the types of album and overall sales volume in the store and arrived at a ranking of the 200 albums that were listed in the chart. (This methodology did vary a little over time, but the basic principle remained the same.)

Although the methodology at the time was better than that of rivals, field participants alleged that it could be "influenced" in a variety of ways by record companies (Dannen, 1991; Denisoff, 1986; Karshner, 1971). Reporting stores could be bribed to report less of rivals' sales and more of their own. Blandishments to boost advertising in the magazine (or contrarily, threats to withhold the same) could sway chart position by a few points.

In practice, *Billboard*'s survey methodology was not so scientific or sound, as revealed by the emergence of a new chart-compilation technology (Anand & Peterson, 2000). In 1987, two entrepreneurs, Mike Fine and Mike Shallet, started a company they called SoundScan to develop a rival methodology that was based on measuring sales by aggregating point-of-sale data captured by scanning machines in retail checkout counters. SoundScan moved aggressively to sign up as many music-retailing outlets as possible.

The new methodology was such a significant technical improvement that it immediately won ringing endorsements from key constituents in the field, largely because it was designed to have more integrity and was not as easily corruptible as the previous one could be. Although SoundScan did not set out to develop an alternative to the *Billboard* albums chart (the firm intended to pool and sell market research data to record companies), its chart began to be published by *Billboard* as the album chart from May 25, 1991.

The introduction of the new, more rational measure proved to be the cause of a profound jolt to sense making within the field. The biggest change by far noticed within the field was the revealed strength of the country music genre. Whereas the previous compilation methodology reported an average of 17 albums per week in the quarter before the changeover, afterward it almost doubled to 32 albums per week. The new methodology also hurt the movement of smaller and independent labels, and that of new artists. In the new regime, the dynamics of charting changed as well, with albums climbing more swiftly to the top of the chart, and staying in the slot for a much shorter period. Overall, the introduction of the SoundScan-compiled *Billboard* chart provided field participants with a significantly different understanding of the market for commercial music.

MARKET-SHAPING CONSEQUENCES OF INFORMATION REGIMES

Attention

Market information regimes provide a highly visible focus of attention. Although a market information regime simplifies and routinizes stimuli within a field, the consequence of attention paid to such symbolic and data-laden information is far reaching (Feldman & March, 1983). Attending to the chart can become a field's defining habitus. Narrowing the focus of attention within a field through ranking charts has its benefits as well as its drawbacks (Gioia & Corely, 2002).

To start with, compiling a simple metric of performance among a set of organizations provides the essential function of defining the field in terms of those that consume such information. It stimulates competition, which stems from the desire to be ranked well. External constituents become empowered to use the metric to ask the awkward questions that make organizations more accountable. Ranking charts may compel organizations to consider useful strategic and tactical adaptations that may benefit the field as a whole. Finally, charts may contain accurate information about the relative worth of entities within the field being compared.

One flaw with narrow metrics such as ranking charts is that they tend to be overweighted as signals of performance. Perceivers rarely pause to check the reliability and validity—or lack thereof—of such measures. The dimensions, values, or qualities traded off to create a simple measure may lack accuracy or generalizability. Visible criteria may obscure more encompassing latent criteria that are more predictive of performance. For example, teaching-based MBA rankings can be easily mistaken as an index of the research quality of a school.

Categorization

Categories enshrined in market information regimes confer legitimacy (Zuckerman, 1999). When particular domains of activity within a field are inappropriately or not at all categorized, they suffer from lack of attention and are perceived to be less attractive. A publicly quoted company that does not neatly fit into security analysts' categorization schemes is penalized with a discounted value.

Seen in this light, the various categories of *Billboard*'s charts are more than mere labels reflecting the industry's market segments—they are party to attempts by actors to reproduce and reshape the field. For new genres seeking legitimacy, obtaining their own category of *Billboard* chart symbolizes a significant step forward. Supporters of the grunge-style "alternative" heavy rock music, which they thought of as different from pop or "soft" rock, declared a victory of sorts when *Billboard* inaugurated the Modern Rock chart in 1988 because it was critical to consolidating their social movement. Similarly, when the SoundScan chart revealed the commercial importance of country music albums, *Billboard* magazine

changed the name of the Top Pop Albums to Top 200 Albums, dropping "pop" from the title at the behest of country music record executives.

Aspiration

Market information regimes implicitly command those subjected to ratings and rankings, in a very self-serving way, to aspire to chart well. Field participants who do not perform as well as expected in a ranking exercise might experience threats to their social identity and find various ways of coping, including a reassessment of their relative standing and reframing or discounting of market information (Elsbach & Kramer, 1996).

One powerful but unintended consequence of such an aspiration is tacit encouragement of maladaptive behaviors focused on improving a social actor's ranking position. An extreme example: Kevin Hughes, a Nashville-based chart compiler for *Cash Box* magazine was allegedly murdered in 1989 because he refused to comply with a record promoter's threats to assign a "bullet" to a record. A benign albeit insidious consequence of the aspiration to chart well may be that leaders that are on a short leash in an organization may focus too much on seeking short-term improvements in rankings and thus may misallocate resources that can ensure long-term success.

Commensuration

Market information regimes help participants make sense of particular product markets within a field. The various charts in *Billboard* magazine help readers understand the dynamics of particular genres such as pop, rock, and R & B. Ennis (1992) showed that readers' commensuration of such dynamics—that is, whether one market is more or less active than another—is very much guided by purposive choices that staff at *Billboard* magazine make in creating a particular chart that can be compared with others. In presenting particular product markets, the magazine has to constantly make judgment calls about categorizing producers into markets as appropriately as possible. For example, a country single should be shown charting in the country chart rather than the R & B chart.

However, products that are anomalous with existing categories prompt intense commensuration activity that can be a source of product market innovation within the field (Rosa, Porac, Runser-Spanjol, & Saxon, 1999). Market information regimes contain highly standardized and predictable categories. When a new product appears in a field but does not neatly fit an existing product category, the fact of its anomaly prompts sense making about its most appropriate category, especially if it is commercially successful.

For example, when auto manufacturers began introducing truck-like cars and car-like trucks in the early 1980s, various auto trade periodicals struggled to classify the new products as cars or trucks. Eventually, a new category called "minivan" was created by the periodicals to make sense of the new product and this

helped cohere sense making on related field activity. The incommensurability of the minivan with the category of car or truck prompted auto producers to create a new and coherent niche for it.

Rationalization

The influence of market information regimes within a field is pervasive because they furnish categories "to think with" rather than categories "to think of" (Douglas, 1986). In providing the cognitive infrastructure of an organizational field, market information regimes seek to do their work invisibly as possible (Bowker & Star, 1999). However, each regime is underpinned by particular choices of scope, methodology, and political tone that become visible whenever changes are promoted and enacted by concerns of technical rationality (Anand & Peterson, 2000). In the case of the *Billboard* chart, as measurement technology evolved to encompass scanner data from retail outlets, replacement of the outmoded survey-based album chart by the technically superior SoundScan chart became inevitable given the valorization of rationality in Western cultural accounts of the world (Meyer, Boli, & Thomas, 1987).

When the methodology of chart compilation changed, the scope of the older *Billboard* album chart became apparent—it was geared to listing top-selling albums from current artists. Canonical albums by dead or disbanded artists such as Elvis Presley and the Beatles have always sold well enough to be on a chart of top 200 albums by sales, but these were excluded from the *Billboard* chart. The adoption of the SoundScan chart prompted the creation of a new chart for "catalog" album sales that, in addition to providing a more accurate reading of the market, also helped create a focused niche for such products. The SoundScan chart also revealed that fewer new artists broke into the Top 200 when compared to the survey methodology. The reduction in new artists in the albums chart—generally considered lifeblood of the industry—became a political minefield. *Billboard* coped by creating a new chart called "Heatseekers," exclusively devoted to the bestselling debut artists in order to help field participants apprehend and deal with significant new actors that were making their mark.

CONCLUSION

Anderson (1991) argued that nothing defines a community as well as a printing press. In large communities, where members are unlikely to meet each other face to face, the printing press (and later, its electronic version) helped to spread news of mutual importance, to inculcate common values, to serve as an archive of shared history, and to set the agenda for a collective future. Trade publications have played a vital role in the evolution of the modern culture industries. *Publishers Weekly* (131 years old and counting), *Variety* (99 years old), and *Advertising Age* (73 years old) have each, in their own way, shaped the development of publishing, popular entertainment, and advertising respectively.

Traditional accounts of the evolution of organizational fields and industries have highlighted the role of the nation-state, regulatory agencies, professional and occupational associations, and special interest groups of producers or consumers as key players. As I have shown here with the case of *Billboard* magazine, trade publications do more than report news and reflect opinion; they help members of an organizational field interact with each other in a profound and meaningful way. Trade publications such as *Billboard* magazine are an overlooked but equally important institution in shaping the development of modern culture industries.

REFERENCES

Anand, N., & Peterson, R. A. (2000). When market information constitutes fields: Sense making of markets in the commercial music field. *Organization Science, 11,* 270–284.
Anderson, B. (1991). *Imagined communities.* London: Verso.
Bowker, G., & Star, S. L. (1999). *Sorting things out: Classification and its consequences.* Cambridge, MA: MIT Press.
Bronson, F. (1994, November 1). In the grooves. *Billboard,* 257–262.
Cyert, R. M., & March, J. G. (1963). *A behavioral theory of the firm.* Englewood Cliffs, NJ: Prentice-Hall.
Dannen, F. (1991). *Hit men: Power brokers and fast money inside the music business.* New York: Random House.
Denisoff, R. S. (1986). *Tarnished gold: The record industry revisited.* New Brunswick, NJ: Transaction Books.
DiMaggio, P. J., & Powell, W. W. (1983). The iron cage revisited: Institutional isomorphism and collective rationality in organizational fields. *American Sociological Review, 48,* 147–160.
Douglas, M. (1986). *How institutions think.* Syracuse, NY: Syracuse University Press.
Durkheim, E. (1965). *The elementary forms of the religious life.* New York: Free Press.
Elsbach, K. D., & Kramer, R. M. (1996). Members' responses to organizational identity threats: Encountering and countering the *Business Week* rankings. *American Science Quarterly, 41,* 442—476.
Ennis, P. (1992). *The seventh stream: The emergence of rock 'n' roll in American popular music.* Hanover, NH: Wesleyan.
Espeland, W. N., & Stevens, M. L. (1998). Commensuration as a social process. *Annual Review of Sociology, 24,* 313–343.
Feiler, B. (1998). *Dreaming out loud: Garth Brooks, Wynonna Judd, & Wade Hayes and the changing face of Nashville.* New York: Avon.
Feldman, M. S., & March, J. G. (1981) Information in organizations as signal and symbol. *Administrative Science Quarterly, 26,* 171–186.
Friedland, R., & Alford, R. R. (1991). Bringing society back in: Symbols, practices, and institutional contradictions. In W. W. Powell & P. J. DiMaggio (Eds.), *The new institutionalism in organizational analysis* (pp. 232–266). Chicago: University of Chicago Press.
Gioia, D. A., & Corley, K. G. (2002). Being good versus looking good: Business school rankings and the Circean transformation from substance to image. *Academy of Management Learning and Education, 1,* 107–120.
Hill, A. (1994, November 1). A voice for black performance. *Billboard,* 64–68.
Hoffman, A., & Ocasio, W. (2001). Not all events are attended equally: Toward a middle-range theory of industry attention to external events. *Organization Science, 12,* 414–434.

Karshner, R. (1971). *The music machine.* Los Angeles: Nash.
March, J. G., & Simon, H. A. (1958). *Organizations.* New York: Wiley.
Meyer, J., Boli, J., & Thomas, G. (1987). Ontology and rationality in the western cultural account. In G. Thomas, J. Meyer, R. Francisco, & J. Boli (Eds.), *Institutional structure: Constituting state, society, and the individual* (pp. 1–37). Newbury Park, CA: Sage.
Nelson, H. (1994, November 1). J. A. Jackson's page. *Billboard,* 74–76.
Newman, M. (1994, November 1). Meet me at the fair. *Billboard,* 41–50.
Ocasio, W. (1997). Towards an attention-based view of the firm. *Strategic Management Journal, 18,* 187–206.
Peterson, R. A. (1997). *Creating country music: Fabricating authenticity.* Chicago: University of Chicago Press.
Ridgeway, V. (1956). Dysfunctional consequences of performance measurement. *Administrative Science Quarterly, 2,* 240–247.
Rosa, J. A., Porac, J. F., Runser-Spanjol, J., & Saxon, M. S. (1999). Sociocognitive dynamics in a product market. *Journal of Marketing, 63,* 64–77.
Sanjek, R., & Sanjek, D. (1996). *Pennies from heaven: The American popular music business in the twentieth century.* New York: Da Capo.
Schlager, K. (1994, November 1). On the boards 1984-1920. *Billboard,* 18–34.
Scott, W. R. (2001). *Institutions and organizations* (2nd ed.). Thousand Oaks, CA: Sage.
Simon, H. A. (1947). *Administrative behavior.* New York: Macmillan.
Townley, B. (2002). The role of competing rationalities in institutional change. *Academy of Management Journal, 45,* 163–179.
Zuckerman, E. (1999). The categorical imperative: Securities analysts and the illegitimacy discount. *American Journal of Sociology, 104,* 1398–1438.

CHAPTER

10

Are they Playing Our Song? Programming Strategies on Commercial Music Radio

Jarl A. Ahlkvist
University of Denver

Robert Faulkner
University of Massachusetts, Amherst

They're definitely bullies, no question about that. They've truly become the evil empire.

—Ed Levine, Galaxy Communications (Boehlert, 2001, p. 2)

They're all about quantity, not quality.

They've taken the value out of radio and turned it into a commodity.

—Marv Nyren, Phoenix Communications (Boehlert, 2001, p. 2)

For many critics of deregulation and ownership concentration, industry giant Clear Channel Communications, owner of over 1,000 radio stations in the United States, epitomizes all that is wrong with commercial radio today. Clear Channel's radio empire (whether evil or not) was made possible by the 1996 Telecommunications Act, which significantly deregulated the commercial radio industry. The Telecom Act, as it is commonly known, formalized a "shift in the definition of public interest from something determined by regulators to something determined by the marketplace" (Bates & Chambers, 1999, p. 23). The rapid ownership concentration that accompanied this shift has fueled concerns—even among prode-regulation conservatives—about the homogenization of programming on commercial radio stations and calls for reregulation of the radio industry.

The 1996 Telecommunications Act formally lifted restrictions on the number of stations licensed to a single owner and legalized duopolies—the licensing of multiple stations in the same market to a single owner. In the wake of the Telecom Act, mergers and acquisitions accelerated as owners sought to establish radio station clusters in markets that would allow them to minimize competition and more rationally target demographics attractive to advertisers. As a result, many commercial radio stations (especially those in larger markets) formerly owned independently or by modest multistation radio groups became part of corporate radio groups like Clear Channel, Infinity, Cumulus, and Entercom that collectively account for the majority of programming available in major formats in markets across the United States (Wirth, 2001). The impact of these dramatic increases in ownership concentration on the diversity of music programming in and across markets is less clear. Research evidence is mixed regarding the consequences of ownership concentration and group ownership on direct format competition in local radio markets (Berry & Waldfogel, 2001; Chambers, 2003; Drushel, 1998; Wirth, 2002) and programming homogenization (Ahlkvist & Fisher, 2000; Greve, 1996; Lacy & Riffe, 1994; Riffe & Shaw, 1990).

While cautioning that several programming philosophies coexist in the industry, Ahlkvist (2001b) suggested that corporate radio's hegemonic "techno-rational" focus may in fact encourage more conservative music-programming decisions. A key factor in this rationalization of programming has been the increased reliance on research-based selection criteria for deciding on programming content. The research in question involves collection of data on targeted listeners' response to records either through phone surveys—known as "callout" research—or auditorium tests in which demographically specified samples of potential listeners are brought together to rate elements of a station's music programming. Ownership concentration encourages the use of research—often overseen by industry consultants—because group owners can employ economies of scale when conducting research, data can be shared among stations in clusters and radio groups, and music-programming decisions based on research can be more easily centralized and systematized.

It seems reasonable to assume that programming choices for stations owned by corporate radio groups are more likely to be rationally developed and bureaucratically managed than they would be at independent mom-and-pop stations. However, when we look more closely at how music programmers do their jobs—how they use recorded music to produce broadcasts that position stations in music formats and markets in particular ways—the accompanying assumption that ownership concentration therefore leads directly or inevitably to programming homogenization appears less reasonable.

In this chapter we draw on our ongoing research on radio programmers that began prior to the Telecommunications Act (1996) in order to shed light on music-programming repertoires at a time when corporate radio groups like Clear Channel dominate the industry and most markets. After reviewing relevant scholarship on music formats on commercial radio, we reprise a typology of programming repertoires that we identified through interviews with programmers working at radio stations in different markets and music formats (Ahlkvist & Faulkner, 2002). Aided by this conceptual framework, we explore some of the key implications of ownership concentration and market oligopolies for radio programmers and the programming they produce.

MANAGING MUSIC FORMATS

Previous studies of music radio have focused on the way programmers weigh input from record companies, along with information about records' popularity and audience preferences when making record-selection decisions (Ahlkvist & Fisher, 2000; Berland, 1990; 1993; Hennion & Meadel, 1986; Negus, 1992, 1993; Rothenbuhler, 1985, 1987; Rothenbuhler & McCourt, 1992; Turner, 1993). However, little is known about variation in how programmers working in different structural contexts seek to coordinate recording industry pressures, information on records' potential, and indicators of audience demand. We argue that understanding how music reaches the commercial airwaves requires that variation in programmer practices be explained. Pivotal to such understanding is acknowledging that music programmers mediate between the recording industry and their audiences. In this role, programmers must navigate a course between programming music that works for the station's format and is effective in targeting desired listeners, and pressure from record companies that can not only supply programmers with records to play, but also provide promotional support for the station.

As one program director put it, a radio station and a record company are "two different companies going in different directions" but "where we intersect is that they want a hit record, we want a hit record. We want a hit because we want everybody to listen to us to hear the hit, they want a hit because it sells more units." In our research we seek to distinguish particular sets of practices that programmers use to address the tension between what record companies would like them to play and what music they think will make their stations successful. Accordingly, we identify four ideal types of programming repertoires that programmers employ and discuss the ownership, market, and format conditions under which each is likely to be predominant.

Contemporary commercial radio stations in the United States program music in a variety of formats such as Adult Contemporary (AC), Top 40 or Contemporary Hit Radio (CHR), Adult, Album Alternative (AAA or Triple A), Country, and Modern Rock. Greve (1996) defined radio formats as "a combination of program content, announcer style, timing of programming and commercial material, and methods for listener feedback and quality control" (p. 39). Radio stations' music formats are the basis of the "uneasy symbiosis" between radio and the recording industry, in which record companies use radio to promote their records and stations use music to target listeners that are attractive to advertisers (Barnes, 1988, p. 39).

To varying degrees, programmers seek record service—a reliable free supply of the latest music—and promotional added value—such as advertising time buys, contest prizes, merchandise giveaways, and concert sponsorship—from record companies in exchange for playing their records. Record company promotions staff—reps, record people, promoters—and independent promoters (indies) encourage radio programmers to add records to their playlists to expose them to the station's listeners and as part of the promotional push to move records up the charts published weekly in trade magazines like *Radio and Records* (*R & R*), *Gavin*, and *Billboard*. Stations that report their playlists to trade magazines, or have their programming monitored electronically by BDS (Broadcast Data Systems), are especially influential because their airplay provides the raw data for the weekly trade charts. The trade charts are important to record companies because programmers are thought to consider a record's movement on the charts when deciding whether or not to add it to their station's playlist. According to Negus (1992, 1993), radio programmers' response (or lack thereof) to promoters' sales pitches has important consequences for record company agendas and their policies regarding signing, recording, and promoting artists.

Most previous studies of music radio employ an analytical perspective that focuses on the selection criteria used by programmers to screen records. Conceptualizing music programming as a selection process and programmers as gatekeepers who decide which records make it through the gate onto the air has led researchers to emphasize programmer isomorphism and selection criteria based on conservative programming practices. From this perspective, programmers are depicted as relying on research, consultants, and trade publications in an effort to rationally reduce uncertainty about which records are viable for attracting a specific target audience (Berland, 1990, 1993; Negus, 1992, 1993, 1999; Rothenbuhler, 1985, 1987; Rothenbuhler & McCourt, 1992; Turner, 1993). Historical case studies emphasize that reliance on such programming practices stems from the shift toward what Berland (1990) described as a "techno-rational" industry logic (Barnard, 1989; Miller, 1992; Peterson, 1978, 1993; Wallis & Malm, 1993).

Only two previous studies of music radio considered that, despite the industry's consolidation and rationalization, all programmers might not act alike. Criticizing the prevailing pessimistic perspective on music radio for "undervaluing its varied modes of production," Grenier (1990, p. 231) contrasted how programmers incorporate the same record into different formats. More recently, in a study of professional discourse on music programming, Ahlkvist (2001b) examined the different orienting "programming philosophies" articulated by radio programmers. In our research we examine programmer variation by focusing on the practices used to attract listeners and negotiate relations with record companies.

METHODOLOGY

This study is based on interviews with 32 programmers at 28 commercial music stations in three accessible geographic regions in the United States.[1] These interviews ranged from 1 to 2.5 hours in length, with most lasting about 1.5 hours. Interviews were tape-recorded and subsequently transcribed. An interview guide was used so that all programmers were asked about the same range of topics, but the basic protocol was adapted to suit variation in the programmers' experiences and concerns. Questions focused on programmers' career in radio, methodology for selecting records for the playlist, use of research, and relations with record companies. In addition, we asked programmers about the organization, ownership, and format of the station they currently worked for. Informal conversations with members of stations' programming and on-air staff, observation of programmers and on-air talent at work, attendance at music meetings, and material from station web sites were used as supplemental data. Articles and editorials published in trade magazines, radio textbooks (Carroll & Davis, 1993; Keith, 1996), how-to guides (MacFarland, 1997; Norberg, 1996), and programmer memoirs (Ladd, 1991; Sklar, 1984) helped us put our primary data into a broader industry context.

In order to interview programmers working in different markets, we focused on stations in three regions. Each region contained a primary market area identified by Arbitron, the industry ratings service. However, each region also included stations that were either located in an adjacent Arbitron market or were operating in small, unrated markets. In the first region, six stations competed in an urban market with a population of about half a million people and one operated on the periphery of this market. The second region included two stations in a medium-sized market with a population of approximately 700,000, and six stations were contained in an Arbitron top-10 urban market with over 6 million residents. It is important to note, however, that three of these large market stations were located on the periphery of the metropolitan area and were secondary players in the urban market. Eleven of the stations in the third region competed for audience share in a top-20 urban market with a population of almost 4 million. The remaining two stations in this region were located in adjacent small markets and primarily targeted audiences in communities on the periphery of the urban market. All but four of the large market stations we studied were licensed to corporate groups.[2] Of these four independently owned stations, however, only one targeted a metropolitan audience, whereas the others catered primarily to suburban communities on the urban periphery. Seven of the eight medium-market sta-

[1]Typically, the program director has primary responsibility for the station's music programming and has the last word on what records should be added to the playlist. Many stations, especially those in larger markets, also have a music director who usually has input into the music selection process, but whose primary responsibility is managing the station's music library.

[2]The corporate groups that owned stations in this study were Ackerly Group, CBS/Infinity, Entercom, Fisher Broadcasting, Saga Broadcasting, and Sandusky Radio.

tions studied were owned by small radio groups that are quite modest when compared with the station holdings and earnings of the corporations that owned the majority of the large-market stations.

A TYPOLOGY OF PROGRAMMING REPERTOIRES

Studying how radio programmers make music-programming decisions reveals, contrary to much of the extant literature, that they do not all use the same practices. As defined by Tilly (1995), cultural repertoires identify "a limited set of routines that are learned, shared, and acted out through a relatively deliberate process of choice" (p. 42). Accordingly, we describe analytically distinct sets of programming practices as programming repertoires. In this section we use excerpts from interviews with programmers to describe four types of programming repertoires in commercial radio. As ideal types, these programming repertoires are analytical constructs that seek to specify distinctive sets of programming practices that are not employed in their pure form by any individual programmer (Muggleton, 2000; Weber, 1949). We develop such a typology in an effort to improve upon prior research on music radio, which has tended to portray all programmers as embodying a techno-rational industry logic. We argue that it is variation in programming repertoires, rather than record selection criteria or programming practices per se, that accounts for differences in stations' music programming.

The Subjective Repertoire

The subjective repertoire describes a set of programming practices grounded in the programmer's personal musical sensibility and taste: Programming practices are based on the programmer's aesthetic evaluation of records and artists' credibility. Passion and love for the music they program help the programmer provide listeners with the best music possible. Accordingly, the subjective repertoire features practices that allow programmers to educate listeners by exposing them to new and unfamiliar music, balance their musical preferences with programming that is viable for the station, and maintain relations with record companies that do not compromise the format's integrity. In combination, these programming practices are geared to promoting the programmer's musical preferences. This is a programming repertoire that, as one music director put it, "harkens back to seventies progressive radio. What was that about? Well, it was about the music and we try to keep it focused on that."

In this repertoire, quality programming is synonymous with innovation and the emphasis is on breaking new records—being one of the first stations to play them—that programmers judge worthy of being heard on the air. A primary reason for breaking records is programmers' passion for a song or artist. As one programmer explained: "Not every record is going to be number one and every once in while there'll be a record you know is not going to work [become a hit], but you *need* to play it because it's a format-defining record. It's something that stands up and is groundbreaking and maybe people aren't going to get it, but we need to play it."

This drive to innovate and take chances with new music makes research a secondary factor. As one programming director explained, "I find music research to be inherently flawed because they base so much of it on familiarity and that's just inherently contradictory to what this format is all about, which is new music." In this repertoire research is no substitute for being a music fanatic: "You know what? At the end of the day it's just a tool and if you really love something you're going to keep playing it, you're going to figure out a way of doing it."

In order to be useful to programmers working in commercial radio, however, the subjective repertoire must also offer a way to curb their aesthetic judgments so that they are not "too hip for the room." Consequently, the repertoire incorporates practices that enable programmers to compromise their personal standards to some degree and play records they do not personally think measure up. Programmers must acknowledge that there is a gap between their musical tastes and what the majority of the station's listeners want to hear. Records that programmers view as lacking in quality may be added to the playlist if they are seen as records that the station cannot afford to ignore because listeners expect them to play them. Here is how one programmer explained why she recently put a "pretty generic record" into heavy rotation: "It didn't strike me passionately, but it's a good radio song and as far as the alternative charts go, it's a number-one song." Another programmer put this more strongly: "This is a good example, this song that's on the air right now I detest, I detest! And we're testing it [playing it in slow rotation] because it is [points it out as a hot single on the *R & R* chart] *this* song.... So I can't say no because after a while that just becomes my ego trying to keep a song that people like off the air."

Even programmers who count on their subjective ear for musical quality realize that programming a commercial station requires a degree of sensitivity to audience conceptions of a record's suitability for the format—reflected in the trade charts—that are different from their own.

In this repertoire, relationships with record companies are founded on the understanding that programmers cannot be pressured into playing records. One program director described herself and her programming staff as "moral bastards: We don't add records for money, we don't add records for promotions, we don't add records for much other than the merit of the records, and that's a dying breed of programmer." Programmers' desire to maximize the aesthetic quality of their station's music programming encourages relationships with record promoters who have a better appreciation of the format's aesthetic potential.

As one programmer explained, "You get to know the record company people over the years. Some of them have a good sense of the radio station and others don't, and in a way you temper it [decisions about which records to add to the playlist] with what that person's sense of judgment is like." When record promoters don't respect or understand the station's format or the programmer's priorities, however, the repertoire dictates a hard-line stance: "And I don't let myself get bullied ... [As a programmer] I'm a total hard ass.... I know what's right for my radio station, the record label doesn't." Even when relations between programmers and record people are good, however, conflicts do occur when promoters are under pressure to get adds. One country programmer who described her staff as "a little tougher" on record promoters than other stations discussed how she deals with pressure from record companies:

> There are times when they'll call us and say, "Are you out of your mind? You can't hear this? This is the biggest hit since 'Achy Breaky Heart,' the biggest hit since LeAnn Rimes' 'Blue' and you can't hear it? You're the only person in the whole country who can't hear it!" Well I'm sorry, we have a lot of other choices and we've chosen to go with this [another record] instead. It's hard because you want to try to help if you can and we want to expose new artists and new music as much as anybody else but we are totally at odds with the record labels in terms of goals: Their goal is to sell records, our goal is to keep listeners.

The Analytical Repertoire

In contrast to the subjective programming repertoire, the analytical repertoire is based on the assumption that what matters in the profession is an ability to objectively assess audience demand and record viability, rather than an ear for music. This programming repertoire is characterized by the use of research data as the primary factor in music selection, a conservative approach toward breaking new records, and practices that maximize autonomy from the recording industry. This programming repertoire encompasses the practices commonly decried by critics of corporate radio as complementing ownership concentration and responsible for the increased standardization and decreased quality of music programming.

According to the analytical repertoire, the best way to ensure that programming is listener driven—an impartial response to scientifically measured target audience demand—is to base music selection decisions on research data. As a programmer explained, programming records that "test well" is "a way of making sure that before you submit listeners in your area to a record, it's as viable as can be known." Interestingly, even programmers who are committed to grounding their work in research acknowledge that this practice compromises the quality of music programming.

Talking about the records that make it onto his station's playlist, one program director reflected: "I hate to say it but, it's the tested music, the music that's come through [being tested]. Is it smart? Yes. Is it great radio? No. Not in my opinion." Such "smart" programmers' tastes in music and sense of aesthetic quality have little to do with their work in radio. It is their ability to use research data that makes them good programmers. Once they have interpreted the numbers, programming is just a matter of playing records that the research suggests the station's target demographic will respond to positively and avoiding records that get too many negatives. In the analytical repertoire, finding out as precisely as possible what the targeted audience wants to hear is the key challenge because, as one programmer noted, "you've got to make sure that you have the right product out there in front of your listener.... There's a lot of money to be made here and we're going to test all this stuff and we're going to make sure we have the best product."

In the analytical repertoire, if one has good data there is little point in taking risks with new records and artists. It makes more sense to follow, rather than to try to lead, the industry trends reflected in the trade charts because it is assumed that listeners prefer familiar records and are more likely to punch to another station if they hear something unfamiliar. Watching and waiting are upheld as the smart way to program a station, whereas taking unnecessary risks with unproven material is considered unprofessional. Referring to colleagues who break a lot of new records, one programmer pondered, "Why do these people do it? Generally it's because they're not real good programmers." When asked how such stations survive, the same programming director shook his head and replied, "They play a lot of crap, they'll get killed eventually." Of course, if programmers wait until every record they play is beginning to get burnt (overplayed), the station begins to sound stale. However, as one AC station's program director explained, it is possible to minimize the risk of playing new records:

> I don't jump out on songs usually that are by unknown artists.... [However,] "Music" by Madonna [an established artist] is probably a good choice right now because Top 40 and Hot AC are both starting to play that record. Well, we can slot that into our call-out without even playing it and get a read from our audience and we can say, "Well, 50% say it's familiar, they really don't know what it is yet, let's hold off another couple of weeks." And then we put it back in and you never know. We did that with "Oops I Did It Again" by Brittany Spears. She's a Top 40 artist, a teenybopper artist. We put that song in [the call-out survey] and it came back number one and we said, "I think we can play this record!"

As this programmer's comments illustrate, the analytical repertoire includes practices geared to making sure that new records are safe to play.

The analytical repertoire also promotes avoidance of close relationships with record promoters, which are seen as a threat to the programmer's objectivity. Unlike the subjective repertoire, this repertoire includes no practices for determining the viability of a record before it breaks, making programmers unlikely to cooperate with record company promotional agendas for new records and artists. Acknowledging that many programmers "can be more or less manipulated by these people [record promoters]," one music director described how he deals with record companies:

> For example, record companies will approach us and say, "Well, we'd love to have your support on this new artist, this new record, and if we were to secure airplay we would arrange this great promotion where we could fly a couple of people to the west coast to see Dave Matthews." It happens all the time and is pretty accepted, but it's just something we don't do, we just avoid that kind of thing. Some radio people say,

> "I get beat up by these record people all the time," but I don't feel that way: it's our radio station and we're going to do whatever the hell we want with it. I would just hate to be in a situation where I felt I had to play a record because I owed somebody a favor, so we just avoid it.

The analytical repertoire downplays the importance of getting promotional extras from record companies because this is seen as a guaranteed way to lose autonomy and end up playing too many stiffs, records that do not work for the station's format and increase the tune-out factor. In this repertoire the risk of playing stiffs outweighs any advantage gained from record companies' supplements to the station's promotional budget. The problem for programmers who accept record company promotions, according to one programmer who avoids them, is that "they have a lot of promotions *and* they have a lot of stinky records on their stations." Not surprisingly, relations with record promoters are characterized by programmer hubris, as in the case of the programmer who explained that, "The record companies work for me.... They are lucky that they have us to talk to. Record companies need us more than we need them.... I don't need record companies for shit!"

The Populist Repertoire

The populist programming repertoire is made up of a set of practices that enable programmers to be the institutional ears of their target audience, selecting records based on criteria similar to those used by the station's listeners. Meeting audience demand depends neither on programmers' subjective evaluation of records nor on their reliance on research data. Instead, this programming repertoire's practices enable programmers to listen like a listener, avoid becoming dependent on research, and negotiate quid pro quo relationships with record companies. We describe this programming repertoire as populist because it defines a set of practices designed to cater to the audience by minimizing the gap between the radio professional and the listener.

In the populist repertoire, the programmer's primary goal is to manage the format to fit the expectations of the local audience. In this repertoire, programming music is, as one programmer explained, "a black art. It is not a science." In practicing this art, "a sense of the [listening] community is more important than an infallible sense of music." Neither research-based analysis nor subjective music appreciation guides programmers using this programming repertoire. Rather, programmers are to rely first and foremost on their affective reaction to records: "I pick music by feeling, music is emotional basically, if it strikes something in me, hopefully it will strike something in our listeners too." This programmer is not, however, suggesting that he selects records based on personal taste or subjective aesthetic criteria, but on his sense of how a typical listener might respond to a record. As he went on to explain: "[I] think of the one guy who's driving his Volvo home from his day at the law office and he's got your radio station on. Does he want to hear this [record]? Who cares if everyone in [the city] wants to, does this guy want to hear this?"

The ear that matters is an ear for what a listener will hear in a song: "I've been blessed with a good ear to be able to hear good bridges and good chords and good songs.... Songs stick out and 'You know what? I'm singing this song in my head I bet our audience would do the same thing.'" The target audience is imagined based on programmers' intuitive sense of the demographic that they themselves reflect, albeit imperfectly. Comparing his station's core listeners and his programming staff, a programmer explained, "Because we grew up together, we know what's going on in terms of music, in terms of what music will make somebody feel good. We have an idea of what, musically, will work with my generation." Another veteran programmer echoed this sentiment and added, "I'm lucky because I personally like most of the stuff we play, but I'm not going to let my personal likes or dislikes affect what we do because at the end of the day it's up to the audience to play what they like, not what I like. People have tried to educate listeners for years and it's always been a failure."

In the populist repertoire, determining who the target audience is and what they want to hear on the air is based on knowing your audience, insight that research alone cannot provide. Being sensitive to the sound that local listeners similar to themselves expect from the station's format also means being skeptical about the usefulness of information on how records are testing in other markets. "I'm maintaining that a guy from Seattle, Washington doesn't know what this [Northeast market's] listening audience wants as much as I do," argued a programmer while explaining why he is skeptical of consultants' programming advice. He went on to add:

> The consultant will tell you, "This song is testing well, this song isn't testing well, you should drop this song, you should move this song into heavy [rotation]." Sorry, you get back to regionality where some songs do better around here than they do out west and I don't care what so and so from California or New York is telling me—that this song is testing well. If it's testing well for you, it may not be testing well for us.

The populist repertoire commits programmers to conceptualizing the local audience as requiring customized music programming through a format that is not replicated in other markets. Accordingly, programmers should not be concerned with conforming to industry expectations about music formats, as illustrated by the programmer who dismissed the significance of his station's format designation in the trade magazine *Gavin* as little more than "a buzz word that advertisers like to hear."

The importance of the programmer being tuned in to what listeners want to hear on the station is complemented by ambivalence about working with record companies: "It's kind of a love-hate relationship. You'd almost rather not deal with them. But if you don't, you won't get the stuff you need." Rather than cultivating close relationships with promoters, however, the populist repertoire specifies a need for quid pro quo relationships. One programmer described such relationships bluntly: "The record companies basically whore themselves. There's no other way to put it.

I do them a favor, they do me a favor. I play a piece of garbage sometimes that I shouldn't be playing ... [but] you never know when you're going to need them." To get reliable record service and promotional support in order to make sure listeners get the music and added value they desire, programmers must sometimes play ball with promoters who they view as "The kings of bullshit ... the *worst* salespeople you've ever seen in your life! You know, the guy who sticks his foot in the door?"

The Collaborative Repertoire

The final programming repertoire in our typology brings together practices that anchor music-programming decisions in collaborative relations with record companies. Rather than independently—either via research or according to programmer judgment—determining which records to put on the air, the collaborative repertoire is so named because it is made up of practices that align programming decisions with record company promotional agendas. This programming repertoire includes practices that minimize breaking records that turn out to be stiffs, maximizing promotional added value, and weighing record companies' sales pitches against other information.

The collaborative repertoire prioritizes cooperating with record companies to break records and expose new artists. Programmers describe their stations as integral to record promotion: "We're a good launching point," "we start a lot of projects that work out real well," "we sell a lot of records." The programmer is expected to follow the record company's promotional agenda by playing and promoting the current single. As one music director explained:

> For example with the new Eminem album there's songs I like better than the new single, but it wouldn't make sense not to play the new single because MTV's behind it, he's performing it on TV and things like that ... so you're only going to help yourself and help the record be more familiar if you stay in the game plan.

Following the record company's game plan often involves a trade-off in which the programmer agrees to get on board to play a hard-to-break work record in exchange for promotional added value. One programmer offered a clear example of this while discussing her sister station's recent promotional coup:

> JAM just did their big "JAM Fest" [an annual concert sponsored by the station] and in order for them to get Korn, a big, big, huge, enormous band right now, the label would say, "Okay, we'll give you Korn, but you have to play my blah blah blah record." And it's up to the individual programmer to figure out how much of that they want to do and how much of that they can do without sacrificing what the sound of their radio station is.

The risk to programmers of breaking records that may turn out to be stiffs is minimized to some degree when the record company gets behind the project promotionally. Such support improves the chances that the record will be a hit and at least cushions the negative impact on the station's music mix if the song tanks.

The collaborative repertoire not only offers programmers a way to offset the risk of breaking records, it also includes practices designed to help the station get the most out of promotional incentives available from record companies. For example, a programmer whose music programming is monitored by *Billboard* explained how she convinced a record company to compensate the station for taking a chance on a new artist's record and spinning (playing) it a lot:

> We've spun this song 379 times, which is more than any other station on the [monitored] panel [of stations]. So, when it comes time for them to play [a concert in] our market [another station in the market] wanted to copromote that show. And what I can do is say [to the record company], "Hey, we played this song more than any other station in the country, you'd better not let them have anything to do with that show." And they [the other station] don't and we're owning the show. It's all a leverage thing when you have this kind of power to contribute to the charts.

In addition to playing records with the most hit potential, programmers collaborate with record companies to promote artists and records that they can own—that become identified with the station through promotions and airplay. A music director contrasted such an artist with one that offered the station less promotional mileage:

> For instance, we have this band Shivery and they have a song on the station that's just making people go mental every time they hear it: [in high voice] "Oh my whoa, whoa, God what is that?" So we're like, "Something's really happening here and this could be a good band for us." Let's bring them to town and do a show and the label will bring them in for free and we'll record it and get a song for our upcoming [CD] sampler. We wouldn't do it with a band like this that's on the radio right now, Travis, because we can't own them, they're getting played on too many stations.

The collaborative repertoire encourages programmers to come through for record companies when they need help on a promotional project and this sometimes involves playing subpar records. However, as one programmer explained, "You have to know when you can do a favor for a label and help them out and when they can help you out and what the limits of that are." When a programmer is contemplating adding a likely stiff to their playlist an important consideration is whether the promotional benefits are worth it: "Oftentimes if a label is coming at you with a lot of incentives to play the record, it means the record is shit and the only way you're going to get that record played is by giving all these incentives and doing all this stuff. And then you have to weigh it." But, as a music director confessed, "Sometimes you make mistakes and end up playing a record that you never should have because you know it's a priority for the label." To guard against this undesirable outcome, programmers with friends in the record business need to stay objective:

> You get so close [to record promoters] that you don't really have an objective look at things and that's the thing you really have to pay attention to ... Dada has a new song out now that I don't particularly think is all that great. And we love Dada and we like the label, but today we're not going to play that one because I don't think it's worth taking up a spot on my playlist for. So, I think it's very important that you stay objective.

To remain objective and not let close relationships with record promoters get the best of them, programmers using this repertoire pay close attention to industry indicators of how records that promoters want them to add are doing at other stations and on the trade charts. As one program director of a rock station explained, "On a national level if the key modern rock stations are banging the shit out of a song that is a pretty good, influential piece of information for us." The collaborative repertoire positions the radio industry as a key reference point for programmers to help balance the promotional spin from record companies.

PROGRAMMING REPERTOIRES AND MUSIC FORMATS

Although previous research on music radio describes key aspects of the record-selection process, the structural conditions that make different programming repertoires logical and the consequences the use of these repertoires have for stations' music formats are not well understood. Our typology of programming repertoires reveals how programming practices are related to music format variation and helps us trace the role of structural factors in promoting or constraining the use of each repertoire. Ahlkvist and Fisher (2000) showed that larger market stations, especially those licensed to group owners, employ more conservative music-selection strategies and produce more standardized programming than those in smaller markets that are more likely to be independently owned. Accordingly, we also discuss the way that market size and station ownership coincide with programmers' use of each repertoire.

The subjective repertoire's emphasis on practices that draw on the programmer's musical taste and expertise produces formats that are music intensive. Although such music formats are oriented toward niche audiences, they encompass a relatively wide range of music within the format's genre boundaries, reflecting programmer commitment to broadening listeners' musical horizons through innovative music programming.

Among the stations we studied, the use of the subjective repertoire was most apparent among programmers managing rock-based formats such as Adult, Album, Alternative (AAA), and Modern Rock. Whether targeting an older or younger demographic, these formats are characterized by relatively low repetition and high levels of record diversity. These are stations with extensive music libraries and often feature specialty programming that comes close to being free-form and includes music from nonrock genres such as techno, jazz, and world music.

We identified programmers using this repertoire in the large, medium, and small markets that we studied. However, because these formats require an audience of music-intensive listeners, stations in less populated markets cannot afford to be as niche oriented as those in larger markets. To use the subjective repertoire in smaller markets, programmers must either make compromises to broaden the station's appeal or tolerate a smaller audience share. In larger markets programmers managing these formats have access to sizable audience segments and can afford to be more committed to the subjective repertoire while maintaining their ratings. In larger markets these formats have the potential to bring in respectable advertising revenues because they target more affluent or high-consuming demographics, making stations programmed via the subjective repertoire suitable additions to corporate groups.

Using the analytical repertoire results in programming that features high repetition and low musical diversity because programmers focus on playing safe hit records in the hopes of reaching a mass audience. This programming repertoire is useful for managing variants of the Top 40/CHR and AC formats, including hybrids such as Hot AC, all of which stress playing the hits and abide by the mantra that "you're never hurt by what you're not playing." These formats are the ancestors of the tight research-based Top 40 jukebox formats developed in the mid 1950s (Denisoff, 1986).

Among the interviewed programmers, those most committed to applying the practices associated with the analytical repertoire worked for large- and medium-market stations that were part of corporate radio groups. This is largely explained by the fact that the objective repertoire requires the use of expensive research that corporate groups are best able to afford and use efficiently. The analytical repertoire justifies the expense of research with the promise that it is the most effective way to reach a large and profitable mass audience.

The populist repertoire can be traced back to the independent, locally focused, personality-driven formats that emerged to compete with radio networks in the 1950s (Leblebici, Salancik, Copay, & King, 1991). Using a repertoire that is distinguished by the centrality of programmer similarity and responsiveness to the local audience produces very different mass-appeal formats than reliance on the analytical repertoire. The music formats of the stations we identified as managed by programmers relying on the populist repertoire's programming practices could be described as AC and Country, although the programmers felt these labels were too restrictive to describe their stations' formats. Reliance on the populist repertoire results in music programming that is more idiosyncratic than that offered by the cookie-cutter formats produced by programmers favoring the analytical repertoire. Given that programmer intuition for what listeners want to hear on the air takes priority over research in this repertoire, music programming strays from the format mainstream reflected in the trade charts. Although familiarity is important, musical repetition is curtailed in an effort to maximize time-spent-listening ratings and listener loyalty to the station. Listener exclusivity was important for programmers using populist practices to manage their formats because they all operated in small markets or on the margins of large markets where there was minimal competition for a mass audience. Unsurprisingly, these programmers' stations were owned independently or by small radio groups. It is unlikely that most corporate groups would find this programming repertoire and the resulting music formats compatible with their financial objectives. In fact, such stations may be at risk for being bought out by corporate groups and automated to play mass-appeal jukebox programming developed outside the market by programmers drawing on the analytical repertoire (Fairchild, 1999).

Finally, programmer use of the collaborative repertoire dampens the innovation and diversity fostered by the subjective repertoire. In addition to rock-based formats, we identified programmers relying on the collaborative repertoire to manage dance-rhythm, smooth jazz, and country formats. These formats use relatively heavy repetition of familiar records to provide a safe backdrop for introducing new music. This requires a format with narrow aesthetic parameters that constrains the range of styles and artists that can be heard on the station.

Among the programmers we studied, those most committed to the programming practices encompassed by the collaborative repertoire worked for corporately owned stations located in large and medium markets. Successful use of the collaborative repertoire requires a large enough audience to make targeting a narrow fragment profitable. This programming repertoire appears to complement ownership concentration in commercial radio. Companies that own stations in similar formats in multiple markets may have greater leverage in negotiating for promotional extras due to their increased playing power and ability to help break records.

The process through which radio stations help to transform records into popular music has been described as a sequence in which smaller market stations break records, helping to move records up the trade charts and providing promoters with a story to encourage larger market stations to add the record (e.g., Barnes, 1988; Negus, 1992). Our study reveals that this process is based on the use of different programming repertoires. The subjective repertoire is important for breaking records and generating the buzz that will encourage more conservative programmers to take risks with new records and artists. Despite the initial importance of getting such stations to add records to their playlists, promoters rely on programmers using the collaborative repertoire to generate the adds and spins that will make a record a hit in a niche format.

The ultimate goal of record companies is usually to have a record cross over to mass-appeal formats where they will be heard by a wider range and larger number of potential record buyers. Programmers using the populist repertoire can often be persuaded or pressured to introduce niche format hits to their more mainstream audiences. However, the esoteric mass-appeal formats that these programmers manage are less useful to record promoters than formats managed by programmers employing the analytical repertoire who can provide airplay at larger market stations. The analytical repertoire leads programmers to be very conservative, and skeptical about what programmers using the populist repertoire are playing. These programmers add records only once research indicates that they will perform for the station. With the possible exception of the populist repertoire, each set of radio-programming practices serves an important function in the production of popular music in today's corporately dominated radio industry.

PROGRAMMING REPERTOIRES IN THE 21ST CENTURY

Our typology of programming repertoires offers a framework for understanding programmer methodologies, constraints on their use, and their consequences for programming content. Since we began studying commercial music radio in the early 1990s, much has changed in the industry and on the air due to ownership concentration and market oligopolies. Given the focus of our research on programmer decision making, we are particularly interested in developments that shape programmers' ability or willingness to draw on the programming repertoires we have outlined. Two such recent developments stemming from these twin structural changes are station clusters and a new form of payola. We briefly discuss these two developments because they illustrate how the prevailing organization of corporate radio groups threatens programmer autonomy and constrains their effective and creative use of programming repertoires, making standardized programming an increasingly likely outcome of the programming decision-making process. In our conclusion, we consider the organizational causes of these developments and the possibility of radio groups reengineering their cultural production process.

Rationalization of programming implies increased input into decision making about what goes on the air from those higher up in the organizational hierarchy, and less from those at the lower end (ironically, those in closest proximity to the actual broadcast). In station clusters, there is the further possibility of locating programming decision making outside individual stations so that programming is done at the cluster or even corporate level. Those who see radio as a fundamentally local medium decry such shifts in programming up the corporate chain of command and, in light of our typology of programming repertoires, we would expect such a shift to encourage use of the analytical and collaborative repertoires because these are most amenable to rationalization.

If people higher up in the corporate hierarchy are making programming decisions, we assume that research and coordination with record companies are strategically prioritized in considering the market and format positioning of the corporations' stations in relation to each other. In contrast, there is less room for programmer use of subjective and populist repertoires, because these imply hands-on programming.

Based on interviews with programmers working in station clusters owned by several major radio groups in a large market, Ahlkvist (2001a) observed a number of commonalities that are suggestive of how programmers are affected by market oligopolies. First, programmers reported losing decision-making autonomy in the face of increased scrutiny from station and cluster managers, programming consultants, and company programmers outside the cluster. Programmers talked about the fact that there is less room for programmers who are passionate about music, as they are increasingly pressured to take more of a business perspective based on research and input on the numbers from those higher up in the organizational hierarchy.

Second, programmers described their jobs as increasingly "administration intensive" as they had to shift their attention toward the bottom-line concerns and away from programming decisions. When asked about the impact of these developments on station programming, most of the interviewed programmers admitted that they probably have not been good for listeners—playlists are tighter, there are more commercials, and there is less regionality. Veteran programmers reminisced about the good old days when music programming was their only concern, when direct format competition motivated them to take more risks and pay closer attention to what local listeners wanted to hear on the air because they were fighting over audience share.

Critics of deregulation and recently even some formerly proderegulation policy makers like Senators Trent Lott and John McCain have raised concerns that radio deregulation has unleashed "evil empires" like Clear Channel that have grown so large that they are fundamentally restructuring the programming production process in ways that serve only their own financial interests. Key accusations are usually leveled at Clear Channel, the largest radio group by far with well over 1,000 stations, and include charges that the major companies have increased advertising rates and ad volume, encouraged on-air indecency to boost ratings, homogenized programming content, centralized programming decisions, and used "cyberjocking" to replace local DJs with canned shows produced by company jocks that are edited to sound local. However, given our focus on the centrality of the relationship between stations and record companies in programming decision making in music radio, it is renewed concerns about payola that draw our attention.

At issue here is the ability of radio groups to use their size to leverage the recording industry, which has serious implications for what is heard on the air and programmers' role in selecting music and artists to put on the air. Although play for pay, or payola, is hardly a new phenomenon in radio, with a critical mass of stations vital to breaking records and cultivating hits and music sales in the hands of a few large radio groups, record companies are at a clear disadvantage when it comes to using radio to promote their records and artists.

As detailed by journalists like Boehlert (2001a), independent (so-called indie) record promoters working for major promotional firms collect an increasingly high toll from record companies to get records on the air at the stations they work with and share the wealth with cooperative radio stations in the form of promotional payments. The leverage that large radio groups have over record companies fundamentally unbalances the symbiotic relationship between radio and record companies that has been a hallmark of music promotion in the radio format era. These practices undermine even the much-criticized programmer reliance on research and ironically exaggerate the influence of record companies in music-selection decisions characterized by the collaborative programming repertoire. Although record companies may be forced to spend large sums of money (Boehlert estimated that an add at a key trend-setting station costs at least $1,000) to get their artists and records airplay at group-owned stations, the fact is that these payments buy record companies influence over radio playlists and reduce the autonomy of radio programmers in the process.

As highlighted by our typology of programming repertoires, payola in the era of corporate radio threatens radio stations' ability to effectively position themselves in markets, because programming—the product used to attract listeners—is compromised. Even the collaborative repertoire, which certainly accommodates a degree of quid pro quo exchange with record companies and promoters, is premised on the fact that programmers must make sure that the benefits of engaging in such exchanges with actors working in the recording industry outweigh the damage they may do to the station's programming. Payola-driven programming threatens the objectivity that programmers say is vital in productively using a collaborative repertoire in the interests of the station.

Why might radio groups engage in practices that marginalize programmers and place programming decisions in the hands of business rather than music people? Loomis and Albarran's (2004) research on general managers of station clusters indicates that the shift toward ownership concentration and market oligopolies did not trigger business process reengineering at major radio groups. General managers at the 25 largest radio groups remain task rather than process oriented, focused on "making as much money for their company as they were able" (Loomis & Albarran, p. 63) rather than product quality. Such reengineering "usually requires that established hierarchies become flattened" (p. 65), and should it occur in radio groups, Loomis and Albarran speculated that corporate programmers and managers would leave music-selection decisions to local programmers, even including DJs as part of the programming team. In this scenario, we would expect that the analytical and collaborative repertoires would be balanced by the subjective and populist repertoires, with the outcome being more innovative and diverse programming. Furthermore, such reengineering of the programming process would be at odds with payola, compromising the quality of the playlist and programmer autonomy.

The forces that might encourage radio groups to reengineer their programming process are not clear, but will likely be related to increased competition for access to radio listeners. Short of major reregulation of the radio industry, competition in the industry may be increased if alternatives to commercial broadcast radio get a foothold. Satellite radio, Internet radio, and Lower Power FM (LPFM) stations may be able to draw significant numbers of listeners away from commercial broadcast stations by offering alternatives to their radio formats.

In contrast to a broadcast radio industry dominated by corporate groups and market clusters, these three variants of radio are likely more conducive to uses of the subjective and populist programming repertoires. Subscription satellite radio services like XM and Sirius offer commercial-free niche programming. According to Larry Rebich, Vice President of programming and market development for Sirius, "We are free of conventional music-programming practices. The emphasis is on music experts and knowledge of the music. Our stream designers—as we call them here—are musicologists, journalists, musicians and people who have radio programming backgrounds" (Clark, 2003, p. 1). Similarly, Internet radio (especially via wireless webcasting), a form of radio based on narrowcasting and offering a theoretically infinite variety of formats and opportunities for most anyone to create their own Internet radio station, offers more music-driven programming than radio groups are currently likely to produce.

Finally, in theory at least, if advocates of local and public radio can overcome resistance from the National Association of Broadcasters on behalf of commercial radio, LPFM stations may offer a viable alternative to commercial radio and provide fertile soil for use of the populist repertoire. However, Hamilton (2004) cautioned that the Federal Communications Commission tends to view LPFM as complementary to, rather than an alternative to, commercial radio: "By requiring and/or rewarding a bureaucratized form of organization, the LPFM proposal discourages experimentation in format, personnel, and participation" (p. 55).

Deregulation and ownership concentration have enabled radio to remain a profitable player in the new media era, but at what cost? Our research on programmers suggests that corporate control and techno-rational hegemony leave some room for multiple ways of programming music and positioning stations in markets. However, the trail that radio giants like Clear Channel are blazing seems increasingly antagonistic to this variety of approaches to music programming and perhaps even the conventional role of programmers themselves. Although it seems unlikely that commercial broadcast radio will be significantly reregulated or that ownership concentration will decrease in the near future, our research does suggest the possibility that radio can be invigorated, even in the oligopoly era, if local programmers are given the autonomy and authority to employ programming repertoires to manage station formats.

REFERENCES

Ahlkvist, J. (2001a, August). *Cookie cutter radio? Economic concentration and music programming in a large market.* Paper presented at the Pacific Sociological Association meetings, San Francisco.

Ahlkvist, J. (2001b). Programming philosophies and the rationalization of music radio. *Media, Culture and Society, 23,* 339–358.

Ahlkvist, J., & Faulkner, R. (2002). Will this record work for us? Managing music formats in commercial radio. *Qualitative Sociology, 25,* 189–215.

Ahlkvist, J., & Fisher, G. (2000). And the hits just keep on coming: Music programming standardization in commercial radio. *Poetics, 27,* 301–325.

Barnard, S. (1989). *On the radio: Music radio in Britain.* Milton Keynes, UK: Open University Press.

Barnes, K. (1988). Top 40 radio: A fragment of the imagination. In S. Frith (Ed.), *Facing the music* (pp. 8–50). New York: Pantheon.

Bates, B. J., & Chambers, T. (1999). The economic basis for radio deregulation. *Journal of Media Economics, 12,* 19–34.

Berland, J. (1990). Radio space and industrial time: Music formats, local narratives and technological mediation. *Popular Music, 9,* 179–192.

Berland, J. (1993). Radio space and industrial time: The case of music formats. In T. Bennett, S. Frith, L. Grossberg, J. Shepard, & G. Turner (Eds.), *Rock and popular music: Politics, policies, institutions* (pp. 104–118). New York: Routledge.

Berry, S. T., & Waldfogel, J. (2001). Do mergers increase product variety? Evidence from radio broadcasting. *Quarterly Journal of Economics, 116,* 1009–1025.

Boehlert, E. (2001a, May 14). Pay for play. *Salon.com.* Retrieved June 15, 2004 from http://dir.salon.com/ent/feature/2001/04/30/clear_channel/index.html

Boehlert, E. (2001b, April 30). Radio's big bully. *Salon.com.* Retrieved June 15, 2004 from http://dir.salon.com/ent/feature/2001/04/30/clear_channel/index.html

Carroll, R. L., & Davis, D. M. (1993). *Electronic media programming: Strategies and decision making.* New York: McGraw-Hill.

Chambers, T. (2003). Radio programming diversity in the era of consolidation. *Journal of Radio Studies, 10,* 33–45.

Clark, R. (2003, May 1). Radio radio! *Mix.* Retrieved June 3, 2004 from http://mixonline.com/newmedia/internetaudio_radio_radio/index.html

Denisoff, R. S. (1986). *Tarnished gold: The record industry revisited.* New Brunswick, CT: Transaction Books.

Drushel, B. (1998). The telecommunications act of 1996 and radio market structure. *Journal of Media Economics, 11,* 3–20.

Fairchild, C. (1999). Deterritorializing radio: Deregulation and the continuing triumph of the corporatist perspective in the USA. *Media, Culture and Society, 21,* 549–561.

Grenier, L. (1990). Radio broadcasting in Canada: The case of "transformat" music. *Popular Music, 9,* 221–233.

Greve, H. R. (1996). Patterns of competition: The diffusion of a market position in radio broadcasting. *Administrative Science Quarterly, 41,* 29–60.

Hamilton, J. (2004). Rationalizing dissent? Challenging conditions of low-power FM radio. *Critical Studies in Media Communication, 21,* 44–63.

Hennion, A., & Meadel, C. (1986). Programming music: Radio as mediator. *Media, Culture and Society, 8,* 281–303.

Keith, M. C. (1996). *The radio station.* Boston: Focal Press.

Lacy, S., & Riffe, D. (1994). The impact of competition and group ownership on radio news. *Journalism Quarterly, 71,* 583–593.

Ladd, J. (1991). *Radio waves: Life and revolution on the FM dial.* New York: St. Martin's Press.

Leblebici, H., Salancik, G. R., Copay, A., & King, T. (1991). Institutional change and the transformation of interorganizational fields: An organizational history of the U.S. radio broadcasting industry. *Administrative Science Quarterly, 36,* 333–364.

Loomis, K. D., & Albarran, A. B. (2004). Managing radio market clusters: Orientations of general managers. *Journal of Media Economics, 17,* 51–69.

MacFarland, D. T. (1997). *Future radio programming strategies: Cultivating listenership in the digital age.* Mahwah, NJ: Lawrence Erlbaum Associates.

Miller, J. (1992). From *radio libres* to *radio privees*: The rapid triumph of commercial networks in French local radio. *Media, Culture and Society, 14,* 261–279.

Muggleton, D. (2000). *Inside subculture: The postmodern meaning of style.* New York: Berg.

Negus, K. (1992). *Producing pop: Culture and conflict in the popular music industry.* London: Arnold.

Negus, K. (1993). Plugging and programming: Pop radio and record promotion in Britain and the United States. *Popular Music, 12,* 57–68.

Negus, K. (1999). *Music genres and corporate cultures.* New York: Routledge.

Norberg, E. (1996). *Radio programming: Tactics and strategy.* Boston: Focal Press.

Peterson, R. A. (1978). The production of cultural change: The case of contemporary country music. *Social Research, 45,* 292–314.

Peterson, R. A. (1993). The battle for classical music on the air. In J. Huggins Balfe (Ed.), *Paying the piper: Causes and consequences of art patronage* (pp. 271–286). Chicago: University of Chicago Press.

Riffe, D., & Shaw, E. F. (1990). Ownership, operating, staffing, and content of "news radio" stations. *Journalism Quarterly, 67,* 663–671.

Rothenbuhler, E. (1985). Programming decision making in popular music radio. *Communication Research, 12,* 209–232.

Rothenbuhler, E. (1987). Commercial radio and popular music: Processes of selection and factors of influence. In J. Lull (Ed.), *Popular music and communication* (pp. 78–95). Newbury Park, CA: Sage.

Rothenbuhler, E., & McCourt, T. (1992). Commercial radio and popular music: Processes of selection and factors of influence. In J. Lull (Ed.), *Popular music and communication* (2nd ed., pp. 97–114). Newbury Park, CA: Sage.

Sklar, R. (1984). *Rocking America: How the all-hit radio stations took over.* New York: St. Martin's Press.

Telecommunications Act of 1996. Public Law No. 104-104. 110 Stat. 56 (1996).

Tilly, C. (1995). *Popular contention in Great Britain, 1758-1834.* Cambridge, MA: Harvard University Press.

Turner, G. (1993). Who killed the radio star? The death of teen radio in Australia. In T. Bennett, S. Frith, L. Grossberg, J. Shepard, & G. Turner (Eds.), *Rock and popular music: Politics, policies, institutions* (pp. 142–155). New York: Routledge.

Wallis, R., & Malm, K. (1993). From state monopoly to commercial oligopoly: European broadcasting policies and popular music output over the airwaves. In T. Bennett, S. Frith, L. Grossberg, J. Shepard, & G. Turner (Eds.), *Rock and popular music: Politics, policies, institutions* (pp. 156–168). New York: Routledge.

Weber, M. (1949). *The methodology of the social sciences.* New York: Free Press.

Wirth, T. L. (2001). Nationwide format oligopolies. *Journal of Radio Studies, 8,* 249–270.

Wirth, T. L. (2002). Direct format competition on the radio dial and the telecommunications act of 1996: A five-year trend study. *Journal of Radio Studies, 9,* 33–50.

CHAPTER

11

Skating on Thin Ice: Confronting Knowledge Ambiguity in the U.S. Motion Picture Industry

Jamal Shamsie
Michigan State University

Nobody knows anything.

—William Goldman (1983, p. 39)

These words from William Goldman have been cited extensively to describe the current status of the U.S. motion picture industry. Yet it is hard to believe that people who hold positions of power within the Hollywood establishment do not have much knowledge about the development, production, marketing, and distribution of motion pictures. In view of the recent rate of turnover among the top management at most of the studios, it is not clear how anyone may be able to hold onto their position if they have not been able to gather sufficient knowledge about the workings of their own industry. If we accept that most studio executives must at least possess the knowledge that they need to survive, we must question what may have led Goldman to make such a statement.

In order to figure out the meaning of Goldman's statement, it must be pointed out that he has built a career based on writing screenplays for the Hollywood studios. He has had a lot of experience with the responses of these studio executives to the screenplays that he has pitched to them over years. He came to the realization that there are few, if any, clear guidelines for evaluating a script. This means that most of the executives running the Hollywood studios have little, if any, idea of which scripts might lead to a blockbuster film. In fact, Hollywood archives are full of examples of films such as *Star Wars, Home Alone,* and *Forrest Gump* that became huge hits for a studio that chose to pursue them only after other studios had rejected them.

Decisions can be hard to make, especially when they deal with the development of new products whose true market potential may not be known. However, there is an added aspect of ambiguity that Hollywood executives face in determining what factors can contribute to the eventual success of a film in the market. Various researchers have stressed the ambiguities and uncertainties that confront executives within such industries, particularly in terms of what will work in the market (Bjorkegren, 1996; Hirsch, 1972; Lampel, Lant, & Shamsie, 2000; Wolf, 1999). Because of the heavier experiential component of cultural products, it is harder to predict how audiences will be affected by the various attributes of the plot, characters, or setting. This makes it extremely difficult to make predictions about their overall response to a particular film.

Given this level of ambiguity and uncertainty, it is reasonable to assume that studio executives would have better knowledge if they had access to more or better information. This assumes, however, that these individuals lack information that could help them to figure out what is needed to make a film perform well in the market. Yet there is ample evidence that studio executives are in fact provided with a vast amount of new information that arrives on an almost daily basis. Trade papers provide daily information about the status of the films that are being developed or produced and about the performance of films that are already in the market.

In order to be of much use, however, this regular stream of incoming information must be organized by these individuals in some meaningful way. Knowledge can only result from the interpretation that they give to and the conclusions that they draw from the information that they receive (Boisot, 2002; Choo, 1998; Crossan, Lane, & White, 1999; Huber, 1991; Weick, 1995; Zack, 1999). But Hollywood executives usually find it difficult to assess the prospects for a film because of the relative ambiguity of most of the information that they receive. Even after a film such as *Titanic* or *Shrek* is successful, it is difficult to identify the precise factors that may have been responsible for its stellar performance.

Under these conditions, most of the knowledge that is acquired by motion picture industry executives is highly influenced by the specific information that they choose to focus on and the particular interpretation that they choose to make. It is this uncertain aspect of the knowledge that they accumulate over the years that poses problems even for the well-seasoned studio executive. Many of these executives do not feel secure or confident about any of the knowledge that they may hold. Consequently, studio executives find it hard to figure out the potential of a film when it is in planning, while it is being made, and even after it has been finished.

In fact, because of the relatively ambiguous nature of most of the information, Hollywood executives find themselves having to choose between interpretations that appear to pull in diametrically opposite directions. Any attempt to assess the relative merits of each of these different pulls can be a very difficult and time-consuming process. It is quite likely that the magnitude of this task can make motion picture industry executives experience a strong sense of paralysis.

In the next part of this chapter, we examine the most salient set of polarities that confront the studio heads as they attempt to understand what specific steps may allow them to identify the particular movies that could achieve blockbuster status. Next, we focus on some of the key developments within the U.S. motion picture industry that have made it difficult for these executives to sort through these ambiguities. In many ways, the disintegration of the old studio system has resulted in a greater need for more useful forms of tacit knowledge. At the same time, the same disintegration has also made it harder for any individual within the studios today to develop such a form of knowledge.

THE AMBIGUOUS NATURE OF INFORMATION

Although all Hollywood executives are not equally informed, most of them are not likely to be held back by their lack of information. Instead, they face their greatest challenge in trying to determine how to use the wealth of information that they have accumulated from their years of experience within the industry. The problem with the knowledge that they can derive from this information is that it often pulls them in very different directions as they attempt to assess the merits of each of the films that they are considering. As they struggle with their decisions about the films they choose to make, these executives must also try to figure out how to deal with these different pulls.

Each of the opposing directions takes the form of a polarity that represents a particular combination or set of industry realities. Studio executives must therefore make critical judgements about which set of industry realities they must base their decisions on. They must try to figure out how they can draw on this conflicting set of realities in order to make firm decisions regarding the movie projects that they are considering. In order to do this, they must find a way out of the contradictions that are represented by each set of opposing polarities. This chapter outlines a few of the most salient polarities, although there are many others.

Follow Versus Lead Market Trends

On the one hand, film executives realize the importance of following market trends. It is extremely important to follow the tastes of consumers, particularly in an industry where these tastes are quite fickle and are subject to continuous change. On the other hand, these executives are also aware that their films can help to shape consumer tastes, leading to the creation of new trends in the market. By releasing specific films into the market, the studios are not only responding to existing tastes, but are also attempting to cultivate new ones. If it is successful, a film that is sufficiently different from all others can help to create a fresh trend among movie watchers.

In recent years, many studio executives have been pushing too heavily on following existing trends, which has frequently led them to make films that are quite similar in content and that go after the same market. This has been particularly true of horror films that are targeted towards the teenage market. A category within this genre has been the "blank from hell" films. This has taken the form of the lover from hell, the nanny from hell, the roommate from hell, and the tenant from hell. Although the risks of imitating something that has already worked may be lower, there are limits to the appeal that variations on the same formula may hold for the movie audience.

The tendency to follow market trends must therefore be balanced by an attempt to create new trends. Many films do well in the marketplace because they offer something to the audience that most other current films do not. Several adult-themed films have done well because they were sufficiently different from most of the other teenage fare that was available. A serious drama or a romantic comedy can do well during a summer in which most of the movies are catering to the action-oriented youth market. War dramas such as *Courage Under Fire* and *Saving Private Ryan* or romantic comedies such as *The Bridges of Madison County* and *Notting Hill* did well because they offered an alternative to most of the typical summer fare.

It is clear that studio executives must always try to stay in touch with the market. The success of their films will be dictated by their ability to anticipate what the vast majority of consumers are looking for. But recent trends only demonstrate the particular kinds of films that have been offered and that audiences have flocked to. They do not reveal the other kinds of films that audiences may have been looking for and have not found. However, a heavy reliance on creating new trends exposes the studio to the risk of having misread the potential audience for a different kind of film. The success of studio executives therefore lies in their ability to strike a balance between the use of both of these strategies in developing their slate of films.

Attract Audiences Through Differentiation Versus Innovation

Film industry executives are usually under considerable pressure to find new ways to attract attention to the films that are being released by their own studios. Given the number of films that typically compete for audiences on any given weekend, each studio desperately needs to make its films stand out in a crowd. One of the best ways to achieve this is by differentiating their movies through some form of branding. In the motion picture industry, branding can most easily be accomplished through the creation of franchises. But the success of any franchise depends on the ability of the filmmakers to keep the audience interested enough to keep coming back. Audiences usually look for novelty in films because they are seeking new forms of experiences. Studio heads are therefore also aware that they need to be on constant lookout for films that would stand out because they try to be truly innovative by breaking some new ground.

Relying on franchises for differentiation is hard to resist in an industry where the success of most films is hard to predict. A franchise allows the studio executive to develop movies for which there is an assured audience. If it is executed well, films that build on prior successes can rework old themes, but do so in interesting new ways. This has been well illustrated by the many sequels that have done better than the originals. *Lethal Weapon 2* did much better than the first *Lethal Weapon*; *Toy Story 2* outperformed the original *Toy Story*. Similarly, some of the most successful films have either been based on characters such as James Bond and Indiana Jones or on themes such as *Star Wars* and *Star Trek*.

But studios usually find it difficult to keep coming up with fresh ideas to keep a franchise going. Without some fresh touch, such films begin to look tired and fail to provide audiences with anything that is really new. Critics constantly complain that many of the films from the Hollywood studios look similar because they stick close to old formulas. Spurred on by such criticism, studio executives know that they must also try to find films that differentiate themselves by being truly innovative. Frequently this has led them to take chances with films that have found great success because they managed to break new ground. Recent examples of such films include *Forrest Gump, Shakespeare in Love,* and *American Beauty*. Yet there are considerable risks attached to trying out truly innovative ideas in films. Their novelty makes it much more difficult to develop an effective marketing strategy and even harder to anticipate the eventual response of the audience.

What this suggests is that motion picture industry executives must strike a balance between the more subtle and the more innovative forms of differentiation within their portfolio of films. It is clearly true that much of the successes of a studio come from new twists that they can give to existing characters and themes. Although audiences do look for novelty, they also expect this novelty to be accessible and familiar. But from time to time, audiences can be captured by something that is really new. By sticking with the completely familiar, the studio head runs the risk of losing ground to rivals who are able to offer something in their films that is really fresh.

Draw on Industry Wisdom Versus Intuitive Insight

Most seasoned motion picture industry executives know too well that they must follow industry wisdom. Industry wisdom establishes general patterns that reduce the risk of decision making. By sticking close to such patterns, a studio head is less likely to be criticized for any failures. At the same time, executives who do not try to use their intuitive insight to move away from established industry patterns are also not likely to find great success. It is by making calculated departures from traditional thinking that a studio manages to create a phenomenal hit that is also highly profitable.

As the perceived uncertainty grows, movie executives are sticking closer than ever to industry wisdom. Above all, this leads them to make blockbuster films that they try to release during months when movie attendance tends to be high. This mentality has led to the rapid increase in the production and marketing costs of the average movie. These costs are largely driven by the desire on the part of studios to ensure a hit by working top stars, special effects, fast action, and exotic locations into their films. It has also led all of the studios to increasingly squeeze their big films into certain time periods of the year. A recent example of this was provided by the pitching of *The Perfect Storm* against *The Patriot* around the holiday weekend at the beginning of July.

This can be contrasted with the decision of Disney to make a movie called *The Sixth Sense* and move its opening up from fall into the last days of summer. The movie was so different from a conventional blockbuster that Disney only made it once it had a financing partner. But its decision to open it in late August when all other studios were dumping their weaker summer fare onto the screens proved to be very successful. The film made more money than most other blockbusters because it had been made relatively cheaply and with little in the way of profit participation deals.

As much as industry wisdom can provide the studio executives with much-needed guidance, spectacular successes are also the result of some meaningful insights that may be gained regarding the subjective experience of movie watchers. Individuals in high positions must make crucial decisions about where to break with established industry practices. They cannot do it often, as David Putnam quickly found out when he briefly took charge of Columbia Pictures. But they must occasionally try to do so and only when they have enough confidence in their own intuitive insights into the working of the industry. If their intuition proves to be even partly correct, they might do better than by always sticking with industry wisdom.

Use Planning Versus Adaptation as a Management Tool

Given the level of complexity and relatively high expenses that are associated with most film projects, studio heads are well aware that they must resort to planning in order to maintain some degree of control. Much publicity is given to those projects that seem to spin out of control, resulting in expenses going well beyond preestablished budgetary levels. But most film projects take a long time to complete, during which they require the collaboration of many different creative individuals at various stages. It is therefore important for the top management to accept that some degree of accommodation or adaptation is also essential in order to ensure the successful completion of each project.

There are clear reasons to maintain control over each film project. Movies such as *Heaven's Gate, Ishtar,* and *Babe 2* provide good examples of the speculator failures that can result when the studio gives too much power to individual directors. However, studio executives must also understand that excessive control may stifle the creativity that is needed to make a good movie. Much of the planning must occur around key early decisions such as the talent that is to be hired and the budget that is to be allocated. As the project gets underway, freedom has to be given to key individuals to use their creativity to shape the film.

Most seasoned film industry executives are aware that successful films typically represent the result of an effective collaboration between several different creative people. Even a classic such as *The Wizard of Oz* was the result of the creative ideas that came from several screenwriters, whose filming was directed by five different directors who worked at various stages of the film, all of which were supervised by as many as three producers. The film clearly benefited from the ability of the studio to draw on the creative abilities of all of these individuals. Although there was a great deal of planning, much of the project simply evolved within certain carefully defined parameters.

Film making is a highly ambiguous and uncertain activity. Nobody really knows what makes a film successful, although it is clear that it always requires a certain minimum level of creativity. Under these conditions, some amount of planning is essential to define some of the key parameters of each film project. Without the laying of some ground rules, the project runs the risk of getting out of control. But beyond this, the studio head must be able to allow the creative talent to gradually develop the film on the basis of their collective vision.

Frame Strategic Decisions Broadly Versus Narrowly

In this world of media conglomerates, studio executives are well aware that each film can be used to create several different streams of revenue through exploiting its content in many forms across many markets. They must therefore make their decisions regarding the films that they choose to make with these potential opportunities in mind. But these individuals must also accept that the performance of their films in domestic theaters is a key determinant of the revenue streams that will be generated from all other sources. A film that is clearly viewed as having bombed in its initial theatrical release is likely to produce much lower overall returns to the studio.

In other words, there are clear benefits to thinking more broadly about the prospects of each film that is being considered by the movie industry executive. Today, films can hardly just be regarded as films. It is just as important to think about the possibilities of different revenue streams that can be generated by a reasonably successful movie. The huge worldwide success of Disney's *The Lion King* in theaters, on video, and on television paved the way. Disney even did well with sales of the film's soundtrack, with sales of assorted merchandise, and with its adaptation into a Broadway play. This has led most studio heads to be more inclined to give the go-ahead to those films whose success can be exploited in other forms by the other business units.

At the same time, the focus can never really move away from thinking narrowly about how well a film will actually work when it is initially released into theaters. A film has to work as a film in theaters before it can work anywhere else. Without this foundation to build on, all other revenue streams begin to dry up. This means great attention has to be given to the details that will help with the successful execution of an appealing concept or idea. As mentioned earlier, the studio has to ensure that many different components will work well together throughout a lengthy and cumbersome process to actually transfer an interesting idea into a film that audiences would want to see. Once the audience enjoys the experience of viewing a film in theaters, they will be motivated to revisit this experience in many other forms.

In other words, the studio head must resist the pressure from the media conglomerates to simply produce content that can feed its growing pipelines. Content per se is not valuable. Content becomes valuable only if there is large enough audience that wants to see it. What makes content work for audiences is not just a high concept or a brilliant idea, but a concept or an idea that is executed well. Again, this suggests that studio executives must think narrowly about what would make a movie work as a movie while they also think more broadly about the various other ways they can exploit its success.

RISING ABOVE THE AMBIGUITY

As mentioned earlier, studio executives have to make critical decisions on a regular basis about the specific films that they will move ahead with. They need to have a full line-up of films that they can use to compete for the box office revenues that are generated each year. In order to make these decisions, studio heads have to gather the relevant information and then convert this into a practical form of knowledge that can actually guide their decision making (Choo, 1998; Dervin, 1992; March & Olsen, 1976; Weick, 1979, 1995). Although information must be assembled, interpreted, and applied, these sequential processes are actually highly interconnected.

In the case of cultural products such as films, however, each one of these may be viewed as a separate product that can be distinguished from all others along many dimensions. In the broadest possible terms, movies differ from each other in the type of genre they represent, the appeal of the talent that they use, and the basic elements of the story line. In order to evaluate the potential for success of any movie, these different aspects of a movie have to be considered individually as well as collectively. What is the potential of the particular genre? What is the appeal of the top star? Can this star do well within this genre? Such a process of evaluating movies can be extremely time consuming without much of a guarantee for producing results.

In the face of these difficulties, most of the Hollywood executives have been searching for simple rules that may allow them to avoid the difficult process of having to take apart and critically examine the various components of each movie in order to assess its potential for success in the market. This has led to a growing reliance on explicit forms of knowledge that is likely to be shared by most of the studios within the industry (Grant, 1996; Matusik & Hill, 1998). The problem with this approach, as we have already pointed out, lies with the difficulties in the interpretation of information at the industry level. There are sufficient examples to support various explanations for the basic elements that lie behind the development of a successful movie.

In many ways, most of the information at the industry level suggests that the many different forces that can explain the success of a particular film often tend to run counter to each other. For the sake of simplicity, studio heads try to deal with this by selecting one of these explanations over the other. More careful scrutiny of these forces would reveal that both of these apparently opposing explanations are likely to be valid. But this would force these executives to take into account the many differences, both subtle and not so subtle, that may exist between the different movies that the studios turn out over the course of each year.

It is possible to argue that, to some extent, the relative absence of any useful tacit knowledge about the market potential of any given film has resulted from a couple of developments in the U.S. motion picture industry. On the one hand, the disintegration of the so-called vertically integrated studio system has resulted in a greater need for studio executives to develop and use tacit forms of knowledge that can usually be derived from their own experiences within their particular firms. At the same time, the disintegration of the studio system has made it more difficult for executives to create and apply such a form of knowledge in order to guide their decision making.

Loss of Effective Control

As mentioned earlier, the key challenge that faces top executives in the motion picture industry today lies in the way that they must deal with the contradictory nature of the information on which much of their knowledge is based. But this problem is hardly new. Studio executives have had to make critical decisions based on knowledge that is highly ambiguous and relatively uncertain since the emergence of the industry. However, even though the nature of this knowledge has not changed, the dependence of these executives on this knowledge has become much more critical.

During the so-called studio system, motion picture industry executives were better equipped to deal with the ambiguity and uncertainty that was associated with their knowledge. Several factors had converged to provide them with a greater amount of control over their firm and their industry (Gomery, 1991; Mast, 1992; Miller & Shamsie, 1996; Schatz, 1988). To begin with, each of the studios had various types of talent locked up for many years under long-term contracts. They were able to discover the best possible uses for this talent and to extract value through using them in a similar way for several years. The biggest studios also had exclusive access to the most profitable theaters in the country, which represented the only distribution outlets at the time for all kinds of films. Finally, all of the firms could count on a high level of demand for films, as audiences had few alternatives available to them for their entertainment.

Today, studio executives operate in a dramatically different environment. Their control over their firm and over their environment is much more precarious. They must continuously strive to attract talent and can only hold on to them by giving them greater autonomy and better financial deals. Their films must derive revenues from multiple sources in many different markets, making access to the market a much more difficult issue. Securing various forms of distribution in each market has become essential in order to squeeze the greatest possible revenues out of each film. And in most cases, audiences face an ever-increasing array of choices for their entertainment needs, making it harder to attract them to movies.

The dramatic shift in control has made it much more difficult for studio heads to be able to make key decisions. They can no longer fall back on resources that they have acquired or developed within their firm or on markets that are easy to cater to and whose tastes might be easier to identify. They are not as familiar with the critical resources on which they rely for the success of each movie because they are rarely able to hold on to them for the long term. Finally, because of increasing importance of a growing number of distribution channels in a multitude of markets, they need to try to keep in touch with the changing market for films through tapping into multiple sources of information both inside and outside their firm.

On the whole, their decision making has become much riskier given their lack of visible control. With far fewer controls at their disposal, motion picture industry executives are even more heavily dependent on various forms of information in order to make critical decisions about the films that they pursue. Each film that they approve represents a gamble that they are taking and that they hope will work. Under the weight of such pressures, they would like to be more certain about the knowledge that they hold.

Lack of Tacit Knowledge

This need for a greater level of certainty is unlikely to be met by the reliance on explicit forms of knowledge that circulates across the industry. Knowledge that is formed at the industry level tends to be rather ambiguous in the motion picture industry, given that there are several possible methods to increase the commercial potential of a film. On the surface, many of these appear to be contradictory, requiring these executives to try to pick one of these approaches over the other.

In order to move away from such pressures, studio heads must try to develop a more tacit body of knowledge that is created within the firm. Knowledge creation can best be viewed as an attempt by a group of individuals to create some sense of their own specific external environment (Crossan et al., 1999; Grant, 1996; Huber, 1991). In this process of sense making, individuals try to determine what information they must focus on, how they should interpret this information, and the way that it should be applied. The manner in which individuals make choices is highly subjective, which led Weick (1979) to develop the concept of enactment.

In order to move in this direction, Hollywood executives must focus on the various elements of each film in deciding how or why they might work in the market. Some films may be successful in drawing back audiences to a genre that may have lost its appeal. *Chicago* was successful in reviving an interest in musicals. *Gladia-*

tor was similarly successful in demonstrating the potential for historical films. A well-developed plot, interesting characters, and appealing cast can allow such movies to do well at the box office, especially if they are released at a time of the year when they will face less intense competition. But these movies were not successful simply because they offered up a fresh genre, but because they possessed specific attributes that managed to attract audiences to a genre that may otherwise have had less appeal. The more recent example of *Troy* clearly indicates that the use of a historical setting was not enough to emulate the success of *Gladiator.*

Other movies may offer more potential to be developed into a franchise that could lead to a series of films that build on each other's success. In many cases, it may be possible to generate additional revenues from books, music, video games, and other merchandise based on these films. But it requires some effort to figure out how and why sequels may work. Although studio executives have begun to bank on the success of a movie that is based on an earlier success, many sequels fail to live up to their promise. A sequel generally works only if the story can be developed further with some additional fresh elements. For every *Spiderman 2* or *Shrek 2*, there are many others such as *Speed 2* or *Charlie's Angels 2* that fail to generate much of the expected interest from audiences.

When knowledge is developed and applied by individuals in this manner, it tends to move away from the simple rules that typically result from efforts to speed up decision making. Furthermore, this subjective interpretation of information at the tacit level can lead to a more useful form of knowledge. It can result in a more fluid, dynamic, and open process of knowledge creation (Boisot, 2002; Crossan et al., 1999; Davenport & Prusak, 1998; Nonaka & Takeuchi, 1995). Individuals can focus on different pieces of information, combine them in various ways, and give them new meanings. In creative arenas such as the motion picture industry, this is the form of knowledge that may serve as a better guide for executives to make their critical decisions about what films they should make.

Absence of Managerial Vision

Many studios suffer from the relative lack of tacit knowledge that has been developed from the actual experiences of the firm. To some extent, this loss can be attributed back to the disintegration of the old studio system. The studios have begun to focus for the most part on the initial financing and development and the eventual marketing and distribution of films. They have moved away from the actual production of their films, relegating this crucial activity to a host of smaller production companies. Sony Pictures, in fact, recently contracted with Revolution Studios to deliver most of the movies that they will offer.

This trend on the part of the studios to distance themselves from the actual process of making films has clearly resulted in the loss of some of the crucial tacit knowledge about what makes a particular movie work (Conner & Prahalad, 1996; Helfat, 1997; Lampel & Shamsie, 2003). The development of a successful movie must be viewed as a craft that requires some degree of hands-on experience. It is through this type of experience that managers in firms can develop the subjective know-how, insights, and intuitions that can provide them with some valuable tacit knowledge over time.

The Hollywood studios could have compensated for this by concentrating on the development of a strong and stable management team that would have worked consistently with a set of production firms as their partners. Working together, each studio would have developed a better sense of the kinds of films that they were developing and obtained a greater understanding of why some of their films were more successful than others. In the old Hollywood, each of the studios was headed by a strong visionary leader such as Louis B. Mayer, Darryl Zanuck, or Harry Cohn who worked with other prominent in-house talent to select the movies that they would develop, market, and distribute each year. Some form of tacit knowledge was likely to be developed within each of these firms as a result of their own particular shared experiences over time (Choo, 1998; Crossan et al., 1999; Grant, 1996; Nonaka & Takeuchi, 1995). These would result from the regular interaction between a relatively stable group of individuals who were involved in the movie development and selection process.

However, as industry observers will be keen to point out, the studios have moved away from such a form of visionary leadership. To begin with, power is more likely to be shared among several individuals, many of whom may change on a regular basis. Critical decisions about which movies will be made are debated at many levels within the studio, resulting in a process that can often take several years. Over that period, many elements of the film, such as talent involved with it and even the story line and characters, can change several times.

Due to these conditions, a film is not likely to move ahead unless the risks that are attached to it can be minimized. But this can more easily be accomplished through reliance on a more explicit form of knowledge that has gained considerable acceptance within the industry. As Zack (1999) pointed out, the more implicit type of knowledge tends to be subconsciously understood and applied because it is particularly difficult to articulate. This makes it harder for studio executives to explain or justify their decisions to various boards or committees.

There are still some examples of strong individuals who may be able to sort their way through the conflicting information to develop and pursue their own particular vision of the kind of movies that they should support. Bill Mechanic, who ran 20th Century Fox for several years, was one such individual. He was the kind of man who really wanted to strike a meaningful balance in his decisions. Mechanic made more conventional fare such as *Independence Day*, but took chances with films like *There's Something About Mary*. He knew he had to use his authority to ensure that *Titanic* did not self-destruct, but he compromised by allowing James Cameron to release a version that was much longer than the studio had stipulated. And he weighed several different elements as he struggled with his decisions to make movies that other studios would have been reluctant to back, such as *Waiting to Exhale* and *Fight Club*.

It is possible that people like Mechanic take too many chances. A string of high-budget disasters such as *Fight Club, Anna and the King,* and *Titan A. E.* does raise some questions about the costs of his mistakes. Mechanic resigned from his post in large part because of the losses that the Fox studio racked up from these bad choices. But shortly before he left, Mechanic pronounced that the studio system was broken. There is little doubt that he was referring to the extremely difficult position that most Hollywood executives tend to find themselves in today. They must move quickly to firm up their knowledge about how to generate a string of successful films, but tend to be given little room to make mistakes.

However, without the chance to develop and test the effectiveness of subjective tacit knowledge, motion picture executives are much more likely to deal with the ambiguity and uncertainty of their information by choosing to play it safe. In terms of the polarities, however, playing it safe implies that they are pulled completely in one of the directions at the expense of the other. This means following the market instead of trying to lead it. It also means sticking with differentiation rather than risking innovation, trying to make a movie by a blueprint rather than by allowing it to develop, staying close to industry traditions rather than pursuing intuitive hunches, and thinking of a movie as a revenue stream rather than as a movie that people may really want to see.

More so than ever before, today's studio heads must be supported in trying to develop tacit knowledge within their teams in order to find a suitable balance between the pressures that can pull them in completely different directions. Without this support, more and more of the motion picture executives are likely to be pulled toward protecting themselves by sticking with what is more certain although it may not produce any memorable films. In the process, they will be giving up on taking chances with groundbreaking films such as *It's a Wonderful Life* and *Casablanca* that will continue to attract audiences for many generations.

REFERENCES

Bjorkegren, D. (1996). *The culture business.* London: Routledge.

Boisot, M. (2002). The creation and sharing of knowledge. In C. W. Choo & N. Bontis (Eds.), *The strategic management of intellectual capital and organizational knowledge* (pp. 65–78). New York: Oxford University Press.

Choo, C. W. (1998). *The knowing organization: How organizations use knowledge to construct meaning, create knowledge, and make decisions.* New York: Oxford University Press.

Conner, K. R., & Prahalad, C. K. (1996). A resource-based theory of the firm: Knowledge versus opportunism. *Organization Science, 7,* 519–532.

Crossan, M. M., Lane, H. W., & White, R. E. (1999). An organizational learning framework: From intuition to institution. *Academy of Management Review, 24,* 522–537.

Davenport, T. H., & Prusak, L. (1998). *Working knowledge: How organizations manage what they know.* Boston: Harvard Business School Press.

Dervin, B. (1992). From the mind's eye of the "user": The sense-making qualitative-quantitative methodology. In J. D. Glazier & R. R. Powell (Eds.), *Qualitative research in information management* (pp. 61–84). Englewood, CO: Libraries Unlimited.

Goldman, W. (1983). *Adventures in the screen trade.* New York: Warner Books.

Gomery, D. (1991). *Movie history: A survey.* Belmont, CA: Wadsworth.

Grant, R. M. (1996). Toward a knowledge-based view of the firm. *Strategic Management Journal, 17,* 109–122.

Helfat, C. (1997). Know-how and asset complementarily and dynamic capability accumulation. *Strategic Management Journal, 18,* 339–360.

Hirsch, P. (1972). Processing fads and fashions: An organization-set analysis of cultural industry system. *American Journal of Sociology, 77,* 639–659.

Huber, G. P. (1991). Organizational learning: The contributing processes and the literatures. *Organization Science, 2,* 88–115.

Lampel, J., & Shamsie, J. (2003). Capabilities in motion: New organizational forms and the reshaping of the Hollywood film industry. *Journal of Management Studies, 40,* 2189–2210.

Lampel, J., Lant, T., & Shamsie, J. (2000). Balancing act: Learning from organizing practices in cultural industries. *Organization Science, 11,* 263–269.

March, J. G., & Olsen, J. P. (1976). *Ambiguity and choice in organizations.* Bergen, Norway: Universitetsforlaget.

Mast, G. (1992). *A short history of the movies* (Rev. ed.). New York: Macmillan.

Matusik, S. F., & Hill, C. W. L. (1998). The utilization of contingent work, knowledge creation and competitive advantage. *Academy of Management Review, 23,* 680–697.

Miller, D., & Shamsie, J. (1996). The resource-based view of the firm in two environments: The Hollywood film studios from 1936 to 1965. *Academy of Management Journal, 39,* 519–543.

Nonaka, I., & Takeuchi, H. (1995). *The knowledge-creating company: How Japanese companies create the dynamics of innovation.* New York: Oxford University Press.

Schatz, T. (1988). *The genius of the system.* New York: Holt.

Weick, K. E. (1979). *The social psychology of organizing.* New York: Random House.

Weick, K. E. (1995). *Sensemaking in organizations.* Thousand Oaks, CA: Sage.

Wolf, M. J. (1999). *The entertainment economy: How mega-media forces are transforming our lives.* New York: Times Books.

Zack, M. H. (1999). Managing codified knowledge. *Sloan Management Review, 21,* 45–53.

IV

The Role of Technology

Cultural industries are subject to frequent bouts of nostalgia for a time when technology was simpler and easier to handle. Audiophiles shop for turntables and vacuum tube amplifiers, all the while declaring vinyl records to be musically superior to compact disks. Movie stars reject the screen for the immediacy of live audiences on Broadway or West End stage. And television producers relinquish the security of prerecording and editing for the dangers of live television. Inevitably the impulse wanes and nostalgia gives way to realism: The audiophiles enthusiastically resume their love affair with new sound-reproduction technologies, movie stars rediscover the advantages of reaching a global audience, and television producers forego the excitement of live television for the flexibility of being able to reshoot and edit.

The relationship of cultural industries to technology has always been one of ambivalence. Artists, managers, and consumers love what technology can do for them, but they also distrust what technology can do to them. Technology is valued as the great enabler. It makes possible the rise of cultural industries in the first place, it provides the tools for artistic creation, and it supplies the means for reaching far and wide. But technology is also feared. It is feared for the way it often undermines established business patterns, it is feared for reducing the value of skills, and it is feared simply for the uncertainty that it can create.

Ambivalence usually begets anxiety. In the case of cultural industries, ambivalence about technology creates anxiety about the control of intellectual property rights. Technology clearly represents a force that facilitates the creation and distribution of cultural products. But technology can also open the way for the unauthorized use and misappropriation of copyrighted products that are a central pillar of the industry's wealth.

The three chapters in this section show that, faced with the unintended consequences of technology, owners of property rights in the cultural industries have traditionally sought to reassert control by resorting to a variety of legal, political, technological, and business strategies. In almost every instance these strategies have been misguided and ultimately doomed to failure. But as all three chapters suggest, there is no indication that the lessons of history are likely to change the thinking and behavior of the individuals and managers who wish to maintain the status quo in the face of rapidly changing technologies.

In chapter 12, Jones examines not only the unintended impact of technology on the evolution of the film industry, but also the unintended consequences of early industry pioneers fighting to maintain their control over the industry. Jones shows how battles over patent rights during the very early days of the film industry initially reinforced industry consensus about technology as the dominant source of advantage in the industry.

After enduring and costly legal battles, the main holders of the rights to the film technology decided to pool their patents. Having set their differences aside, pioneers who owed their success primarily to their technology saw the increase in demand for films as an opportunity to reap greater rewards by carefully restricting access to this technology. Faced with the widespread unlicensed use of their technology, members of the patents pool—or trust as they were known at the time—engaged in concerted efforts to attack independent producers and exhibitors who operated outside their group.

These efforts were ultimately fruitless, but they had two unintended consequences. First, by focusing their efforts on maintaining control of their technology, members of the trust lost sight of the creative potential of film as an artistic medium. Second, their vigorous assault on independent producers and exhibitors encouraged these new entrants to develop strategies that bypassed the trust's control. When the dust settled, most of the technological pioneers were out of business and the independent producers and exhibitors became part of the dominant oligopoly that formed what became known as the Hollywood motion picture industry. The cornerstone of the Hollywood motion picture industry has been and still is the control of content rather than the control of technology.

In chapter 13, Dowd explores the relationship between control of technology and control of content from another perspective. He shows how producers of cultural products, in this case record companies, use their control of technology to maintain control of content. Dowd explores the successive generations of technical designs used to capture and deliver recorded music. Throughout this technological evolution, the companies that owned the intellectual property rights to the music were firmly convinced that free access to their music—via radio, private recording of music, or music file swapping on the Internet—should be resisted and if possible stopped altogether.

The chronicle of these efforts go back to the 1930s when record companies engaged in concerted efforts in the courts and in the U.S. Congress to prevent radio stations from playing prerecorded music on the air. By contrast, the record companies embraced jukeboxes precisely because they allowed for control and monitoring of music in public areas. It was only the entry and subsequent success of Capitol Records that demonstrated to the industry that, contrary to conventional wisdom, playing records on the air increased rather than decreased sales.

The symbiotic relationship between free airplay and record sales, to which the industry owes its explosive growth in the last 50 years, should have changed attitudes, but this has not been the case. The lessons of the battle against the emerging radio industry have not been applied to private recording of music, or to the more recent advent of music file swapping over the Internet. Both are seen as threats to property rights, and both are resisted with all the massive financial and political resources that are at the disposal of the large record companies.

Finally, in chapter 14, Lant and Hewlin also look at the relationship between content and technology as a disruptive force, but this time from the perspective of a rising rather than an established industry. The paper explores the rise of Silicon Alley, a cluster of New York City firms dedicated to the creation and distribution of digital media. The rise of Silicon Alley was greatly facilitated by the emergence of CD-ROMs as the primary vehicle for delivering digital media. From the point of view of intellectual property rights, CD-ROMs have the same advantage as records in the music industry. They must be bought as discrete units, and their distribution and sale can be easily managed and monitored, and in addition, they can be designed to prevent easy reproduction, a feature that ensures against piracy.

Above all, however, the use of CD-ROMs as the main vehicle for delivering digital content concentrates power in the hands of the publisher. Providers of content may be dispersed, but when it comes to putting together the final CD-ROM the publisher acts as a creative and commercial hub for the final product. The hub function of publishers encourages the formation of clusters. This pattern is familiar to record companies and book publishers and it is a pattern that seemed to be shaping the evolution of the multimedia industry.

Unfortunately, as Lant and Hewlin suggest, the evolution of this pattern was aborted by the rise of the Internet in the late 1990s. The Internet provided a far cheaper and more effective means of distributing digital media. It did away with the need for physically embedding digital content for purposes of delivery, and in the process practically eliminated the role of publishers as hubs. Confronting the loss of distinct advantage, Silicon Alley began to cast about for a new role and a new identity. Lant and Hewlin show how members of Silicon Alley use their proximity to one of the most powerful media concentrations in the world, the New York newspaper and broadcasting cluster, to promote their image as a cluster with unique content-creating capabilities. This chapter leaves one with the distinct impression that this sustained attempt at differentiating New York digital content creators from the rest of the world is not likely to succeed.

However, a close reading of all three chapters suggests that, when it comes to examining the role of technology in cultural industries, unintended consequences of radical changes have been the rule rather than the exception. Assessing the impact of technology on content—and vice versa—is a guessing game that defies even the experts. What is certain, as these chapters persuasively demonstrate, is that attempting to use technology to maintain control over content is in the long run doomed to failure.

CHAPTER

12

From Technology to Content: The Shift in Dominant Logic in the Early American Film Industry

Candace Jones
Boston College

The history of cultural industries is littered with successful incumbents who, failing to see or respond to dramatic shifts in their competitive landscapes, were replaced by newcomers. In essence, cultural industries showcase how one dominant logic—the means and practices for achieving desired goals (Bacharach, Bamberger, & Sonnenstuhl, 1996; Prahalad & Bettis, 1986)—is replaced by another dominant logic. For example, early technology firms, which dominated the film industry from 1895 to 1911, dismissed the importance of films containing stories and stars, only to be replaced by content firms that focused on stories and stars and attracted larger audiences (Jones, 2001). In publishing, firms shifted from a craft to business logic (Thornton, 2002), replacing CEOs and executives in doing so (Thornton & Ocasio, 1999). In the music industry, country music was ignored as a viable genre until new consumer tracking of products made explicit to decision makers its popularity with consumers (Anand & Peterson, 2000). In short, dominant players were unable to see the value of resources and alternative strategies that newer entrants brought into the industry and how these resources and strategies shifted the basis of competitive advantage.

Why is it that dominant players are unable to see and adapt to shifts in their environments, opening the door for new players who eventually replace them? Managerial attention is a scarce resource (Ocasio, 1997), creating competitive blindspots or judgmental mistakes (Zajac & Bazerman, 1991), when attention is restricted to existing competitors and practices. Two conditions are likely to focus incumbents' managerial attention on existing resources and practices: intense rivalry among dominant firms and shared career backgrounds of top decision makers.

Intense rivalry among established competitors means that firms possess similar resource endowments and have similar products and customers (Chen, 1996). Given their resource, product, and customer overlap, they are aware of and focus their attention on one another. When their rivalry is intense, they reduce their scanning of the environment and focus on maintaining their position within an already-established group; thus, they are less likely to see as rivals competitors who possess different resource endowments, allowing newcomers to get established and more easily alter the rules of competition. Industry evolution is driven by an ecology of competition, where actions taken by one firm have implications for actions taken by rivals (Huygens, Baden-Fuller, Van Den Bosch, & Volberda, 2001), creating community rather than individual firm competitive processes (Mezias & Kuperman, 2000).

Careers are a form of environmental imprinting (Boeker, 1988; Stinchcombe, 1965) because a career is a "repository of knowledge" (Bird, 1994) that shapes what problems are seen and how these problems should be resolved. When top decision makers share similar career backgrounds, they enact similar organizational strategies and share logics of actions (Bacharach et al., 1996; Boeker; Fligstein, 1991). The more similar the dominant players' backgrounds, the more likely they are to interact in industry forums, build overlapping social networks, and develop taken-for-granted rules of competition, creating an industry macroculture that may be maladaptive (Abrahamson & Fombrun, 1994). When tacit rules are shared among dominant players, alternatives are neither seen nor imagined (Scott, 1995). Because careers link persons to institutional fields through occupations and organizations, careers provide insight into how stability and change within industries and institutions occur (Jones & Dunn, in press).

We use a case study of the film industry from 1895 to 1920 as it shifted from technology to content to explore how rivalry of industry incumbents focused attention on established competitors, ignoring newcomers and new resources, and how careers imprinted particular logics of action that were hard to alter. Both rivalry and careers restricted the attention of dominant technology firms, leading them to dismiss changes in consumer preferences. Once new competitors and resources gained enough momentum to come into incumbents' awareness, incumbents actively resisted them. However, incumbents' inertia to changes in industry allowed a new community of players to become established and shift institutional logics (Mezias & Kuperman, 2000). This dynamic led to competitive obsolescence by technology firms and their replacement by content providers within the early American film industry.

FROM TECHNOLOGY TO CONTENT: RIVALRY AND CAREERS AS SOURCES OF INCUMBENT INERTIA

To understand how rivalry and careers coevolve with an industry and become a source of incumbent inertia, we place competitive moves among firms within their historical context. The American film industry experienced a shift from technology to content, which was driven by two types of entrepreneurs: technology and content. These entrepreneurs became rivals from 1909 to 1916, battling for control over the industry (this synopsis of industry history is drawn from Jones, 2001). We examine their intense rivalry and how their careers determined those to whom incumbents attended.

Sources of Incumbent Inertia: Rivalry as Focusing Firms' Attention

The industry shift from technology to content was reflected in perceptions of who were rivals at different points in time. Rivalry refers to the microprocesses of specific moves and countermoves of one firm against another, whereas competition refers to generic industry- or market-level phenomenon (Chen, 1996). Litigation is one type of move. Litigation over patent, copyright, and trademark infringements were prevalent during the industry's early history, allowing us to identify rivalry and shifts in rivalry among firms.

As can be seen in Table 12.1, before 1909, rivalry, in terms of litigation, occurred primarily between technology firms. Data about litigation information came from Musser (1990), the Edison Archives at Rutgers University and Bowser (1994). From 1910 to 1918, rivalry shifted to technology versus content firms, which competed with one another for control of the industry. The time periods of 1895 to 1918 are compared in Table 12.1 because after 1920, most technology firms had exited the industry.

TABLE 12.1
Firm Rivalry Over Time: Competitive Moves Through Litigation

Rivalry	1895–1908	1909–1918	Total
Technology-technology	93	4	97
Technology-content	9	23	32
Content-content	0	1	1
Total	102	28	130

Table 12.1 shows the shift in rivalry and competitive dynamics, which raises the question of what precipitates the awareness of a rival by a focal firm. To understand when and how technology entrepreneurs shifted their rivalry from one another to content entrepreneurs, we need to understand the intense rivalry among technology entrepreneurs.

For technology entrepreneurs, Edison's practices set the industry's initial trajectory and defined who was considered a rival. In December 1897, Edison launched patent infringement suits against every major competitor and exhibitor, arguing that anyone who used film equipment needed to pay him a royalty (Musser, 1990). Edison attempted to control anyone who used film equipment; his rivalry was seen in the extensiveness of his patent litigation. Edison, it should be noted, purchased rather than invented most of these patents (Musser, 1990, 1991) and much of his legal wrangling involved attempts to control the benefits from technological solutions. Edison's most intensive competitive moves were against technical entrepreneurs who could develop alternatives to the technological solutions he sought to control through patent rights.

Each of Edison's patent infringement suits was met by a countermove of his archrival Biograph, run by his former employee W. K. L. Dickson. Biograph and Edison held approximately 28% and 17% of the market respectively. They were the first two entrants, and also held key patents in film technology. In December 1901 the lower court upheld Edison's claims. Biograph, Edison's main competitor, appealed. In March 1902, Judge Wallace of the Court of Appeals supported Biograph, dismissing Edison's patent right. He declared, "It is obvious that Mr. Edison was not a pioneer" (Musser, 1991, p. 196). Edison reissued patents and appealed the Biograph decision. Litigation rampaged until 1907, when the United States Appellate Court ruled that "the moving picture apparatus of all the numerous companies in this country, with one exception, is an infringement on the patents covered by the Edison Co." (Musser, p. 334). The one exception was Biograph, which used a friction-feed system invented by Edison's prior employee W. K. L. Dickson.

Paradoxically, the intense rivalries among technology entrepreneurs, seen in their lawsuits, became the basis for collaboration. Judge Dickson noted that "their desire to allay bickerings and recriminations among themselves" (*United States v. Motion Picture Patents Co.*, 1915, p. 808) was a motive for forming the industry's first strategic network. Initially Edison tried to exclude Biograph from participating in a jointly held trust, hoping to put his former employee and nemesis out of business. However, Biograph held too much of the market to be excluded (Musser, 1991). Reluctantly, Edison allowed Biograph to join the Trust as an equal partner.

In January 1909, almost 2 years after the lawsuit granting Edison and Biograph equal status and patent rights, 10 firms holding 16 key patents pooled their patents, forming the Motion Picture Patents Company or "Trust" (called the "Trust" because patents were held in trust). The Trust's members operated as independent entities but coordinated their production. The reduction in lawsuits and enhanced coordination of production radically increased film product from these 10 firms. Their combined output went from 598 films in 1906, to 1,287 in 1907, 2,227 in

1908, 2,821 in 1909, and 3,128 in 1910. Finally, the technology entrepreneurs could focus their attention on production rather than their rivalry and competition amongst themselves.

By this time, however, content entrepreneurs had moved backward in the value chain; their production of films equaled that of technology entrepreneurs in 1910. By 1910 technology and content entrepreneurs had extensive overlap in their resource similarity, bringing them into awareness of one another as rivals. As technology and content entrepreneurs moved into greater resource similarity and imitation of one another, their rivalry shifted from within groups to between groups. Initially, technology entrepreneurs were so consumed with their in-group rivalry that new competitors and resources did not enter their awareness as a force until their within-group rivalry had been resolved and their new competitors had moved into greater resource similarity.

These historical events allow us to understand how intense within-group rivalry may fuel an incumbent's inertia, delaying competitive responses to a new group of entrepreneurs with competing logics because incumbents focus on similar rivals until it is often too late to combat new rivals effectively. Next, we examine how similar careers are a form of cultural imprinting, shaping who and what is attended to and how this influenced incumbent inertia.

Sources of Incumbent Inertia: Careers as Cultural Imprinting

The American film industry was born in 1895 when social trends of extensive innovations in mass communication (e.g., telegraph, stock ticker, phonograph, and telephone; Musser, 1990) opened new opportunities and technically skilled entrepreneurs entered to take advantage of these opportunities. Entrepreneurs who cultivated opportunities and claimed value from these technical challenges had specific skill sets, reflected in their careers before entering the industry. The first three American entrants and dominant industry members—Biograph, Edison, and Lubin—came from careers in manufacturing; indeed, most early entrepreneurs called their firms "manufacturers" (Bowser, 1994). Of the first 12 entrants into the film industry, 5 were technically oriented (e.g., inventors, optician) with manufacturing backgrounds (see Table 12.2).

Because the context of the emerging industry was one of resolving technical challenges in film equipment and stock, film content was of secondary importance to dominant technology firms. These entrepreneurs had logics of action steeped in gaining efficiencies and emphasizing volume and product turnover. Films were undifferentiated product and treated as a commodity; they were sold by price per foot regardless of quality or cost of production. Films were short and simple snapshots of life events (e.g., coronations, train wrecks) or staged events (e.g., a couple dancing, a woman tossing her salad), called "actualities." However, starting in about 1904, consumer preferences started to shift toward a narrative content: pictures that told a story.

The social trend of immigration is important for understanding why film content changed from actualities to narratives. Because immigrants did not share a common

TABLE 12.2
Careers of Top Eight Technology and Content Entrepreneurial Firms

Entrepreneur	Entry	Founders' Careers
Technology	Equipment and production: 1893–1903	63% (5 of 8) Manufacturer or inventor
	Distribution: 1909	37% (3 of 8) theater
	Exhibition: never	
Content	Exhibition: 1903–1907	50% (4 of 8) retail
	Distribution: 1909–1914[a]	25% (2 of 8) film distribution or production
	Production: 1909–1916	25% (2 of 8) other

[a]In 1909 Carl Laemmle set up IMP, which was the forerunner to Universal. He released his first film in October 1909. In 1914 William Hodgkinson founded Paramount, the first firm to provide national distribution of films.

language (the three largest immigrant groups came from Germany, Russia, and Italy), they needed an easily understandable form of story telling, which is a narrative. From 1903 through 1907 immigration rates peaked at 12% of the population; this increase in immigration coincided with increased consumer preferences for narratives. For example, Edison's production records reveal that from 1904 to 1907, his firm sold acted films at 3.5 the rate of actualities (Musser, 1990, p. 375). Narrative films exemplified by dramas went from 67% of films in 1907 to 96% in 1908 and 97% in 1909 (Allen, 1985, p. 78), culminating in the feature film, which became the industry standard by 1912 (Bowser, 1994). Immigrants also became exhibitors within film, primarily because film was a new industry that served immigrants, providing greater opportunities relative to established industries (Balio, 1985; Bowser, 1994; Gabler, 1988). Immigrants were an important audience for films, making exhibition the fastest growing sector of the market. Nickelodeons, where films were shown, mushroomed from 350 in 1905 to 3,500 in 1908 (Balio), becoming the dominant outlet for films between 1905 and 1914 (Merritt, 1985). Nickelodeons were associated with ghetto dwellers—immigrants and blue-collar workers (Merritt).

Although the Trust, which controlled movie production and exhibition through its patent rights (e.g., the making or showing of a movie required patent permission), had seen skyrocketing demand for movies, it licensed only about two thirds of exhibitors, believing that demand would stabilize and that it could control the market (Balio, 1985; Musser, 1991). This was a strategic miscalculation. From 1909 to 1913, the number of independent movie theaters surged from 2,500 screens to 8,306 (330%), whereas Trust-licensed theaters increased 4,000 to 6,877 (170%; Anderson, 1985, p. 144). Exhibition was a sector in which technology entrepreneurs had neither experience nor ownership. In contrast, content entrepreneurs, who had retail backgrounds and were more attuned to and cultivated consumer preferences (see Table 12.2), entered the industry through exhibition.

Their income from exhibition fueled their backward integration into distribution and production. The rise and dominance of the feature film from 1910 through 1915 occurred after massive immigration to the United States. With the increasing standardization of technology and changing consumer preferences in film content, the skills that provided competitive advantage shifted from resolving technical problems to identifying and cultivating consumer tastes.

Because technology entrepreneurs focused their attention on patents and saw film content as irrelevant, they actively resisted and denied the change in consumer preferences from actualities to narratives. When Kleine, a member of the Trust who was an importer not an inventor, saw that imported European films generated impressive box office revenues (over $1 million for three films in 6 months), he suggested that the Trust move toward feature films. In a memo to him, the head of the Trust explained that "feature subjects of more than five reels ... [are] too long for the average picture theaters" and that he wanted programs of no longer than three reels (Anderson, 1985, p. 150). Adolph Zuckor, a content entrepreneur, applied for a production license from the Trust in 1912 for feature films. The Trust refused, telling him "the time is not ripe for feature films, if it ever will be" (Gabler, 1988, p. 30).

Technology entrepreneurs insisted on short film formats that frustrated their creative talent. For example, director D. W. Griffith left Biograph in 1913 over this issue (Katz, 1994, p. 560) and Edison lost Edwin Porter, its primary director and cameraman, in 1910 over creative conflicts (Musser, 1991). The creative talent of directors provided coherence to a film's story and was thus a source of competitive advantage. For example, in 1909 Biograph hired D. W. Griffith as its director and "the sudden improvement in the quality of Biograph product that resulted from Griffith's innovations did not go unnoticed by the public. Attendance at theaters that featured Biograph films rose dramatically" (Katz, p. 560). Technology entrepreneurs also downplayed the creative talent of stars. For example, Biograph was the first to develop a star, called the "Biograph girl" (so the brand would accrue to the firm). However, Biograph refused to promote its star Mary Pickford as an individual. Biograph reported to the *New York Dramatic Mirror* that "it was not the personality of a particular player that made for successful motion picture production but rather 'first the story, second the direction, and third competent people as a class not as individuals'" (Balio, 1985, p. 156). In 1910 content entrepreneur Carl Laemmle enticed Pickford to switch from technology firm Biograph to his content firm, Universal. Technology and content firms differed significantly in what resources they saw as critical and how they managed their creative talent.

The shift in capabilities from technology to content is seen in how only 25% of top-20 technology firms, which had the resources and industry experience, became top producers in feature films. In contrast, Eastern European Jewish immigrants became 50% of top-20 producers or distributors in feature films from 1911 to 1920 (see Table 12.1). In essence, the dominant technology firms refused to acknowledge the consumer demand for a new product, the feature film, which was fueled by talents of stars and directors, and which shifted industry competitive advantage. Trust members' reluctance to engage in feature film production hindered their ability to sustain market dominance. By 1918 8 of 10 Trust members (except Pathé and Vitagraph) were either bankrupt or had left the industry. Technology entrepreneurs' career logic of action was a source of competitive inertia.

CONCLUSION

By examining entrepreneurs' careers and in-group rivalry, we gained insight into sources of incumbents' inertia. Technology entrants came from manufacturing careers and imported an economizing logic of action, which they were reluctant to relinquish. They spent enormous energies in litigation with one another to establish dominance and control over property rights in the industry. This consumed their attention, resources, and energies, allowing newcomers to gain a foothold in a new and rapidly growing industry. In contrast, content firms came from retail experiences and imported a marketing logic. Technology entrepreneurs did not attend sufficiently to content entrepreneurs until they competed head to head as producers, moving into greater resource similarity (Chen, 1996). Technology and content entrepreneurs held distinct logics of action that defined what resources they pursued, what capabilities they developed, and how competitive dynamics within and between the two groups of entrepreneurs unfolded.

When entrepreneurs and top decision makers restrict their focus of attention to either technology or content, this provides an opportunity for smaller or newer competitors to exploit this restricted focus of attention. Ironically, the bit player among the content firms was Warner Brothers, who by developing sound technology in 1927 revolutionized and consolidated its place in the film industry. Currently, media conglomerates are battling for survival with smaller films such as Lucas' Industrial Light and Magic, which seeks to make digital technology the standard in the industry. By doing so, Lucas will radically alter and reduce the entertainment giants' control over distribution, which has been their source of competitive advantage since the 1930s. Technology developments drive content, such as the rise of computer animation and Disney's current challenge of retraining their animators to create a specific look and appeal to young audiences raised on computer games. Content may in turn drive technological developments such as the use of computers to capture and create spectacular special effects that are central to action-packed films. The rapid pace of technological advancement for creating and distributing content such as the Internet and the enormous appeal of content makes the promulgation of movies viable in multiple technological formats such as DVD, movie houses, cable television, and Internet access. In today's media environment, technology and content are finding new ways in which they may live off of and extend one another, requiring that top decision makers attend to both technology and content.

REFERENCES

Abrahamson, E., & Fombrun, C. J. (1994). Macrocultures: Determinants and consequences. *Academy of Management Review, 19,* 728–755.

Allen, R. C. (1985). The movies in vaudeville: Historical context of the movies as popular entertainment. In T. Balio (Ed.), *The American film industry* (2nd ed., pp. 57–82). Madison: University of Wisconsin Press.

Anand, N., & Peterson, R. A. (2000). When market information constitutes fields: Sensemaking of markets in the commercial music industry. *Organization Science, 11,* 270–284.

Anderson, R. (1985). The motion pictures patent company: A reevaluation. In T. Balio (Ed.), *The American film industry* (2nd ed., pp. 133–152). Madison: University of Wisconsin Press.

Bacharach, S., Bamberger, P., & Sonnenstuhl, W. J. (1996). The organizational transformation process: The micropolitics of dissonance reduction and the alignment of logics of action. *Administrative Science Quarterly, 41,* 477–506.

Balio, T. (1985). A novelty spawns small business, 1894–1908. In T. Balio (Ed.), *The American film industry* (2nd ed., pp. 3–25). Madison: University of Wisconsin Press.

Balio, T. (1985). Stars in business: The founding of United Artists. In T. Balio (Ed.), *A novelty spawns small business, 1894–1908* (2nd ed., pp. 153–172). Madison: University of Wisconsin Press.

Bird, A. (1994). Careers as repositories of knowledge: A new perspective on boundaryless careers. *Journal of Organizational Behavior, 15,* 325–344.

Boeker, W. P. (1988). Organizational origins: Entrepreneurial and environmental imprinting at the time of founding. In G. R. Carroll (Ed.), *Ecological models in organizations* (pp. 33–51). Cambridge, MA: Ballinger.

Bowser, E. (1994). *The transformation of cinema: 1907–1915.* Berkeley: University of California Press.

Chen, M. J. (1996). Competitor analysis and interfirm rivalry: Toward a theoretical integration. *Academy of Management Review, 21,* 100–134.

Fligstein, N. (1991). The structural transformation of American industry: An institutional account of the causes and consequences of diversification in the largest firms, 1919–1979. In W. W. Powell &. P. J. DiMaggio (Eds.), *The new institutionalism in organizational analysis* (pp. 311–336). Chicago: University of Chicago Press.

Gabler, N. (1988). *An empire of their own: How the Jews invented Hollywood.* New York: Anchor.

Huygens, M., Baden-Fuller, C., Van Den Bosch, F. A. J., &. Volberda, H. (2001). Co-evolution of firm capabilities and industry competition: Investigating the music industry, 1877-1997. *Organization Studies, 22,* 971–1011.

Jones, C. (2001). Coevolution of entrepreneurial careers, institutional rules and competitive dynamics in American film, 1895-1920. *Organization Studies, 22,* 911–944.

Jones, C., & Dunn, M. T. (in press). Careers and institutions: The centrality of careers in organization theory. In H. Gunz & M. Pieperl (Eds.), *Handbook of career theory.* Oxford: Oxford University Press.

Katz, E. (1994). *The film encyclopedia.* New York: Harper Perennial.

Merritt, R. (1985). Nickelodeon theaters, 1905–1914: Building an audience for the movies. In T. Balio (Ed.), *The American film industry* (2nd ed., pp. 83–102). Madison: University of Wisconsin Press.

Mezias, S. J., & Kuperman, J. C. (2000). The community dynamics of entrepreneurship: The birth of the American film industry, 1895–1920. *Journal of Business Venturing, 16,* 209–233.
Musser, C. (1990). *The emergence of cinema: The American screen to 1907.* Berkeley: University of California Press.
Musser, C. (1991). *Before the nickelodeon: Edwin S. Porter and the Edison Manufacturing Company.* Berkeley: University of California Press.
Ocasio, W. (1997). Towards an attention-based view of the firm. *Strategic Management Journal, 18,* 187–206.
Prahalad, C. K., & Bettis, R. A. (1986). The dominant logic: A new linkage between diversity and performance. *Strategic Management Journal, 7,* 485–501.
Scott, W. R. (1995). *Institutions and organizations.* Thousand Oaks, CA: Sage.
Stinchcombe, A. L. (1965). Social structure and organization. In J. G. March (Ed.), *Handbook of organizations.* Chicago: Rand McNally.
Thornton, P. H. (2002). The rise of the corporation in a craft industry: Conflict and conformity in institutional logics. *Academy of Management Journal, 45,* 81–101.
Thornton, P. H., & Ocasio, W. (1999). Institutional logics and the historical contingency of power in organizations: Executive succession in the higher education publishing industry, 1958-1990. *American Journal of Sociology, 105,* 801–843.
United States v. Motion Picture Patents Co. et al. District Court, Pennsylvania 1915. *Federal Reporter,* pp. 800–812.
Zajac, E. J., & Bazerman, M. H. (1991). Blindspots in industry and competitor analysis: Implications of interfirm (mis)perceptions for strategic decisions. *Academy of Management Review, 16,* 37–56.

CHAPTER

13

From 78s to MP3s: The Embedded Impact of Technology in the Market for Prerecorded Music[1]

Timothy Dowd
Emory University

Most researchers often emphasize technology when explaining the dramatic transformation of markets (Fischer, 1992; Nelson, 1994). Their common emphasis does not denote a consensus regarding how technology contributes to market transformation. In fact, a divide exists regarding this issue. Some herald the causal impact of technology, where the rise of superior technologies spurs transformation. Others stress its contingent impact, where successful strategies for exploiting technology prompt transformation. This divide not only entails divergent opinions about technology, I suggest that it also reflects fundamentally different approaches to markets.

Scholars tend toward either atomized or embedded depictions when approaching markets (Dacin, Ventresca, & Beal, 1999). Atomized depictions are

[1]I thank Maureen Blyler, Cindy Hinton, Kathy Liddle, Kim Lupo, Tracy Scott, and Pat Wehner for their comments and suggestions on earlier drafts. I especially thank Jamal Shamsie for his outstanding editorial guidance and support.

common in, but are not limited to, neoclassical economics. They posit that individual actors—be they people or firms—negotiate markets in relative isolation by heeding universal laws of efficiency and self-interest. Contextual factors, such as interfirm relations and state policy, play minimal roles in market activity, as they either reinforce universal laws or are eliminated via natural selection (Adams & Brock, 1991; Yonay, 1998).

Atomistic depictions likewise treat technology as driven by universal laws and as little shaped by contextual factors. Technologies that provide optimal solutions to problems (e.g., production costs) diffuse and transform markets by altering how their respective firms operate. Diffusion is not problematic because firms are willing and able to exploit new technologies (Silverberg, Dosi, & Orsenigo, 1988; Smith & Marx, 1994). As Disco and van der Meulen (1998, p. 4) lamented about such a depiction, "technologies develop according to an inner logic ... and are therefore more or less impervious to human influence. On this view you can't hurry technology, but neither can you constrain it once its time has come."

Scholars from diverse traditions, including economic sociology, object to atomistic depictions. Their embedded depictions posit that markets can vary widely by context and, hence, do not reflect universal laws. The pursuit of efficiency and self-interest, for example, can entail drastically different prescriptions in one context versus another (Dobbin & Dowd, 2000; Roy, 1997). Indeed, contextual factors play key roles in market activity. Interfirm relations help create markets by shaping competition, prices, and resource allocation (Uzzi, 1997). State policy helps create markets by stipulating the property rights that enable exchange and by delimiting the strategies that firms can embrace (Dobbin & Dowd, 1997; Edelman & Suchman, 1997).

Embedded depictions likewise treat technology as contextually contingent: Successful strategies regarding technology—rather than new technologies per se—prompt market change (Bijker & Law, 1992; Disco & van der Meulen, 1998; Fischer, 1992). This treatment is supported by empirical regularities. First, patent law limits which firms may exploit a given technology, shaping (if not slowing) the diffusion of new technologies (e.g., Conant, 1960). Second, firms that possess the right to exploit new technologies face the dilemma of how to do so. This is of major importance, as new technologies can languish for years or fade into obscurity (e.g., Cusumano, Mylonadis, & Rosenbloom, 1992; Lewis, 1991). Finally, widespread adoption of certain technologies can preclude the adoption of equally optimal or superior technologies, as sunk costs involved in adopted technologies may make their abandonment unlikely (e.g., McGuire, Granovetter, & Schwartz, 1994).

SCOPE OF THIS CHAPTER

This chapter demonstrates the embeddedness of technology via the historical case of the U.S. market for prerecorded music, which the recording industry has serviced since 1890 (Dowd, 2003). The case mostly emphasizes the period from 1940—when the recording industry had fully recovered from its near demise—to the early 1990s—when the industry momentarily basked in the success of the compact disc. However, it also addresses the context that preceded 1940, and it comments on the unresolved flux that emerged in the late 1990s (e.g., Napster, MP3s).

The prerecorded music market provides an ideal case because discussions of it abound with atomistic depictions. Indeed, much conventional wisdom suggests that new technologies—such as tape recorders and compact discs—provide the main (if not sole) impetus for epochal shifts in the production of prerecorded music. Drawing on archival and secondary sources, this case demonstrates the opposite. Transformations of the prerecorded music market resulted from the interplay between technology and contextual factors (e.g., copyright law), with the latter having the decisive impact. A particular variant of the embeddedness literature informs this case study—the new institutionalism in organizational sociology (Scott, 1995). I highlight salient aspects of this theory before presenting the case.

Institutional Convergence and Product Conceptions

Institutionalists argue that firms confront an ambiguous marketplace that contains no certain paths to success. Firms cope with this ambiguity and uncertainty by monitoring a limited range of elements (DiMaggio, 1997). In order to select which elements they should monitor, firms collectively develop conceptions of how their market works. Their set of conceptions addresses such domains as competitive strategies (Fligstein, 1996), labor relations (Dobbin, Sutton, Meyer, & Scott, 1993), and organizational boundaries (Davis, Diekmann, & Tinsley, 1994). Each conception is "simultaneously a worldview that allows actors to interpret the actions of others and includes a reflection of how the market is structured" (Fligstein, 1996, p. 658).

When documenting how U.S. broadcasters make sense of radio technology, Leblebici and colleagues (Leblebici, 1995; Leblebici, Salancik, Copay, & King, 1991) demonstrated the importance of collective conceptions regarding the product. Among other things, they showed how broadcasting firms came to agree on two key elements: the technological format of their product (e.g., AM vs. FM signals) and the uses of this format by other business (e.g., ship-to-shore communication vs. advertisement). Their findings resonate with past institutional work in several ways, of which I mention two.

First, change in the collective conception about radio's product mostly follows the process detailed in many institutional studies (Dowd & Dobbin, 1997). Some firms innovate a new format or use that favors their respective position; they can politick for other firms to follow their lead. If the new format or use appears to generate success for the innovator, then other firms imitate. Issues of power surface when actors, such as the state, coerce other firms to adopt a new format or use. The process culminates when firms institutionalize a new format or use, rendering a market that diverges from its previous incarnation. That is, firms treat the new conception as an objective fact that defines the nature of their market.

Second, a newly institutionalized format or use need not rest on superior technologies, as is the case for a wide assortment of institutions (Meyer, Boli, &

Thomas, 1994; Meyer & Rowan, 1977). In fact, given the role that power plays in the institutionalization process (Dobbin & Dowd, 2000; Roy, 1997), firms can embrace a new format or use that favors the interests of particular actors rather than the interests of efficiency or technological superiority—as when powerful actors delayed the emergence of FM radio (Lewis, 1991).

I follow the example of Leblebici et al. (1991) and examine the collective conception that record firms hold for their product of prerecorded music. I document their evolving consensus about the product's technological formats (e.g., compact disc). These formats are what record firms exchange with consumers and, consequently, provide crucial income for record firms. I also document their evolving consensus about the uses of their product by nonproducing firms—those businesses that occupy an intermediary position between record firms and consumers (e.g., radio stations). Such uses provide a potential source of income, and hence, are of great concern to recording firms (witness the Napster case). I use *product conception* to denote institutionalized consensus among recording firms about their products' formats and uses. A new product conception occurs when record firms adopt a form or use that entails a logic that sharply diverges with the past logic. I make such a distinction so as not to confuse incremental changes (e.g., the successive adoption of the eight-track tape and cassette tape formats) with the epochal changes (e.g., the shift from analog to digital formats) that concern institutionalists.

The historical case addresses, after 1940, three occasions where record firms institutionalized a new product conception. Atomistic depictions suggest that such major shifts would follow the facile diffusion of new and superior technologies. This was not borne out in the prerecorded music market. Each product conception diffused only after the coercing or politicking of powerful actors, and each relied on technological formats that were old or nonsuperior, or both. Although I only document product conceptions in the prerecorded music market, I expect that such conceptions are salient for all media markets. In fact, as much history reveals, epochal shifts in media formats or uses result from a contested rather than efficient process (e.g., Balio, 1990; Cusumano et al., 1992; Kerr, 1990; Leblebici et al., 1991).

THE EMERGENCE AND DOMINANCE OF A SINGLE FORMAT, 1900 to 1940

RCA Victor, Columbia, and Decca (the Big Three) dominated the prerecorded music market in the early 1940s, accounting for nearly 99% of recordings manufactured in the United States (U.S. Congress, 1942). Their conception of the product, then, had great import. Regarding its technological format, the Big Three held that prerecorded music should generate income via flat discs that rotated at 78 revolutions per minute (rpm) and that were made of a shellac compound. However, the 78-rpm shellac disc was not the only viable format, nor was it technologically superior.

The format embraced by the Big Three was rooted in the turn of the century. The selling of prerecorded music on 78s began around 1894, grew common in the early 1900s, and became standard in the 1910s; the shellac compound was first used for 78s in 1897 and became the norm in the early 1900s (Garlick, 1977; Isom, 1977; Sutton, 2000). Despite its long history, the 78-rpm shellac disc had notable limitations. The 10-inch configuration provided less than 5 minutes of prerecorded music per side. Lengthy compositions (e.g., orchestral music) required numerous discs, as well as the interruptions that occurred when listeners changed discs (Goldmark, 1973).

Record firms would later finesse this limitation by emulating the photo album and creating the record album—a leatherette-bound volume with multiple paper sleeves, with each sleeve containing a disc (Garlick, 1977); they also devised automatic record changers that allowed a speedy transition from one disc to another (Kogen, 1977). The shellac compound posed further limitations: "The largest deficiency of shellac record was its surface noise ... a partial blessing for it masked many other faults. Shellac records were full of blisters and unfilled grooves which produced ticks and pops in the sound" (Isom, 1977, pp. 720–721). The compound also was extremely brittle. Some firms responded by shipping 78s in wooden crates, in order to minimize breakage (Isom, 1977).

Developments in other industries (i.e., film, radio) during the 1920s and 1930s revealed that the 78-rpm shellac disc was but one alternative for the prerecorded music market. In 1925, Western Electric developed a device that allowed a reel of film to be synchronized to a disc of prerecorded sound, the Vitaphone. Western Electric did not utilize 78s because of their limited playback time (a reel of film exceeded 10 minutes); instead, it perfected a 16-inch disc that rotated at 33 1/3 rpm and provided 15 minutes of sound per side. This disc amazed audiences at the showing of *Don Juan* in 1926 and *The Jazz Singer* in 1927 (Barrios, 1995). The Vitaphone soon faded from the film industry, as studios now recorded sound on film, but its disc quickly diffused to the radio industry (Bachman, 1977; Barrios, 1995).

From 1928 on, a growing number of radio stations relied on 33 1/3 rpm discs for electrical transcriptions—recordings of live programming manufactured by Western Electric and others. These 16-inch discs allowed, among other things, stations to air a program from one time zone at a convenient time in other time zones (Morton, 2000; U.S. Congress, 1942). Their 15-minute duration was attractive for radio programming, especially when compared to the short duration of 78s (Hyde, 1994; Morton, 2000). These 33 1/3s became more attractive in the 1930s, when Western Electric and others shifted to a compound of vinyl rather than shellac. This shift yielded a notable improvement in sonic quality and an unbreakable product that could easily be mailed (Isom, 1977; Khanna, 1977). Although Vitaphone discs and electrical transcriptions could not be played on home phonographs of the day (Barrios, 1995; Hyde, 1994), both demonstrated superior advances over the format found in the prerecorded music market. Nevertheless, the Big Three and other record firms relied on the 78-rpm shellac disc in 1940 and would do so for years.[2]

OPPOSITION TO RADIO AIRPLAY AND ACCEPTANCE OF THE JUKEBOX, 1920 to 1940

Historical developments in the 1920s (the rise of commercial radio) and the 1930s (the resurgence of jukeboxes) forced record firms to grapple with the uses of their prerecorded product. The Big Three concurred that radio stations should not broadcast their 78s. Instead, they wanted stations to prompt sales of prerecorded music by airing live broadcasts of the Big Three's respective songs and performers. They also conceded that businesses could buy prerecorded discs for use in jukeboxes

The opposition of the Big Three to the broadcasting of their 78s was rooted in the recording industry's economic turmoil of the 1920s and early 1930s. From the earliest days of radio, stations broadcasted the prerecorded music of record firms. Some thought that this would benefit both industries, providing cheap programming for the infant radio industry and free promotion for the robust recording industry (Hyde, 1994; Sanjek, 1988). However, the fortunes of both industries soon diverged. The number of record firms sharply declined while the number of stations swelled into the thousands (Leblebici et al., 1991; Sutton, 2000). The frailty of record firms was matched by declining output: Their total production value plummeted from $105.6 million in 1921 to $5.5 million in 1933 (Recording Industry Association of America [RIAA], n.d.). Concurrently, the annual number of commercial radio stations rose dramatically (Sterling, 1984).

This turmoil shaped what would become the Big Three. The forerunners of RCA Victor, and Columbia—Victor Talking Machine and Columbia Phonograph—were stalwarts of the early prerecorded music market (Gellat, 1977) and were among the first U.S. firms to establish multinational operations (Chandler, 1990). Their decades of success evaporated in the 1920s, and each floundered before eventual acquisition by a radio giant (Millard, 1995; Schicke, 1974). Victor was purchased in 1929 by RCA, the parent company of the NBC network. Columbia experienced several ownership changes, the final one occurring when the CBS network acquired it in 1938 (Federal Communications Commission, 1941; Sutton, 2000).

---

[2]In 1931, RCA developed 10- and 12-inch shellac discs that rotated 33 1/3 rpm and were compatible with existing home phonographs. Exploiting the extended duration of these discs, RCA developed a catalogue that included lengthy orchestral pieces (Atlas, 1950; Fagan, 1982; RCA, 1953). These discs were plagued by technical difficulties, such as unsteady rotation, and were commercial failures (Bachman, 1977; Goldmark, 1973; Schicke, 1974). RCA ceased their production in 1934 because of supposed "apathy on the part of the buying public" (RCA, 1953, p. 31). Heeding its failure, RCA continued to stress 78s for the prerecorded music market—as would Columbia and Decca (Atlas; Isom, 1977).

The last of the Big Three (Decca) would navigate the turmoil, in part, by providing business establishments with prerecorded music for use in jukeboxes. The placement of coin-operated phonographs in establishments dated back to 1889, and their use by establishments waxed and waned in subsequent decades before growing moribund in the late 1920s (Bodoh, 1977; Dowd, 2003). The 1933 repeal of prohibition revived coin-operated phonographs in the form of jukeboxes. The proliferating number of bars and clubs used these machines to provided ambience and easy income; diners, malt shops, and other establishments soon followed suit (Bodoh, 1977; Lynch, 1990). Decca Records (est. 1934) targeted establishments that used jukeboxes. This provided them with inexpensive records (21 cents each versus the once-common retail price of 75 cents). Decca's strategy led to great success and its inclusion in the Big Three. By 1938, roughly 60% of U.S. record sales were to establishments that used jukeboxes, and Decca accounted for some 75% of those sales (Ennis, 1992; Millard, 1995; Sanjek, 1988).

Amid the economic turmoil of the 1920s and 1930s, recording personnel drew conclusions about uses of their product. They concluded that record firms suffer when stations broadcast prerecorded music (Sanjek, 1988). This conclusion rested on what would later prove to be a flawed assumption: Consumers would not buy records when they could hear them for free on radio (Schicke, 1974). It also rested on an accurate evaluation of U.S. copyright law.

When broadcasting prerecorded music, radio stations must pay royalties to the composers, lyricists, and publishers of the music but not to the record firms or performers that generate the recording (American Society of Composers, Authors, and Publishers, 1933; Ringer, 1961). In other words, stations can generate income by repeatedly playing hit records and, aside from the initial purchase price, they need not compensate record firms. They also concluded that record firms benefit when businesses use prerecorded music in jukeboxes (Ennis, 1992; Schicke, 1974). Their acceptance of jukeboxes was somewhat at odds with their rejection of radio airplay, as coin-operated phonographs were exempt from copyright since 1909. As was the case in radio, then, record firms saw no share of the jukebox profit that resulted from the repeated play of hit records (Sanjek, 1988). Flaws and inconsistencies aside, the first conclusion provided a ready explanation for the near demise of the prerecorded music market in the 1920s and the second one offered an explanation for the success of Decca in the 1930s.

Given such conclusions, the Big Three devised an approach to radio that discouraged the airplay of records. Beginning in 1933, RCA Victor and Columbia inscribed prohibitions on their 78s to prevent radio stations from broadcasting their prerecorded product. These inscriptions included "Not Licensed for Radio Broadcast" and "Licensed for Non-Commercial Use on Phonographs in Homes." Beginning in 1937, Decca inscribed similar prohibitions on its 78s (Sanjek, 1988; Sherman & Nauck, 1998).

Powerful actors in government and broadcasting likewise opposed the broadcasting of prerecorded music. Since the 1920s, federal officials preferred that radio serve the public via broadcasts of live programming; one of their reasons was that live entertainment and information (unlike 78s) were not widely available to all (Hyde, 1994; Morton, 2000).[3] CBS and NBC also advocated live broadcasting. Corporate documents reveal that both networks championed live programming because it demonstrated radio's reach, immediacy, and potential for edification (e.g., NBC Advisory Council, 1930, p. 7). Both networks discouraged (if not forbade) owned and affiliated stations from airing the 78s of record firms (Hyde; U.S. Congress, 1942).[4] Finally, in the late 1930s, supreme courts in three states required that particular stations cease airplay of records that bore prohibitive inscriptions (Hayes, 1982; Ringer, 1961; U.S. Congress, 1978).

By the end of the 1930s, the product conception of the Big Three was institutionalized. For example, it was now common practice for record firms to evaluate success in the prerecorded market by attending simultaneously to *Variety* charts that detailed the bestselling 78 discs, *Billboard* charts that detailed the songs and performers that garnered the most live performances on radio, and *Billboard* charts that detailed which records did well in jukebox play (Ennis, 1992; Whitburn, 1986). This product conception, however, rested on an old and nonsuperior technological format (i.e., the 78-rpm shellac disc) and on a conservative approach to a new technology (i.e., opposition to radio airplay). Given the dominance of the Big Three, and the opposition to airplay found in quarters of government and broadcasting, this product conception seemed firmly entrenched.

ACCEPTANCE OF RADIO AIRPLAY, 1940 to 1947

A series of developments in the early 1940s challenged the Big Three's product conception, thereby creating an opportunity for the emergence of a new product conception. Several of the developments pertained to broadcasting. In 1940, the New York Supreme Court ruled that once radio stations purchased a record, they were free to broadcast it, even when it bore a "Not Licensed for Broadcast" inscription (Hayes, 1982; Ringer, 1961). Big Three managers were not pleased with this ruling, and they unsuccessfully pursued ways of obtaining fees from broadcasters that aired their recordings (Sanjek, 1988). Meanwhile, the Federal Communications Commission (1941) issued a series of rulings that were meant to curtail the power of radio networks, including those that limited the ability of networks to in-

[3]Federal officials had additional concerns: Stations can use prerecorded music to feign a live performance and, thereby, deceive listeners. Stations that rely on inexpensive 78s, furthermore, have a competitive advantage over those that rely on costly live programming (Hyde, 1994; Morton, 2000).

[4]The National Association of Broadcasters (NAB, 1978) favored live broadcasts as well, but not as vigorously as CBS and NBC. NAB standards only required that stations not broadcast phonograph records between 6:00 and 11:00 p.m. By "phonograph records," it meant the 78s manufactured by record firms and not the electrical transcriptions used by broadcasters. It made this distinction, as many in radio did, to emphasize the quality of transcriptions and to placate federal concerns (e.g., transcriptions were not sold to the public and, thus, not widely available; Hyde, 1994; Morton, 2000).

fluence the programming of affiliated stations. Shortly thereafter, federal officials admitted that their opposition to radio airplay was difficult to enforce (U.S. Congress, 1942). These developments meant that network and nonnetwork stations alike were soon able to pursue the broadcast of prerecorded music.

Two other developments pertained to the production of prerecorded music. First, wartime restrictions sharply curtailed the production of recordings. For example, the government limited the production of record firms because their shellac was needed for warfare production. Although record firms were allowed to retain their current stocks of shellac, future purchases of shellac were dependent on the amount that government warehouses could allow (Millard, 1995; Sanjek, 1988).

Second, the American Federation of Musicians (AFM, est. 1896) exacerbated these wartime restrictions. AFM leadership feared that the prerecorded music would reduce employment opportunities for its members (Leiter, 1974; U.S. Congress, 1948). As a result, it announced that "from and after August 1, 1942, the members of the American Federation of Musicians will not play or contract for recordings, transcriptions, or other forms of mechanical reproductions of music" (U.S. Congress, 1942, p. 6). In other words, the vast majority of American instrumentalists would not be available for the prerecorded music market. This ban would continue until record firms agreed to pay a royalty to its unemployment fund (Ennis, 1992; Sanjek, 1988). Rather than concede to the AFM, the Big Three attempted to wait them out by drawing on their large backlog of unreleased recordings. As the ban continued, the Big Three quickly ran out of new products. The ban ended in 1944 when the last of the Big Three agreed with the stipulations of the AFM (Leiter, 1974), but not before production levels had dropped to low levels. Columbia Records, for instance, went from releasing more than 2000 records in 1940 to only 62 in 1944 (U.S. Congress, 1958).

Capitol Records (est. 1942) offered an innovation that undermined the extant product conception. Before doing so, however, it first had to cope with the AFM ban and the shellac shortage. Ironically, these two developments helped Capitol deal with another obstacle—succeeding in a market dominated by the Big Three. In particular, the AFM ban and shellac shortage constrained the range of material that the Big Three could release and the number of copies that they could manufacture. As a result, the newly formed Capitol gained a visibility it might not have enjoyed under different circumstances. "Everything that should have held us back, worked for us," wrote cofounder Johnny Mercer. "The war and even the musicians strike only made our little company better known and more quickly recognized ... we got heard a lot" (Grein, 1992a, p. C2).[5]

While skillfully dealing with the shortage of material and musicians, Capitol executives believed that the broadcasting of recordings would stimulate rather than harm sales. They chose to ignore the lessons that recording personnel had

[5]Regarding the AFM ban, the founders of Capitol had a month to prepare before it was implemented. Working round the clock, they generated an admirable supply of recordings (Grein, 1992a, 1992b; Sanjek, 1988).

drawn from the turmoil of the 1920s and 1930s. As a result, Capitol became the first record firm regularly to deliver free recordings to disk jockeys (Grein, 1992a; Sanjek, 1988). As cofounder Glenn Wallichs recalled:

> We devised a personal sample record for about 50 of America's most influential jockeys. We typed up special labels with their names on both sides ... and then had our limited employee force drive around and distribute each sample personally. It was a service that created a sensation... We made the jock a Big Man. (Dexter, 1969, p. 58)

Capitol's reliance on radio airplay soon reaped success. By the end of 1942, consumers and jukebox owners were buying Capitol's recordings in numbers that were comparable to those of the Big Three. By the time that wartime restrictions and the AFM ban had subsided, Capitol had garnered sales in excess of $2 million. Indeed, Capitol had joined the ranks of the dominant firms, turning the Big Three into the Big Four (Grein, 1992a, 1992b; Moody's Investor Services, 1950; Sanjek, 1988).

The success of Capitol's innovative use held ramifications for the prerecorded music market. On the one hand, the Big Three begrudgingly ceased their quest for attaining fees whenever broadcasters aired recordings and likewise courted DJs with free recordings (Ennis, 1992; Sanjek, 1988; U.S. Congress, 1958, 1960). On the other hand, a growing number of firms entered the recording industry, imitating the use that Capitol innovated. In fact, this new use dramatically altered the logic of the market for prerecorded music: If small or new firms could attain sufficient airplay for one recording, the resulting attention could, in turn, lead to sales that subsidized future operations—as Capitol Records had clearly demonstrated (U.S. Congress, 1958). The diffusion of this new use was made possible by government and court actions, which eventually forced those in the radio and recording industries to accept the airplay of prerecorded music.

By early 1945, record firms still agreed that their product should be reproduced on 78-rpm discs (i.e., format). They now agreed, however, on a new use: Recordings should be broadcast in order to stimulate sales. The institutionalization of the new product conception was apparent in February, when *Billboard* initiated a new popularity chart, "Records Most-Played by Disk Jockeys." Record firm managers now evaluated success by monitoring which recordings received the most retail sales, jukebox purchases, and radio airplay (Whitburn, 1986). Thus, a new use of an old technology rather than a new technological format transformed the market for prerecorded music.

RISE OF MULTIPLE FORMATS, 1948 to 1982

The broadcasting of prerecorded music on the radio allowed a flood of new entrants to come into the recording industry; this resulted in the Big Four becoming the Big Six, as the record labels of Mercury and MGM quickly prospered, and it led to a decrease in market shares for the largest recording firms (Dowd, 2004;

Sanjek, 1988). Amid dissipating market shares, two of the largest firms contemplated a new technological format that would supplant the 78-rpm disc. CBS (Columbia) unveiled its 33 1/3-rpm long-playing (LP) disc in 1948. The LP was made of nonbreakable plastic (vinylite) and could store more than 20 minutes of music per side, a significant improvement over the short-playing and brittle 78-rpm disc. RCA debuted its vinylite 45-rpm disc shortly thereafter. Although this disc stored less than 5 minutes of music per side, it was inexpensive and small, as was its $29.95 record player (Gellatt, 1977; Millard, 1995).

Each firm hoped that its new disc would become the market standard. As a result, each launched multimillion-dollar campaigns to promote their respective discs. Furthermore, both firms freely licensed their respective technology to any interested record firm, thus temporarily foregoing the usual patent royalties in the pursuit of allies (Gellatt, 1977; Millard, 1995). These free licenses, furthermore, proved to be a boon for small record firms, especially because they lowered production costs ("Cap Promotion Push," 1950).

Record firms, radio stations, and consumers quickly favored CBS's LP disc over RCA's 45 rpm. In January of 1950, RCA seemed to sound defeat when announcing that it likewise would offer LP recordings. However, this announcement signaled the beginning of its "Operation TNT." RCA personnel now advocated a two-speed market and launched a massive advertising campaign in support of this idea. RCA's efforts soon garnered support from various quarters. Record firms, for example, used LPs for soundtracks and used 45-rpm discs for singles played on the radio. In fact, jukebox operators and radio stations eventually relied on 45-rpm discs. Thus, it appeared that the market would discard the 78-rpm disc in favor of both LPs and 45-rpm discs ("Diskeries Wary," 1954; "Hard Trek for Diskers," 1950; "Jukes Will Test New-Speed Disks," 1950; "Majors and Subsids Switch," 1954; "1,092 Stations," 1950; "Standardization Advances," 1950; "Stations to Get 325,000 R. P. M. Records," 1954; "Who're Pressing What Speeds," 1950; see also Gellatt, 1977; Millard, 1995; Sanjek, 1988; Simon, 1950).

Two European developments complicated the shift to a two-speed market. First, magnetic-tape recording grew more viable as U.S. manufacturers gained free access to the German developments made during World War II. By 1949, the majority of record firms used this new technology for "recording music first on tape and later transcribing it to a master disk from which pressings are made" ("Men Behind the Microphones," 1952, p. 57; Millard, 1995). RCA and Capitol began marketing prerecorded tapes for consumers in 1953 ("Diskeries Wary," 1954). Second, two British firms—British Decca and EMI—introduced two incompatible formats of stereo technology (Boehm, 1958; Gray, 1986; Sanjek, 1988). Both developments suggested that the formats of prerecorded music would entail more than a two-speed market.

In 1957, record firms revised their product conception concerning the format of their product while retaining their old assessment concerning its uses. Following the politicking of CBS, RCA, and others, they now agreed that recordings should be reproduced in multiple formats, including 33 1/3 discs (in mono and stereo),

45-rpm discs, and prerecorded tapes (which now accounted for $7 million in sales; see Millard, 1995; Morton, 2000). The institutionalization of the new product conception was demonstrated by two formal changes. In October, *Billboard* initiated its popularity charts for LP albums to complement the extant charts for hit songs. In December, the RIAA established a market-wide standard for stereo production ("Best Selling Pop LPs," 1957; Boehm, 1958; Millard, 1995; Sanjek, 1988).

The new product conception was notable for its treatment of technology. First, record firms now expected to truck in multiple formats. Consequently, a variety of new formats were later introduced into the market without disruption (e.g., cassettes). In fact, various tape and disc formats coexisted throughout the 1960s and into the 1970s. Second, record firms did not embrace a new technology that was superior. Instead, they compromised by embracing a variety of new technologies, some of which proved to be far from superior (e.g., eight-track tapes; "Are Cassettes Here to Stay?," 1969; Millard, 1995; see also Christman & Terry, 1990).

Production levels increased dramatically under this new product conception and the dominance of the Big Six rebounded as they adapted (Dowd, 2004). Their adaptation occurred in a piecemeal fashion. First, the Big Six found that their sheer number of units rose by factors of two or more as they released the same song on LPs, 45-rpm discs, cassettes, and other formats. Second, they found that such heightened production created a logjam among their distributors. Third, they responded to this logjam by devising and expanding their own distribution systems.

By the mid-1960s, each firm operated its own distribution in heavily populated areas and relied on independent distributors in sparsely populated areas. By the late 1960s, each of the Big Six had severed its reliance on independent distributors and relied on its own system of distribution (Denisoff, 1986; King, 1966). Finally, the sprawling distribution systems of each firm required a steady supply of products. Each of the Big Six responded by pursuing contracts with smaller record firms, whereby they would distribute the records of smaller firms in exchange for fees and royalties. Such arrangements could easily give way to consolidation (and often did), as the Big Six acquired financial interest in the firms that they distributed. The end result was that a growing percentage of products entered the prerecorded music market under the aegis of the Big Six (Denisoff; Dowd, 2004).

The expanding prosperity of both the Big Six and the recording industry eventually faced a challenge. The industry recession of 1979 signaled a dramatic change in the fortunes of the prerecorded music market, for production levels and sales had risen at a fairly steady pace since World War II. This fairly steady increase accelerated in the mid to late 1970s, as production and sales levels reached new plateaus. By 1978, the market produced more than 700 million recordings and generated $4 billion in sales. The 1978 boom, however, turned to bust in 1979. Total sales of recordings declined by almost a $500 million in less than a year. The recession continued until the end of 1982, when Michael Jackson's *Thriller* signaled the end of the recession (Denisoff, 1986; Dowd & Blyler, 2002).

THE RISE OF A NEW DOMINANT FORMAT AND A NEW USE 1982 to the 1990s

A number of analysts proposed reasons for the sudden recession, including the aging of the baby boomers, the dearth of new performers, the emergence of video games, and the overabundance of disco records. Nevertheless, the Big Six blamed the recession on the cassette tape. In particular, they claimed that consumers were "illegally" taping recordings rather than purchasing them. Warner Communications—now one of the Big Six—estimated that home taping cost all record firms some $2.8 billion a year. Although a government study found no support for the deleterious impact of home taping, recording personnel were adamant that home taping was the source of the recession (Denisoff, 1986; U.S. Congress, Office of Technology Assessment, 1989).

Although the origins of the recession were less than clear, its impact was obvious. On the one hand, the recession of 1979 prompted consolidation in the prerecorded music market in two ways. First, Big Six firms acquired the record divisions of many firms that exited during the recession. Second, an increasing number of smaller firms, such as A & M and Motown, turned to the Big Six for distribution as the recession decimated the independent distribution that once served them (Denisoff, 1986; Dowd, 2004; Sanjek, 1988). On the other hand, the recession also created an opportunity for record firms to reassess the nature of their market's products. In the face of such economic hardship, one record firm innovated a new technological format for the product, whereas another innovated a new use. In doing so, both firms ultimately undermined the extant product conception.

Philips (the owner of Mercury) offered the compact disc (CD) to consumers in 1982. Unlike previous formats, the CD would not deteriorate after repeated use; moreover, its 75 minutes of music offered a substantial improvement over existing discs and tapes. Despite its obvious technical superiority, the CD debuted only after Philips had convinced manufacturers and musicians of its marketability. One year after becoming available, 308 million CD units were sold. By 1986, more CD units were sold than LP albums. In fact, Columbia Records—the initial champion of the LP album—would eventually offer fewer than 12,000 vinyl albums (McGahan, 1991; Millard, 1995; Puterbaugh, 1992; RIAA, 1987, 1995).

The second innovation resulted from a joint venture between Warner Communications and American Express: the emergence of Music Television (MTV) in 1981. As was the case with the CD, MTV personnel previously campaigned to convince firms of the marketability of music videos. Most, but not all, of the Big Six responded positively to this promotional campaign by delivering videos for broadcast. By 1983, various consumer surveys showed that MTV videos stimulated album purchases. As a result, video production soared: The original 570 videos played on MTV ballooned to a library of more than 8,000 (Banks, 1996; Denisoff, 1986, 1988; Giles & Mundy, 1991).

Record firms had revised their product conception in the wake of politicking by Philips, Warner, and others. Regarding the formats, record firms now offered recordings in analog (e.g., cassettes), digital (e.g., CDs), and video formats. Regarding the uses, record firms now promoted sales via both radio and television airplay. Recording personnel maintained that prerecorded music in one format would stimulate the demand for such music in another format. Video renditions of songs, for instance, would persuade consumers to buy the sound-recording counterparts. The institutionalization of this new product conception was demonstrated in 1983 when, first, the RIAA began gathering data on the production and sales of CDs, and, second, *Billboard* initiated its airplay charts for music videos (RIAA, 1987; "Video Programming," 1983). By the end of the 1980s, these video charts showed that some 80% of hit songs also had an accompanying video (Dowd & Blyler, 2002).

It is tempting to portray this product conception as driven by superior technology, given the CD's rise to prominence. However, such a portrayal is not accurate for several reasons. First, the widespread acceptance of the CD did not lead to the demise of the analog cassette, which is demonstrably inferior to the CD in a number of ways (Morton, 2000). Second, record firms took active steps to ensure that another superior technology did not diffuse throughout the prerecorded music market. Recalling their perceived peril of home taping, record firms petitioned Congress in the 1980s to block the sale of digital audiotape (DAT) machines to consumers (U.S. Congress, Office of Technology Assessment, 1989). This format would have allowed consumers to make CD-quality tapes, which record firms feared would damage the vibrant sales of CDS.

After a protracted struggle, record firms finally won a victory. The Home Recording Act of 1992 imposed a royalty on the sale of both DAT machines and blank DAT tapes. The resultant funds were distributed among a variety of interested parties (e.g., composers, performers), with record firms receiving a share (U.S. Congress, 1987, 1992). Record firms remained concerned, however, and did not release prerecorded music on DAT. Finally, record firms likewise were less than enthusiastic about Philips' introduction of the Digital Compact Cassette and Sony's MiniDisc, as were consumers, with neither format becoming a mainstay for prerecorded music (McGahan, 1991; Morton, 2000). Hence, the product conception that arose in the early 1980s drew on one digital format, yet it did not draw on other digital formats that were patently superior to the analog cassette tape.

The largest record firms mostly thrived under this product conception and continued the emphasis on distribution formed during the previous product conception. The largest firms pursued distribution contracts so fervently because they each sought to broaden their range of products, provide a constant product flow for their massive distribution systems, and increase their market share (Dowd, 2004). Indeed, their dominance would grow more pronounced as a round of mergers and acquisitions reduced the Big Six to the Big Five. Thus, as the new millennium opened, the Big Five would consist of AOL Time Warner, Bertelsmann, EMI, Sony, and Vivendi Universal (Roberts, 1995; Standard and Poor's, 2000). Each of these firms was well poised for producing and distributing multiple formats, yet none of them was ready for what would occur on the Internet.

THE UNRESOLVED FLUX OF THE NEW MILLENNIUM

In the late 1990s, record firms encountered a new format that proved far more challenging than DAT—the MP3. While record firms were grappling with DAT, a group of German researchers were improving sound transmission for high-definition television. Their efforts resulted in a technology that reduces the size of digital sound files by a factor greater than 10. This innovation became the standard for the Moving Picture Experts Group, with its initial label of "MPEG 1 Layer 3," giving way to the moniker of "MP3." Although created for television, MP3 soon became the format of choice for those wishing to exchange musical files. Such individuals often took the digital music found on CDs and created MP3 copies. The compressed size of the MP3s, in turn, facilitated their distribution via e-mail. These individuals had therefore attained what the record firms had hoped to prevent: digital copies of prerecorded music. Moreover, their copies could be widely disseminated with little effort (Drummond, 2000; Keefe, 2000).

Various entrepreneurs sought to exploit the distribution of MP3s, with the Napster web site providing the most infamous example. It originated, in part, from the idea of Shawn Fanning, a one-time student at Northeastern University who created a program for sharing musical files. The operation of Napster was elegantly simple. It offered its users free access to musical recordings by linking together the hard drives belonging to the community of Napster users. This, in turn, allowed users to search for and download, without payment, digital files of music found on their peers' computers. Many of these downloaded files contained songs copied from commercial recordings—copies made without the permission of record firms.

As the number of exchanged MP3s exploded into the millions, the RIAA filed suit against the web site in December 1999, alleging that Napster facilitated copyright infringement. The allegation received support when a court ordered Napster to prevent its users from trading copyrighted music. Unable to devise a means for preventing copyright infringement, and failing in the court of appeals, the first incarnation of Napster ground to a halt ("The Industry Responds," 2000; Levy, 2000; "Music Publishers," 2001; "Napster Downloads Drop 36 Percent in April," 2001; Stone, 2000; Zeidler, 2000b).

The Napster ruling did not solve the recording industry's troubles. Subsequent peer-to-peer systems (e.g., Kazaa) proved more immune to legal action than had the first incarnation of Napster ("Not-so-Jolly Rogers," 2003), and the circulation of commercial recordings without payment to copyright holders continued at a startling pace—with more than 5 million individuals sharing some 250 million songs per week by the end of 2003 (Nelson, 2004). Meanwhile, firms beyond the recording industry eventually launched online sites, such as Apple's iTunes and Roxio's recent incarnation of Napster, that provided commercial recordings for a minimal price (e.g., 99 cents per downloaded song) and without copyright infringement (Kloer, 2003). These sites sold some 25 million songs in early 2004, with Apple's iTunes accounting for the most (Belson, 2004; Levy, 2004).

The success of iTunes and other sites suggested that consumers were ready to embrace a legal approach to online music. Concurrently, the recording industry endured a dramatic decline in the sales of prerecorded music, dropping more than 12 % from 2000 to 2003 (Nelson, 2004). Still, the industry had yet to devise a product conception addressing online music. Universal Music's move to cut the price of prerecorded CDs ("Not-so-Jolly Rogers," 2003), for example, was more a modification of the old product conception than the creation of a new conception. The flurry of lawsuits that the RIAA brought against individuals who engage in illegal downloads (Schwartz, 2004a) was more reactive than proactive—designating what consumers should not do with regard to online music. Amidst this flux and uncertainty, the Big Five moved to become the Big Four; after regulators blocked merger attempts among these large firms, a merger between Sony and Bertelsmann seemed eminent ("Not-so-Jolly Rogers," 2003; "Fightback," 2004).

Although issues surrounding the online distribution of music are far from resolved, these issues suggest that a new product conception will eventually appear. Heeding both the formats and uses of prerecorded music provides some purchase on why there is currently such flux. Though incredibly slow in accepting the online distribution of music, the dominant record firms have embraced the idea (Keefe, 2000). They have not, however, embraced the MP3 because of its lack of copy protection (Hillis, 2000; Rose, 2000; Ziedler, 2000a). Instead, they seek to "create piracy-proof specifications for a standard or family of standards for digital music" (Drummond, 2000; p. 158; see also Scwhartz, 2004b). That is, they hope to avoid the problems that they experienced in the late 1970s, when, as they claimed, excessive copying of prerecorded music raised all sorts of difficulties for the recording industry.

These record firms therefore face the challenge of devising such a format and then persuading consumers to adopt it. Record firms are likewise concerned with the uses of online music. Though still not entitled to compensation whenever their recordings are broadcast on radio (RIAA, 1995), as a result of the Digital Millennium Copyright Act of 1998 (UCLA, 2003), they are entitled to compensation when their recordings are conveyed via the Internet. They will likely be vigilant in securing this right, perhaps motivated by distant memories of free music found on radio nearly destroying the recording industry. Nevertheless, record firms face the challenge of securing such income from various parties ("Music Publishers," 2000; Tedeschi, 2004; Zeidler, 2000c).

The formats and uses of online music are far from institutionalized. As in previous periods, this epochal change will depend on the innovations of particular firms, and the politicking and coercion that follow. Such change will have major implications for the market for prerecorded music. For example, a few record firms now dominate the market for prerecorded music, in large part, because of their extensive distribution systems, which can ship a voluminous supply of prerecorded music to retailers in the United States and abroad. Moving to a product conception where digital files are distributed online, we may see a weakening of these firms and the emergence of a modern day Decca or Capitol that grows to dominance by championing a new product conception. Whatever the outcome, the new logic of doing business will not merely result from the facile diffusion of a superior technology—for instance, the typical MP3 is not the optimal format for sound quality (Captain, 2004)—but will emerge from the interplay between technology and contextual factors.

CONCLUSION

In atomized depictions, markets are governed by universal laws that transcend a given sociohistorical context. Producing firms negotiate their respective markets in relative isolation, for they each operate by heeding efficiency and profit concerns rather than by collaborating with other producers; superior technologies easily diffuse, as efficient and profit-maximizing firms eagerly exploit these optimal innovations. Though appealing in their parsimony, atomistic depictions gloss over the difficulties that producing firms face in real world markets. As one institutional economist noted, "The implication of this setup is that time and place (space) do not matter.... This is what makes the [depictions] so neat and elegant, but also so bloodless and without the noise and fight that we know from real life" (Myrhmann, 1989, p. 41).

The case of the prerecorded music market reveals a cognitive process that is lacking in atomized depictions, whereby market producers must decipher how they are to employ new and old technologies. Such a cognitive process, however, is at the core of neo-institutional theory and at the heart of the present study. Institutionalists suggest that the potential for market change emerges when producers conceive of technology in a manner that sharply breaks with past conceptions, as when Capitol Records personnel envisioned radio airplay as stimulating rather than hampering record sales. Institutionalists also suggest that actual change occurs when most producers embrace such a new conception, as when small firms emulated Capitol Records by seeking radio airplay and the Big Three begrudgingly followed suit.

Institutionalists find that the progression from new conception to widespread acceptance, however, can entail coercion or politicking by powerful actors (Leblebici et al., 1991). Such coercian occurred when U.S. courts forced radio stations to cease broadcasting records that contained prohibitive inscriptions. Such persuasion occurred when CBS and RCA convinced record firms to adopt the LP and 45-rpm disc while abandoning the 78-rpm disc. The transformation of the prerecorded music market, then, did not arise as isolated firms embraced new technology, as atomized depictions suggest. Instead, transformation arose as producing firms collectively reassessed the nature of old and new technology.

REFERENCES

Adams, W., & Brock, J. W. (1991). *Antitrust economics on trial.* Princeton, NJ: Princeton University Press.

American Society of Composers, Authors, and Publishers. (1933). *How the public gets its music.* New York: Author.

Are cassettes here to stay? (1969). *High Fidelity, 19,* 46–53.

Atlas, B. (1950, May 13). RCA's Sarnoff tangles with Rosenman. *Billboard, 62,* 1, 11, 16.

Bachman, W. S. (1977). The LP and the single. *Journal of the Audio Engineering Society, 25,* 821–823.

Balio, T. (Ed.). (1990). *Hollywood in the age of television.* Boston: Unwin Hyman.

Banks, J. (1996). *Monopoly television.* Boulder, CO: Westview.

Barrios, R. (1995). *A song in the dark.* New York: Oxford University Press.

Belson, K. (2004, April 19). Infighting left Sony behind Apple in digital music [Electronic Version]. *The New York Times,* p. C1.

Best selling pop LPs. (1957, October 7). *Billboard, 69,* 40.

Bijker, W. E., & Law, J. (Eds.). (1992). *Shaping technology/building society.* Cambridge, MA: MIT Press.

Bodoh, A. G. (1977). The jukebox, the radio, and the record. *Journal of the Audio Engineering Society, 25,* 836–842.

Boehm, G. A. (1958, August). Stereo goes to market. *Fortune, 58,* 108–111,165.

Cap promotion push in works to build bands. (1950, February 18). *Billboard, 62,*16.

Captain, S. (2004, April 1). All the world's a soundstage as audio formats evolve [Electronic version]. *The New York Times,* p. X.

Chandler, A., Jr. (1990). *Scale and scope.* Cambridge, MA: Belknap.

Christman, E., & Terry, K. (1990, June 30). Label execs say cassette will endure. *Billboard, 102,* 7, 92.

Conant, M. (1960). *Antitrust in the motion picture industry.* Berkeley: University of California Press.

Cusumano, M. A., Mylonadis, Y., & Rosenbloom, R. S. (1992). Strategic maneuvering and mass-market dynamics. *Business History Review, 66,* 51–194.

Dacin, M. T, Ventresca, M. J,. & Beal, B. D. (1999). The embeddedness of organizations. *Journal of Management, 25,* 317–356.

Davis, G. F., Diekmann, K. A., & Tinsley, C. H. (1994). The decline and fall of the conglomerate firm in the 1980s. *American Sociological Review, 59,* 547–570.

Denisoff, R. S. (1986). *Tarnished gold.* New Brunswick, NJ: Transaction.

Denisoff, R. S. (1988). *Inside MTV.* New Brunswick, NJ: Transaction.

Dexter, D. (1969, December 27). 1930–1945, disk jockey. *Billboard, 81,* 56, 58.

DiMaggio, P. J. (1997). Culture as cognition. *Annual Review of Sociology, 23,* 263–287.

Disco, C., & van der Meulen, B. (1998). Introduction. In C. Disco & B. van der Meulen (Eds.), *Getting new technologies together* (pp. 1–13). Berlin: de Gruyter.

Diskeries wary of entering tape field. (1954, February 20). *Billboard, 66,* 16.

Dobbin, F., & Dowd, T. J. (1997). How policy shapes competition. *Administrative Science Quarterly, 42,* 501–529.

Dobbin, F., & Dowd, T. J. (2000). The market that antitrust built. *American Sociological Review, 65,* 631–657.

Dobbin, F., Sutton, J. R., Meyer, J. W., & Scott, W. R. (1993). Equal opportunity law and the construction of internal labor markets. *American Journal of Sociology, 99,* 396–427.

Dowd, T. J. (2003). Structural power and the construction of markets. *Comparative Social Research, 21,* 147–201.

Dowd, T. J. (2004). Concentration and diversity revisited. *Social Forces, 82,* 1411–1455.

Dowd, T. J., & Blyler, M. (2002). Charting race. *Poetics, 30,* 83–106.

Dowd, T. J., & Dobbin, F. (1997). The embedded actor and the invention of natural economic law. *American Behavioral Scientist, 40,* 478–489.
Drummond, M. (2000, December 12). Big music fights back. *Business 2.0, 5,* 154–165.
Edelman, L., & Suchman, M. C. (1997). The legal environment of organizations. *Annual Review of Sociology, 23,* 479–515.
Ennis, P. H. (1992). *The seventh stream.* Hanover, NH: Wesleyan University Press.
Fagan, T. (1982). Notes and comments on the 1931 to 1934 listing of RCA Victor's pre-LP-33 1/3 rpm recordings. *Association of Recorded Sound Collections Journal, 14*(3), 41–61.
Federal Communications Commission. (1941). *Report on chain broadcasting.* Washington, DC: Superintendent of Documents.
Fightback or death-rattle? [Electronic version]. (2004, April 2). *The Economist,* x.
Fischer, C. (1992). *America calling.* Berkeley: University of California Press.
Fligstein, N. (1996). Markets as politics. *American Sociological Review, 61,* 656–673.
Garlick, L. (1977). The graphic arts and the record industry. *Journal of the Audio Engineering Society, 25,* 779–784.
Gellatt, R. (1977). *The fabulous phonograph, 1877–1977.* New York: MacMillan.
Giles, J., & Mundy, C. (1991, December 12). Yearbook. *Rolling Stone, 619/620,* 18–95.
Goldmark, P. C. (1973). *Maverick inventor.* New York: Saturday Review Press.
Gray, M. H. (1986). The birth of Decca stereo. *Association for Recorded Sound Collections, 18*(1–3), 5–13.
Grein, P. (1992a, June 13). Capitol Records. *Billboard, 104,* C2, C4, C30–C32, C36.
Grein, P. (1992b). *Capitol Records, fiftieth anniversary.* Hollywood, CA: Capitol Records.
Hard trek for diskers: Tax figures though fight in '49—New look in 1950. (1950, January 7). *Billboard, 62,* 3, 12.
Hayes, H. C. (1982). Performance rights in sound recordings. *Copyright Law Symposium, 27,* 113–153.
Hillis, S. (2000, January 7). RealNetworks, Universal joins in web music. *Reuters.* Retrieved January 7, 2000, from http://dailynews.yahoo.com/h/nm/2000107/en/music-relnetworks_1.html
Hyde, J. L. (1994). *Adversaries to allies.* Unpublished doctoral dissertation, University of Alabama, Tuscaloosa.
The industry responds to Napster. (2000, April 15). *Billboard, 112,* 1, 105.
Isom, W. R. (1977). Record materials, part II. *Journal of the Audio Engineering Society, 25,* 718–723.
Jukes will test new-speed disks: 45's and 33 1/3's to get trial start April 1. (1950, March 4). *Billboard, 62,* 18, 84.
Keefe, B. (2000, October 2). Napster verdict. *Atlanta Journal Constitution,* pp. C1–C2.
Kerr, C. E. (1990). Incorporating the star. *Business History Review, 64,* 383–410.
Khanna, S. K. (1977). Record materials, part III. *Journal of the Audio Engineering Society, 25,* 724–726.
King, A. B. (1966). *The marketing of phonograph records in the United States.* Unpublished doctoral dissertation, The Ohio State University, Columbus.
Kloer, P. (2003, October 24). Downloading 2.0. *Atlanta Journal Constitution,* pp. C1, C8.
Kogen, J. H. (1977). Record changers, turntables, and tone arms. *Journal of the Audio Engineering Society, 25,* 749–758.
Leblebici, H. (1995). Radio broadcasters. In G. R. Carroll & M. T. Hannan (Eds.), *Organization in industry* (pp. 308–331). New York: Oxford University Press.
Leblebici, H., Salancik, G. R., Copay, A., & King, T. (1991). Institutional change and the transformation of interorganizational fields. *Administrative Science Quarterly, 36,* 333–363.
Leiter, R. D. (1974). *The musicians and Petrillo.* New York: Octagon Books.

Levy, S. (2000, June 5). The noisy war over Napster. *Newsweek, 135,* 46–53.
Levy, S. (2004, July 26). iPod Nation. *Newsweek, 144,* 42–50.
Lewis, T. (1991). *Empire of the air.* New York: Harper Perennial.
Lynch, V. (1990). *American jukebox.* San Francisco: Chronicle Books.
Majors and subsids switch to 45's for pops to deejays. (1954, June 5). *Billboard, 66,* 14, 26.
McGahan, A. M. (1991). Philips' compact disc introduction. *Harvard Business School Case Study,* #9-792-035. Cambridge, MA: Harvard Business School.
McGuire, P., Granovetter, M., & Schwartz, M. (1994). Thomas Edison and the social construction of the early electricity industry in America. In R. Swedberg (Ed.), *Explorations in economic sociology* (pp. 213–246). New York: Russell Sage Foundation.
Men behind the microphones. (1952, September 8). *Newsweek, 40,* 56–59.
Meyer, J. W., Boli, J., & Thomas, G. M. (1994). Ontology and rationalization in the western cultural account. In W. R. Scott & J. W. Meyer (Eds.), *Institutional environments* (pp. 9–27). Newbury Park, CA: Sage.
Meyer, J., & Rowan, B. (1977). Institutionalized organizations. *American Journal of Sociology, 83,* 340–363.
Millard, A. (1995). *America on record.* New York: Cambridge University Press.
Moody's Investor Services. (1950). *Moody's manual of investments.* New York: Author.
Morton, D. (2000). *Off the record.* New Brunswick, NJ: Rutgers University Press.
Music publishers record labels reach internet pact. (2000, October 10). *Reuters.* Retrieved October 11, 2000, from http://dailynews.yahoo.com/h/nm/20001010/en/music-riaq_1.html
Myhrmann, J. (1989). The new institutional economics and the process of economic development. *Journal of Institutional and Theoretical Economics, 145,* 38–58.
National Association of Broadcasters. (1978). NAB code of ethics and standards of commercial practice. In F. J. Kahn (Ed.), *Documents of American broadcasting* (pp. 63–66). Englewood Cliffs, NJ: Prentice-Hall.
NBC Advisory Council. (1930). *The president's report and resume of programs fourth annual meeting.* New York: Author.
Nelson, C. (2004, February 23). CD sales rise, but industry is too wary to party [Electronic version]. *The New York Times,* p. C1.
Nelson, R. R. (1994). Evolutionary theorizing about economic change. In N. J. Smelser & R. Swedberg (Eds.), *The handbook of economic sociology* (pp. 108–136). Princeton, NJ: Russell Sage.
Not-so-Jolly Rogers [Electronic version]. (2003, September 10). *The Economist,* X.
1,092 stations can play LPs. (1950, February 4). *Billboard, 62,* 16.
Puterbaugh, P. (1992, October 29). Gone but not forgotten. *Rolling Stone, 642,* 28.
Radio Corporation of America. (1953). *The 50 year story of Radio Corporation of America.* New York: Author.
Recording Industry Association of America. (n.d.). *Recording manufacturers' dollar shipment of phonograph records, 1921–1966; dollar shipment of discs and tapes, 1967–1982.* Unpublished manuscript.
Recording Industry Association of America. (1987). *Inside the recording industry.* Washington, DC: Author.
Recording Industry Association of America. (1995). *(R)evolution.* Washington, DC: Author.
Ringer, B. (1961). *The unauthorized duplication of sound recordings.* Washington, DC: U.S. Government Printing Office.
Roberts, J. L. (1995, April 17). Hey Edgar, why MCA? *Newsweek, 125,* 58–60.

Rose, S. (2000, September 11). Warner Music, RealNetworks in digital music act. *Reuters.* Retrieved September 12, 2000 from http://dailynews.yahoo.com/h/nm/20000911/en/music-warner_2.html
Roy, W. G. (1997). *Socializing capital.* Princeton, NJ: Princeton University Press.
Sanjek, R. (1988). *American popular music and its business.* New York: Oxford University Press.
Schicke, C. A. (1974). *Revolution in sound.* Boston: Little, Brown and Co.
Schwartz, J. (2004a, January 22). Music industry returns to court, altering tactics on file sharing [Electronic version]. *The New York Times,* p. C1.
Schwartz, J. (2004b, March 8) A software aimed at taming file-sharing [Electronic version]. *The New York Times,* p. C7.
Scott, W. R. (1995). *Institutions and organizations.* Thousand Oaks, CA: Sage.
Sherman, M. W., & Nauck, K. R., III. (1998). *Note the notes.* New Orleans, LA: Monarch Record Enterprises.
Silverberg, G., Dosi, G., & Orsenigo, L. (1988). Innovation, diversity, and diffusion. *Economic Journal, 98,* 1032–1054.
Simon, B. (1950, May 20). Indies losing LP gravy. *Billboard, 62,* 14.
Smith, M. R., & Marx, L. (Eds.). (1994). *Does technology drive history?* Cambridge, MA: MIT Press.
Standard and Poor's. (2000). *Industry surveys.* New York: Author.
Standardization advances: Disks, players settling down to 3 speeds. (1950, January 14). *Billboard, 62,* 20.
Stations to get 325,000 45 R. P. M. records free. (1954, July 3). *Billboard, 66,* 3, 11.
Sterling, C. (1984). *Electronic media.* New York: Praeger.
Stone, B. (2000, November 13). The odd couple. *Newsweek , 136,* 56–57.
Sutton, A. (2000). *American record labels and companies.* Denver, CO: Mainspring Press.
Tedeschi, B. (2004, March 22). E-commerce report. *The New York Times,* p. C7.
UCLA Online Institute for Cyberspace Law & Policy (2003). *The digital millenium copyright act.* Retrieved July 9, 2003 from http://www.gseis.ucla.edu/iclp/dmca1.html
U.S. Congress. (1942). *Use of mechanical production of music.* Washington, DC: Government Printing Office.
U.S. Congress. (1948). *Restrictive union practices of the American Federation of Musicians.* Washington, DC: Government Printing Office.
U.S. Congress. (1958). *Amendment to Communications Act of 1934 (prohibiting radio and television stations from engaging in music publishing or recording business).* Washington, DC: Government Printing Office.
U.S. Congress. (1960). *Responsibilities of broadcasting licensees and station personnel.* Washington, DC: Government Printing Office.
U.S. Congress. (1978). *Performance rights in sound recordings.* Washington, DC: US Government Printing Office.
U.S. Congress. (1987). *Copyright issues presented by digital audio tape.* Washington, DC: US Government Printing Office.
U.S. Congress. (1992). *Audio Home Recording Act of 1992.* Washington, DC: US Government Printing Office.
U.S. Congress, Office of Technology Assessment. (1989). *Copyright and home copying.* Washington, DC: Government Printing Office.
Uzzi, B. (1997). Social structure and competition in interfirm networks. *Administrative Science Quarterly, 42,* 35–67.

Whitburn, J. (1986). *Pop memories, 1890–1954.* Menomonee Falls, WI: Record Research.
Who're pressing what speeds. (1950, January 21). *Billboard, 62,* 14.
Yonay, Y. P. (1998). *The struggle over the soul of economics.* Princeton, NJ: Princeton University Press.
Zeidler, S. (2000a). BMG launches music download venture with Lycos. *Reuters.* Retrieved October 11, 2000, from http://dailynews.yahoo.com/h/nm/20001010/en/music-bertelsmann_1.html
Zeidler, S. (2000b, May 8). RIAA scores early win in battle vs. Napster. *Reuters.* Retrieved May 10, 2000, from http://dailynews.yahoo.com/h/nm/20000508/en/music-napster_6.html
Zeidler, S. (2000c). RIAA to develop identifier systems for music on internet. *Reuters.* Retrieved October 14, 2000, from http://dailynews.yahoo.com/h/nm/20001012/en/music-riaq_2.html

CHAPTER

14

Silicon Alley.com: Struggling for Legitimacy in New Media

Theresa K. Lant
New York University

Patricia F. Hewlin
Georgetown University

The businesses emerging around the creation of new media often face a unique set of challenges. Not only do they need to convince resource holders that their individual firms are worthy of investment, but they also need to create resource holder confidence in the new medium on which they are building their businesses. Each new medium must become legitimate in the eyes of artists who might use the medium, consumers who will experience culture via the medium, and stakeholders who provide resources to maintain the viability of the medium.

The importance of legitimacy as a precondition for the formation of cultural industries is strikingly illustrated in the emergence of Silicon Alley, an agglomeration of firms and institutions in the New York City area that focus on new media. Initially, these organizations emphasized CD-ROMs as the main mode of distribution, but subsequently the Internet became the driving force of this new media district. The lexicon used in New York to refer to Internet-based businesses, new media as opposed to e-commerce, emphasizes the existing identity of New York City.

New York is a major media center, with a large number of media firms, including publishing, entertainment, journalism, broadcasting, cable, and advertising. This expertise is reflected in the human resources that populate the city. The majority of firms founded in New York during the Silicon Alley era (1990–2000) were engaged in digital media, web-page design, and advertising. Most were engaged in some form of content creation, content distribution, or services associated with using the new medium of the Internet.

This chapter explores how entrepreneurial actors in New York City attempted to legitimize this new medium through collective action and evangelism akin to the creation of a social movement. The key theme that we explore is how entrepreneurial actors create forums for interaction among each other as a way of creating and communicating a collective identity that was both distinct from the way in which other regions were using the Internet and yet credible enough to attract resources. This chapter also asks whether the creation of a distinctive identity is sufficient to sustain a region devoted to a new medium from the threats of economic turndowns, competition, and technological change.

Although the use of the Internet as a medium for providing entertainment and information has diffused broadly, the fate of Silicon Alley as a regional center of Internet content creation is less certain. Following the financial market downturn of April 2000 and the attack on the World Trade Center in New York in September 2001, Silicon Alley ceased to exist as a distinct and unique agglomeration of new media entrepreneurial activity: "Places like Silicon Alley captured and fermented the energies, resources, aspirations of the moment, but they were not built for the ages" (Ross, 2003, p. 236).

COGNITIVE LEGITIMACY AND EMERGING CULTURAL MEDIA

Entrepreneurs working to establish new industries must establish legitimacy for their industry and product in addition to promoting their individual businesses (Aldrich, 1999; Aldrich & Fiol, 1994). Potential resource holders may not fully understand the nature of the new venture, potential customers may not understand the nature and value of products and services being offered, and potential employees may view jobs in the new population with a mixture of skepticism and distrust. To succeed, founders must find strategies to raise the level of public knowledge and acceptance of new activity, or cognitive legitimacy (Aldrich). In order to attract resources to their nascent firms, entrepreneurs must make sense of their businesses for resource holders. Resource holders need to understand the potential market that the firm will serve, the value of the product or service that the firm will provide, and the nature of competition that the firm will face (Pollock & Rindova, 2002).

In emerging industries, there is a great deal of ambiguity with respect to all of these factors. The nature and value of products and services are not understood. It is often unclear how one firm's product compares with another, or if two firms are even competing in the same product category. This is because both the nature of products and their potential value are in flux; the relative positions of firms offering these evolving products are also evolving.

A well-known example of such ambiguity and the evolution of product or service definitions can be seen in the way firms that emerged as Internet search engines have added features such as information categorization, content agglomeration, and e-mail over time. Potential customers and competitors experienced significant uncertainty regarding the nature and value of these services, how to use them, and which firms should be considered direct competitors (Lant, 2003).

The level of ambiguity is even greater in emerging cultural industries. Cultural industries are characterized by high levels of ambiguity about product characteristics that are associated with quality and about the strategies of firms that are successful (Lampel, Lant, Shamsie, 2000). The distinctive characteristics of entertainment markets make the establishment of any new media industry especially difficult.

FOSTERING COGNITIVE LEGITIMACY THROUGH COLLECTIVE ACTION

In this emerging arena of Internet-based new media, actors were struggling to make sense of a field in which market segments and the rules of the game were not yet established. We found that the actors in this field were engaged in a process of trying to make sense of who they were, what their product or service was, what the potential market was, and with whom they should form relationships. In this process of trying to simultaneously create and make sense of this new arena of social and economic activity, the interaction among individuals across firms is as critical as interaction within firms. It is a field in which cooperation as well as competition flourishes and network linkages are critical for organizational survival.

Before the world had ever heard of Silicon Alley, a number of actors were sowing the seeds that would produce a recognizable social and economic community based on creating new Internet-based media businesses. Entrepreneurial actors in Silicon Alley attempted to create cognitive legitimacy by engaging in two related types of activity: creating forums for interaction among diverse sets of actors, and through these interactions, attempting to create a distinct yet credible identity for New York City as a successful new media center and the most important location for new media content creation. This chapter explores these activities by illustrating the types of actions, speech, and networking activities pursued by Silicon Alley entrepreneurs.

Creating Forums for Social Interaction

Starting as early as 1990, communities of writers and artists were interacting about the potential of using new media as a canvas for their work. For instance, Stacy Horn, a graduate of New York University's Interactive Telecommunications Program, founded ECHO, an online community for writers and artists. In 1992 Mark Stahlman, a retired investment banker who had taken AOL public in 1992, started CyberSalon, a "monthly dinner party for people interested in computer-related, network related activities in New York." In 1994, Stahlman, along with Brian Horey, a local venture capitalist, founded NYNMA, the New York New Media Association, a nonprofit trade association.

Brian Horey recalled:

> NYNMA formed because this new media thing was starting to happen, and we were concerned that New York wouldn't play the role in it that it should. At the time we got it started, CD-ROM development was still the leading edge of the new media industry, and we thought too much of it was going to the West Coast. We needed more infrastructure and a sense of community if we were going to build something here.
>
> NYNMA's mission, according to Stahlman, was "to galvanize a community in New York." According to a published quote from the founders of NYNMA: "We formed NYNMA so that we could stop flying to California every other week to do business" ("Building a New Media Community," 1998, p. 3).

At its peak in 1999, membership in NYNMA had reached nearly 7,000 individuals in approximately 2,500 companies. Members worked in a variety of fields, such as broadcasting and publishing, web-site development, design, entertainment, education, and professional and financial services. One of NYNMA's goals was to promote Silicon Alley as a leading global center for new media business (NYNMA web site). NYNMA initially formalized networking among new media participants by holding regular Cybersuds meetings at local nightclubs such as the Roxy. NYNMA defined Cyberuds as "a chance to meet people from the regional new media community in a casual atmosphere—exchange ideas, business opportunities, and gossip" (Cybersuds announcement). Alice Rodd O'Rourke, Executive Director NYNMA, stated, "I've worked in four industries, and I've never seen networking the way this industry networks. It's very purposeful: Don't you want to know? Don't you want to share? Don't you want to be part of this? It's got a spark in it that is very exciting."

Many other formal and informal networking forums were created during this time. Many were initiated by a self-proclaimed group of "Early True Believers." They are "the closest thing Silicon Alley has to an indigenous population ... they're brainy math-and-music types with impressive liberal-arts educations, mostly upper-crust backgrounds, and birthdays in or around 1966" ("Silicon Alley 10003," 2000, p. X). They held social networking events called "CyberSlacker parties" ("Silicon Alley 10003," 2000). Jamie Levy, hostess of the Cyberslacker parties, described them as "bringing together animators and programmers. It was a party atmosphere, but we would have computers set up." Many of the friends and attendees are the founders of Silicon Alley firms such as MTVi, Feed, Razorfish, Pseudo.com, StockObjects, Nerve, and the Silicon Alley Reporter. Another networking event was "Cocktails with Courtney" (social columnist and Pulitzer heir), "monthly parties where dot-com execs, top-level managers, analysts, programmers, investors, and media professionals could meet in a friendly and elegant social networking environment."

Other venues for interaction followed, and became increasingly formalized. In March 1997, the Global Community Sandbox opened at 55 Broad Street in downtown Manhattan. The image of a sandbox is that of converging and shifting and blurred boundaries among its components. This exemplifies the interaction among actors with different backgrounds who meet at the Sandbox to share ideas. These interactions are also exemplified by advertisements for the Silicon Alley 1998 conference, which looks like a Venn diagram illustrating the interaction of different sets of people and businesses.

Diverse actors engage in cooperative efforts to facilitate new media in New York. Actors in Silicon Alley come from a wide variety of professional backgrounds and industries, including advertising, graphic design, publishing, digital technology, software development, visual and performing arts, and journalism. Professional boundaries and definitions created by traditional media and other industries started falling away as interaction among players from different arenas increased.

Figure 14.1 provides an example of the way in which actors from different industries and types of institutions interacted at these boundary-crossing events. By creating forums for interaction such as the "Alley to the Valley" conference, new media entrepreneurs were able to communicate their vision to potential resource holders in established media business, established firms in complementary industries, financial institutions, and potential investors. In these forums, entrepreneurs could communicate their uniqueness while developing legitimacy for new ways of doing business.

Creating Boundaries, Categories, and Identity

Facilitated by social networking, these actors moved quickly to spread the word about the possibilities for new media business and about how and why New York was both different and the place to be for new media. These new media evangelists used several means to spread the word.

The following quote from the September 1997 editorial of the *Silicon Alley Reporter* illustrates the way in which actors in the region were taking collective action to create cognitive legitimacy for their products and their community:

> There is a camaraderie amongst the Interactive advertising community. It goes something like this: this will never be a viable industry unless we shift huge amounts of advertising dollars from TV, print and radio to Interactive. Fighting over experimental advertising budgets is not going to rise the tide. In order for all the boats to rise the community needs to evangelize the potential of online advertising. (Silicon Alley Reporter, p. 2)

The parties, conferences, seminars, and networking events were opportunities to communicate about New York new media's distinctive identity. One good illustration is the August 12, 1998 CyberSplash, billed as follows:

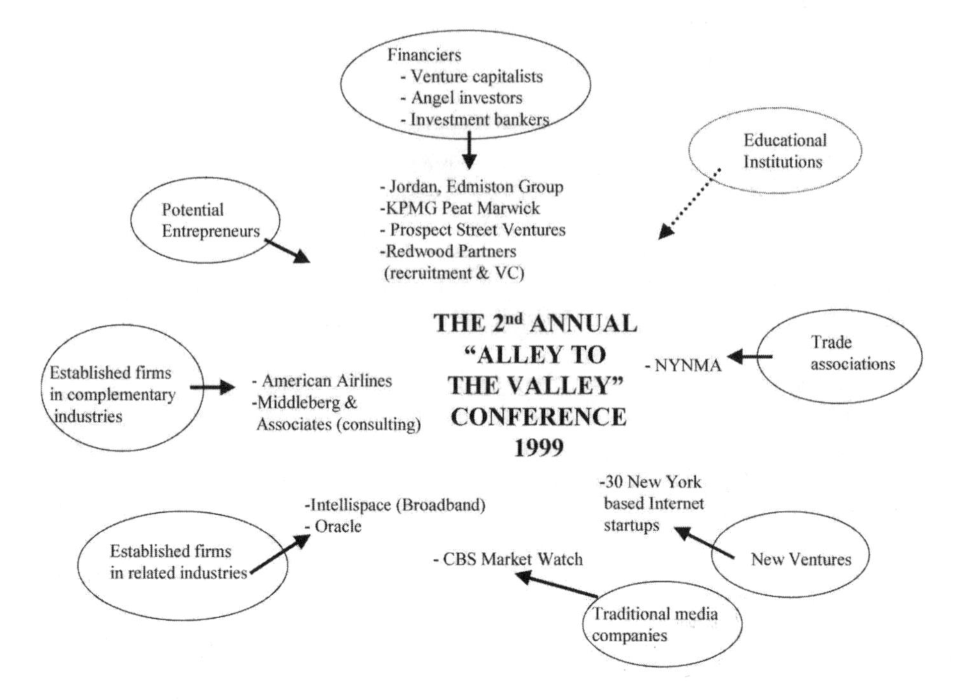

FIG. 14.1. Groups of actors represented at the second annual Alley to the Valley conference.

> NYNMA & Ad Club—Floating Towards the Millennium ... the networking event united the best of NYC's traditional media organizations with companies on the cutting edge of the Internet. With only 506 days to go until the Millennium, these two communities came together to forge synergies that will shape the online advertising industry in the next century. ("NYNMA & Ad Club," 1998, p. 2).

NYNMA also helped to reduce the ambiguity around new media products and services by creating product and business categories; members were asked to identify themselves within various categories, which evolved over time, and then organize their membership directories according to the categories. Actors sponsoring formal conferences, such as the Silicon Alley 1998 conference, also facilitated this categorization process. A communiqué from the organizer of the conference stated, "Many of the companies [participating in the conference] are not yet categorized.... If your company is one of them please let me know which category you would like to be listed under (commerce, content, interactive, agency, etc.)" (J. M. Calacanis, personal communication, February 12, 1998 e-mail to all Silicon Alley Reporter subscribers).

The fact that Silicon Alley identified itself with media content is significant not only because it reflects the culture and expertise of the city, but also because media are a vehicle for communication and information diffusion. Whereas firms in all industries use media to communicate about their products ("Intel inside") and their corporate image (e.g., "Cisco—are you ready?"), media firms are readily able to publicize their own products and image. Thus, it is no surprise that a major vehicle for spreading the word about the unique identity of New York new media was the use of old and new media. Together, old and new media both competed and cooperated with each other in attempts to enhance the legitimacy and distinctiveness of Silicon Alley.

New media advertising proliferated in old media print publications, broadcast radio and television, and cable. Opinion leaders in the media also used their positions to try to shape the cognitive understanding of the emerging field. This pattern of actions suggests that the media, both old and new, played a key role in attracting attention to and generating legitimacy for the emerging new media businesses in New York. Each publication not only provides information, but also contributes frames of reference, interpretations, and evaluations. The information they provide is not value-free. Rather, it is heavily laden with content that offers a point of view. The choice of what appears in the publications and what does not frames what is important and what is not. Furthermore, the content that is included is framed in a variety of ways.

A frame that was used frequently is the creation of lists, in particular, lists of firms or people that the publication has identified as being important or deserving of media attention. Established print media played a role in this. For example, *Crain's New York*'s "Top Cats" listed "players shaping Silicon Alley" ("Growing Up," 1997, p. 19). New online publications also played their part. The *@NY—The New York Internet Newsletter*, an online publication dedicated to news about Silicon Alley, which also featured daily e-mail updates to subscribers, said about their top-25 list that "the AtNewYork.Com 25 has historically tended to reward ideas" (@NY, 1997, www.atnewyork.com)

"In the early days of the local Internet business, ideas were all we had, and AtNewYork.com took it upon itself to analyze the best of the companies pursuing those ideas and to single them out, to make the list in 1999 a company had to be big; it had to be a marketplace leader or damn near a marketplace leader in its space" (The atnewyork.com, 25). The attention and legitimacy produced by these lists can be very powerful. The publications have a great deal of discretion in deciding whom to reward with such resources.

The manner in which information was communicated by the media also influenced the perceived identity of Silicon Alley. Much of what was written focused on what made New York new media distinctive. In 1996, a local entrepreneur started a print publication to cover both the business and social side of Silicon Alley, called *The Silicon Alley Reporter*. The editor of *The Silicon Alley Reporter* was the Alley's self-proclaimed evangelist. He used his bully pulpit to influence the identity of the new emerging New York media environment. The broad legitimizing role of *The Silicon Alley Reporter* was exemplified by the move to nationwide distribution in mid-1998. The following snapshots from his editorials between 1997 and 1999 illustrate the efforts of this publication to characterize New York new media as unique and powerful:

> Without getting too emotional on you, this is an unprecedented time in history. Young people with energy and dreams can take their shot. You don't need to wait in line, or beg someone at NBC or William Morris to take your call. You don't need to ask permission from anyone, you can just do it.... Whatever you do, don't put yourself in the position twenty years from now—when over a billion people are on the Internet—of kicking yourself for not taking a chance.... No one has made the equivalent of Citizen Kane on the Internet, but there's no reasons you can't be the Orson Welles of the Net. ("Editors Page," 1997, p. 2)

> Ten years from now people will laugh when they read about all the attention given to the browser wars. Give me a break, is Sienfeld funnier on a Sony TV rather than a JVC? New York and Los Angeles are becoming the driving force in the Internet Industry for a very simple reason: they are the talent and media capitals of the world. Sure, content and community are going to take longer to play out than the tools to make them. Right now, L.A. and NYC may be on the bottom of the food chain by the Red Herring's and Upside's standards because we don't have the immediate revenues that make myopic venture capitalists drool. But there's no place on the food chain I'd rather be. Would you rather have made the camera that shot "Citizen Kane," or make "Citizen Kane?" ("Editors Page," 1998, p. 2)

> A bunch of granola eating hippies from San Francisco were going to dictate the most powerful medium of all time? Give me a break. I'll tell you who's going to dictate the most powerful medium of all time—New Yorkers and people in Los Angeles, because they've always dictated what's happened to big mediums. ("Meta Tags," 1999)

THE DOUBLE-EDGED SWORD OF DISTINCTIVE IDENTITY

Our grounded exploration of the process of legitimizing new media in Silicon Alley highlights the important role played by collective action among early participants and their use of old and new media. The media were used to raise awareness, disseminate information, and help create an identity for Silicon Alley as well as the firms within it. Early in the life of Silicon Alley, advertising firms were reluctant to use new media. Like other forms of media, such as radio and TV broadcast, cable, and print media, advertising is a crucial revenue stream that enables media to survive. The very survival of new media, likewise, depended on convincing advertisers to use new media. The initial success of this strategy can be seen in Figure 14.2, from the rapid rise in the number of ad pages sold by *The Silicon Alley Reporter*, from 12 in a typical 1997 issue to almost 100 in late 1999.

Once traditional media accepted new media as legitimate, everything was set for the next stage of legitimization. Other resources such as human and financial capital were necessary to support the growth of the region. Increases in both forms of capital can be seen in the growth of jobs and the growth of venture capital in 1998 and 1999. The number of firms receiving venture capital increased from 32 in 1998 to 110 in 1999. The size of the venture capital deals increased also, from an average of $8.1 million per deal in 1998, to $11.5 million in 1999. The number of IPOs has also increased in a similar pattern, from 8 in 1998 to 41 in 1999. The

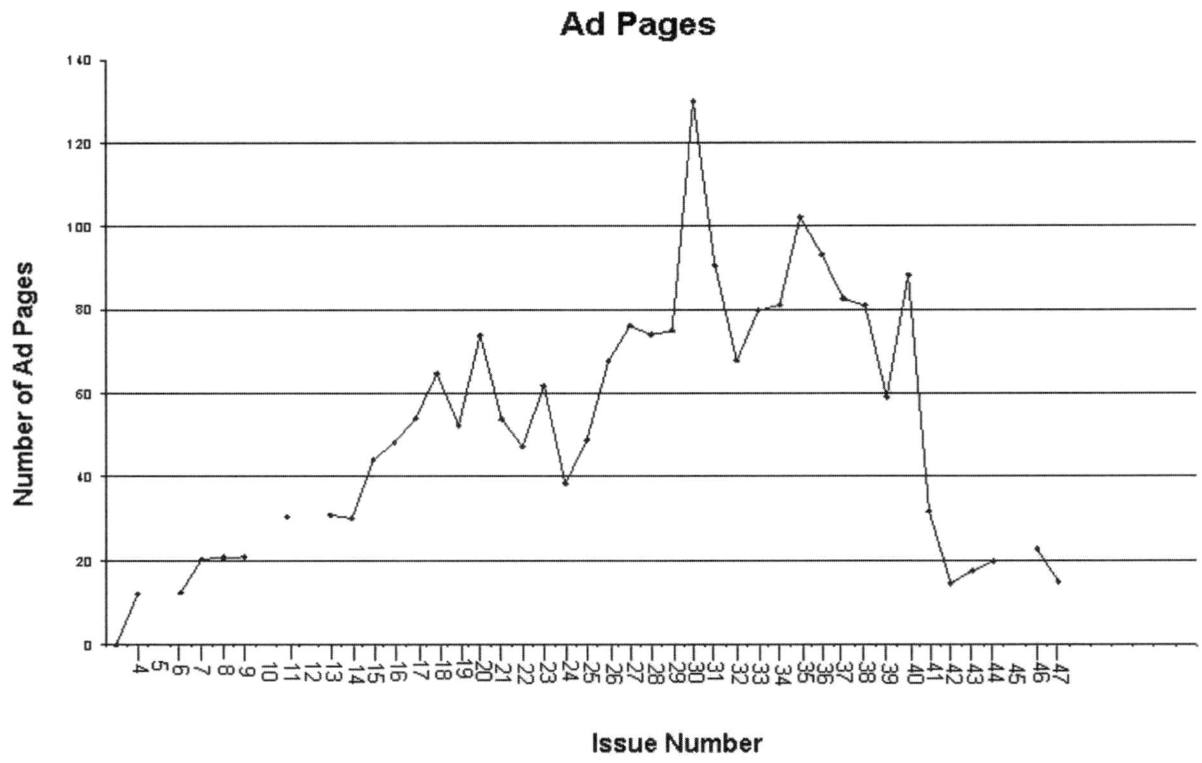

FIG. 14.2. *Silicon Alley Reporter* number of advertising pages between 1997 and 1999.

money raised per IPO also increased, from an average of $32.5 million in 1998, to $85.1 million in 1999 (PriceWaterhouseCoopers, 1999).

Our exploration of the process of legitimizing a new medium and creating a viable market for its products has yielded several insights. First, new media gain legitimacy by using existing media to grab visibility and attention. Because existing forms of media were already seen as legitimate, new media forms could obtain legitimacy by appearing in legitimate publications. Second, in order to attract resources, the entrepreneurs developing a new medium must be evangelists. They must use a variety of forums (including existing media) to communicate the value of using the new medium. Finally, a viable market is created through this process of educating and convincing resource holders to invest their time, attention, and money in the new medium. Thus, once consumers, advertisers, and investment bankers believed in the viability of the new medium, the market for cultural products on the Internet became a reality.

However, the creation of cognitive legitimacy that depended on claims of uniqueness was enough to sustain a viable new media industry in New York. The challenge that faced these aspiring new media businesses was made tougher as a result of the shortage of new venture capital following the stockmarket decline of April 2000 and the overall decline of the New York City economy following the attacks on the World Trade Center in September 2001. Once the flows of external resources dried up, the vitality of Silicon Alley declined rapidly (Arikan, 2004).

Although some of the entrepreneurial firms have survived, most of the innovative uses of new media have diffused to established media firms in what true believers would call a watered-down form. This decline is mirrored in the decline of media dedicated to following the Silicon Alley phenomenon, such as *The Silicon Alley Reporter.* Figure 14.2 shows the decline in ad pages in 2000 and 2001. Ultimately, the publication ceased to exist. Membership in NYNMA also declined, and it too has subsequently merged with a software trade association.

The creation of cognitive legitimacy was crucial to bringing resources to support new media into New York City. Such resource flows are critical to the emergence of a new industry and also to its sustainability. However, cognitive legitimacy may be a necessary but insufficient condition for the success of an industry. For an industry to succeed, it must also hold its own against forces such as substitutes, technological change, and direct competitors. In order for a regional industry to be sustainable, enthusiasm for and legitimacy of businesses leveraging the Internet for the creation and distribution of cultural content need to be backed up with sound business models.

As noted in *Crain's New York*, the buzz created by the evangelizing entrepreneurs in Silicon Alley exceeded their business acumen: "With unproven technologies and half baked business models, a generation of technophiles has received vast sums of money because venture capitalists, who would have required exacting credentials of any fledgling manufacturer or retailer, have applied few of the standard tests when it comes to new media" ("Gold Rush," 1998, p. 52). Lacking the management sophistication and resource base of established media firms, these new media entrepreneurs created excitement, buzz, and legitimacy for using the Internet as a new medium of cultural creation and distribution, but many were not able to create sustainable business enterprises to capture the value that they created.

CONCLUSION

Throughout history people have used various media to express ideas. The media available for use, however, have multiplied over time. Every form of cultural expression was a new medium at one time. Each new form of media has some unique qualities and tends to influence the nature of cultural expression in some new way. Media that we now take for granted, whether paper, radio, television, or film, were all path breaking in their time. There was no market for television before the television was invented. Once television was a technological reality, the existence of a television broadcast market depended on the adoption by consumers and programmers of both the technology and the type of content that it carried. In recent years, we have seen a similar pattern in the emergence and adoption of Internet-based cultural content.

The case example of Silicon Alley demonstrates a conundrum for new media entrepreneurs. Their efforts at creating a social movement to create excitement about and legitimize a new medium are crucial to the adoption of the medium. These efforts are not enough, however, to sustain their claims of uniqueness in the long term. New media diffuse into societal culture and business markets. What was once new becomes taken for granted, cognitively legitimate, and thus, becomes established, acceptable, and widely copied by entrepreneurs and established firms in other geographic regions. Thus, the efforts of early entrepreneurs are key to the widespread adoption and diffusion of a new medium. The irony is that, at least in the case of Silicon Alley, most of the entrepreneurs were not able to capture the value that they produced.

REFERENCES

Aldrich, H. E. (1999). *Organizations evolving.* Newbury Park, CA: Sage.

Aldrich, H. E., & Fiol, C. M. (1994). Fools rush in? The institutional context of industry creation. *Academy of Management Review, 19,* 645–670.

Arikan, A. (2004). *Entrepreneurial regions as complex entrepreneurial systems: A socio-cognitive model of emergence.* Unpublished doctoral dissertation, New York University.

"Building a New Media Community." (1998, November 23). *The New York Times.* Retrieved online.

Calacanis, J. M. (1998, February 12). E-mail communiqué.

"Editor's Page." (1997, May). *Silicon Alley Reporter, 4,* 2.

"Editor's Page." (1997, September). *Silicon Alley Reporter, 7,* 2.

"Editor's Page." (1998, April). *Silicon Alley Reporter, 13,* 3.

"Gold Rush." (1998, November 16). *Crain's New York Business,* p. 52.

"Growing Up." (1997, November 24). *Crain's New York,* p. 219.

Lant, T. K. (2000). *"The rise of Silicon Alley."* New York: Stern School of Business in *SternBusiness* available at: http://www.stern.nyu.edu/sternbusiness/fall.winter.2000

Lant, T. K. (2003), Strategic capabilities in emerging fields: Navigating ambiguity, leveraging social capital, and creating identity in Silicon Alley. In C. Helfat, (Ed.) *The evolution of organizational resources and capabilities: Emergence, development, and change* (pp. 110–118). London: Blackwell.

Lampel, J., Lant, T., & Shamsie, J. (2000). Balancing act: Learning from organizing practices in cultural industries. *Organization Science, 11*(3), 263–269.

"Meta Tags." (1999, June 11). *Shiftonline.* Retrieved June 11, 1999 from http://www.shiftonline.com

"NYNMA & Ad Club." (1998, September 15). *NYNMA News,* p. 2. Retrieved from http://www.nynma.org

Pollock, T., & Rindova, V. (2003). Media legitimation effects in the market for initial public offerings. *Academy of Management Journal, 46,* 631–642.

PriceWaterhouseCoopers, LLP. (1999). *New York media industry survey* (3rd. ed.). New York: Price Waterhouse Coopers.

Ross, A. (2003). *No collar: The humane workforce and its hidden costs.* New York: Basic Books.

"Silicon Alley 10003." (2000, March 6) *New York Magazine.*Coverstory, by Vanessa Grigoriadis. Retrieved from http://www.newyorkmag.com

V

The Impact of Globalization

Deeply moved by a BBC documentary on the 1984 Ethiopian famine, Bob Geldof, the singer and songwriter of the rock group The Boomtown Rats, organized two simultaneous concerts under the name Live Aid, one in London and one in Philadelphia. Live Aid became the biggest music event in history, drawing an estimated 1.5 billion television viewers world wide. The concert generated donations and royalties of over $140 million toward African famine relief. But beyond this, it inspired 45 musicians, including 21 of the top American performers such as Lionel Richie, Michael Jackson, Tina Turner, Bob Dylan, and Bruce Springsteen to gather at the A & M Recording Studios in Hollywood in order to record "We Are the World." Written by Lionel Richie and Michael Jackson and produced by Quincy Jones, the song and record went on to win the 1985 Grammys for both Song of the Year and Record of the Year and to sell more than 10 million copies, raising $50 million for famine relief.

Live Aid and "We Are the World" provide a compelling demonstration of the power of cultural industries to make the world a better place. Artists in the United Kingdom and the United States are able to mobilize worldwide support through song and performance for a stricken and remote region that few if any of them has ever visited. Live Aid and "We Are the World," however, also illustrate an aspect of globalization in cultural industries that has raised considerable concern and criticism. A closely intertwined popular music establishment based in the United States and the United Kingdom was able to use its vast network of communications and its ties to powerful corporate sponsors to impose its interpretation of the world on countries as far apart as Japan and Chile.

There are therefore two sides to globalization, one positive and the other negative. But to complicate matters, there are also two vantage points: that of producers and that of consumers. The rise of large global entertainment and media companies has, in the minds of many producers, been at the expense of local communities that are crushed under the flood of technically sophisticated and commercially appealing products from the great centers of cultural production in Europe and North America. Against this pessimistic assessment, there are others who see the story of globalization in cultural industries as the progressive coming together of distant creative communities leading to the opening of new opportunities for cultural industries that in the past were confined by their national boundaries.

The same difference of views can also be found in analyses of the impact of globalization on consumers. The pessimistic view argues that globalization in the cultural industries is commercializing the world's cultural heritage, replacing local cultural diversity with globally homogeneous products. The optimistic perspective sees globalization of cultural industries as stimulating innovation, promoting cross-fertilization, and increasing the diversity of products and experiences available to everybody worldwide.

Because globalization of cultural industries is an ongoing process, the verdict on these debates is essentially one on whether globalization should be encouraged or constrained. But debating the impact of globalization, is in this respect, is not simply an academic exercise. It represents a process that forces communities and polities to ponder whether and how they should react to globalization in industries that are so vital to their cohesion and identity. The chapters in this section represent a contribution toward this complex four-sided debate. They are about the benefits as well as the ills of globalization in the cultural industries.

In chapter 15, Lampel and Honig examine the sustained efforts by the Children's Television Workshop (CTW) to bridge the bitter divide between Israelis and Palestinians by sponsoring a bilingual and bicultural joint production of its flagship program *Sesame Street*. Lampel and Honig examine the evolution of the venture from several perspectives. The first perspective examines the three-way venture as an example of the formation of a small network, one in which CTW acts as sponsor and catalyst. The second perspective examines the struggle to persuade Palestinians and Israelis to work together, and the difficult journey that both sides had to undertake to bring the program to successful completion. The third perspective examines the mismatch between American intentions and Middle Eastern realities.

As an American organization, CTW is steeped in multiethnic inclusion and is dedicated to bringing different cultures into the American fold. The tragedy of the Israel-Palestine conflict, however, is one of two national groups struggling to create and sustain separate national identities. They are intent on separation, not inclusion. And their conflict is about how to achieve this separation without sacrificing their vital interests.

CTW therefore finds itself caught between its own values and those of the people it is trying to help. And although CTW did not set out to impose American values on the Middle East, it could not get away from the central assumption of globalization: that people everywhere are essentially the same, and that they ultimately share a desire for the same products and the same experiences.

CTW's persistence and ingenuity triumphs in the face of difficult circumstances. *Rechov Sumsum-Shara'a Sumsum*, as the Israeli-Palestinian version of *Sesame Street* came to be known, was produced and eventually aired. The venture, however, has not made a discernable impact as far as peace between Israelis and Palestinians is concerned. Nevertheless, it does demonstrate the way in which global centers of cultural production can exercise considerable local influence.

This local influence has also been increasingly felt in the motion picture industry. In chapter 16, Guild and Joyce examine the strategic adaptation of Australian film producers to the challenge of Hollywood. Although the American motion picture industry has long occupied a dominant global position, a combination of trade barriers and state subsidies has kept the market share of Hollywood motion picture industry in most countries in check. Many countries could boast a vibrant domestic motion picture industry for most of the 20th century, but this picture has changed as trade barriers were negotiated down and state subsidies gradually phased out. In country after country, domestic motion picture production has come under attack from a better financed and commercially more savvy Hollywood competitor.

Guild and Joyce point out that Australian film producers, like those in many other countries, have relied on government subsidies in order to compete against Hollywood films. However, faced with government refusal to provide subsidies without matching private financing, Australian film producers are being forced to become more market oriented by shifting the style and content of their movies in a more commercial direction.

Guild and Joyce explore how Australian film producers have struggled to come to terms with the artistic and commercial ramifications of the new environment. Their research provides a snapshot of a period in the history of the Australian film industry when resistance and adaptation, defiance and resignation, coexist. Reluctantly, they suggest that the era of art-house film making in Australia may be coming to a close, and that the artistic and commercial survival of the Australian film industry depends on its ability to discover a way of attracting sizable audiences without having to give up on its unique artistic voice.

If Guild and Joyce provide a snapshot of a cultural industry in transition, and urge adaptation to the inevitable march of Hollywood, chapter 17 by Lampel and Shamsie argues that we should not be hasty to judge where globalization in the cultural industries is heading. They suggest that it is best to forgo ideological passion when discussing the future of the cultural industries. Thus, instead of allowing projected negative or positive outcomes of globalization to dominate analysis, we should look at the current process of globalization as essentially open-ended.

It is open-ended because the issues that are the heart of the debates of the future of cultural industries are susceptible to different interpretations of the forces that are shaping the evolution of these industries. More specifically, debates on the future of the cultural industries often revolve around two key issues: The first issue concerns the foundations of competitive advantage in the cultural industries, and the second the impact of globalization on the cultural space in which these industries operate. Each issue elicits a different point of view, and each point of view suggests a different direction for the evolution of the cultural industries.

The result, as is often the case in strategy, is a map of the future made up of four distinct evolutionary scenarios. Lampel and Shamsie outline and discuss these scenarios from the point of view of producers as well as consumers, but their main interest is in the type of organizations that will inhibit a world dominated by each of these scenarios. Some of these organizational types have long been with us, and others may emerge as a result of new technologies. It is ultimately for the reader to judge which type of organization will dominate which cultural industry.

Taken together, the three chapters suggest that cultural industries, like several others, are clearly being affected by the ongoing process of globalization. This process is pushing these industries to respond through the development of new forms of strategies and new types of organizations. However, as all of the chapters indicate, it is still difficult to make any clear predictions about the eventual impact of globalization on cultural industries.

CHAPTER

15

Let the Children Play: Muppets in the Middle of the Middle East

Joseph Lampel
City University, London

Benson Honig
Wilfred Laurier University

Observers of the cultural industries are often struck by the ability of transnational corporations to use their power to reshape local cultures to suit their strategic needs. The size and visibility of these corporations, however, often obscures the emergence of networks of small enterprises that congregate regionally in clusters of intense cultural production and innovation. Key to the survival of these regional clusters are norms and practices that facilitate transactional coordination by creating a substantial level of familiarity and trust among potential trading partners (Storper, 1997, p. 80). In the cultural industries, the emergence of these small firm networks (SFNs) reduces the inevitable barriers to trading that arise when potential partners from different cultures and with different values have to exchange or share resources that are by their very nature intangible and difficult to protect.

The juxtaposition between transitional corporations and regional clusters suggests a division of labor: Large corporations operate globally and regional clusters operate locally. The former internalize operations precisely because cultural goods are difficult to trade, whereas the latter are only able to operate locally precisely because proximity is the only way in which they can create an ecology where trust can reduce the higher than normal transaction costs that are endemic to cultural industries.

We argue that networks of small firms in the cultural industries need not be confined regionally, but are capable, under certain conditions, of reaching out across the globe (Fisher, 1992; Scott, 1997). An important mechanism for overcoming the difficulty of forming such networks is the emergence of hub organizations that can broker the relationship between potential partners (Hargadon & Sutton, 1997). The task of the hub organization is to create conditions that facilitate agreement by inducing trust and reducing transaction costs that often arise when potential partners come to the relationship with different expectations and different sets of values. The role is often catalytic rather than simply a question of imposing an agreement. Hub organizations therefore do much more than provide inducements to the formation of relationships; they seek to shape attitudes and overcome value differences.

In this chapter, we explore a case in which an organization acts as a hub organization, playing the role of joint-venture champion in an intensely political context. The organization in question is the Children's Television Workshop (CTW), and the case on which we focus is a joint venture between Israelis and Palestinians to produce a bilingual and bicultural version of the well-known American program *Sesame Street*. The joint venture is the brainchild of Lewis Bernstein, an executive producer at CTW. It is part of an international strategy that goes back to CTW's early days when the organization started exporting its flagship program *Sesame Street* via a network of coproductions with foreign broadcasters (Gettas, 1990). The Israel-Palestine joint venture represents an effort on the part of CTW to encourage joint ventures between its coproducers. The declared aim of this strategy is social and political, rather than economic: "To encourage contact and dialogue between communities which have been divided by bitter conflict" and to "teach mutual respect to preschool children living in Israel and the Palestinian Territories" (from interview with Lewis Bernstein, New York, March 19, 1998).

Our case study is based on archival data and interviews with the key protagonists in Israel, the West Bank, and the United States. Interviews were conducted shortly after the successful production of the joint-venture programming, but before it was distributed and publicly aired. Respondents included the Israeli and Palestinian producers, as well as two senior American CTW representatives responsible for the activity, beginning with its inception. All critical interviews were recorded and transcribed for subsequent analysis.

We begin our analysis with a discussion of the motives that lead organizations to pursue hub strategies. We then look at CTW's international strategy, and the historical origins of the Israel-Palestine joint venture. We next focus our attention on the difficulties that CTW confronted in gaining support and commitment for the joint venture from parties on both sides of the Middle East divide. We show that even when this interest was forthcoming, CTW played an essential role in building trust and facilitating the implementation of agreements. We conclude with a discussion of how the joint venture influenced CTW's long-term strategy.

HUB ORGANIZATIONS AND THE FORMATION OF TRIADIC NETWORKS

SFNs arise as a result of individual firms pursing localized self-interest, but their creation produces forces that are collective in orientation (Perrow, 1992; Perry, 1999). In networks that are part of regional clusters the proximity of firms enhances the formation of multiple relationships by providing complementary products, increasing the flow of information, and creating a pool of transactional experience that forms the basis for common norms and practices (Porter, 1998). In networks that are not embedded in the same regional geography, dyadic formation of linkages are strategic in orientation, and are based largely on the calculus of costs and benefits—without taking into account factors that are not relevant to the dyad itself (Galaskiewicz, 1985; Lei, 1993).

Discussion of SFNs, however, suggests that network dynamics can influence dyad formation (Herrigel, 1993; Richter, 1999). The influence, as the literature on joint venture and alliances tends to suggest, is largely covert (Rowley, 1997): Most organizations engaged in the formation of direct relations focus their attention exclusively on the specific linkage involved, with little thought given to how the formation of these linkages fits into the network as a whole (Astley & Brahm, 1989; Gulati, 1998; Human & Provan, 1997).

Possible exceptions to this are hub organizations whose strategies depend on performing brokerage roles in networks (Hargadon & Sutton, 1997). Such organizations form and manage their own networks, and often seek a central position in such networks. These organizations develop strategies that seek to establish a network position, giving them more discretion and influence than others in the network. This position is based, initially, on the firm's first-order linkages, linkages with organizations with which it has direct dealings. However, beyond network advantages that arise from first-order linkages, a firm can also derive influence by leveraging second-order relationships, which emerge as organizations that it deals with directly from relationships of their own. In effect, hub organizations can architect networks by facilitating the formation of triadic relationships with themselves as hub and catalytic agents. For strategically minded actors, this strategy can generate the following gains:

1. Hub organizations that encourage second-order linkages can improve their position within the network (Boje & Whetten, 1981; Skytte, 1992). This strategy is often pursued by organizations wishing to increase the density of their ties to the rest of the network (Burt, 1976). By fostering the formation of second-order linkages, these organizations shift the flow of financial and creative resources in a way that puts them in a better bargaining position vis-à-vis other organizations in the network (Wiewel & Hunter, 1986). Hub organizations that

foster the formation of second-order ties can capture resources generated by the formation and operation of such ties. This brokerage activity goes beyond traditional middle-man activity where organizations collect brokerage fees for bringing parties together. It entails efforts to become middle partners in long-standing relationships. Firms in areas such as entertainment or investment banking often pursue brokerage activity systematically (Burnett, 1995; Rubin, Schweizer, & Stephen, 1996). Looking at networks, brokering organizations in these industries pursue a strategy of identifying and developing second-order ties from which they then capture rents on an ongoing basis.

2. In addition to capturing rents generated internally to the networks, hub organizations fostering second-order ties can capture network rents (Bensaou & Venkatraman, 1995). Networks are engaged in an active resource exchange with their larger environments (Baker, Faulkner, & Fisher, 1998). Organizations that are members of such networks benefit differentially from the exchange. An increase in the number of participants in the network can increase the total amount of resources that accrue to the network, or change the distribution of resources (Gimeno & Woo, 1996). Hub organizations may choose to foster the formation of second-order ties for one or both of these reasons. The hub may calculate that working to improve the network's position in the larger environment will be advantageous to itself. Alternatively, it may pursue the formation of second-order linkages as a way of capturing more of the resources flowing into the network.

3. Hub organizations that encourage the formation of second-order linkages can shape the development of the network in line with their own policies or values (Nee, 1998; Park, 1996). From a resource-dependency standpoint, brokering organizations can negotiate greater control over the structure and content of second-order relationships if they play an important role in their formation (Burt, 1992). Hubs can also expect to exert a considerable influence on the development of these linkages if their support is necessary for the viability and effectiveness of these linkages. This opens the way for hub organizations to externalize their policies, making it more likely that other organizations in the network are acting under the hub umbrella, rather than pursuing independent policies of their own.

To be successful, however, hub strategies must overcome a number of barriers. An obvious barrier to the spontaneous formation of triadic networks is an imbalance between the costs and benefits that each organization believes it can derive from such a relationship. Organizations are unlikely to form relationships if the benefits do not measure up to the costs of setting them up. In many instances, however, triadic networks will not form even when the potential benefits are clear because the organizations that make up a potential triadic network are deterred by concerns that gains and costs will be unfairly distributed (Yamagishi, Gillmore, & Cook, 1988). This may occur when one party believes that a power imbalance will result in unfair terms, or because there is a suspicion that under the cover of agreement one party will opportunistically exploit the vulnerability or resources of the other (Larsson, Bengtsson, Henriksson, & Sparks, 1998).

Such concerns are acute when the parties belong to different cultural groups with values that are different in orientation. Because value differences cannot be easily articulated, bargaining may become bogged down as the parties attempt to translate transactional nuance into contractual terms. Different values can also contribute to mistrust when the transaction itself deals with products that are culturally sensitive in a way that one party (or both) is not fully able to appreciate. This is often the case with cultural products, where economic valuation and social valuation are incommensurate.

The task of the hub organization, therefore, is to create conditions that facilitate agreement by inducing trust and reducing transaction costs. Research suggests that hubs have the following methods at their disposal:

Persuasion: Hub organizations can actively attempt to persuade parties with whom the hub has first-order linkages that a second-order linkage among themselves is to their mutual advantage. Transaction cost theory suggests that bounded rationality can raise the costs of negotiating and writing contracts. When the parties involved are unable, by virtue of their respective cognitive limitations, to explore the possibility of forming relationships, a hub organization can step in and provide these parties its own analysis and assessment of the relationship (Kanter & Myers, 1991). This would amount to underwriting some of the costs of transacting, thereby making the formation of the relationship less costly to those involved.

Resource provision: Hub organizations can provide resources as incentives, thereby making the relationship more attractive. In many instances, organizations see the costs of the relationship as outweighing the advantages (Lei & Slocum, 1991; Lincoln, 1984). Attempts by the hub organization to use persuasion may fail, leaving the hub organization with no alternative but to shift the costs-benefits calculus. The hub may do this by offering inducements such as direct cash transfers, expanded access to critical resources, or the promise of future business activity.

Confidence building: Hub organizations may act to reduce transaction costs by alleviating the fear of opportunism (Provan & Gassenheimer, 1994). It is not uncommon for parties to have a negative view of each other, and thus a pessimistic assessment of the merits of successfully forming a relationship. Their lack of confidence may be due to past experience, or it may be due to a general climate of distrust (Zaheer & Venkatraman, 1995). A hub organization can act in a number of ways to deal with this problem. It can act as a trusted go-between, providing assurances to each organization about the other's intentions. It can work to reduce fear of opportunism, by improving the climate in which negotiations are being conducted. And finally, it can become an active mediator, resolving disputes and bridging gaps in perceptions.

These three ways of fostering the formation of triadic networks are not mutually exclusive. Hub organizations can employ all three. There is, however, a qualitative difference between persuasion and resource provision on the one hand, and confidence building on the other. Whereas persuasion and resource provision depend on the actions of the hub organization alone, confidence building depends on a reciprocal relationship of trust between the hub organization and its first-order partners (Saxton, 1997). This is summarized in Figure 15.1.

The hub organization uses persuasion and resources to lower the transaction barriers between A and B in Fig. 15.1. These methods, however, are costly to the hub organization. An attractive alternative that is potentially less costly is to use the trust that A and B have in the hub organization. This allows the hub to build the level of confidence these parties need to successfully negotiate and implement agreements. As we see in the case study described later, all three methods are used. In this case, the last method, that of confidence building, turns out to be crucial.

THE INTERNATIONAL EXPANSION OF CTW

The CTW began producing *Sesame Street* in a Manhattan studio in 1969. Over the subsequent 30 years, countless children's programs have come and gone, victims of changing tastes.

CTW's *Sesame Street* represents a major exception. It currently penetrates more than 120 million viewing households in over 130 different countries, with the

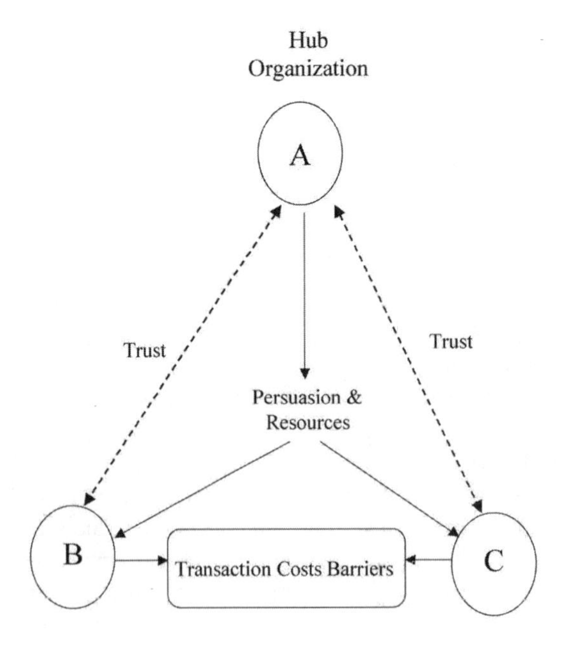

FIG.15.1. Role of brokerage in formation of Triadic Networks.

ubiquitous characters of Big Bird, Oscar the Grouch, Bert, and Ernie, and their many various indigenized Muppet friends and relations (Cole & Richman, 1997).

The pedagogical success of the *Sesame Street* model has been well documented and researched, and has been an integral component of the program since its inception (Rice, Hurston, Truglio, & Wright, 1990). Multiple studies have demonstrated increased vocabulary, letter recognition, number recognition, and printed-word identification among viewers from 6 months to 5 years of age (CTW, 1991). The deceptively simple recipe—a fast pace, short vignettes, exaggerated characters, songs and stories—represents a highly successful curriculum referred to as "the CTW model," which has been designed and refined by child psychologists, educators, producers, and other researchers.

Shortly after *Sesame Street* began broadcasting, there was considerable international interest in exporting, coproducing, and otherwise adapting the model to various other countries. An international division was thus formed, with the task of licensing and regulating the product to other environments. The division quickly developed policies that both protected the proprietary interests of CTW and promoted the core beliefs in preschool education and cultural relevancy so important to *Sesame Street*'s success.

Characteristically for CTW (and bucking media trends of the era), commercial advertising was not to be allowed on any international programming (Gettas, 1990). Rather, *Sesame Street* was to gain resources from two commercially well-proven techniques (Raugust, 1999). First, it would have international royalty rights from ancillary products such as games, toys, and stuffed animals—CTW has authorized more than 10,000 items worldwide through 300 licensing agreements. Second, and to a lesser extent, it would act as a children's television consulting firm, training and disseminating the CTW model throughout the world, and through promotional partners such as Nestlé for Ulitsa Sezam in Russia and General Electric for Zhima Jie in China.

Whereas the first efforts to export *Sesame Street* consisted of dubbing and minor programmatic supplements to existing material, subsequent efforts entailed considerable reworking of the content and theme, including contextual alterations more appropriate to the host countries involved. A Spanish-language version was adapted by Mexico and exported throughout Latin America in 1973, followed by coproductions in Brazil, Holland, Germany, Spain, Kuwait, Israel, Sweden, the Philippines, Portugal, Turkey, and Norway. In all cases, CTW played an instrumental role in training and disseminating the model abroad. For example, the Muppets, the CTW-Jim Henson-designed puppets used in all *Sesame Street* programs throughout the world, are exclusively produced at CTW studios and exported to each particular market from the United States.

Programming content is also critically vetted to ensure CTW quality and educational standards are rigorously met. No coproducer can go on the air until CTW approves the program. All scripts must be translated into English and approved by a CTW committee in New York. In a process that can take as long as a year, the head of research at CTW goes to the foreign country and invites local top educators to clarify the specific needs of their communities. Foreign scriptwriters are invited to a CTW workshop that trains them in their approach. Each approved writer is assigned specific goals for a module. Although they may write in their own language, the script must be subsequently translated into English, after which it goes to a CTW committee for approval. As with the script writing, CTW conducts auditions for puppeteers, after which it trains them in the *Sesame Street* Muppet method.

As a result of CTW's pioneering activities, it is not only a major contributor of children's educational TV worldwide, but also functions as key agent in promoting and diffusing educational broadcasting. For example, CTW has actively worked with the United Nations Educational and Social and Cultural Organization (UNESCO), despite the fact that the United States is not a UNESCO member. Worldwide, academic researchers regularly utilize both CTW's facilities and products when investigating developmental psychology and early childhood learning (CTW, 1991; Cole & Richman, 1997).

Through careful marketing, controlled distribution, and copyright enforcement, CTW has effectively established itself as a network hub in the global children's educational market. This position is the result of the economic predicament confronting independent broadcasters. The economics of television production are such that independent production of children's programming in most countries is either not economically feasible, or if feasible, tends to deliver a substandard product (Gettas, 1990). For social policy reasons, educational authorities in most countries desire children's programming that meets the highest possible standards. Attaining these standards, however, is often only possible by collaborating with organizations such as CTW that can provide crucial high-quality content inputs.

As a result, there are currently over 17 international coproductions among the 90 countries viewing *Sesame Street* (Cole & Richman, 1997). CTW has used its formidable technical lead toward systematic model development. For example, CTW has identified nearly 600 goals, broadly grouped into four categories (Children of the World, Human Diversity, Symbolic Representation, and Cognitive Organization) that form part of an educational model. Each of the categories is associated with research streams and seminars that help the CTW mission diffuse to an ever-larger worldwide audience. The CTW system of goals, associated with formative and summative research, also provides expert legitimacy in disseminating practices throughout the network. This adds considerable credibility in obtaining foundation support, thus extending the network and further establishing CTW's role as a hub agent.

SESAME STREET IN THE MIDDLE EAST

Research Methodology

Examining network formation from the perspective of socially embedded characteristics, such as trust, required our utilizing a qualitative case study approach. We elected to interview primary and ancillary stakeholders in each of the three nodes of the triad, the American, Israeli, and Palestinian production teams. Interviews were conducted on location in New York, Tel Aviv, and in the West Bank, specifically in Ramallah. In addition to a number of supporting actors, extensive interviews were conducted with Bernstein (American producer) and Kuttab (Palestinian producer) in English, and with Dolly Wolbrun (Israeli producer) in Hebrew. Our goal was to examine the accumulated accounts of the network conception, formation, execution, and current status. Whereas the critical interviews were conducted at the location of the respective places of business, telephone interviewing was also conducted with various support members of the production team. All interviews were recorded, transcribed, and analyzed for both complementary and contradictory perspectives.

Utilizing these three sources provided a degree of triangulation generating additional reliability regarding the historical facts of the case. In addition to the interviews, we also examined internal documents provided by CTW, as well as information obtained from the popular press regarding the historical sequence of events, including critical obstacles and barriers. Open coding of the interviews allowed us to isolate critical themes using a grounded theory method (Glaser & Strauss, 1967). Both researchers independently read the transcripts, compared interpretations, and, where clarifications were necessary, returned to the data for additional analysis. A telephone interview was also conducted with Bernstein's assistant on the project, and this was also transcribed, providing further reliability. In light of the small and unusual sample, as well as the inductive nature of the research, our findings should be considered preliminary. Issues related to validity and generalizability await further confirmatory analysis.

The Roots of the Joint Venture

CTW first started a coproduction with Israeli government-sponsored educational television in 1982, adapting the then-familiar model to the Israeli cultural context. In all, 200 episodes were produced with a broadly defined theme of diversity and mutual respect in the heterogeneous Israeli environment. Although the program was quite popular, it had been relying on somewhat dated reruns for nearly 10 years, and was in need of updating and attention to contemporary themes, such as the recent immigration from the former Soviet Union, now representing 18% of the Israeli population. Unfortunately, there were insufficient budgetary funds to address the cleaning up and modernizing necessary for the program's rejuvenation.

When Arafat and Rabin shook hands after Oslo in 1993, Lewis Bernstein, an executive producer at CTW and former director of the Israeli coproduction, immediately recognized an opportunity to form a unique joint CTW production involving both Palestinians and Israelis. Although management at CTW was somewhat skeptical of the concept, CTW applied for and received a grant to conduct a feasibility study from the Carnegie Foundation. The outcome of the study indicated that a joint Palestinian-Israeli project would be much more difficult than CTW anticipated. For example, it discovered that there were four, not three, groups necessary to involve in the project. In addition to CTW, the Israelis, and the Palestinians, CTW learned that it would be necessary to include Palestinian Israelis, the CTW term for Israeli Arabs. When it determined that external funding might be available, CTW proceeded to write a complete proposal that was eventually supported by 18 different foundations, including Carnegie, Ford, Revson, Gruss, North Star, and the Dutch and Israeli governments.

OVERCOMING BARRIERS THROUGH CONFIDENCE BUILDING

Bernstein was well aware, when he set out to create a joint venture between Israelis and Palestinians, that the history of the conflict between these two peoples made his task especially difficult (Tsur, 1998). In principle, initiating a joint-venture process depends on a readiness from the parties to look at the idea positively. In the case of many firms, there are often cognitive and informational barriers that slow the process. Firms may ignore cooperation as a strategic move because it runs counter to their perceptions of the environment, or because they may simply be unwilling to explore the time and resources necessary to evaluate such opportunities. A hub organization can remedy these problems by performing the analysis itself, and then providing the results to the organizations involved.

In the case of the Israel-Palestine joint venture, however, deep-seated political antagonisms made it difficult to get the process started. The mere idea of a joint venture—even in an area as benign as children's television—was something that the Israelis found difficult to contemplate, and the Palestinians regarded as anathema. Making a case for the project, therefore, amounted to an attempt to expand a rationality bounded not only by the cognitive constraints that usually hamper analysis, but also by what each side considered to be technically and politically feasible.

Bernstein's main problem was the deeply entrenched assumptions that each side had about the other, which stood in the way of objective evaluation of the project. Dolly Wolbrum, the Israeli producer, did not believe it would be possible to find Palestinians willing to work with them on such an undertaking. Her skepticism was born out when Bernstein met with the representatives of the Palestinian Broadcasting Corporation (PBA, the symmetrical arm to Israeli Broadcasting). The PBA gave the proposal a cool reception. A new organization still negotiating with various donors in Arab countries, the PBA leadership believed that doing a joint Israeli-Palestinian production as a first project would be politically unwise. The PBA wished Bernstein well with his venture, but insisted that it was politically impossible for them to participate.

Persuasion failed. Resources, however, proved to be the critical lever that moved the whole process forward. When Bernstein approached the Israelis, he came with an offer to assist with a substantial portion of the $4.9-million budget, and received a very supportive, if skeptical, response. The Palestinians, on the other hand, refused to come aboard. Daoud Kuttab, Bernstein's key interlocutor and the man who eventually became the Palestinian executive producer, resisted the offer. He was concerned that the Palestinians would be allocated a secondary role in the venture, thereby affirming their subordinate political position vis-à-vis the Israelis. He was also concerned that the venture would provide the Israelis with symbolic capital at the expense of the Palestinians. Beyond these calculations, however, Kuttab had deep reservations about the venture's basic theme of bringing people together. As he put it: "The basic thrust of the Palestinian-Israeli peace agreement was more of a divorce than a marriage, in that the Palestinians want a separate state."

Kuttab made the case for a separate Palestinian program. Bernstein pointed out that whereas the Israelis had produced television for 30 years, the Palestinians had no experience, and for them to take on such a project was well beyond their present capabilities. In any case, he argued, there was no money to do a Palestinian production on its own. The Palestinians had an opportunity to do a joint production immediately. If Kuttab was unwilling to help, CTW would find other Palestinians willing to go ahead with the project. Kuttab remained uncommitted.

Realizing that he was not making headway with Kuttab, Bernstein decided to bypass him for the moment and make his offer to key Palestinian actors, artists, animators, and media technicians. In a series of meetings he presented the venture, and discussed what CTW was willing to offer Palestinian participants in terms of technical skills and training for the project. The Palestinians had recently organized an animation workshop, so Bernstein contacted the participants and brought them into the process as well. Bernstein's strategy, as it emerged, was to generate grassroots support among Palestinians who stood to benefit from the joint venture, and then to bring this support to bear on Kuttab.

The strategy worked, and Kuttab was persuaded to participate as coproducer. As Kuttab indicated, "Some of the people who I asked, and that wanted to participate in this, convinced me that we could do it ... that there was enough talent, and with proper training ... and the willingness of the Americans to allow Palestinians to help themselves without any veto power from the other side." At the same time, he imposed a number of conditions that CTW had to meet as a price for his support:

1. His group would be the only Palestinians CTW would work with (Bernstein had identified an Israeli public relations company that was trying to contact other Palestinians who might want to participate—this apparently concerned Kuttab).
2. The Palestinians wanted genuine participation from the moment of inception until the program was complete, with a budget, writing staff, other personnel, and so on.
3. Acknowledging the asymmetry of experience between the Israelis and the Palestinians, he wanted help in raising their level of skills to provide an approximate symmetry.

4. There was to be no censorship and no veto power on content beyond artistic or educational criteria.

The lure of resources may have succeeded in getting Palestinians to participate. Participation and successful outcome, however, are two different things. Transforming an agreement in principle into a workable relationship presented Bernstein and CTW with a host of new problems, some predictable and others wholly unpredictable.

To launch the project, CTW envisioned bringing the key Israeli and Palestinian actors to New York for a curriculum workshop, in order to develop the necessary goals, themes, and educational aims for each episode. Convening a joint meeting, however, proved to be a problem. Discussions with the Palestinians and the Israelis proceeded along separate tracks. The Palestinian Israelis who wanted to attend both discussions were caught in the middle. The latter group reflects a historic artifact particular to the Arab-Israeli conflict. They are the Arabs that remained in Israel after partition in 1948 and have dual identities, as citizens of Israel and as Palestinian non-Jewish Arabs, typically sympathetic to the cause of Palestinian nationalism. CTW discovered that this dual identity required participation in negotiations with both parties, effectively increasing the size of the network. It was only after a number of separate meetings were conducted that CTW finally succeeded in bringing all of the parties together in a single room.

The meetings CTW organized were meant to plan a curriculum seminar leading to the development of educational goals for each episode, as each show was meant to teach a basic concept. CTW thought about the project in general terms, never considering the possibility of objections, particularly political objections, that might be voiced by any of the parties. In conducting the preliminary meetings, CTW found that the Palestinians were never in agreement with the Israelis, and vice versa.

Serious negotiations took place, for example, regarding where and how the Muppets would meet each other (Marcus, 1997). At first, a common park was suggested. "Who would own the park?," asked the Palestinians. Meeting at a wall separating the two communities was also considered. As Kuttab stated, "We wanted a mix between being rooted in the reality of the situation and not being overly optimistic." Finally, negotiations concluded with two separate streets, with different names and characters, where invited guests might interact with each other (Mifflin, 1996). Mirroring the political climate at large, the Palestinians were uncomfortable depicting Israelis visiting their street without invitation, much as soldiers and settlers currently did in the real world.

As the project proceeded, CTW began to see themselves not as disseminators, as they had been in their other coproductions, but increasingly as catalysts. The new role presented unusual constraints that CTW learned to navigate, but took considerable time. Whereas typical coproduction programs take 18 months to 2 years to produce, *Rechov Sumsum/Shara'a Sumsum*, the Hebrew-Arabic title of *Sesame Street*, took more than twice as long. The additional time and expenditure, however, were necessary to overcome the barriers of mistrust that separated the two sides. We depict this process in our timeline, Figure 15.2.

In terms of transaction costs, what CTW and Bernstein had to do was reduce the fear of opportunism sufficiently to allow both sides to develop a working relationship. CTW did this by acting as a resource provider, a guarantor and a go-between. As Kuttab stated:

> [CTW] provided us with the very top quality artistic means that we needed.... I don't think it would have worked without them because there's too much animosity between Palestinians and Israelis ... a third party well recognized for their product

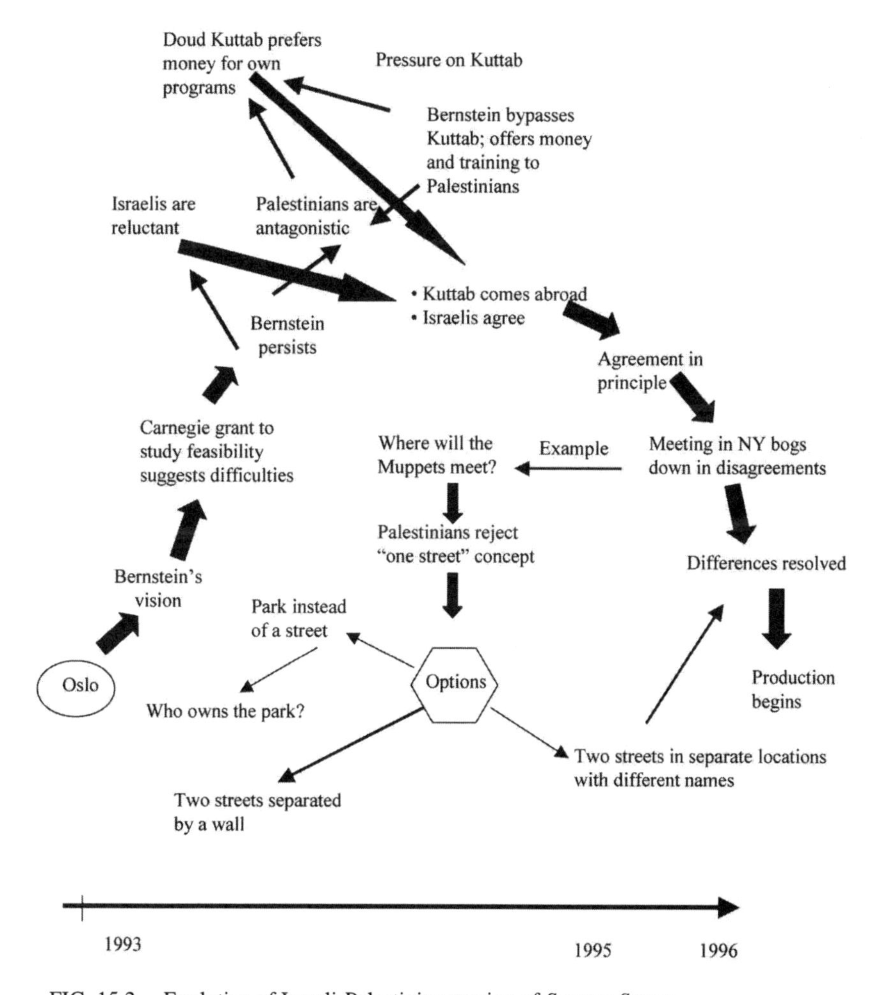

FIG. 15.2. Evolution of Israeli-Palestinian version of *Sesame Street*.

made it easier for us to do this type of program ... you almost needed somebody like an American to develop good relationships and credible relationships between both sides ... you needed a third party.

CTW'S STRATEGY IN THE AFTERMATH OF THE JOINT VENTURE

Promoting goodwill between the Israelis and Palestinians was the main goal motivating CTW's sponsorship of the joint venture. To the extent that this goal was achieved, peace in the Middle East probably benefited. From an organizational point of view, however, peacemaking alone is rarely a sufficient motive for undertaking such a complex and costly effort. Other benefits must be derived for the effort to be deemed worthwhile. Thus, the question naturally arises: Did CTW benefit directly from the joint venture, and if it did, how have these benefits influenced its strategic thinking as a hub organization?

In the first part of the chapter we outlined a number of ways in which hub organizations such as CTW can expect to benefit from the formation of triadic networks. Going back to these benefits, we find the following:

1. There is no indication that the Israel-Palestine joint venture helped CTW improve its position within the network. CTW was already the key player in the network, and its position was not likely to become more central as a result of this joint venture.

2. CTW generates much of its revenues through royalties for ancillary products such as games, toys, and stuffed animals. The joint venture does not seem to have increased the sale of such products significantly, and there is no evidence that the participants had such sales in mind when they embarked on the joint venture.

3. The joint venture generated considerable interest and financial support from foundations and governments. This financial support represents a net flow of new resources from the larger environment into the network. Most of the support was used to fund the network, but to the extent that it represented a contribution to CTW's overhead, it can be considered a positive motivation to proceed with the joint venture. It is difficult to say whether CTW would have scaled back its efforts had this support not been forthcoming. What is clear is that having this support meant that internal champions, such as Bernstein, had less to fear from critics who could argue that CTW had no business expanding into an area traditionally the province of diplomats.

4. The joint venture represented an affirmation of CTW's core organizational values, and beyond that, an expression of the values of the venture's champion: Lewis Bernstein. Bernstein's vision of bringing people together was consistent with CTW's basic philosophical belief that children, unlike their parents, are essentially apolitical. Left to interact freely, they form relationships that are devoid of the mistrust and acrimony from which the adult world is unable to escape. Un-

> fortunately, it quickly became clear that the Middle East is inherently an inhospitable environment for this vision of childhood. CTW had to adjust its values to suit the situation. The core values of the organization therefore did not prevail.

The successful production of the programs vindicated CTW's and Bernstein's belief that the organization could make a contribution that went beyond education and entertainment. At the same time, the success was not unalloyed. The programs showed that the two societies could coexist, but only by first disengaging. It was not a celebration of commonality, as CTW and Bernstein hoped, but at best a respectful recognition by each side of the other's right to be different. What CTW discovered was that the concept of "separate but equal," which stood for segregation and discrimination in the United States, was precisely the one that found favor in the Middle East, where the right to be distinct and self-governing is the essence of self-determination.

CTW entered the joint venture with strong assumptions that are rooted in American conceptions of multicultural and multiethnic society. From CTW's point of view, children are basically the same everywhere, even if their vocabularies and customs reflect the place in which they are born: They are curious, fun loving, tolerant, and open to other peoples and other cultures. The world of children is separate from the world of adults. The latter may intrude on the former, but left to develop without interference, children are able to transcend barriers that hamper relationships in the adult world.

In the United States, and in other countries that share the American espousal of multiethnic and multicultural values, *Sesame Street* enjoys additional prestige precisely because it seeks to do more than just educate and entertain children. This prestige is useful to *Sesame Street*, not only when negotiating with their first-order linkages, but also when attracting resources and talent. In many societies, support for *Sesame Street* is support for ideals that these societies would like to inculcate in future adults. By the same token, working for *Sesame Street* is not just a job, it is participating in moral education and social reform—goals that many artistic professionals regard as central to their vocation.

In a wide variety of countries, however, CTW enjoyed a great success in exporting *Sesame Street* because of its technical and artistic excellence, and not because these countries always accepted the values intrinsic to *Sesame Street*. Daoud Kuttab reflected the ambivalence at the heart of the show in the following way:

> Sesame Street is a copyrighted American product, it is no different than Coca Cola, in the sense that they have produced something that people like. Even though they are nonprofit whereas Coca Cola is for profit, they basically go around the world finding people who are interested in their product. They will adapt it to that country's needs, just like Coca Cola will write their sign in Arabic, on its bottle, but in the end, when you drink Coca Cola in Tel Aviv or in Damascus, or New York City it tastes the same. When you see a *Sesame Street* copyrighted program it might sound different, the characters might live in a different environment, but it will have the basic style,

> which is a magazine style, puppets are the key players, education connected with entertainment, short videos that are colorful, educational, and entertaining. They spend a lot of money and make everybody spend a lot of money to make sure that they stay on that standard.

CTW's involvement in the joint venture between Israelis and Palestinians had wider repercussions for the organization. Mintzberg and Waters (1985) pointed out that strategies can be both deliberate and emergent. What resulted inadvertently from the experience was a new set of values about children's programming in highly politicized contexts (Lei & Slocum, 1992). These values, in turn, have become important as CTW pursues the formation of second-order linkages in other contexts. Subsequent to the Israeli-Palestinian project, CTW began to pursue similar activities elsewhere. The move bears the hallmarks of an emergent strategy: The publicity generated queries from regions as far afield as South Africa and Russia.

Television broadcasters in countries where bitter communal and ethnic conflict has been endemic were intrigued by the Israel-Palestine joint venture. CTW, for its part, began to see the Israel-Palestine venture as a model that could be applied in other parts of the world. It is still too early to say to what extent the model is applicable, given the peculiarities of the Israeli-Palestinian conflict. All that can be said at this point is that CTW and its sponsors are committed to attempting this venture in other parts of the world. If successful, this represents a strategic change for CTW. Initially a television production house, focusing solely on the education and entertainment needs of children, it will begin to take into account the wider social and political issues that affect not only children, but their parents as well.

CONCLUSION

The ability to develop and maintain trust is a critical resource in an era of increasing globalization (Lewicki, McAllister, & Bies, 1998). Trust is essential for forming alliances and relationships in industries where transactional problems stand in the way of efficient bargaining and contractual enforcement. This is frequently the case in cultural industries—not only because the resources involved are often intangible and easily appropriated, but also because the value-laden character of cultural products increases the likelihood of contractual disputes.

In this chapter we examined the actions of one organization, CTW, which deliberately set out to promote a joint venture between organizations with a long history of mistrust. To overcome the legacy of mistrust, CTW had to employ a strategy that attacked this issue indirectly rather than directly. This meant breaking the process of collaboration into discrete steps, and then working to underwrite and guarantee each step of the relationship as it evolved.

Dyadic trust, according to Mayer, Davis, and Schoorman (1995), is the result of three factors: ability, benevolence, and integrity. Ability refers to the skills, competencies, and characteristics of the trustee that inspire such trust; benevolence refers to the intrinsic, noninstrumental motivations of the trustee toward the trusting person; and integrity is the perception of credible principles attributed to the trustee by the trusting person (Mayer et al., 1995). The triadic network, which emerged as a result of the Israel/-Palestine joint venture, owes much to CTW's organizational ability, benevolence, and integrity, but it also benefited greatly from the efforts of individuals such as Lewis Bernstein who understood implicitly a political logic that was new to CTW.

The intentional creation of SFNs in the cultural industries creates strategic opportunities that are often crucial to the development of this sector, and hence are of considerable interest to public policy. Our study highlights the benefits that flow from the creation of such a network: Information was shared, mutual learning took place, experience was diffused, resources were acquired and distributed, and potential long-term relationships were established.

The situation that we examine is unique, but the lessons that emerge out of the Israel-Palestine joint venture raise questions that are pertinent for all cultural industries. Cultural industries in liberal societies on the whole avoid direct political involvement (Bjorkegren, 1996). They may use politics as background, as vocabulary, or as a source of narrative and plot, but are generally averse to taking political stands that can alienate large segments of the population. Corporate actors that enter political arenas do so at their peril. Culture and politics however cannot be easily divorced. In a world where crafting and selling culture are able to transform collective experience into rich expression, social responsibility comes with the power to influence social and political change.

REFERENCES

Astley, W. G., & Brahm, R. A. (1989). Organizational designs for post-industrial strategies: The role of interorganizational collaboration. In C. C. Snow (Ed.), *Strategy, organization design, and human resource management* (pp. 233–270). Greenwich, CT: JAI Press.

Baker, W., Faulkner, R., & Fisher, G. (1998). Hazards of the market: The continuity and dissolution of interorganizational market relationships. *American Sociological Review, 63,* 147–177.

Bensaou, M., & Venkatraman, N. (1995). Configurations of interorganizational relationships: A comparison between U.S. and Japanese automakers. *Management Science, 41,* 1471–1492.

Boje, D., & Whetten, D. (1981). Effects of organizational strategies and contextual constraints on centrality and attributes of influence in interorganizational networks. *Administrative Science Quarterly, 26,* 378–395.

Bjorkegren, D. (1996). *The culture business.* London: Routledge.

Burnett, R. (1995). *The global jukebox: The international music industry.* London: Routledge.

Burt, R. (1976). Position in network. *Social Forces, 55,* 93–122.

Burt, R. S. (1992). *Structural holes: The social structure of competition.* Cambridge, MA: Harvard University Press.

Children Television Workshop. (1991). *What research indicated about the educational effects of CTW Sesame Street.* New York: Author.

Cole, C., & Richman, B. (1997). *Sesame Street around the world: Vol. 7. Research Roundup.* New York: Children's Television Workshop.

Fisher, R. (1992). *Arts networking in Europe.* London: Arts Council of Great Britain.

Galaskiewicz, J. (1985). Interorganizational relations. *Annual Review of Sociology, 11,* 281–304.

Gettas, G. (1990). The globalization of Sesame Street: A producer's perspective. *Educational Technology Research and Development, 38*(4), 55–63.

Gimeno, J., & Woo, C. (1996). Economic multiplexity: The structural embeddedness of cooperation in multiple relations of interdependence. *Advances in Strategic Management, 13,* 323–361.

Glaser, B., & Strauss, A. (1967). *The discovery of grounded theory.* Chicago: Aldine.

Gulati, R. (1998). Alliances and networks. *Strategic Management Journal, 19,* 293–317.

Hargadon, A., & Sutton, R. (1997). Technology brokering and innovation in a product development firm. *Administrative Science Quarterly, 42,* 716–749.

Herrigel, G. (1993). Power and the redefinition of industrial districts: The case of BadenWurttemberg. In G. Grabher (Ed.), *The embedded firm* (pp. 227–251). London: Routledge.

Human, S., & Provan, K. (1997). An emergent theory of structure and outcomes in small-firm strategic manufacturing networks. *Academy of Management Journal, 40,* 368–403.

Kanter, R. M., & Myers, P. S. (1991). Interorganizational Bonds and intraorganizational behavior. In A. Etzioni & P. R. Lawrence (Eds.), *Socio-Economics: Toward a new synthesis* (pp. 329–344). Armonk, NY: Sharpe.

Larsson, R., Bengtsson, L., Henriksson, K., & Sparks, J. (1998). The interorganizational learning dilemma: Collective knowledge development in strategic alliances. *Organization Science, 9,* 285–305.

Lei, D. (1993). Offensive and defensive uses of alliances. *Long Range Planning, 26*(4), 32–41.

Lei, D., & Slocum, J. (1991). Global strategic alliances: Payoffs and pitfalls. *Organizational Dynamics, 19*(3), 44–62.

Lei, D., & Slocum, J. (1992). Global strategy, competence-building and strategic alliances. *California Management Review, 35,* 81–97.

Lewicki, R., McAllister, D., & Bies, R. (1998). Trust and distrust: New relationships and realities. *Academy of Management Review, 23,* 438–458.

Lincoln, J. (1984). Analyzing relations in dyads: Problems, models, and an application to interorganizational research. *Sociological Methods and Research, 13,* 45–76.

Marcus, A. (1997, June 5). Ernie uses Hebrew, Bert speaks Arabic; Moses, he's a grouch. *Wall Street Journal Europe,* 1.

Mayer, R., Davis, J., & Schoorman, D. (1995). An integration of organizational trust. *Academy of Management Review, 20,* 709–729.

Mifflin, L. (1996, June 11). An Israeli-Palestinian *Sesame Street. New York Times,* C15.

Mintzberg, H., & Waters, J. (1985). On strategies, deliberate and emergent. *Strategic Management Journal, 6,* 257–272.

Nee, V. (1998). Norms and networks in economic and organizational performance. *American Economic Review, 88*(2), 85–89.

Park, S. (1996). Managing an interorganizational network: A framework of the institutional mechanism for network control. *Organization Studies, 17,* 795–824.

Perrow, C. (1992). Small-firm networks. In N. Nohria & R. Eccles (Eds.), *Networks and organizations* (pp. 445–470). Boston: Harvard Business School Press.

Perry, M. (1999). *Small firms and network economies.* London: Routledge.

Porter, M. (1998). Clusters and the new economics of competition. *Harvard Business Review, 76*(6), 77–90.

Provan, K., & Gassenheimer, J. (1994). Supplier commitment in relational contract exchanges with buyers: A study of interorganizational dependence and exercised power. *Journal of Management Studies, 31,* 55–68.

Raugust, K. (1999, October). Can you tell me how to get to Sesamstrasse? Local co-productions fuel Sesame Street's international expansion. *Animation World Magazine, 7,* 10–12.

Rice, M., Hurston, A., Truglio, R., & Wright, J. (1990). Words from Sesame Street: Learning vocabulary while viewing. *Developmental Psychology, 26,* 421–428.

Richter, F. J. (1999). *Business networks in Asia.* New York: Quorum Books.

Rowley, T. (1997). Moving beyond dyadic ties: A network theory of stakeholder. *Academy of Management Review, 22,* 887–910.

Rubin, E., Schweizer, U., & Stephen, F. (1996). The phenomenology of contract: Complex contracting in the entertainment industry. *Journal of Institutional and Theoretical Economics, 152,* 123–153.

Saxton, T. (1997). The effects of partner and relationship characteristics on alliance outcomes. *Academy of Management Journal, 40,* 443–461.

Scott, L. (1997). Networks: New tools for innovation and exploration. In M. Fitzgibbon & A. Kelly (Eds.), *From maestro to manager: Critical issues in arts and culture management* (pp. 297–318). Dublin, Ireland: Oak Tree Press.

Skytte, H. (1992). Developing and sustaining competitive advantages through interorganizational relations between retailers and suppliers. *International Review of Retail, Distribution and Consumer Research, 2,* 155–164.

Storper, M. (1997). *The regional world.* New York: Guilford Press.

Tsur, S. (1998, April 3). Puppets of peace. *The Jerusalem Post,* 02.

Wiewel, W., & Hunter, A. (1986). The interorganizational network as a resource: A comparative case study of organizational genesis. *Administrative Science Quarterly, 30,* 482–496.

Yamagishi, T., Gillmore, M., & Cook, K. (1988). Network connections and the distribution of power in exchange networks. *American Journal of Sociology, 93,* 833–851.

Zaheer, A., & Venkatraman, N. (1995). Relational governance as an interorganizational strategy: An empirical test of the role of trust in economic exchange. *Strategic Management Journal, 16,* 373–392.

CHAPTER

16

Surviving in the Shadow of Hollywood: A Study of the Australian Film Industry

Wendy L. Guild
University of Colorado, Denver

Mary L. Joyce
California State University, Fullerton

As the Hollywood studios have poured more and more money into their lavish blockbusters, they have begun to rely on revenues from as many sources as possible in order to recoup their heavy investments. Consequently, they have decided to push their products more aggressively in both domestic and foreign markets through the use of wide distribution and saturation marketing strategies. In the process, the major U.S. studios have posed a serious challenge to other film industries that have been developing in various countries around the world. Smaller film industries that had managed to thrive in spite of competition from Hollywood have had to search for strategies to cope with this growing threat.

In many cases, film industries around the globe have responded by focusing on the specific needs of their local markets (Cook, 1990; Gomery, 1991; Nowell-Smith, 1996; Thompson & Bordwell, 1994). In spite of the strong appeal of the extravagant Hollywood blockbuster films, audiences in each country have continued to show considerable interest in films that are tied to their particular cultural context and are made in their own language. Some of the industries, such as those located in India and Hong Kong, have managed to show considerable growth by catering to these localized needs. Others such as those in France and Japan have also managed to rely on local markets to sustain a smaller presence.

However, film industries that are located in other English-speaking countries have found it harder to survive. They have had to develop films that may cater to niche markets, even in their home countries. In this chapter, we examine the nature of the challenge that is being faced by one such country, Australia. In spite of a strong level of demand for movies in their home market, Australian films have found it hard to compete against U.S. blockbusters, rarely managing to claim more than 5% of domestic revenues.

Following the example of many other countries, the Australian film industry managed to obtain considerable support from their government in the form of subsidies in order to survive (International Trade Administration, 2000). But recent cutbacks in these subsidies have forced Australian film producers to turn to more private funding, from both domestic and foreign investors (Australian Film Commission, 2000a). Yet their film industry has been ill equipped to attract substantial funding. More specifically, the Australian film industry has been hampered by inadequate development funds, lengthy development times, a lack of experience curves in film development, and underdeveloped films that are not strong enough to make it to distribution (Australian Film Commission, 2000a, 2000b, 2002).

In the rest of this chapter, we provide a review of the current status of the Australian film industry. We then move on to explore the overall orientation of this industry. We believe that Australian film producers have been pursuing a product-oriented business model, focusing on making the quality films that they have wanted to make. They have tended to pay less attention to a market-oriented business model that would allow them to concentrate more on catering to or developing the tastes of audiences.

We follow this up with interviews with Australian film producers who elaborate on this preference for a product-oriented rather than a market-oriented business model. Our conclusions suggest that the film producers' perspective on their craft could make it difficult for them to sustain their domestic film industry. Much more emphasis on a market orientation (Jaworski & Kohli, 1992, 1993; Kohli & Jaworski, 1990; Narver & Slater, 1989; Slater & Narver, 1992) is needed for Australian film producers to achieve their creative goals and find their own niche in the competitive marketplace.

THE STATUS OF THE AUSTRALIAN FILM INDUSTRY

Australians enthusiastically support the film industry with an annual per capita attendance of 4.85 visits compared with a global average of 1.49 visits (Informa Group PLC, 2001), but the majority of the films that they are attending are made in the United States. Australian-made movies have met with modest success in terms of Australian gross box office receipts. Of 259 films that were released in Australia in 2002, 22 were made in Australia compared to 170 that originated in the United States, many of which were major Hollywood studio releases. In 2002, Australian films earned 4.9% of the total Australian box office of A$844.8 million (Australian), whereas U.S.-sponsored films secured 83.2% of the total Australian box office (Australian Film Commission, 2002).

A major reason that U.S.-made films dominate in Australian theaters is that films from the major Hollywood studios are well financed and intensively marketed relative to Australian films (Informa Group PLC, 2001). For example, the average budget for a major U.S. studio (e.g., Disney, Warner Brothers) film in 2002 was A$95.9 million (US$58.8 million), whereas that of an Australian feature film in the same year was A$7.8 million. The average advertising budget for a U.S. studio film in the U.S. in 2002 was A$49.9 million (US$30.62 million), an amount larger than the average budget of A$7.8 million for an Australian production.

To some extent, Australian films have compensated for their lack of revenue from their home market through success in global markets. Over the past 30 years, Australia has had numerous breakout successes that did capture a sizeable global audience. These have included films such as *Picnic at Hanging Rock, The Adventures of Priscilla: Queen of the Desert, Muriel's Wedding, Strictly Ballroom, Shine, The Dish,* and *Rabbit-Proof Fence.* Australian films released internationally in 2002 were viewed in countries across Asia Pacific, Europe, North America, the Middle East, Africa, and South America. In 2002, Australian films held 3 of the top-50 film slots internationally, which is surprising when compared with the size of Australia's population (just over 20 million according to the Australian Bureau of Statistics, 2002). Most of the rest of the spots were taken by Hollywood films.

In spite of this modest success in both the domestic and global markets, the Australian film producer community must compete for investment from both governmental and private sources. The Australian Film Commission (2000a) estimated that the government invested A$26.9 million (21.1% of the total) in Australian feature films shot in 1999 and 2000. The rest of the financing came from private sources, with Australian private investors contributing A$18.8 million (14.8% of the total) and foreign investors contributing A$81.4 million (64% of the total). This hybrid model of financial investment has allowed the Australian producers to generate a steady stream of films that have managed to generate reasonable revenues, in spite of growing competition from Hollywood blockbusters.

The model has also fostered a long-term perspective that allowed the Australian film industry to develop along the lines of the objectives specified in the Australia Council Act of 1975. These objectives included the following three elements: "a drive for the highest possible standards in artistic creativity, innovation and expression; an opening up of enjoyment of the arts to as wide an audience as possible free from economic and locational barriers; and a further enhancement of the arts' unique role in defining what it means to be Australian [to Australians and the world]" (Throsby, 2001, pp. 14–15). The process for securing government funding, however, requires the guarantee of private investment, from either recognized international sales agents or distributors, before the government will come on board a project (Australian Film Commission, 2000b). Although the Australian government is hopeful that they can stimulate more private investment in Australian films, to date, the private support has been inconsistent (Woods, 2000).

ORIENTATION OF THE AUSTRALIAN FILM INDUSTRY

In this chapter, we focus on the basic orientation of the Australian film producers. Their fundamental underlying orientation guided their decision making and influenced their preproduction, production, and post-production activities on various film projects (Webster, 1992). Careful examination of the orientation of these producers provides some useful clues about the nature of their underlying business model. Although these orientations can take many forms (Churchill & Peter, 1998), the film industry in Australia is struggling to move away from a purely product-oriented business model and to embrace a more market-oriented model.

A product-oriented business model is one in which a decision maker (i.e., film producer) focuses on products (i.e., films), tries to attain the best possible quality, and assumes that markets will respond to this quality. In essence, the producer hopes that the audience will eventually discover the film because of its positive attributes. This orientation is most likely to work in situations where it is difficult to anticipate market trends or there is little need to follow them. Consequently, a product orientation is typically successful in environments that are experiencing rapid change, in environments in which demand exceeds supply, or in arenas in which there is little competition.

By contrast, a market-oriented business model is one where the producer, as decision maker, tries to tailor the films to the market (Jaworski, Kohli, & Sahay, 2000). Producers can pursue a market-driven orientation by anticipating and catering to what they perceive to be the salient needs of a well-defined segment of the audience. Clearly, such an orientation is much more likely to work in situations where market trends are relatively clear and need to be followed. It follows, then, that a market orientation is more successful in environments that are not experiencing rapid change, in environments in which supply far exceeds demand, or in arenas where there is intense competition.

The Australian model of film development has largely been driven by a product orientation. Producers and their teams search for scripts that they consider to be promising, which could be turned into films of sufficiently high quality, and wait for production opportunities to arise (Australian Film Commission, 2000a). Although this has led to some critically acclaimed films, such a product orientation has often failed to generate sufficient box office receipts and long-term profitability because of intense competition, declining government support, and market saturation (Informa Group PLC, 2001).

By contrast, a market-oriented business model appears to have played a relatively minor role in the development of the Australian film industry. Producers have made little effort to focus on the specific attributes that may appeal to particular movie audiences and try to focus on these in order to lure them away from

U.S.-produced films. By neglecting to understand the prevailing trends in audience preferences, most Australian films have faced a more uphill battle in gaining sufficient support from distributors and exhibitors in a marketplace that is becoming more globally competitive.

A STUDY OF THE AUSTRALIAN FILM PRODUCER

In January 2001, we interviewed a sample of 17 Australian producers as a part of a larger project on the Australian film industry. The population of producers who made films in the 1990s for whom contact information was available totaled 33, yielding a response rate of 51%. The sample was evenly distributed across first-time, established, and veteran producers. Nine interviews were conducted face to face, and ranged from 1 to 3¼ hours (averaging 1¾ hours). Five of the interviews were conducted by e-mail (averaging 4 pages), and three were conducted by phone (averaging 25 minutes). Each interview was taped and transcribed. The interviews were semistructured, leading with questions on how the changing financial situation affects the producers and how they manage the tension between art and commerce (Lampel, Lant, & Shamsie, 2000).

We interviewed Australian producers in order to gain a better understanding of the reasons behind their heavier reliance on a product-oriented business model over a market-oriented business model. Although we recognize that there are many players in the Australian film industry (e.g., distributors, international sales agents, and exhibitors), we focused on the producers because they are the primary drivers of film making in Australia. These film producers were deemed to be the best subjects to interview because they are, in effect, responsible for initiating most of the films that get made.

Furthermore, given the project-based management that underlies most film-making efforts (DeFillippi & Arthur, 1998), their leadership has even more impact than in an ongoing organization (Daymon, 2000). In Australia, there is no studio system, such as in Hollywood, with readily available financial backing, access to several production facilities, a network of production and marketing talent, and established distribution channels. Australian producers must actually develop the project, raise the financing, pull together the creative team, oversee the production or shooting, and manage all distribution and marketing arrangements. As such, these producers need to make crucial decisions about where to devote most of their energy: on searching for quality scripts and recruiting well-known talent or on thinking about potential distribution deals and the marketing possibilities.

For the most part, Australian film producers have a highly developed product orientation. They strongly believe that they can only do better by making the best films that they possibly can in terms of the quality of characters, story, and settings. They basically subscribe to a *Field of Dreams* rationale that states, "If you build it, they will come." (Initials refer to interviewee.)

I think the answer is always in the work, and unfortunately it just means that we need to be better and better and better at what we do. (II)

When you find a script with a heart, a heart beating strongly that permeates everything, every character, you have to hold on to it because those are the films that break out. The films with heart, the ones that are unique that speaks to people. (DD)

The product orientation of Australian producers is also apparent in how they talk about the type of movies they make, how they are different from Hollywood, and the passion that drives them to do this work. They have a clear, well-shared idea of the kind of film that can be made in Australia by Australians. The films that succeed are usually original intense dramas or quirky comedies with heart that tap into Australian culture:

[We] are making intense dramas and quirky comedies … (AA)

The films that have been *successful*—*Shine, Strictly Ballroom, Muriel's Wedding, Priscilla*—in hindsight they all have a commercial aspect to them, but they are small stories, small Australian stories—what is known as the quirky Australian film—idiosyncratically Australian. (DD)

They attribute the success of their films to the originality that differentiates them from Hollywood films. This rivalry also helps them in constructing a distinctive identity for their local industry (Porac, Thomas, Wilson, & Paton, 1995). Such a comparison allows them to define the film that they should make by the type of story that it can tell:

Whenever I read a script I always say, "Could Hollywood make this film?" Because if they can, we shouldn't bother. (EE)

I don't think Australian producers should set out to make formulaic, highly commercial [films].… You cannot compete with the studio system and what they have available to them. (FF)

I think everyone aspires to making a film that is outside the American story model that works internationally. (GG)

In the eyes of these producers, Hollywood films are so well resourced, and they do such a good job of creating product that appeals to mass audiences, Australia should stay out of this market and produce films with unusual stories, with available resources in attempts to appeal to a smaller, more art-house market and just hope the film can sell internationally:

We are a fringe industry in the world scene and we are subsidized, but we have terribly terribly low budgets. We are really making films that struggle alongside other independent films in the world to find an audience in that independent and art-house market. (BB)

However, as producers try to stay away from mass-market films, they tend to identify much more with the creative production of movies than with the marketing activities that may be tied to them. They see themselves as being very hands-on in the creative process—they are in the business because they want to tell stories on film, and they stick with it because of their passion for the story:

I think first and foremost it has to be something that absolutely takes your fancy because you have got to be prepared to put lots of time into it.... It's an industry of the heart. It is really made up of people who adore what they do and are prepared to go out on a limb for it. (FF)

I am a filmmaking producer, I mean, of course I'm a deal maker and a businessman, but I hate being those things. I love the organic process of making a movie, of putting it together and getting the script out and hopefully the right director and the right actors and the right crew and putting all that thing together and at the end of it comes a film of which we can all be proud of.... I am intensely hands-on—I can't not be. I'm everywhere, I mean, I have to be. (HH)

I see myself as a creative producer, in the sense that I am not just about raising finance, you know, I want to put the comma in that line of the dialogue, kind of thing. That's why I am making films. (JJ)

In part, Australian film producers have failed to develop a stronger market orientation because their limited budgets do not allow them to spend much on marketing. Proportionally, Australian producers tip their allocations to production over marketing far more than major American studios and some American independent studios (Fleischhauer & von Blumencron, 1999). This has also led to a relative lack of marketing expertise and marketing infrastructure within the Australian film industry:

I don't think in Australia there are very good marketing people. I wish I could have nothing to do with it, because I don't particularly know a lot about it, but we don't have very experienced marketing people and we don't have many, it is a part of the industry that doesn't really exist. (BB)

The relative lack of marketing expertise and infrastructure has also led many producers to develop a certain degree of distrust of marketing. Many of them believe that greater focus on marketing will constrain their ability to make quality films with compelling stories:

The problem is that you have a film and a story that you are passionate about ... most investors ... are going to be saying to how, okay, how can we sell this to America. We can't sell this to America with that character doing that. You know what I mean.... So the film starts to become something else. (GG)

You have to market the film, you have to be there for all the publicity, and you get treated like a sort of nasty trouble by the distributors, because you can't afford to hound them, but you do, over the whole distribution of the film. (FF)

On [one of my films] I tried to get them to scrap the poster, I even offered to pay for a new poster, but they wouldn't, and I hated it.... Sales agents in particular often want to put out a trailer that has nothing to do with the film but they think they are going to bring in particular market. But people who see that trailer are going to be disappointed in the film because it is not that sort of film. And the people who want to see this sort of film aren't going to get it from that trailer and so they're not going to look at it. And there is a terrible tendency to people to misrepresent what the material is, I think. At least that is what I fear as a producer. What you want to present to the world in the best possible way, is what you made. (BB)

At the same time, producers do understand that it is important to develop effective methods for reaching an audience:

We are not constrained by some of the rules of Hollywood films so that we can be even a little bit more adventurous, but never forget that you are making the films for an audience. (II)

I do try to keep abreast of what audiences feel, but if I do not like that feeling I don't follow it. This can mean I will not make certain films. (LL)

In the end, the industry will only survive by finding our audience. (DD)

Now there has to be a greater understanding of what a film can do elsewhere. (FF)

In spite of the importance of reaching an audience, Australian film producers are not sure that conventional Hollywood methods of prescreenings and focus groups would work for the kind of films that they make:

There's never really been a huge culture of testing films here, not like there is in America. I don't necessarily think we need to go down the entire path that the Americans do which is like placing everything on what they say. (GG)

[The distributor] wanted us to do test screening in the United States.... I think it had an edge, a rawness to it that was eventually lost through the process. (KK)

Most Australian film producers also believe that they do not have a meaningful relationship with significant distributors and exhibitors. Furthermore, many of them also believe that any marketing efforts that they can possibly make are unlikely to have any significant impact on these distributors or exhibitors. They feel that their films will never draw the level of audience that will be attracted to a Hollywood blockbuster.

I think more and more distributors appreciate that the filmmakers do have quite a lot to offer, they should be involved in the marketing not only because most of them have some sort of profile that is worth using but also they are best able to talk about the product, they know it intimately and they can talk about to figure out how to best pitch it to a particular audience. (FF)

[Australian distributors] have this whole idea that they have to be seen to be promoting Australian films when 95% of their income comes from releasing American product. That says everything. So their whole focus, their structure, their marketing campaigns, the philosophy behind the release strategy, everything is focused around an American film of a certain budget level of a certain genre. So to walk in and say here's something different, regardless of its commercial potential in Australia, if it doesn't fit that mold, then they are just going to struggle with it, no matter how much they want to do it, how much they love it, it is just not going to work. (GG)

In summary, Australian film producers have developed a strong product orientation but have been reluctant or slow to pursue a sufficient market orientation. They believe that they can best deal with the threat posed by Hollywood by relying on a product orientation to focus on certain types of films that they may be able to excel in. At the same time, they do see how any attempts to develop a marketing orientation may either complement or enhance their product orientation. In large part, this conviction is driven by their inability to discover marketing methods that do not follow the Hollywood model.

IMPLICATIONS AND CONCLUSION

The Australian film industry, like many other smaller film industries around the world, is in a difficult position. Government subsidization waxes and wanes with each election, but there has been a gradual reduction of this support over time. In order to respond to this, Australian producers have needed to secure a regular supply of private funding in order to maintain a level of film production that can allow them to maintain a viable local industry. But higher levels of funding may be difficult to maintain as long as these producers continue to use their product-oriented business models to make specialized films, without much attempt to use a marketing orientation to increase the box office revenues that are generated by these films.

The strong product orientation drives Australian film producers to focus on telling great stories that speak to select audiences. In large part, such a form of emphasis on product orientation has emerged in response to the threat posed by Hollywood blockbusters. Australian film producers have tried to concentrate on making films that would be sufficiently different from the U.S.-produced offerings. By differentiating their films, they hope that these address a different need for potential movie audiences that the Hollywood productions are not able to meet.

At the same time, the relative lack of a market orientation among the Australian film producers has prevented them from actively pursuing and developing the audience to whom these films can speak. In terms of marketing, these producers have failed to search for their own distinctive marketing efforts that would not require them to compete with the traditional Hollywood marketing approaches. If Australian films are really different, then they need to find their own methods of communicating their unique qualities to their prospective audiences.

Instead of rejecting a marketing orientation because it may not be suited to their films, Australian film producers need to discover one that may be more effective. In this goal, they may benefit from pursuing a driving-markets approach rather than the conventional market-driven one (Jaworski et al., 2000). Such an approach would require them to actively build the specialized markets for their films rather than to respond to broader market trends.

The efforts to build the market would require a much more concentrated effort. Besides working on particular types of films that they should support, the Australian film producers would have to combine design, production, marketing, and distribution and align all of these in a manner that would differentiate their entire range of activities from that of Hollywood (Bishop, Case, Axarlis, Plante, & Allsop, 2000). Each of these activities cannot be developed in a vacuum without regard for how it will work with the other. Marketing and distribution must be developed along with the design and production of Australian films.

To develop such an integrated approach, Australian film producers need to move away from the purely product-driven "if you build it they will come" orientation. They cannot simply hope that various partners such as investors and distributors will support their films just because they share the same vision. Instead, producers would do better if they learned to work with various partners in their local industry to understand how their product may serve the needs of their intended market. This will allow them to improve their product and to find better ways of reaching their market.

In particular, Australian film producers need to work with local distributors and exhibitors and with foreign sales agents to create a new business model for developing and marketing films outside the mainstream. Given the current frame of distributors and foreign sales agents, producers need to engage in personal selling, not only of the content of their film, but also of the methods that might be effective in selling their film to a sizeable audience. Only by adopting such an approach can they continue to survive in the shadows of Hollywood and maintain a sustainable local industry.

For many producers, as elaborated earlier, their product orientation reflects their identities as producers of art. They do not identify with the business side of their industry. We argue that this is a luxury that is not sustainable in the long run if they must turn to private financing in order to replace decreasing subsidies from the government. However, this does not mean that producers have to compromise their art in order to sell it. Instead, and consistent with the findings of Gainer and Padanyi (2002), we argue that they could better tailor their art to the audience that it is expected to reach.

Although we have focused in this chapter on the Australian film industry, the challenges that it faces in an industry that is becoming more global in character are certainly not unique. Smaller film industries that are trying to survive in many different countries must confront many of the same issues. Each of them must search for a more appropriate model for both making and selling their films that works for the markets they are trying to reach. It is only through the development of a somewhat unique configuration of activities that many of these film industries will be able to sustain themselves in the long run in the presence of Hollywood studios' market dominance.

REFERENCES

Australian Bureau of Statistics. (2002, December). *Australian demographic statistics.* Retrieved March 10, 2004, from http://www.abs.gov.au/Ausstats/abs@.nsf/ca79f6302ec2e9cca256886001514d7/35ca51458e2fe133ca2568a900143aa5!OpenDocument

Australian Film Commission. (2000a, November). *Development: A study of Australian and international funding and practice in the feature film industry.* Sydney: Author.

Australian Film Commission. (2000b). *National production survey 1999/2000.* Sydney: Author.

Australian Film Commission. (2002). *Australian films: 2002 box office share.* Sydney: Author.

Bishop, R., Case, D., Axarlis, S., Plante, J., & Allsop, D. (2000). *Innovation in the Australian film Industry.* Retrieved month, day, year, from Prime Minister's Science, Engineering, and Innovation Council's web site: http://www.dest.gov.au/science/pmseic/documents/Film.pdf

Churchill, G. A., & Peter, J. P. (1998). *Marketing: Creating value for customers.* Burr Ridge, IL: McGraw-Hill.

Cook, D. A. (1990). *A history of narrative film* (2nd ed.). New York: Norton.

Daymon, C. (2000). Leadership and emerging cultural patterns in a new television station. *Studies in Cultures, Organizations, and Societies, 6,* 169–196.

DeFillippi, R. J., & Arthur, M. B. (1998). Paradox in project-based enterprise: The case of film making. *California Management Review, 40,* 125–139.

Fleischhauer, J., & von Blumencron, M. M. (1999). Kassensturz in Hollywood. *Der Spiegel, 5*(16), 84–86.

Gainer, B., & Padanyi (2002). Applying the marketing concept to cultural organizations: An empirical study of the relationship between market orientation and performance. *International Journal of Nonprofit and Voluntary Sector Marketing, 7*(2), 182–193.

Gomery, D. (1991). *Movie history: A survey.* Belmont, CA: Wadsworth.

International Trade Administration. (2000, September). *The migration of U.S. film and television production: Impact of "Runaways" on workers and small business in the U.S. film industry.* Retrieved March 15, 2004, from http://www.ita.doc.gov/media/filmreport.htm

Informa Group PLC. (2001). *Global film: Exhibition and distribution, 4th Edition.*

Jaworski, B. J., & Kohli, A. K. (1992). *Market orientation: Antecedents and consequences.* Cambridge, MA: Marketing Science Institute. (Working Paper No. 92-104, 1–36) Cambridge, MA: Marketing Science Institute.

Jaworski, B. J., & Kohli, A. K. (1993). Market orientation: Antecedents and consequences. *Journal of Marketing, 57,* 53–70.

Jaworski, B. J., Kohli, A. K., & Sahay, A. (2000). Market-driven versus driving markets. *Academy of Marketing Science, 28,* 45–54.

Kohli, A. K., & Jaworski, B. J. (1990). *Market orientation: The construct, research propositions, and managerial implications.* (Working Paper No. 90-113, 1–40) Cambridge, MA: Marketing Science Institute.

Lampel, J., Lant, T., & Shamsie, J. (2000) .Balancing act: Learning from organizing practices in cultural industries. *Organization Science, 11,* 263–269.

Narver, J. C., & Slater, S. F. (1989). *The effect of market orientation on business profitability.* (Working Paper No. 89-120, 1–35) Cambridge, MA: Marketing Science Institute.

Nowell-Smith, G. (Ed.). (1996). *The Oxford history of world cinema.* Oxford. UK: Oxford University Press.

Porac, J. F., Thomas, H., Wilson, F., & Paton, D. (1995). Rivalry and the industry model of Scottish knitwear products. *Administrative Science Quarterly, 40,* 203–227.

Slater, S. F., & Narver, J. C. (1992). *Market orientation, performance, and the moderating influence of competitive environment.* (Working Paper No. 92-118, 1–35) Cambridge, MA: Marketing Science Institute.

Thompson, K., & Bordwell, D. (1994). *Film history: An introduction.* New York: McGraw-Hill.

Throsby, D. (2001). Public funding of the arts in Australia: 1900 to 2000. In D. Trewin (Ed.), *2001 Yearbook Australia.* Canberra: Australian Bureau of Statistics.

Webster, F. E. (1992). The changing role of marketing in the corporation. *Journal of Marketing, 56,* 1–17.

Woods, M. (2000, July 7). Oz's private coin strategy a bust at $13 mil [Electronic version]. *Variety.* Available at http://www.variety.com/index.asp?layout=upsell_article&articleID=VR1117783390&cs=1

CHAPTER

17

Uncertain Globalization: Evolutionary Scenarios for the Future Development of Cultural Industries

Joseph Lampel
City University, London

Jamal Shamsie
Michigan State University

The Walt Disney Company has been delivering happiness to millions of kids for many years with such animated masterpieces as *Cinderella, Bambi,* and *The Lion King.* In spite of this accomplishment, the firm has drawn considerable hostility from many who have accused Disney of pillaging their culture to make a fast buck (Didcock, 1997). The Greeks are up in arms over the portrayal of their ancient hero in *Hercules.* The Danes are indignant at Disney's transformation of their most cherished national fable *The Little Mermaid.* In France, Disney's animated treatment of Victor Hugo's classic *The Hunchback of Notre Dame* was greeted with howls of protest. Disney changed the name to *Notre-Dame de Paris*, made the ending more upbeat, and, to add insult to injury, failed to mention that Victor Hugo had anything to do with the story in the first place (Hainer, 1997). Not surprisingly, the film attracted angry reaction from Victor Hugo's descendants who denounced the Disney movie as "vulgar globalization."

The concerns over what has come to be known as cultural globalization have largely been driven by arguments that corporations such as Disney represent a future in which large megacorporations will dominate our cinemas, rule our airwaves, and own our bookstores. Opposing this perspective are observers and scholars who argue that organizations in the cultural industries are not masters of their domain, that ultimately markets are driven by what consumers decide to buy rather than by what producers decide to offer (Held & McGrew, 2002; Robertson, 1992). Much of the debate, however, is driven by extrapolation from today's headlines. This allows anxiety about what cultural globalization will do to our society to override any deep analysis of what globalization will do to the business of culture itself.

In this chapter, we argue that in order to fully appreciate the impact of globalization on the business of culture, we must begin with an understanding of the evolution of cultural industries from an organizational perspective. The organizations that produce, distribute, and market cultural products operate at the cutting edge of globalization. Globalization has created the choices that these organizations confront and it shapes the choices that these organizations eventually make. But these choices do not simply represent some form of automatic response to technological, economic, and social forces. Instead, most of these choices are shaped by certain underlying beliefs and assumptions that these organizations may hold about the potential impact of globalization on cultural industries.

In cultural industries, as elsewhere, organizational concerns about the possible impact of globalization have been fueled by divergent interpretations. To understand these interpretations, we must focus on two distinct areas that are of considerable importance to organizations as they attempt to respond to the movement toward globalization. First, organizations are concerned about the potential impact of globalization on the sources of competitive advantage in cultural industries, and second, they are trying to understand what impact globalization is likely to have on the patterns of production and the consumption of cultural products.

Our analysis of globalization in the cultural industries suggests that both of these areas are undergoing change, but that the direction of change is at present uncertain. Globalization may increase the competitive advantage of holding resources, or it may require organizations to forego holding resources, and instead base strategic advantage on preferential access to resources. By the same token, globalization may lead to homogenous cultural products and uniform cultural tastes, or it may produce the very opposite: greater product innovation and more diverse cultural tastes.

Organizations in cultural industries cannot wait for the outcome of globalization to conclusively show which of these scenarios is correct. They must act decisively when the trends are uncertain precisely because they wish to occupy a strong position in the future. But ironically, because they are deciding to act early, the collective decisions of these firms are shaping the very outcomes that they are trying to predict. These outcomes give rise to evolutionary scenarios that we explore in the last part of the chapter. But these evolutionary scenarios, it is worth noting, do not represent any futuristic predictions. They are extrapolations based on decisions that are currently being made by organizations in the cultural industries in response to the challenge of globalization.

GLOBALIZATION IN CULTURAL INDUSTRIES

All cultural industries—with the possible exception of computer games—began life as national industries. Although globalization did not have much influence on cultural industries for many years, it gradually began to exercise considerable influence, more slowly in the case of literature and art, but more quickly in the case of motion pictures and recorded music. The increase in tempo can partly be attributed to the growth of trade. There has been a close relationship between an increase in trade and a movement toward globalization in cultural industries.

Trade depends on efficient communications and transportation, and these make it possible for people and ideas to span geographical boundaries. As geographical boundaries fall, a relationship is formed between the producers of one country and the cultural tastes of another. European literature shapes American literary tastes; American jazz has an influence on European musical tastes; Japanese art on sale in Paris inspires French impressionists; and French films that are shown in Tokyo have an impact on Japanese animation (Kirschbaum & Vasconcelos, 2004).

As the boundaries that separate different cultural products across various national markets begin to break down, there is a gradual movement toward globalization. In this chapter, we argue that two key issues are central to our understanding of how the pull of globalization could impact organizations in cultural industries. The first issue deals with the influence of globalization on the development of competitive advantage in cultural industries. The nature and form of this influence can vary, depending on two contrasting views of the roots of competitive advantage in cultural industries.

One view contends that firms use globalization in order to gain control of a large number of vital creative and economic resources. An opposing view argues the roots of competitive advantage in cultural industries are not to be found in control of creative and economic resources that tend to depreciate in value quickly, but in the ability to gain access on advantageous terms to creative and economic resources that will grow in value in the future.

The second issue concerns the impact of globalization on the cultural space in which cultural industries operate. Cultural industries encourage the mingling of cultures, some of which is unintentional and some of which can be quite deliberate. The result of this mingling, however, is to bring together ideas and themes from cultural spaces that were previously separated from each other by geographical and political barriers.

One view argues that globalization will promote convergence and uniformity of cultural products. Thus, homogeneity will displace diversity as cultural forms fuse to produce uniform creative standards. The opposing view argues the global cultural space is primarily an arena for interaction and trade. It exists as another level where cultural producers exchange ideas and explore opportunities that will in fact encourage greater variety and diversity.

Evolution of Competitive Advantage

Globalization poses a fundamental challenge to what constitutes competitive advantage in the cultural industries. This challenge is especially urgent when it comes to decisions on how resources should be acquired and deployed. The development, production, marketing, and distribution of cultural products call for combining creative resources such as writers, composers, and performers, and economic resources such as financial capital, production facilities, and distribution networks. Competitive advantage clearly requires both creative and economic resources. But given the fundamentally different character of creative and economic resources, a key question that faces firms is the steps that they must take to garner the resources that are necessary for competitive advantage within a more global context.

The answer to this question depends on evaluating the relative importance of controlling creative and economic resources, as opposed to acquiring access to these resources on favorable terms. This depends on judging trends, rather than fixing the roots of competitive advantage once and for all. Thus at one extreme we find researchers and observers who argue that competitive advantage in cultural industries is increasingly based on controlling of resources, in particular downstream resources such as distribution and retail. For proponents of this view, economic resources are the source of power because they mediate between the intangible creative resources on the one hand and the more tangible economic resources on the other.

This position allows the owners of economic resources to dictate terms to creative resources, and hence to extract maximum rents from their use. Inevitably, these rents are invested in wider distribution scope and greater marketing efficiency. This begets better financial performance that will in turn allow owners of economic resources to raise additional financial resources that can be used to reinforce their distribution and marketing operations.

Central to the view that economic resources can dictate terms to creative resources is the assumption that creative resources are abundant. Caves (2000) pointed out that the supply of creative resources far outstrips the demand. Music schools award some 14,000 degrees whereas symphony orchestras may hire 300 musicians. Twentieth-Century Fox considers 10,000 proposals and produces 12 films a year. Before the era of literary agents, Doubleday received 10,000 unsolicited manuscripts a year and published 4.

These statistics, however, simply indicate the abundance of creative resources that may be available, but it is clear that all of these resources do not have equal value. In fact, it is usually only a small percentage of published authors, of released movies, and of recorded music that account for the lion's share of the market. To make matters worse, the value distribution of creative resources is not only skewed, it is also unstable. Four young men from Liverpool with cheap guitars can unleash a revolution that unsettles the recording industry. The movie industry invests millions in popular themes that fail to attract audiences, only to see maverick film makers with handheld equipment roaming through apparently haunted woods grab the box office.

In other words, economic resources allow firms to mobilize creative resources but not to guarantee their value. For many, however, the value of creative resources is the key to competitive advantage in cultural industries. This gives rise to an opposing view that argues that any analysis of competitive advantage in the cultural industries should not begin with an assessment of which firms control the most resources, but with which have differential access to the most valuable creative resources. This perspective points to a focus on networks and relationships. It puts a premium on information and expert judgment and therefore highlights the development of specialized roles and key competencies that are necessary for identifying and mobilizing valuable creative resources.

An interesting example from the video game industry demonstrates the difference between the two perspectives. The video game industry is currently dominated by companies with their own teams of game developers under contract. Game publishers typically sign up a development house to work on a project based on an original concept or acquired intellectual property such as Spider Man or Harry Potter. Firms therefore attempt to create a competitive advantage by tying up as many talented developers as possible with long-term contracts.

But as the industry grows, it is evolving in a direction that is familiar to the motion picture industry: Developers are becoming increasingly attracted by the economic and creative advantage of negotiating projects on a deal-by-deal basis. This entails rejecting the corporate umbrella of game-development companies and striking out on their own. The shift puts game publishers in a position similar to that of the Hollywood studios: Access to talent becomes more important to competitive advantage than control of talent.

The shift is helped along by talent agencies that specialize in assembling and packaging deals. Seamus Blackley, who works for CAA, one of Hollywood's premier talent agencies, sees access to talented developers as increasingly the true source of competitive advantage. The role of agents, he argued, is "to be able to bring to publishers heaps of creative people that they would not be able to assemble themselves, that they would not have access to or even knowledge of" (Heavens, 2004, p. 9).

Evolution of Cultural Space

Cultural industries connect market activity and social life to a degree that is rarely seen in other industries. These industries came into existence in a preexisting cultural space that consists of beliefs, symbols, and ideas that are at the heart of human and social reality. The growth of large-scale cultural commercial activity—backed by powerful systems of production, distribution, and marketing—is changing the dynamics and structure of traditional culture spaces. The nature and direction of this change is a matter of conflicting interpretation.

One view argues that the economic and technological strategies that sustain competitive advantage in cultural industries dominate the creation and appreciation of cultural products. This view is predicated on the belief that it is commercial and technological necessity rather than long-standing cultural preferences that drive what firms produce and what consumers learn to enjoy. Commercial and technological necessity point to economies of scale, and economies of scale are reinforced by standardization of tastes.

From this it follows that globalization in cultural industries should vastly increase economies of scale, and subsequently promote standardization of tastes. The more people have access to the same books, music, and movies, so the argument goes, the more their tastes tend to converge (Bryman, 2004; Ritzer, 2004). The more their tastes converge, the more there is market pressure to offer products that cater to standardized tastes. The paradox of expansion, in terms both of sheer volume of products and greater access, is that it seems to reinforce the tendency to cater to the largest number of people with similar tastes.

Globalization increases scale, but it also erodes geographic and national boundaries (Augè, 1995). Increasing travel and improved communications bring disparate cultures into closer contact. This mélange of cultures becomes an important input into the creative process: Producers tap talent and ideas wherever they can find them, and then use both to create products that have wide appeal precisely because they fuse diverse cultural elements into relatively homogenous products. In effect, cultural industries dominate and transform the cultural space in much the same way that other industries dominate and transform our tastes in clothes and food.

An opposing view argues that cultural production and consumption retain a measure of autonomy vis-à-vis the business of culture. The process of creating and appreciating cultural products is too deeply embedded in unique cultural settings to be fundamentally altered by scale and technology. From this it follows that local uniqueness and cultural specificity that existed prior to the rise of cultural industries do not quickly or easily disappear (Robertson, 1990). Economies of scale need not result in fusion and homogeneity. Instead, exposure to different cultures creates new tastes, and new tastes create a potential for diversity that economies of scale can satisfy.

The manifestation of this diversity depends on how different cultures interact. As creative artists from different cultures come into contact with each other there is greater scope for experimentation and innovation. The French and Cubans develop their own jazz style. The Japanese take film animation and comics in a completely different direction. Modern dance in the West forms new synthesis from Balinese and South Asian traditions (Pieterse, 1995). Hybrids proliferate as cultures meet and converse, borrowing from each other, and adapting each other's ideas to their local context (Chanda, 2000; Eriksen, 2003; Zhang, 2000).

EVOLUTIONARY SCENARIOS

Debates about the impact of globalization have touched not only on how these forces may be shaping the cultural industries at present, but also on what cultural industries could look like in the future. In this respect, each of the issues we discussed earlier—the sources of competitive advantage and the dynamics of cultural spaces under the impact of globalization—suggests two contrasting positions. These positions are not merely points of view; they are also assumptions in various possible evolutionary scenarios for cultural industries. When managers and experts analyze and predict the future of the cultural industries in a time of rapid globalization they are essentially taking positions in debates defined by these key issues.

Because each of these issues, and its associated debate, has led to the development of two conflicting positions, the range of possible views can be defined by a four-fold conceptual space. When this conceptual space is used to examine the impact of globalization on cultural industries, we end up with four possible evolutionary scenarios that are depicted in Table 17.1. In the remainder of this chapter we examine these scenarios. We look at the organizations that are going to populate this matrix, at what they will look like, and how they will operate. We brave the descriptions of these future evolutionary scenarios on the basis of what we can see

TABLE 17.1
Scenarios of Globalization in the Cultural Industries

	Fusion	Hybridization
Control	**Monolithic conglomerations**	**Symbiotic conglomeration**
	- Large hierarchical conglomerates controlling most cultural industries	- Large hierarchical conglomerates control distribution and retail
	- Control exercised from source to market through pervasive vertical integration	- Production of cultural goods is largely in the hands of loosely affiliated small entrepreneurial independents with high mortality rate
Access	**Dominant agglomeration**	**Virtual agglomeration**
	- Cultural industries are dominated by powerful production clusters	- Cultural industries are shaped by a complex web of networks linking different locales and different artistic communities
	- These clusters cooperate to shape relatively standardized products for global consumption	- New technologies, in particular the Internet, permit complete disintermediation; cultural producers and consumers can communicate directly without the mediation of commercial entities
	- Power in this scenario is based on access to cluster	- The same technologies permit remote collaboration and exchange of ideas
	- Clusters are dominated by a mixture of strong firms supported by an ecology of small firms	

today. Ultimately, our hope is that these descriptions will provide the basis for serious discussion and policy debate.

Scenario 1: Monolithic Conglomerations

The first scenario flows directly from the assumption that competitive advantage in cultural industries comes directly from control of creative and economic resources, and from the second assumption that cultural spaces are becoming increasingly uniform and homogenous. This scenario sees cultural industries as increasingly coming under the domination of large and highly centralized conglomerates. Using economies of scale and scope and an advantageous access to capital markets, these conglomerates will vertically integrate the value chain of successive cultural industries, taking control of these industries from the creative source to final consumers.

The concentration of economic resources, in particular distribution and marketing resources, will not only give these conglomerates inordinate control over the creative process, it will also make it possible to subordinate the creative process to market imperatives. To make the most of their market power, centralized conglomerates will seek economies of consumption by standardizing tastes. This in turn will be used to create product complementarities (i.e., synergies) across business lines in different cultural industries. The overall effect will be to gradually reduce the barriers that separate the value chains of different cultural industries. Carried to its logical conclusion this scenario sees the evolution of a single culture industry dominated by a handful of transnational media-entertainment giants that exercise almost total control over standardized and homogenized cultural space.

Scenario 2: Symbiotic Conglomerations

This scenario is based on the assumption that competitive advantage in cultural industries comes directly from control of creative and economic resources, and on the second assumption that contact among cultural producers will produce a proliferation of hybrids and diversity. The scenario sees an emerging division of labor in the cultural industries between small business units that originate cultural products and large conglomerates that focus on downstream activities such as distribution and retail.

Small business units emerge through external entrepreneurial activity, or are generated from within conglomerates through a process of internal venturing. The relationship between the large conglomerates and these units runs the gamut from direct ownership with a degree of divisional autonomy, to an equity position that accords managers quasi-independence, to an arms-length market relationship.

The dynamics of cultural industries under symbiotic conglomeration is based on recognition that market power can be used to extract maximum rents from cultural products with proven value, but is limited in efficacy when it comes to identifying and creating cultural products that are valuable. The exercise of power by large conglomerates is therefore tempered by awareness of their dependence on the specialized skills and insight of the small business units that populate the upstream part of the value chain. The small business units, for their part, are aware that their continued existence depends on their ability to detect new cultural trends and create new tastes. Their exploratory and innovative activities promote hybridization by actively experimenting with combinations of different cultural forms and different tastes.

Scenario 3: Dominant Agglomerations

This scenario is based on the assumption that competitive advantage in cultural industries is sustained by gaining access to creative resources, and on the second assumption that trade and international contacts lead to homogeneity and uniformity of tastes and cultural products. The departure point for this scenario is the view that current technological change is restructuring the relationship between creative and economic resources.

An increasing number of distribution technologies and proliferation of media outlets are allowing owners of creative resources to communicate directly with final consumers. As power shifts to creative resources, the challenge is no longer reaching the market but being the first to identify and mobilize valuable creative resources.

The emphasis on first-mover advantage changes the nature of competition in most cultural industry. The key to success is access to creative resources in their formative phase. Competition for access puts a premium on physical proximity to talent and the creative process. Owners of economic resources therefore position themselves in areas of high creative activity and their presence attracts inflow of creative talent. The result is a process of agglomeration in which creative clusters emerge to dominate the production of cultural goods.

This domination is based not only on a higher concentration of creative talent, but on the standardization of tastes and accelerating homogenization of the cultural space worldwide. The creative clusters are hot areas of creative activity that are closely linked to global systems of distribution and marketing. The standardization of tastes ensures that the creative activity is concentrated in few locations and is aligned with the preferences of consumers that are widely dispersed.

Standardization and homogeneity are also reinforced by the mobility of creative talent that tends to give creative clusters a global dimension. However, although talent is recruited worldwide, it is assimilated into a monolithic culture: Clusters borrow and adopt what other cultures have to offer, but their outputs are relatively standardized in line with the needs of distribution and marketing efficiencies.

Scenario 4: Virtual Agglomerations

This scenario is based on the assumption that competitive advantage in cultural industries is sustained by gaining access to creative resources, and on the second assumption that contact among cultural producers will produce a proliferation of hybrids and diversity. Behind this scenario is the view that the same technological change that is breaking the boundaries between owners of creative resources and final consumers is also allowing creative talent to form new structures of collaborative creativity.

Communications infrastructure, in particular, the Internet, is making it possible for creative talent to abolish the barriers that traditionally separated creative workers from different cultures. These linkages coalesce into networks that in turn promote the formation of virtual creative communities. Creative resources are both localized in their respective geographic locations and globalized through their dense interconnectivity. With individuals and firms having a wide range of options when it comes to exchanging ideas and forming collaborative alliances, their strategy consists of staking positions in this interactive space, and then using this position to assemble bundles of resources either singly or in partnership with others.

The emergence of virtual agglomerations signals a transformation. The term *cultural industries* becomes increasingly archaic as industry boundaries begin to disappear and economic resources become more highly dispersed. The organizational division of labor between creative and economic resources likewise begins to disappear. As information costs and economies of scale fall, hierarchies give way to a wide variety of new organizational forms that are virtual, perform hub functions, and are frequently managed by artists and entrepreneurs.

Final markets also undergo a profound transformation. Interactivity promotes product variety and market fragmentation. With more choices available, consumers become explorers of new tastes and codevelopers of new products. Though mass markets continue to exist, they lose their dominance, and with the dominance of mass market in decline, the creative process explores with considerable vigor the possibilities inherent in hybridization—not only between different cultures, but also between different cultural products.

CONCLUSION

Cultural industries have burst their national boundaries and are now increasingly global. The impact on cultural products has been dramatic. To a degree unprecedented in history, the cultural products that we enjoy are crafted with commercial intent by firms that are not part of our cultural life. This transformation has given rise to an acrimonious debate, pitting many who attack what they see as the packaging and vulgarization of culture in the interests of profit-seeking corporations, against others who point to the cornucopia of books, music, and films that globalization has made available to every child and adult across the world.

In this chapter, we argued that the impact of cultural globalization on consumers is inseparable from the impact of globalization of producers. In fact, discussion of the former without a full understanding of the latter is speculative at best, and little more than polemics at its worse.

Turning our attention to how cultural industries are developing under the dynamics of globalization, we argued that two issues are crucial for understanding the future of cultural industries. The first calls into question the basis of competitive advantage in cultural industries, and the second tackles the dynamics of the cultural space under globalization. To us it is clear that these two issues are contestable. In other words, they are shaped by a complex interaction among technology, organization, ideology, and political action. Rather than predetermine how this interaction will turn out, we outline four scenarios that we believe can be logically derived by taking a rather extreme interpretation of how each issue may play itself out in the years to come.

Our four scenarios should therefore be seen as pure types that are unlikely to occur but are nevertheless useful for revealing interesting properties. It is a safe bet that reality will be more complex. Cultural industries will probably exhibit a mixture of these types, though perhaps not equally. Thus, symbiotic conglomeration is likely to coexist with dominant agglomeration (e.g., the movie industry), and dominant conglomeration may coexist with virtual agglomeration (e.g., the music industry).

The dynamics of mixed scenarios may already be detectable in the way that cultural industries are organized and managed today. In this respect therefore our analysis should not be seen as an exercise in predicting the future, but rather as an attempt to look at the present as history in the making.

REFERENCES

Augè, M. (1995). *Non-places: Introduction to an anthropology of supermodernity.* London: Sage.

Bryman, A. (2004). *The Disneyization of society.* Thousand Oaks, CA: Sage.

Caves, R. (2000). *Creative industries: Contracts between art and commerce.* Cambridge, MA: Harvard University Press.

Chanda, T. (2000). The cultural "creolization" of the world, interview with Edouard Glissant. *Label France, 38,* available http://www.diplomatic.gouv.fr/label-France/ENGLISH/INDEX/i38.html

Didcock, B. (1997, December 31). Is Disney determined to destroy western culture? *The Scotsman,* 11.

Eriksen, T. H. (2003). Creolization and creativity. *Global Networks, 3,* 223–237.

Hainer, C. (1997, March 11). Novelist's heirs decry Disney's quasi-culture. *USA Today,* 1D.

Heavens, A. (2004, July 12). Managing the profits of doom. *Financial Times, 9.*

Held, D., & McGrew, A. (2002). *Globalism/anti-globalization.* Cambridge, UK: Polity Press.

Kirschbaum, C., & Vasconcelos, F. (2004, July). *Jazz: Structural changes and identity creation in cultural movements.* Paper presented at the 20th EGOS-Colloquium. Ljublijana, Slovenia.

Pieterse, J. (1995). Globalization as hybridization. In M. Featherstone, S. M. Lash, & R. Robertson (Eds.), *Global modernities* (pp. 45–67). London: Sage.

Ritzer, G. (2004). *The globalization of nothing.* Thousand Oaks, CA: Sage.

Robertson, R. (1990). Globalization: Time-space and homogeneity-heterogeneity. In M. Featherstone (Ed.), *Global culture: Nationalism, globalization and modernity* (pp. 25–44). London: Sage.

Robertson, R. (1992). *Globalization: Social theory and local culture.* London: Sage.
Zhang, Y. (2000, October). *Cinematic remapping of Taipei: Cultural hybridization, heterotopias, and postmodernity.* Paper presented at the Fifth Annual Conference on the History and Cultural of Taiwan, Los Angeles.

Conclusions

CHAPTER

18

Untangling the Complexities of Cultural Industries: Directions for Future Research

Joseph Lampel
City University, London

Jamal Shamsie
Michigan State University

Theresa K. Lant
New York University

There is no business like show business.

—Irving Berlin

Many industries believe that they are unique, yet few express this belief with such lyrical conviction. The business of culture may be different, but ultimately it is a business. This side of the cultural industries may be unpalatable for some entrepreneurs and creative individuals for whom the old motto of MGM, "Ars Gratia Artis" (Art for Art's Sake), may supersede all other considerations. But economic success is usually vital, if not as an end in itself, then as a precondition for obtaining the resources needed to sustain creative activity.

Because this book is dedicated to the business of culture, it is fitting that we should conclude by examining why the pursuit of market success in the cultural industries is not only so important, but also the subject of so much reflection and controversy. Accordingly, we begin with a discussion of the reasons why business success in cultural industries is so fraught with ambiguity and uncertainty. More specifically, we argue that the problem of ascertaining the quality of cultural products prevents the emergence of standards in cultural industries. This, in turn, makes strategy in these industries more uncertain to develop and more difficult to execute than in most industries.

In the second part of this chapter, we argue that these twin problems manifest themselves in a set of polar opposites, imperatives that firms in the cultural industries must navigate with varying degrees of success. More specifically, we outline five polar opposites: artistic values versus mass entertainment, product differentiation versus market innovation, demand analysis versus market construction, vertical integration versus flexible specialization, and individual inspiration versus creative systems.

In the last part of this chapter we turn our attention to future research. Here we seek to identify a number of research topics that we feel clearly represent promising areas for both curiosity-driven research and potential application. More specifically, we propose the following topics: the role of technology in shaping the future of cultural industries; the increasing importance of experts, critics, and other institutions that shape tastes in the cultural industries; the emergence of competitive anomalies such as winner take all; the role of hitherto neglected special events such as festivals and award ceremonies in the life of the cultural industries; the contribution of consumption and production clusters to the growth of the cultural industries; and finally, the implications of new organizational forms for the evolution of the cultural industries.

THE SEARCH FOR SUCCESS IN CULTURAL INDUSTRIES

Business success ultimately depends on creating value for consumers and then obtaining sufficient returns on the resources invested in creating this value to allow the producing organization to meet its obligations and continue its operations. In cultural industries, this general formula runs up against the difficulties of defining value in the first place. Information economists identify three broad categories of goods. The first category is made up of search goods, goods whose quality relative to expectations can be verified prior to purchase. The second category consists of experience goods, goods whose quality relative to expectations cannot be verified prior to purchase, but can be evaluated on consumption. And the third type consists of credence goods, goods whose quality relative to expectations cannot be verified either before or after consumption.

Cultural products are widely regarded as experience goods, but they are clearly different from other experience goods such as automobiles and mattresses. For the most part, these differences stem from the nonutilitarian nature of cultural goods such as motion pictures and recorded music. This nonutilitarian nature of cultural products leads to different processes for establishing their value, and by extension this has an impact on how firms succeed in the marketplace.

The value of goods that are produced with a clearly indicated utilitarian function is judged first and foremost by how well they fulfil this function, and only then by other characteristics. A beautifully designed car may be pleasing to the eye, but for most consumers it is not much of a car if it is constantly breaking down. The car may be put on display for its aesthetic beauty, but it is its utility as a vehicle that defines it as a product. Firms that compete in selling many types of experience goods compete on some measure of performance that is utilitarian in nature.

Though utility may not be the only consideration, it creates a background that allows for the systematic comparison of different products. In markets where efficient processes of comparison are possible, this provides a basis for the emergence of stable and explicit standards of quality. Stable and explicit standards of quality in turn provide focal points for evaluating value for producers and consumers alike. These focal points ultimately permit managers to accumulate reliable knowledge about the causal relationship between the size and nature of investments and the magnitude of success.

Cultural goods, by contrast, are experience goods that lack explicit utility (Bjorkegren, 1996; Hirsch, 1972; Holbrook & Hirschman, 1982). This lack of explicit utility makes it extremely difficult to identify and establish clear standards of quality (Bjorkegren; Lewis, 1990; Turow, 1984). On the whole, basic notions of quality tend to remain highly contestable in cultural industries. Whereas utilitarian producers usually develop a consensus on specific and often measurable standards of quality, producers of cultural industries deal with standards that represent abstract ideals rather than specific product attributes. For example, many consumers may espouse the importance of originality in art or in music, but each of them may attach fundamentally different meanings to the term.

Opinions about quality can diverge so strongly that producers find it hard to figure out why some products do well but others do not. Even when there is a widespread agreement about the relatively high or relatively low level of quality of a particular cultural product, this consensus belies deep disagreements as to why this is the case. This is not only the case before consumers make their purchase decisions, but also afterward.

Ultimately, understanding why products succeed or fail remains forever in the realm of educated conjecture. This is rarely due to the lack of data—plenty of data are usually available—but because these data are susceptible to multiple and contradictory interpretations. Taken as a whole, these contradictory interpretations produce ambiguity that impacts on the ability of managers to make well-informed decisions, but it also promotes the value of insight and intuition to a degree that is rarely seen in other industries.

When trying to make some sense of why consumers of cultural products make the choices they do, managers in cultural industries often rely heavily on their insight into the subjective experience of consumers. What results is more a process of interpretative enactment rather than systematic or rational analysis. For instance, producers of cultural goods know that consumers look for products that can be counted on to entertain, stimulate, and provoke reflection. Trying to satisfy the consumer on these dimensions can pose a tremendous challenge when the relationship between cause and effect is so ambiguous. Hence a common complaint in the cultural industries is about how often organizations fail to get the desired response from customers in spite of going to extreme lengths to ensure that all the right elements are present.

Notwithstanding this ambiguity, producers in the cultural industries do evolve what Spender (1989) called "industry recipes," conventional wisdom about what works and what does not. For instance, producers in the cultural industries know that cultural products are more likely to find market success when they blend familiar and novel elements. Consumers need familiarity to understand what they are offered, but they need novelty to enjoy it.

Going beyond this conventional wisdom, however, is difficult. Blending the familiar and novel depends more on art than technique, more on insight than professional judgment. Not surprisingly, organizations in cultural industries expend considerable resources searching for a formula that can accomplish this goal, but generally find it to be elusive. Tastes are inherently unstable, and what is more, the novel and popular in one period becomes familiar and usually staid during the next.

This problem makes the search for expert knowledge a more difficult process in cultural industries than is often encountered in other industries. Judging what to produce, and how to produce it, not to mention the need to develop the skills necessary to distribute and market these products, are as essential in cultural industries as elsewhere. Individuals who have the requisite knowledge and skills are much in demand. But although there are many who claim to possess the requisite knowledge and skills, sorting and evaluating the best individuals for the job is highly uncertain.

It is hard to find experts in cultural industries in the conventional sense of that term. There are no recognized specialists such as engineers or analysts who can take products apart and point to problems when they arise. Codified knowledge can be useful to tackle problems, but ultimately it is of limited value. Tacit knowledge is more important in cultural industries, making resources such as talent, creativity, and innovation more crucial for success (Jones & DeFillippi, 1996; Miller & Shamsie, 1996). But these are amorphous resources: They cannot be clearly defined, they emerge from unexpected sources, and they lose their value for reasons that are not entirely understood.

Much of the strategy of firms in the cultural industries is therefore oriented toward finding, developing, and maintaining control over these resources. For instance, most record companies have Artist and Repertoire (A & R) units whose main task is to find and develop new artists (Wilson, 1987). The major Hollywood studios have in place systems for screening and evaluating thousands of new movie scripts each year for the few promising ones (Kent, 1991). And publishers have departments whose sole task is to bring authors to the attention of the reading public by orchestrating personal appearances with other promotion and marketing efforts (Coser, Kadushin, & Powell, 1982).

Consequently, the long-term survival of firms in cultural industries depends heavily on building up and maintaining their creative resources. However, because the processes that generate them are poorly understood, there is considerable uncertainty not only about how to detect them, but also about how to replicate and use them. Managerial practices such as professional training and apprenticeship that are useful in other industries are largely ineffective in cultural industries. What is more, resources that have proven value are usually embedded in individuals and groups over which the corporation has much more limited control (Robins, 1993; Saundry, 1998; Stearns, Hoffman, & Heide, 1987).

To ensure that they have these crucial resources when they are needed, organizations must possess capabilities that generate these resources for later use. But developing these capabilities usually puts organizations in cultural industries in the position of having to deal with conflicting demands. On the one hand, organizations must give creative individuals the autonomy they need to be effective, but they must also incorporate these individuals into the strategy of the organization in a way that does not stifle the autonomy that is essential to creativity.

Discovering promising artists and developing highly successful projects calls for managers with exceptional intuition and subtle judgment, but relying on managers with these special talents often leads to opportunistic behavior and empire building. Fulfilling these opposing demands, and doing this while at the same time sustaining successful performance, is probably the key strategic task that perennially confronts organizations in cultural industries. Although this task is typically influenced by changes in technology and shifts in cultural tastes, it is basically framed by a number of key imperatives that remain relatively unchanged.

NAVIGATING OPPOSING IMPERATIVES WITHIN A CULTURAL CONTEXT

In the previous section, we examined the factors that influence market success in cultural industries. In essence, the search for business success in cultural industries confronts two problems: demand patterns that are highly unpredictable and production processes that are difficult to monitor and control. The evolution of cultural industries can be viewed as a persistent search for managerial practices and organizational forms that can address these problems. On the demand side, firms try to shape consumer preferences by expending large amounts of resources on new methods of distribution, marketing, and promotion. On the supply side, firms seek to develop new ways of uncovering and managing creative inputs.

In both respects, organizations in cultural industries have found success to be at best temporary for reasons that are intrinsic to these industries. Shaping consumer tastes is difficult in any industry, but in the case of cultural industries it is made even more difficult by the uncertain foundations of preferences and the volatility of fashion. Finding and managing creative inputs that lead to successful cultural products is equally difficult: The relationship between creative effort and valued products is ambiguous.

Caught between the uncertainty of the level and type of demand and the ambiguity of transforming inputs into outputs, firms in cultural industries find that success depends on navigating between opposing imperatives. Hirsch (1972) suggested that these opposing imperatives arise from the position that organizations in cultural industries occupy between producers and consumers. Cultural industries, he argued, are essentially systems of organizations that mediate the flow of cultural goods between producers and consumers.

Reconciling the demands of artistic production with those of the marketplace is intrinsically an unstable process. The two areas are not only different in character, but are often in opposition—each is shaped by different needs and each is judged by different criteria. The strategies that evolve as a result reflect the opposing pressures exerted at each end of the value chain. To understand how success is attained in cultural industries, in spite of the difficulties, it is therefore important to understand the polarities that shape the choices available to organizations in these industries.

Research on cultural industries, by both scholars and knowledgeable observers, suggests five polar opposites that define the field of action within which organizations in cultural industries operate. We discuss these polarities in the following sections.

Artistic Values Versus Mass Entertainment

Cultural industries combine two realms of human experience. All societies produce culture as a form of individual and collective expression of basic ideas and aspirations. Paintings, dance, theater, and music predate by millennia the formation of commercial cultural businesses. However, it is through their entertainment value that cultural products attract the audiences that can support them. The artistic value of cultural products must be balanced against their entertainment value. Combining these two realms of art and entertainment is a source of continuing tension in cultural industries.

Cultural industries strive to remain loyal to artistic values, but they must also deal with market economics. The question that persistently confronts organizations in cultural industries is: Which one of these imperatives should drive decision making? Should mass entertainment be dictated by artistic values or should artistic values be used to pursue mass entertainment?

In the film industry this dichotomy is responsible for much of the debate between Americans and Europeans. The American motion picture industry sees artistic values as subordinate to mass entertainment. It celebrates artistic achievement, but sees it as a by-product of its main mission: generating healthy sales in the box office. The European motion picture industry, by contrast, sees artistic values as a driving force, and mass entertainment as at best a regrettable necessity.

Product Differentiation Versus Market Innovation

Competition in cultural industries is driven by a search for novelty. However, although consumers expect to find novelty in cultural goods, they also want this novelty to be accessible and familiar. If the story and characters sound familiar, then pushing the technological frontier can create some degree of novelty. This contradiction puts producers in cultural industries in the middle of two opposing pressures.

On the one hand, producers are pushed to seek novelty that differentiates products without making them fundamentally different from others in the same category. This novelty represents a recombination of existing elements and styles that differentiates but does not break with existing artistic and aesthetic conventions. On the other hand, there is the push to pursue innovation past existing limits. This type of novelty breaks new ground, frequently produces new types of cultural products, and may expand if not fundamentally change the market.

The emergence of rock and roll as a distinct musical category illustrates this dynamic. Rock and roll has its roots in jazz, blues, gospel, and country music. Most historians agree that the first recording that can be clearly identified as the musical innovation that eventually came to be known as rock and roll is "Rocket 88." Released in 1951, it was produced by Sam Phillips, composed by Jackie Brenston and Ike Turner, and sung by Brenston. At first the major recording companies disdained rock and roll as a passing fad, a product differentiation rather than a new category of music. But the genre began to establish itself as a separate category with the meteoric rise of Elvis Presley in 1954. With the success of the Beatles and their Apple Records label, the industry finally recognized rock and roll as a distinct market category.

Demand Analysis Versus Market Construction

There is a long-standing dispute in cultural industries between those who see cultural goods as an expression of the needs and desires of consumers, and those who argue that what consumers want is almost entirely shaped by the imagination and creativity of the producers. The debate corresponds to fundamentally different views of why some cultural goods become successful whereas others do not.

Thus, cultural goods may become successful because they deliberately or accidentally tap preexisting consumer preferences. For instance, it is possible to predict that there are market segments where customers have well-defined and specific tastes. This may be movies with the latest action-packed special effects, or recordings of "boy bands." Success depends on finding products that satisfy these tastes, rather than working to change tastes. On the other hand, we have the view that the high road to success consists of shaping tastes to fit the products at hand. Cultural goods become successful because they shape tastes to suit their own production; in effect, they create the standards by which they are judged, and then deliver an experience that meets these standards.

The dilemma of modern symphony orchestras illustrates both positions. Symphony orchestras know from long experience that their main audience looks forward to old classics such as Mozart, Beethoven, or Brahms. At the same time, orchestras rely on experimentation to sustain the distinctiveness and reputation for originality that attracts the indispensable approval of musical critics. To accommodate both, orchestras program old and new music side by side: the old to attract mainstream audience, and the new to please the critics. Critics, however, have an influence on taste formation. So in the long run orchestras are creating tastes for new music and even new categories of music.

Vertical Integration Versus Flexible Specialization

In cultural industries, as in many other industries, organizations often look for gains by trying to exert greater control over both the creation and the delivery of their products. This has invariably led to a drive to integrate all aspects of the value chain under a single corporate umbrella. A strategy of vertical integration increases market power and thus can potentially lower distribution costs, but the administrative difficulties of coordinating multiple business lines can reduce strategic agility, because size and business diversity rarely go hand in hand. Nor is diversity conducive to a quick response to new tastes and new trends that is so essential to long-term advantage in the cultural industries.

We have seen trends pushing in both directions recently. For instance, Pixar, a firm with expertise in digital animation, has maintained some of its independence by creating a strategic alliance with Disney to do a series of films. This arrangement benefits both parties by enabling risk sharing and access to resources not held within each of the respective firms, while each maintains a degree of independence to focus on what they do best. On the other hand, firms such as Time Warner are attempting to control as many aspects of content creation and distribution as possible. Vertical integration allows firms such as Time Warner to capture more rents by exploiting more comprehensively upfront investments in content creation.

The strategic rationale for vertical integration is currently being undermined by technologies such as cable, satellite, and high-speed broadband. In a world in which hundreds of channels compete for viewers, and the mass audience is rapidly fragmenting, small and agile specialists may hold an edge over resource-rich but organizationally constrained generalists. The case for vertical integration seemed unassailable in the 20th century, but by the 21st century the pendulum began to swing the other way: It is now an open question whether vertical integration or flexible specialization will dominate the landscape in the coming century.

Individual Inspiration Versus Creative Systems

There is a persistent debate in cultural industries about the true source of creative value. Is it the individual who is the pivotal element in the value chain, or is it the system as a whole that produces the critical ingredients of successful cultural products? The debate has important repercussions. If the individual is the pivotal element in the creation of value, then the key to success is finding or developing these individuals. Efforts should focus on finding the next Steven Spielberg, Tom Clancy, or Bruce Springsteen. Search criteria would include identifying genius, tacit knowledge, and star quality. If, on the other hand, it is the system, then less emphasis should be placed on individuals, and more on developing structures, processes, and cultures that produce successful cultural products. Efforts should focus on combining resources in unique ways to create core competencies in developing and maintaining creative systems.

The way Disney set up their organization to create and leverage films such as *The Lion King* is a good example of the power of creative systems. Walt Disney does not simply let creative individuals loose with the hope that a high-quality film will emerge. Film content, marketing, merchandising, and theme park potential are carefully coordinated. Success in the box office spurs marketing, is fed into merchandising, then into theme park shows, and subsequently transformed into a Broadway musical. At every step a creative team backed by organizational systems ensures that success in one area is used to promote success in another. Ultimately, the aim, from the very beginning, is not simply to produce and deliver successful products, but to build a franchise that will last for many decades to come.

In many cultural industries one finds examples of organizations that have put their faith primarily in individuals or systems. More often, however, organizations usually try to combine the best of both. There does seem to be a movement of late to reduce the power of artists and stars by focusing on content that is controllable. Reality shows, game shows, and "manufactured" stars are all examples.

A Balancing Act

Strategizing in cultural industries must not only contend with these polarities, it must also deal with the fact that the forces represented by these opposing imperatives can render the strategic paradigm inherently unstable. Although there are frequent attempts to develop a dominant strategic paradigm in cultural industries, and for a while they may be successful, the relative power of one imperative in comparison to its opposite often shifts, and this shift undermines the effectiveness of the paradigm that previously seemed unassailable.

Nevertheless, in cultural industries there is an ongoing debate about which polarity truly dominates. In part because balancing polarities is not a process with clear-cut outcomes, it is tempting to marshal evidence and arguments and decide which polarity is essential for business success and which can be effectively ignored. The cyclical waxing and waning of the different polarities over time, however, suggests that these debates can rarely be conclusive. Thus, when it comes to the practical business of creating and selling cultural goods, firms must proceed with both polarities in mind.

For example, if firms pursue the goal of mass entertainment, they should not lose sight of artistic values. If artistic values dominate, commercial survival dictates that market realities cannot be ignored indefinitely. If firms are intent on creating new genres or new categories of cultural goods, they must bear in mind that most products in cultural industries succeed by differentiating rather than by being revolutionary. And similarly, if they pursue a strategy of marginal product differentiation, me-too products with a minor difference, they should be aware that in the long run they could lose to firms that introduce truly innovative products.

By the same token, firms must analyze the market in order to understand what their consumers are likely to respond to, but they must also try to influence consumers by encouraging interest in attributes in which their products possess an advantage. Analyzing the market accurately ensures that producers can effectively communicate with their consumers; shaping tastes allows producers to construct the market along lines that increase the value of their products. Similarly, new technologies such as the Internet may help to turn flexible specialization into a reality, but this does not undermine the potential advantages of vertical integration. In fact, the ability to digitize content has spurred convergence among previously separate industries, thus encouraging the mergers of media firms. Large media conglomerates may be able to leverage synergies across their business units, but if they attempt to pursue this too far they are likely to stifle the very creativity on which they depend.

Finally, when we turn to the last polarity, individual inspiration versus creative systems, we encounter one of the longest and most vociferous debates in the cultural industries. Individual inspiration is often championed because it is easier to identify (even when it is not so easy to understand), but without the support of a creative system it is unlikely to be fully exploited. Creative systems often seem more reliable and offer a tempting way of eliminating dependence on creative individuals, but without the inspiration of creative individuals, output often degenerates into a poor imitation of past success.

Seeking to strike a balance between opposing polarities usually leads to the combination and extension of existing models rather than to totally innovative approaches. This lesson may contain what is ultimately the truly crucial insight that cultural industries can impart to other industries where environmental conditions are similar but the polarities at play may be fundamentally different: The choices facing organizations are often the result of contrary imperatives. It is important to understand how these imperatives play against each other. By using this understanding, organizations can decide which practices should be modified and which should be discarded, which organizational forms are still viable and which should be abandoned in favor of completely new ones. It is certain, however, that for firms in these industries to be successful, they will need to create dynamic strategies and competencies, those that will enable them to adjust their practices easily as various changes sway the balance of the opposing imperatives in one direction or another.

TOWARD A RESEARCH AGENDA FOR CULTURAL INDUSTRIES

No concluding chapter in a book on cultural industries can be truly conclusive. The reason is not simply that the rate of change in these industries is too rapid to allow for any definitive final statements—this can be said of many industries—it is that, unlike work that has been carried out on other industries, management research on cultural industries is still is in its infancy. Nevertheless, enough studies have been carried out to allow us to outline a substantial research agenda. Our suggestions are, of course, our own. They represent an analysis of the situation that currently exists in cultural industries from the perspective of what we know already. We believe that most of it will be relevant in the near and not-so-near future, but we are also certain that unexpected developments will create new phenomena for researchers to examine.

Impact of Technology

The impact of technology on cultural industries is one of the areas that needs the most intensive investigation. Technology is the key driver for the emergence of cultural industries (Gallagher, 2001; Jones, 2001). Without sound recording, motion picture photography, or the computer, we would not have many of the cultural industries that exist today. The enabling role of these technologies is clear enough. What is less well understood is the complex dynamics between technology and content. In particular, we need more investigation of the mediating role of formats used to package and deliver content.

For example, the emergence of the long-playing record was the result of evolution in recording and playback technology. The long-playing record, in turn, gave rise to compilation, or the album. The album became a standard means of artistic expression, leading to the creation of its own bestseller charts. The recent emergence of online downloading, by contrast, poses a threat to the album. When consumers can sample and download individual songs, they are no longer obliged to buy an entire album. The decline of the album may signal a wholesale return to an earlier era when singles dominated or it may lead to different packaging and different formats.

Dynamics of Consumer Tastes

The pattern of changes in consumer tastes represents another important area for research. Although it has often been said that one cannot argue about tastes, debates about tastes in cultural industries have been with us for a very long time. At the most basic level, the arguments boil down to whether the producers impose tastes on the consumers or whether the consumers force the producers to meet their tastes.

What is often ignored in this debate is the role of experts, critics, and other institutions in defining and shaping tastes (Anand & Peterson, 2000; Lampel & Shamsie, 2000; Wijnberg & Gemser, 2000). The role of critics in the motion picture industry has been crucial for the success of movies that would otherwise be consigned to the margins of the market. Art galleries play an important role in defining new artistic movements, and museums likewise reinforce the status of certain artists at the expense of others. Similarly, bestselling lists, hit charts, and bestsellers have become institutions that shape tastes in their own right.

There are considerable opportunities for research on this issue. We believe that most progress is likely to occur in the intersection of institutional theory and strategy. The first provides a framework for explaining the evolution of normative structures that define and shape tastes. The latter can provide explanations of how individuals and organizations take advantage of these normative structures to further their strategy.

Dynamics of Competition

A third area for promising research lies in the dynamics of competition in cultural industries. Competition in cultural industries must deal with an interesting paradox: On the one hand, cultural products tap intensely private opinions and experiences, but on the other hand they owe their success to an unusual tendency of individuals to be influenced by the opinions and behavior of others in their community (Caves, 2000; De Vany, 2003; Walls, 1997). The prevalence of bandwagon effects in cultural industries often leads to market anomalies such as the "Red Queen" effect, in which incessant competitive battle for dominance by producers of cultural goods results in behavior that threatens the viability of the industry as a whole.

A competitive anomaly that may also have destructive consequences is the so-called winner-take-all effect. This effect has resulted from the vast increase in scale that has accompanied the expansion of cultural industries. This vastly expanded scale has created a skewed distribution of rewards for organizations and artists. A few gain the bulk of resources, leaving the rest struggling for basic survival. From a strategic point of view, this militates against creating balanced portfolios of products and artists, and pushes instead for a ceaseless search for blockbusters or hits. We need more research into the dynamics that produce these anomalies and how individuals and organizations strategically deal with the opportunities and challenges that they create.

Collaborative and Collective Activities

The range of collaborative and collective activities that are carried out in cultural industries presents another promising area for research. Collaborative activities take place at both the bilateral and the network levels. Joint ventures, alliances, and consortia are as pervasive in cultural industries as in many others. They follow similar patterns to those observed in other industries and are similarly motivated by risk and resource sharing.

By contrast, the collective activities that have become widespread in cultural industries are relatively unique in the place they occupy. Special events and award ceremonies are part of the fabric of cultural industries (Anand & Watson, 2004; De Vany, 2003; Schipper, 1992). There are hundreds of film or music festivals, numerous events that are designed to celebrate talent, and various award ceremonies, all of which receive a great deal of publicity.

Although most industries do have some collective events in which information is exchanged and recognition is conferred, in cultural industries these events have evolved into an institutional system in their own right. The institutional system has its roots far back in history, but the sheer number and scope of these events in the past 20 years suggest that we are dealing with an important institutional evolution that needs closer examination.

Consumption and Production Clusters

The fifth area of promising research is also at the industry level and it is also a product of recent historical evolution. The established view of cultural industries tends to emphasize the global reach of the organizations that dominate this sector. The emphasis has been on production, distribution, and marketing for consumers everywhere. This view represents a vision of the marketplace where the creators and providers of cultural products go to the consumers, rather than the other way around.

In preindustrial societies, however, it was far more common for creators and providers of cultural products to congregate in specific locations and for consumers to undertake the necessary travel. During the 20th century, modern technology began to relieve consumers of this necessity: Music could be enjoyed in the comfort of the living room and motion pictures were available in neighborhood cinemas. The old traditions continued to exist in the forms of Broadway and West End theater, but these clusters of cultural production and consumption were regarded as anachronisms.

The rise of mass tourism, however, has created the infrastructure for the resurgence of consumption clusters on a much larger scale. Some of these clusters are pure cultural hubs, as in the case of Nashville for country music, whereas others such as Las Vegas combine culture with other activities like gambling. What is distinct about these clusters is that they serve primarily as entertainment hubs, dominated by consumption, with little or no development of talent or creation of original material.

But alongside consumption clusters there is also the emergence of production clusters (Acheson & Maule, 1994; Coe, 2001; Scott, 2002). Historically, there is nothing new about production clusters. One only has to look back at Renaissance Florence to see a well-established production cluster. One of the best, and earliest, examples of production clusters in the cultural industries is Hollywood: a motion picture production cluster that dominates the industry globally. More recent examples of such clusters can be found in Tin Pan Alley and Silicon Alley, both of which are located in New York City.

Production and consumption clusters have the potential to shape cultural industries in which they operate. In comparison to research on production and consumption clusters in other industries, research on these clusters in cultural industries is still sparse. One of the reasons for this relative neglect is the need to bring together insights from economics, geography, and sociology to explain why they arise and how they function. The other reason may well be that we do not see the organization and strategy of, and within, these clusters as sufficiently important to merit close study. As clusters grow in economic and social terms, however, their relevance to business is bound to grow, and with it will grow the need for detailed research.

New Organizational Forms

The final area of promising research focuses on the emergence of new organizational forms in cultural industries. Organizational experimentation and managerial innovation in a wide range of industries have led many researchers and observers to argue that the dominance of large corporate hierarchies may be coming to an end. No single organizational form is expected to replace the traditional corporate form. Instead, researchers suggest that a wide variety of organizational forms are likely to emerge and that the popularity of these new organizational forms will depend on the technological, operational, and strategic needs of each industry.

Such a trend toward diverse organizational forms appears to be especially pertinent for cultural industries (Eisenmann & Bower, 2000: Robins, 1993). Most cultural industries have come to be dominated by large corporate hierarchies. But many of the difficulties and challenges that were discussed earlier, such as high demand uncertainty, considerable causal ambiguity, and problems with managing creative talent, have all conspired to constrain and undermine traditional corporate practices. In the face of these problems, corporate hierarchies have begun to experiment with new organizational arrangements, both internally and externally.

Along with the emergence of this experimentation, we are also beginning to see an exodus from corporate hierarchies of talented managers who prefer entrepreneurial initiative to managerial sinecure. These managers-turned-entrepreneurs are often open to new organizational practices and their success is likely to propagate new practices in cultural as well as in other industries.

Parting Thoughts

Research in management serves two masters: intrinsic curiosity and practical application. The topics that we have outlined were chosen precisely because they do both to a fairly high degree. The choice is a matter of judgment. Only time will tell which of these topics will prove truly fruitful as areas of investigation. The verdict will be the product of effort by other researchers. All we can say in conclusion is that we hope that our effort will serve to excite and motivate more research, and that this research breaks new ground and ultimately surpasses our agenda.

REFERENCES

Acheson, K., & Maule, C. J. (1994). Understanding Hollywood's organization and continuing success. *Journal of Cultural Economics, 18,* 271–300.

Anand, N., & Peterson, R. A. (2000). When market information constitutes fields: Sensemaking of markets in the commercial music industry. *Organization Science, 11,* 270–284.

Anand, N., & Watson, M. R. (2004). Tournament rituals in the evolution of fields: The case of the Grammy awards. *Academy of Management Journal, 47,* 59–80.

Bjorkegren, D. (1996). *The culture business.* London: Routledge.

Caves, R. E. (2000). *Creative industries: Contracts between art and commerce.* Cambridge, MA: Harvard University Press.

Coe, N. M. (2001). A hybrid agglomeration? The development of a satellite-marshallian industrial district in Vancouver's film industry. *Urban Studies, 38,* 1753–1775.

Coser, L. A., Kadushin, C. A., & Powell, W. (1982). *Books: The culture and commerce of publishing.* Chicago: University of Chicago Press.

De Vany, A. (2003). *Hollywood economics: How extreme uncertainty shapes the film industry.* New York: Routledge.

Eisenmann, T. R., & Bower, J. L. (2000). The entrepreneurial M-form: Strategic integration in global media firms. *Organization Science, 11,* 348–355.

Gallagher, S. (2001). Innovation and competition in standard-based industries: A historical analysis of the home video game market. *IEEE Transactions on Engineering Management, 49,* 67–82.

Hirsch, P. (1972). Processing fads and fashions: An organization-set analysis of cultural industry system. *American Journal of Sociology, 77,* 639–659.

Holbrook, M. B., & Hirschman, E. C. (1982). The experiential aspects of consumption: Consumer fantasies, feelings and fun. *Journal of Consumer Research, 9*(9), 132–140.

Jones, C. (2001). Co-evolution of entrepreneurial careers, institutional rules and competitive dynamics in American film, 1895-1920. *Organization Studies, 22,* 911–944.

Jones, C., & DeFillippi, R. J. (1996). Back to the future in film: Combining industry and self-knowledge to meet the career challenges of the 21st century. *Academy of Management Executive, 10*(4), 89–103.

Kent, N. (1991). *Naked Hollywood.* London: BBC Books.

Lampel, J., & Shamsie, J. (2000). Critical push: Strategies for creating momentum in the motion picture industry. *Journal of Management, 26,* 233–257.

Lewis, J. (1990). *Art, culture and enterprise.* London: Routledge.

Miller, D., & Shamsie, J. (1996). The resource based view of the firm in two environments: The Hollywood film studios from 1936 to 1965. *Academy of Management Journal, 39,* 519–543.

Robins, J. A. (1993). Organization as strategy: Restructuring production in the film industry. *Strategic Management Journal, 14,* 103–118.

Saundry, R. (1998). The limits of flexibility: The case of UK television. *British Journal of Management, 9,* 151–162.

Schipper, H. (1992). *Broken record: The inside story of the Grammy Awards.* New York: Carol.

Scott, A. J. (2002). A new map of Hollywood: The production and distribution of American motion pictures. *Regional Studies, 36,* 957–975.

Spender, J. C. (1989). *Industry recipes.* Cambridge, MA: Basil Blackwell.

Stearns, T. M., Hoffman, A. N., & Heide, J. B. (1987). Performance of commercial television stations as an outcome of interorganizational linkages and environmental conditions. *Academy of Management Journal, 30,* 71–90.

Turow, J. (1984). *Media industries.* New York: Longman.

Walls, D. (1997). Increasing returns to information: Evidence from the Hong Kong movie market. *Applied Economic Letters, 5,* 215–219.

Wijnberg, N. M., & Gemser, G. (2000). Adding value to innovation: Impressionism and the transformation of the selective system in visual arts. *Organization Science, 11,* 323–329.

Wilson, M. (1987). *How to make it in the rock business.* London: Columbus Books.

CHAPTER

19

Promising and Neglected Types of Studies on Cultural Industries

W. Richard Scott
Stanford University

As more organizational scholars are attracted to the study of cultural industries, what are the kinds of research that should be fostered? Every scholar will have his or her own list of candidates, but I want to emphasize the value of two general types of research: comparative structural analysis and structural-cultural analysis.

COMPARATIVE STRUCTURAL ANALYSIS

Most of the empirical work to date has focused on a single organization, population, or field-industry in a single (or brief) period of time. Such studies need to be supplemented with others that provide a comparative perspective on similar units, whether organizations, organizational populations, or organizational fields. The aim of such inquiry is to determine how similar kinds of symbolic services are produced under varying structural arrangements.

The comparative framework might emphasize differences across countries or regions. Far too many studies are limited to the U.S. context. Although geographical boundaries are somewhat arbitrary, they have continuing relevance because they represent differences in political, regulatory, economic, and cultural traditions that exert important effects on the ways in which work is organized and productive activities are conducted. The same activity varies in important respects depending on where—under what institutional conditions—it is carried out (Hofstede, 1991; Lammers & Hickson, 1979).

Comparisons should also be made across organizations in differing fields or industries. In this case, attention is focused on structural similarities and dissimilarities involved in the production of differing symbolic products. Cultural industries differ in the organization and relations among various components of the production or commodity chain. Early seminal studies—for example, by Hirsch (1975) comparing pharmaceutical manufacturing with phonograph record companies and by Powell (1988) comparing a university press and a public television company—provide instructive but largely neglected models of this kind of cross-sectoral comparison. However, Carroll (1987), who compared concentration in the newspaper publishing and music recording industries, pointed out that studies of single firms or selected (usually large) firms provide misleading information on the industry as a whole.

Particularly in times of rapid change, comparisons of structural features of a given cultural industry as they change over time can yield valuable insights. Research at differing levels of analysis—from the most macro to the very micro—can be illuminating. Scholars need to be working at the world-system level, examining the ways in which changes over time in global infrastructures influence the structure and operation of cultural industries. In general, far too little research addresses phenomena at this level even though scholars are well aware that among the most significant developments of our time are the rise of trans-societal associations and organizations. Among the forces to be examined are world conferences and congresses, international nongovernmental organizations, professional networks, and the rapid rise of global corporate forms (Boli & Thomas, 1999; Meyer, 1994). Ideas and other types of symbolic materials travel rapidly, but are also translated and altered in transit (Appadurai, 1996; Czarniawska & Joerges, 1996). The globalization of cultural media industries is well underway (Eisenmann & Bower, 2000).

At the societal level, clear changes are discernable in the structure of cultural industries, as Hirsch (2000) illustrated for the U.S. context. There are also valuable studies of evolution over time in organizational structures at the level of the organizational field. DiMaggio (1982, 1991) provided a compelling analysis of the construction and institutionalization of art museums in the United States at the turn of the 19th century; Leblebici, Salancik, Copay, and King (1991) examined changes in the patterns of dominance and normative frameworks operating in the U.S. radio broadcasting industry during the period from 1920 to 1965; and Thornton (2004) described changes occurring in the field of college text publication between 1958 and 1990.

For rather arbitrary reasons, several comparative studies of newspapers—in a number of U.S. cities, Argentina, Finland, and Ireland—were conducted at the population level. This population was selected, in part, because "newspaper publication leaves dated material products" that allow researchers to examine their vital rates over long periods of time (Carroll & Hannan, 1989, p. 528; for a review of these studies, see Baum, 1996) In addition to examining the effects of density-dependent processes on founding and failure rates, these studies also considered the effects of changes in technology and political turmoil. In addition, organizational ecologists have examined the sources of specialization and concentration in the industry and publisher succession rates (Carroll, 1987).

The examination of structural variation in cultural systems—both cross-sectorally and over time—allows us to consider the multiple ways in which similar activities can be structured. Organizing patterns reflect not only technical concerns but also institutional constraints and patterns operating at world-system, societal, field, population, and organizational levels. Differences is both technical approaches and institutional models may contribute to the existence of multiple structural models. There is much to be learned in empirically examining the joint effect of these forces in different places and times.

STRUCTURAL-CULTURAL ANALYSIS

More attention needs to be given to the ways in which changes in organizational structure affect the nature and meaning of the activities that have been organized. One of the peculiar features of much sociological analysis is that analysts tend to attend to the secondary effects of organizations on a wide range of phenomena—on stratification and power systems, on the satisfaction and morale of workers, on the demographic rates of organizational founding and disbanding—but overlook their effects on the work itself. As Latour and Woolgar (1979) pointed out, sociologists studying science have focused on virtually every topic except the effect of the organization on science itself: the construction of scientific knowledge. Researchers studying cultural industries need to attend closely to the ways in which different institutional and social structural arrangements affect the content and form of their cultural products.

As in all types of organizations, there is a close relation between organizational forms, work processes, and the characteristics, quantity, and diversity of the products produced and markets served. Peterson (1979; see also Peterson & Amand, 2004) reviewed studies that consider the ways in which rewards, evaluation processes, organizational dynamics, technology, and markets influence the particulars of symbol production, although the number of such studies is far too small. Alexander (1996) provided a vivid study of the ways in which changes in the sources of funding have influenced the format of exhibitions and the styles of paintings exhibited by major U.S. museums. The wider structure of the industry can play a role as well. Mezias and Mezias (2000) demonstrated that an increasing concentration of generalist film producers stimulated the emergence of specialists who, in turn, were more active in the creation of new film genres in the United States from 1912 to 1929. Industry structure affects cultural innovation.

The nature of the product can also be affected by the infrastructure of the industry, the role played by intermediaries in the understanding and evaluation of the product. For example, Anand and Peterson (2000) showed how emergence of a "market regime"—the methodology used to collect information on sales—in the phonograph record industry led to a common conception among participants of the nature and characteristics of this field. More importantly, changes in the methodology led to a restructuring of these conceptions and evaluations, with consequences for the types of music produced.

Of the many possible and useful studies examining the determinants and consequences of cultural industries, I believe that a special premium should be placed on structural-cultural analysis. It is especially important that researchers examine the effects of organizational and industry structure on the products and services provided. How does the medium affect the message? After all, the products we are talking about are not shoes or sausages. The products of these industries are ideas, values, truths, and dreams: conceptions of who we are and what we could become. If the structuring of the organizations that create and distribute these products affects them in any way, we must seek to understand why and how.

REFERENCES

Alexander, V. D. (1996). *Museums and money: The impact on funding on exhibitions, scholarship, and management.* Bloomington: Indiana University Press.

Anand, N., & Peterson, R. A. (2000). When market information constitutes fields: Sensemaking of markets in the commercial music industry. *Organization Science, 11,* 270–284.

Appadurai, A. (1996). *Modernity at large: Cultural dimensions of globalization.* Minneapolis: University of Minnesota Press.

Baum, J. A. C. (1996). Organizational ecology. In S. R. Clegg, C. Hardy, & W. R. Nord (Eds.), *Handbook of organization studies* (pp. 77–114). Thousand Oaks, CA: Sage.

Boli, J., & Thomas, G. M. (Eds.). (1999). *Constructing world culture: International nongovernmental organizations since 1875.* Stanford, CA: Stanford University Press.

Carroll, G. R. (1987). *Publish and perish: The organizational ecology of newspaper industries.* Greenwich, CT: JAI Press.

Carroll, G. R., & Hannan, M. T. (1989). Density dependence in the evolution of populations of newspaper organizations. *American Sociological Review, 54,* 524–541.

Czarniawska, B. & Joerges, B. (1996). Travels of ideas. In B. Czaarniawska & G. Sevón (Eds.), *Translating organizational change* (pp. 13–48). New York: de Gruyter.

DiMaggio, P. J. (1982). Cultural entrepreneurship in nineteenth century Boston. (Parts 1 and 2). *Media, Culture, and Society, 4,* 35–50, 303–322.

DiMaggio, P. J. (1991). Constructing an organizational field as a professional project: U.S. art museums, 1920-1940. In W. W. Powell & P. J. DiMaggio (Eds.), *The new institutionalism in organizational analysis* (pp. 267–292). Chicago: University of Chicago Press.

Eisenmann, T. R., & Bower, J. L. (2000). The entrepreneurial M-form: Strategic integration in global media firms. *Organization Science, 11,* 348–355.

Hirsch, P. M. (1975). Organizational effectiveness and the institutional environment. *Administrative Science Quarterly, 20,* 327–34.

Hirsch, P. M. (2000). Cultural industries revisited. *Organization Science, 11,* 357–361.

Hofstede, G. (1991). *Cultures and organizations: Software of the mind.* London: McGraw-Hill.

Lammers, C. J., & Hickson, D. J. (Eds.). (1979). *Organizations alike and unlike: International and inter-institutional studies in the sociology of organizations.* London: Routledge & Kegan Paul.

Latour, B., & Woolgar, S. (1979). *Laboratory life: The construction of scientific facts.* Beverly Hills, CA: Sage.

Leblebici, H., Salancik, G. R., Copay, A., & King, T. (1991). Institutional change and the transformation of interorganizational fields: An organizational history of the U.S. radio broadcasting industry. *Administrative Science Quarterly, 36,* 333—363.

Meyer, J. W. (1994). Rationalized environments. In W. R. Scott & J. W. Meyer (Eds.), *Institutional environments and organizations: Structural complexity and individualism* (pp. 28–54). Thousand Oaks, CA: Sage.

Mezias, J. M., & Mezias, S. J. (2000). Resource partitioning, the founding of specialist firms, and innovation: The American feature film industry, 1912-1929. *Organization Science, 11,* 306–322.

Peterson, R. A. (Ed.). (1979). Revitalizing the culture concept. *Annual Review of Sociology, 5,* 137–166.

Peterson, R. A., & Anand, N. (2004). The production of culture perspective. *Annual Review of Sociology, 30,* 311–334.

Powell, W. W. (1988). Institutional effects on organizational structure and performance. In L. G. Zucker (Ed.), *Institutional patterns and organizations: Culture and environment* (pp. 115–136). Cambridge, MA: Ballinger.

Thornton, P. (2004). *Markets from culture: Institutional logics and organizational decisions in higher education publishing.* Stanford, CA: Stanford University Press.

Author Index

A

Abrahamson, E., 52, *55,* 196, *203*
Acheson, K., 301, *303*
Adams, W., 206, *222*
Adorno, T. W., 6, *13*
Ahlkvist, J., 156, 157, 158, 168, 171, *174*
Albarran, A. B., 173, *175*
Albert, S., 37, *39,* 57, 58, 59, 60, *67*
Aldrich, H. E., 16, *19,* 52, *55,* 105, *116,* 228, *237*
Alexander, V. D., 307, *308*
Alford, R. R., 148, *153*
Allen, R. C., 200, *203*
Allmendinger, J., 60, *67*
Allsop, D., 272, *273*
Anand, N., 17, *21,* 140, 143, 144, 149, 152, *153,* 195, *203,* 300, 301, *303,* 307, 308, *308, 309*
Anderson, A. B., 53, *55*
Anderson, B., 152, *153*
Anderson, P., 106, *117*
Anderson, R., 200,201, *203*
Andrews, P., 52, *56*
Appadurai, A., 306, *308*
Arikan, A., 236, *237*
Aronson, J. E., 122, 124, 125, 127, *133*
Arthur, M. B., 267, *273*
Astley, W. G., 245, *259*
Atlas, B., 210*n*2, *222*
Augè, M., 280, *285*
Avrich, B., 9, *13*
Axarlis, S., 272, *273*

B

Bacharach, S., 195, 196, *203*
Bachman, W. S., 209, 210*n*2, *222*
Baden-Fuller, C., 53, *55,* 196, *203*
Baker, W., 246, *259*
Balio, T., 200, 201, *203,* 208, *222*
Bamberger, P., 195, 196, *203*
Banks, J., 217, *222*
Barbas, S., 8, *13*
Barnard, S., 158, *174*
Barnatt, C., 52, *56*
Barnes, K., 158, 170, *174*
Barrios, R., 209, *222*
Barthes, R., 16, *19*
Bates, B. J., 156, *174*
Baum, J. A. C., 106, *116,* 307, *308*
Bazerman, M. H., 196, *204*
Beal, B. D., 205, *222*
Becker, D., 84, *101*
Becker, H. S., 17, 18, *19*
Bell, D., 8, *13*
Belson, K., 220, *222*
Benford, R. D., 62, *68*
Bengston, L., 247, *260*
Bensaou, M., 246, *259*
Berger, D. G., 53, *55*
Berger, P. L., 16, *20*
Bergesen, A., 16, *21*
Berland, J., 157, 158, *174, 175*
Berry, S. T., 156, *175*
Bettis, R. A., 195, *204*
Bies, R., 258, *260*
Bijker, W. E., 206, *222*

Billington, C., 98n5, *101*
Bird, A., 196, *203*
Bishop, R., 272, *273*
Bjorkegren, D., 5, *13,* 107, *116,* 178, *189,* 259, *259,* 291, *303*
Blau, J., 19, *20*
Blau, P. M., 16, *20*
Blyler, M., 216, 218, *222*
Bodoh, A. G., 211, *222*
Boehlert, E., 155, 172, *175*
Boehm, G. A., 215, 216, *222*
Boeker, W. P., 196, *203*
Boisot, M., 178, 187, *189*
Boje, D., 245, *259*
Boli, J., 152, *154,* 207, *224,* 306, *308*
Bonanno, G., 121, *132*
Borden, A., 66, *68*
Bordwell, D., 263, *274*
Bourdieu, P., 16, 18, *20*
Bower, J. L., 302, *303,* 306, *308*
Bowker, G., 144, 152, *153*
Bowser, E., 47, 48, *55,* 197, 199, 200, *203*
Brahm, R. A., 245, *259*
Brandenberger, A., 78, 80*f*, 98, *102*
Brock, J. W., 206, *222*
Bronson, F., 140, 144, *153*
Brooks, T., 127, 128, *132*
Brown, J. S., 9, *13*
Bryman, A., 8, *13,* 280, *285*
Buckley, W., 15, *20*
Budros, A., 105, 106, *116*
Burnett, R., 246, *259*
Burt, R. S., 245, 246, *259*

C

Captain, S., 221, *222*
Carroll, G. R., 306, 307, *309*
Carroll, R. L., 159, *175*
Case, D., 272, *273*
Cato, J., 10, *13*
Caves, R. E., 43, *55,* 278, *285,* 300, *303*
Chambers, T., 156, *174, 175*
Chanda, T., 280, *285*
Chandler, A., Jr., 210, *222*
Chasen, J. S., 31, *39*
Chen, M. J., 196, 197, 202, *203*
Chiu, R., 83, *103*
Choi, J., 75, *101*
Choo, C. W., 178, 184, 188, *189*
Chou, C., 83, *103*
Christman, E., 216, *222*
Churchill, G. A., 266, *273*
Clark, K. B., 45, *56*
Clark, R., 174, *175*
Cleland, D. I., 43, *55*
Coe, N. M., 301, *303*
Cohen, S., 77, *102*
Cole, C., 249, 250, *260*
Conant, M., 206, *222*
Conner, K. R., 187, *189*
Cook, D. A., 263, *273*
Cook, K., 246, *261*
Copay, A., 169, *175,* 207, 208, 210, 221, *223,* 306, *309*
Corbin, J., 113, *117*
Corley, K. G., 150, *153*
Coser, L. A., 293, *303*
Crane, D., 18, *20*
Crawford, X., 43, 46, *56*
Crossan, M. M., 178, 186, 187, 188, *189*
Cusumano, M. A., 206, 208, *222*
Cyert, R. M., 143, *153*
Czarniawska, B., 306, *308*

D

Dacin, M. T., 205, *222*
Danaher, P. J., 122, *132*
Dannen, F., 147, 149, *153*
Davenport, T. H., 187, *189*
Davis, D. M., 159, *175*
Davis, G. F., 207, *222*
Davis, J., 258, 259, *260*
Davis, R., 29, *39*
Daymon, C., 267, *273*
DeFillippi, R. J., 267, *273,* 292, *303*
Denisoff, R. S., 149, *153,* 169, *175,* 216, 217, *222*
Dervin, B., 184, *189*
De Vany, A., 120, 121, *132,* 300, 301, *303*
Dexter, D., 214, *222*
Didcock, B., 275, *285*
Diekmann, K.. A., 207, *222*
DiMaggio, P. J., 16, 17, 18, *20,* 140, *153,* 207, *222,* 306, *308*
Disco, C., 206, *222*
Dobbin, F., 206, 207, 208, *222, 223*
Dockster Marcus, A., *260*
Dorward, N., 121, *132*
Dosi, G., 206, *225*
Douglas, M., 16, *20,* 152, *153*

Dow, B. J., 29, *39*
Dowd, T. J., 67, *68,* 206, 207, 208, 211, 214, 216, 217, 218, *222, 223*
Drummond, M., 219, 220, *223*
Drushel, B., 156, *175*
Duguid, P., 9, *13,* 42, 53, *56*
Dukerich, J., 37, *39,* 58, *68*
Dunn, M. T., 196, *203*
Durkheim, E., 17, *20,* 144, *153*
Dutton, J. E., 37, *39* , 58, *68*

E

Eaton, B. C., 121, *132*
Edelman, L., 206, *223*
Eechambadi, N. V., 122, 123, 125, 127, *133*
Eisenhardt, K. M., 113, *116*
Eisenman, T. R., 302, *303,* 306, *308*
Eisner, A. B., 106, *116, 117*
Elkin, T., 84, *102*
Elsbach, K. D., 37, *39,* 151, *153*
Emerson, R., 28, 35, *39*
Ennis, P. H., 143, 147, 148, 151, ***153,*** 211, 212, 213, 214, *223*
Eriksen, T. H., 280, *285*
Espeland, W. N., 147, *153*
Evan, W. M., 16, *20*

F

Fagan, T., 210*n*2, *223*
Fairchild, C., 170, *175*
Faulkner, R. R., 52, 53, *55,* 157, *174,* 246, *259*
Feiler, B., 146, 147, *153*
Feldman, M. S., 150, *153*
Finkelstein, S., 52, *56*
Fiol, C. M., 52, *55,* 105, *116,* 228, *237*
Fischer, C., 205, 206, *223*
Fisher, G., 156, 157, 168, *174,* 246, *259*
Fisher, R., 244, *260*
Fleischhauer, J., 269, *273*
Fligstein, N., 196, *203,* 207, *223*
Flynn, L., 110, *116*
Foa, E., 34, *39*
Foa, U., 34, *39*
Fombrun, C. J., 52, *55,* 196, *203*
Foreman, P. O., 60, *68*
Frankel, D., *102*
Freeland, R. F., 52, *55*
Freeman, J., 16, *20*
Friedland, R., 148, *153*
Friedrich, O., 52, *55*

G

Gabler, N., 200, 201, *203*
Gainer, B., 273, *273*
Galaskiewicz, J., 245, *260*
Gallagher, S., 80*f*, *102,* 299, *303*
Gantz, W., 122, 123, *133*
Garlick, L., 209, *223*
Garud, R., 52, *56*
Gassenheimer, J., 247, *261*
Geertz, C., 16, *20*
Gellatt, R., 210, 215, *223*
Gemser, G., 42, 52, *55,* 300, *304*
Gensch, D., 122, 125, 127, *133*
Gettas, G., 244, 249, 250, *260*
Gioia, D. A., 37, *39,* 150, *153*
Giles, J., 217, *223*
Gillmore, M., 246, *261*
Gilmore, J. H., 9, *14*
Gimeno, J., 246, *260*
Glaser, B. G., 113, *117*, 251, *260*
Glynn, M. A., 19, *20,* 42, 53, *55,* 58, 60, 66, *68*
Goffman, E., 17, *20*
Golden-Biddle, K. H., 58, 59, *68*
Goldman, W., 177, *189, 285*
Goldmark, P. C., 209, 210*n*2, *223*
Gomery, D., 46, *55,* 185, *189,* 263, *273*
Graham, J., 30, 31, *39*
Granovetter, M., 206, *224*
Grant, R. M., 184, 186, 188, *189*
Gray, M. H., 215, *223*
Greenberg, B. S., 123, 124, 125, *133*
Grein, P., 213, 213*n*5, 214, *223*
Grenier, L., 158, *175*
Greiner, L. E., 46, *55*
Greve, H. R., 156, 157, *175*
Griliches, Z., *117*
Gulati, R., 245, *260*

H

Hackman, J. R., 60, *67*
Hadju, J., 79, *102*
Hainer, C., 275, *285*

Hall, B. H., *117*
Hamilton, J., 174, *175*
Hannan, M. T., 16, *20, 308*
Hargadon, A., 244, 245, *260*
Haring, B., 110, *116*
Harquail, C. V., 37, *39,* 58, *68*
Hausman, J., *117*
Hay, D. A., 121, *133*
Hayes, H. C., 212, *223*
Head, S. W., 122, *133*
Heavens, A., 279, *285*
Heide, J. B., 293, *304*
Held, D., 276, *285*
Helfat, C., 187, *190*
Hennion, A., 157, *175*
Henriksson, K., 247, *260*
Henry, D., 62, 63, 64, *68*
Henry, M. D., 122, 123, 124, 127, *133*
Herrigel, G., 245, *260*
Hickson, D. J., 306, *309*
Hill, A., 142, *153*
Hill, C. W. L., 95, *102,* 184, *190*
Hill, T., 127, 128, *133*
Hillis, S., 220, *223*
Hills, M., 8, *13*
Hirsch, P. M., 6, *13,* 16, 17, 19, *20,* 107, *117,* 178, *190,* 291, 294, *303,* 306, *309*
Hirshberg, J., 54, *55*
Hirschman, E. C., 291, *303*
Hisey, P., 81, *102*
Hoffman, A., 143, *153*
Hoffman A. N., 293, *304*
Hofstede, G., 306, *309*
Hogg, T., 53, *55*
Holbrook, M. B., 291, *303*
Horen, J. H., 122, 124, 125, *133*
Hotelling, H., 121, *133*
Huber, G. P., 178, 186, *190*
Huberman, B. A., 53, *55*
Human, S., 245, *260*
Hunt, S. A., 62, *68*
Hunter, A., 245, *261*
Hunter, J. D., 16, *21*
Hurston, A., *249*
Huygens, M., 53, *55,* 196, *203*
Hyde, J. L., 209, 210, 212, 212*n*3, *223*

I

Isom, W. R., 209, 210*n*10, *223*

J

Jaworski, B. J., 264, 266, 272, *273, 274*
Jett, Q. R., 106, *116*
Joerges, B., 306, *308*
Johnson, M. E., 81*n*2, *102*
Jones, C., 52, *55,* 195, 196, *203,* 292, 299, *303*

K

Kadushin, C. A., 293, *303*
Kahn, R. L., 15, *20*
Kanter, R. M., 247, *260*
Karl, S., 76, 77, 82, 83, *102, 103*
Karshner, R., 139, 149, *154*
Kasten, A., 80*f*, *102*
Katz, D., 15, *20*
Katz, E., 201, *203*
Katz, M., 75, *102*
Keefe, B., 219, 220, *223*
Keegan, A., 43, 46, *56*
Keith, M. C., 159, *175*
Kent, N., 292, *303*
Kerr, C. E., 208, *223*
Keyton, J., 28, 29, 30, 31, 32, 34, 35, 38, *39, 40*
Khanna, S. K., 209, *223*
King, A. B., 216, *223*
King, T., 169, *175,* 207, 208, 210, 221, *223,* 306, *309*
Kirschbaum, C., 277, *285*
Kittner, J., 76, 77, 82, 83, *102, 103*
Kloer, P., 220, *223*
Kogen, J. H., 209, *223*
Kohli, A. K., 264, 266, 272, *273, 274*
Korn, H. J., 106, *116*
Kotha, S., 106, *116*
Kramer, R. M., 37, *39,* 151, *153*
Ksobiech, K. J., 123, 124, 125, 127, *133*
Kuhn, T., 5, *13*
Kuperman, J. C., 42, *55,* 196, *204*
Kurzweil, E., 16, *21*

L

Lacy, S., 156, *175*
Ladd, J., 159, *175*
Lammers, C. J., 306, *309*

Lampel, J., 17, 19, *20,* 28, *39,* 42, 46, *55,* 120, 121, *133,* 178, 187, *190,* 229, *237,* 267, *274,* 300, *303*
Lane, H. W., 178, 186, 187, 188, *189*
Lant, T. K., 17, 19, *20,* 28, *39,* 42, *55,* 178, *190,* 229, *237, 238,* 267, *274*
Larsson, R., 247, *260*
Latour, B., 18, *20,* 307, *309*
Law, J., 206, *222*
Lawrence, T. B., 6, *13*
Leblebici, H., 169, *175,* 207, 208, 210, 221, *223,* 306, *309*
Lee, H. L., 98*n*5, *101, 102*
Lefton, T., 82, *102*
Lei, D., 245, 247, 258, *260*
Leiter, R. D., 213, *223*
Lenski, G., 16, *20*
Levinson, M., 10, *14*
Levi-Strauss, C., 16, *20*
Levy, S., 219, 220, *224*
Lewicki, R., 258, *260*
Lewis, J., 291, *303*
Lewis, L. A., 8, *13*
Lewis, T., 206, 208, *224*
Lichty, L. W., 127, *133*
Liddle, K., 66, *68*
Lincoln, J., 247, *260*
Lipsey, R. G., 121, *133*
Loomis, G., 66, *68*
Loomis, K. D., 173, *175*
Lounsbury, M., 66, *68*
Luckmann, T., 16, *20*
Lupo, K., 66, *68*
Lynch, V., 211, *224*

M

MacFarland, D. T., 159, *175*
Macgowan, K., 41, 46, *55*
Machan, D., 97, *102*
MacNeil, I. R., 28, *39*
Malm, K., 158, *176*
Manes, S., 110, *117*
March, J. G., 143, 150, *153, 154,* 184, *190*
Marsh, E., 127, 128, *132*
Marx, L., 206, *225*
Mast, G., 185, *190*
Matusik, S. F., 184, *190*
Maule, C. J., 301, *303*
Mawhinney, D. F., 122, *132*
Mayer, R., 258, 259, *260*
McAllister, D., 258, *260*
McCourt, T., 157, 158, *176*
McGahan, A. M., 217, 218, *224*
McGann, M. E., 99, *102*
McGrew, A., 276, *285*
McGuire, P., 206, *224*
McLean Parks, J., 28, 33, 34, 35, 36, 37, *39, 40*
Meadel, C., 157, *175*
Mechanic, D., 28, 36, *39*
Medrek, T. J., 66, 67, *68*
Merritt, R., 200, *203*
Meyer, A., 58, *68*
Meyer, J. W., 16, 17, *20, 21,* 152, *154,* 207, 208, *222, 224,* 306, *309*
Mezias, J. M., 19, *20,* 52, *55,* 307, *309*
Mezias, S. J., 19, *20,* 42, 52, *55,* 106, *117,* 196, *204,* 307, *309*
Mifflin, L., 254, *260*
Millard, A., 210, 211, 213, 215, 216, 217, *224*
Miller, D., 185, *190,* 292, *303*
Miller, J., 158, *175*
Mintzberg, H., 258, *260*
Mitchell, W., 106, *117*
Mohr, J. W., 17, *21*
Morton, D., 209, 212, 212*n*3, 212*n*4, 216, 218, *224*
Mossberg, G., 108, *117*
Mouritsen, J., 19, *20*
Muggleton, D., 160, *175*
Mundy, C., 217, *223*
Musser, C., 197, 198, 199, 200, *204*
Myers, P. S., 247, *260*
Myhrmann, J., 221, *224*
Mylonadis, Y., 206, 208, *222*

N

Narver, J. C., 264, *274*
Nauck, K. R., III, 211, *225*
Nee, V., 246, *260*
Negus, K., 157, 158, 170, *175*
Nelson, C., 219, *224*
Nelson, H., *154*
Nelson, R. R., 105, *117,* 205, *224*
Newman, M., 141, *154*
Noble, D., 53, *55*
Nonaka, I., 187, 188, *190*
Norberg, E., 159, *175*

Norton, L. P., 84, *102*
Norwick, K. P., 31, *39*
Nowell-Smith, G., 263, *274*

O

Ocasio, W., 143, *153, 154,* 195, 196, *204*
Olsen, J. P., 184, *190*
Orsenigo, L., 206, *225*

P

Padanyi, 273, *273*
Padmanabhan, V., 98*n*5, *102*
Park, J., 31, *40*
Park, S., 246, *260*
Parsons, T., 16, *21*
Paton, D., 268, *274*
Perrow, C., 245, *260*
Perry, M., 245, *260*
Peter, J. P., 266, *273*
Peterson, K., 85, *102*
Peterson, R. A., 17, *21,* 53, *55,* 140, 143, 144, 145, 146, 149, 152, *153, 154,* 158, *175, 176,* 195, *203,* 300, *303,* 307, 308, *308, 309*
Pfeffer, J., 36, *40*
Pham, A., 84, *102*
Phillips, N., 6, *13*
Pieterse, J., 280, *285*
Pine, J. B., 9, *14*
Plante, J., 272, *273*
Pollok, T., 228, *238*
Polsson, K., 76, 77, *102*
Ponce, C. L., 8, *14*
Porac, J. F., 151, *154,* 268, *274*
Porter, M. E., 120, 121, *133,* 245, *260*
Powell, W. W., 16, 18, 19, *20, 21,* 140, *153,* 293, *303,* 306, *309*
Power, D., 6, *14*
Prahalad, C. K., 187, *189,* 195, *204*
Pratt, M. G., 60, *68*
Prescott, E. C., 121, *133*
Provan, K., 245, 247, *260, 261*
Prusak, L., 187, *189*
Puterbaugh, P., 217, *224*
Puttnam, D., 42, *56*

Q

Quinn, J. B., 52, *56*

R

Raelin, J. A., 52, *56*
Raghuram, S., 52, *56*
Rao, H., 58, 59, *68*
Rao, V. R., 127, *133*
Raugust, K., 249, *261*
Reddy, S. K., 122, 124, 125, 127, *133*
Rice, M., 249, *261*
Richman, B., 249, 250, *260*
Richter, F. J., 245, *261*
Ridgeway, V., 146, *154*
Riffe, D., 156, *175, 176*
Rigdon, J., 80*f*, *102*
Rindova, V., 228, *238*
Ringer, B., 211, 212, *224*
Rinne, H. J., 122, 123, 124, 127, *133*
Ritzer, G., 280, *285*
Roberts, J. L., 218, *224*
Robertson, R., 276, 280, *285*
Robins, J. A., 53, *56,* 293, 302, *303*
Rorty, R., 16, *21*
Rosa, J. A., 151, *154*
Rose, S., 220, *225*
Rosenbloom, R., 206, 208, *222*
Ross, A., 228, *238*
Rothenbuhler, E., 157, 158, *176*
Rousseau, D. M., 28, 34, *40*
Rowan, B., 17, *20,* 208, *224*
Rowley, T., 245, *261*
Roy, W. G., 206, 208, *225*
Rubin, E., 246, *261*
Runser-Spanjol, J., 151, *154*
Rust, R. T., 122, 123, 125, 127, *133*

S

Sahay, A., 266, 272, *274*
Salancik, G. R., 36, *40,* 169, *175,* 207, 208, 210, 221, *223,* 306, *309*
Sanchez, R., 43, *56*
Sanjek, D., 141, *154*
Sanjek, R., 141, *154,* 210, 211, 212, 213, 213*n*5, 214, 215, 216, 217, *225*

Saundry, R., 293, *303*
Saxon, M. S., 151, *154*
Saxton, T., 248, *261*
Scally, R., 80*f*, *102*
Schatz, T., 45, 50, 52, *56*, 185, *190*
Schein, V. E., 46, *55*
Schiavone, N., *133*
Schicke, C. A., 210, 210*n*2, 211, *225*
Schickel, R., 8, *14*
Schilling, M. A., 75, 76, 77, 79, 82, 83, 85, 95, *102*, *103*
Schipper, H., 301, *303*
Schlager, K., 140, 141, *154*
Schoorman, D., 258, 259, *260*
Schrag, R. L., 29, *40*
Schumpeter, J. A., 115, *117*
Schwartz, J., 62, 65, 66, *68*, *69*, 220, *225*
Schwartz, M., 206, *224*
Schweitzer, U., 246, *261*
Scott, A. J., 301, *304*
Scott, L., 244, *261*
Scott, W. R., 16, 18, *20*, *21*, 148, *154*, 196, *204*, 207, *222*, *225*
Seabrook, J., 8, *14*
Seely Brown, J., 42, 53, *56*
Shaman, P., 122, 125, 127, *133*
Shamsie, J., 17, 19, *20*, 28, *39*, *40*, 42, *55*, 120, 121, *133*, 178, 185, 187, *190*, 229, *237*, 267, *274*, 292, 300, *303*
Shapiro, C., 75, *102*
Shaw, E. F., 156, *176*
Shaw, R. W., 121, *133*
Sheff, D., 77, *103*
Sherman, M. W., 211, *225*
Silverberg, G., 206, *225*
Simon, B., 215, *225*
Simon, H. A., 143, *154*
Sinakin, Y. D., 81, *103*
Skærbæk, P., 19, *20*
Sklar, R., 159, *176*
Skytte, H., 245, *261*
Slater, S. F., 264, *274*
Slocum, J., 247, 258, *260*
smith, f. l., 28, 29, 30, 31, 32, 33, 34, 35, 36, 37, 38, *39*, *40*
Smith, M. R., 206, *225*
Snider, M., 84, *103*
Snow, D. A., 62, *68*
Sonnenstuhl, W. J., 195, 196, *203*
Sparks, J., 247, *260*
Spender, J. C., 292, *304*
Staiger, J., 43, 47, 48, 50, 54, *56*
Stam, A., 122, 124, 125, 127, *133*
Star, S. L., 144, 152, *153*
Starkey, K., 52, *56*
Stearns, T. M., 293, *304*
Stephen, F., 246, *261*
Sterling, C., 210, *225*
Stevens, M. L., 147, *153*
Stinchcombe, A. L., 196, *204*
Stipp, H., *133*
Stone, B., 219, *225*
Storper, M., 53, *56*, 243, *261*
Strauss, A. L., 113, *116*, *117*, 251, *260*
Suchman, M., 59, *69*
Suchman, M. C., 206, *223*
Sutton, A., 209, 210, *225*
Sutton, J. R., 207, *222*
Sutton, R., 244, 245, *260*
Swann, G. M. P., 121, *133*

T

Takeuchi, H., 187, 188, *190*
Tang, C., 98, *101*
Tedeschi, B., 220, *225*
Tempest, S., 52, *56*
Terry, K., 216, *222*
Thomas, B., 47, 48, 51, *56*
Thomas, G., 152, *154*
Thomas, G. M., 208, *224*, 306, *308*
Thomas, H., 268, *274*
Thomas, J. B., 37, *39*
Thompson, K., 263, *274*
Thornton, P. H., 195, *204*, 306, *309*
Throsby, D., 265, *274*
Tiedge, J. T., 123, 124, 125, 127, *133*
Tilly, C., 160, *176*
Tinsley, C. H., 207, *222*
Townley, B., 148, *154*
Towse, R. M., 7, *14*
Trachtenberg, J., 79, 81, *103*
Truglio, R., 249, *261*
Tsur, S., 252, *261*
Turner, G., 157, 158, *176*
Turner, J. R., 43, 46, *56*
Turner, N., 79, *103*
Turow, J., 291,, *304*
Tushman, M. L., 106, *117*

U

Uzzi, B., 206, *225*

V

Vaidhyanathan, S., 54, *56*
Van den Bosch, F. A. J., 53, *55,* 196, *203*
van der Meulen, B., 206, *222*
Vasconcelos, F., 277, *285*
Venkatraman, N., 246, 247, *259, 261*
Ventresca, M. J., 17, *21,* 205, *222*
Visscher, M., 121, *133*
Volberda, H., 53, *55*, 196, *203*
von Blumencron, M. M., 269, *273*

W

Wakshlag, J. J., 123, 124, 125, *133*
Waldfogel, J., 156, *175*
Wallis, R., 158, *176*
Walls, D., 300, *304*
Waters, J., 258, *260*
Watson, M. R., 301, *303*
Weber, M., 160, *176*
Webster, F. E., 266, *274*
Webster, J. G., 124, 125, 127, *133*
Weick, K. E., 178, 184, 186, *190*
Weisenfeld, B., 52, *56*
Whang, S., 98*n*5, *102*
Wheelwright, S. C., 45, *56*
Whetten, D., 37, *39,* 57, 58, 59, 60, *67,* 245, *259*
Whitburn, J., 212, 214, *226*
White, R. E., 178, 186, 187, 188, *189*
Wiewel, W., 245, *261*
Wijnberg, N. M., 42, 52, *56,* 300, *304*
Wilcox, J., 84, *101*
Wildstrom, S. H., 84, *103*
Wilson, F., 268, *274*
Wilson, M., 292, *304*
Winter, S. G., 105, *117*
Wirth, T. L., 156, *176*
Witten, M., 16, *21*
Wolf, M. J., 8, *14*, 178, *190*
Woo, C., 246, *260*
Woods, M., 266, *274*
Woolgar, S., 18, *20,* 307, *309*
Wright, J., 249, *261*
Wuthnow, R., 16, *21*

Y

Yamagishi, T., 246, *261*
Yonay, Y. P., 206, *226*

Z

Zack, M. H., 178, 188, *190*
Zaheer, A., 247, *261*
Zajac, E. J., 196, *204*
Zeidler, S., 219, 220, *226*
Zhang, Y., 280, *286*
Zohoori, A. R., 122, 123, *133*
Zuckerman, E., 150, *154*

Subject Index

Note: *f* indicates figure, *n* indicates footnote, *t* indicates table, *tn* indicates table footnote.

A

A & M, 217
Ackerman, Tom, 145
Adaptation, 182–183
Adventures of Priscilla, The, 265
Ambiguity, 25, 105, 107, 178, 184–189, 207, 228–229, 232, 290, 292, 294, 302
American Federation of Musicians (AFM), 213
Amusement Business, 142
Analog recordings, 218
Ancillary products, 249, 256
Anna and the King, 188
AOL Time Warner, 218
Apple's iTunes, 219
Ars Gratia Artis, 289
Artistic values, 294
Atari, 77–78, 80–81, 81*n*1
Atlanta Symphony Orchestra (ASO), 58, 62–67
Artistic
- freedom, 42
- identity, 57–58, 62, 66

Art-versus-commerce dilemma, 19, 52, 267
As You Desire Me, 49
Aspiration, 143, 146–147, 151
Atomized depictions, 205–208, 221
Attention, 143–144, 150
Audience
- potential, 120
- response, 45, 51
- target, 158, 162, 164–165

Australia Council Act of 1975, 265
Australian Film Commission, 265
Australian Film Industry
orientation of, 266–267
Australian film producers, 264, 267–271
Autonomy, 42
- in cultural industries, 52–54
- of directors, 47–48

Award ceremonies, 290, 301

B

Bakshi, Ralph, 4
Balboa, 48
Beliefs, 8, 16
Ben Hur, 49–50
Benefactor, The, 131
Bernstein, Lewis, 244, 251–257, 259
Bertelsmann, 218
Bestseller charts, 139, 299
Big Five, 218
Big Four, 214
Big Six, 214, 216–218
Big Three, 208–214, 221
Billboard
- chart(s), 136, 139–140, 142, 147–150, 152, 212, 214, 218
  - categorizing domains of activity, 144–146
  - lists, 145*t*

movement, 136
particular market dynamics, 143–144
position, 136, 146–147
magazine, 139–140, 147–148, 150–151
role in field coalescence, 140–142
Billboard Advertiser, The, 140–141
Billboard Music Week, 142
Biograph Company, 47, 198–199, 201
Birth of a Nation, 46
Blackley, Seamus, 278
Bloodworth-Thompson, Linda, 24, 28–38
Bogart, Neil, 147
Boundary spanners, 19
Boy bands, 295
Branding, 180–181
British Decca, 215
Broadcast Data Systems (BDS), 158
Broadcast networks, 73, 120, 122, 126–130, 132
Brokerage roles, 245
Bullet, 146, 151
Burke, Delta, 24, 30–38
Bushnell, Nolan, 77

C

Capitol Records, 139, 213–214
Career backgrounds, 196
Casablanca records, 147
Cash Box, 147–148, 151
Categorical schemas, 144
CBS records, 215
Celebrity
cult of, 8
Central producer system, 42
defined, 43, 45–46
during the Studio Era, 44*f*
evolution of, 46–52
Chaplin, Charlie, 54
Character(s)
control, 27–28
development of, 24, 27, 29
voice of, 38
Charleston Regional Business Journal Online, 114
Cheers, 119
Children's Television Workshop (CTW), 240–241, 244–245
joint venture with Israel and Palestine, 250–256
strategy in the aftermath of, 256–258
international expansion of, 248–250
Clear Channel Communications, 155–157, 172, 174
Coca cola, 257
Cognitive
legitimacy, 228–231, 236
structure, 144
Cohn, Harry, 188
Coleco Vision, 77
Collaborative activities, 300–301
Collective
action, 52, 228–234
activities, 300–301
Columbia (records), 208, 210–211, 217
Columbia Phonograph, 210
Commensuration, 143, 147, 151
Commercial
music field, 140, 144, 148
radio industry, 155–156
Community, 124
Compact Disc (CD), 217–218
Compact Disc Interactive (CD-1), 79
Comparative structural analysis, 305–307
Competitive
advantage, 196, 201–202, 212*n*3, 242, 276–285
blindspots, 196
dynamics, 136, 198, 202
Complex systems, 19
Confidence building, 247–248
overcoming barriers through, 252–256
Conglomerates, 183–184, 202, 281*t*, 282–283
Consumer
demand, 6
psychology, 12
tastes, 52, 180, 201, 293–294, 299–300
Consumption clusters, 301–302
Content
agglomeration, 229
firms, 195, 197, 201–202
Contextual factors, 206–207, 221
Continuity scripts, 50
Control, 182–183
in cultural industries, 52–54
of directors, 47
of exhibition, 46

loss of, 185–186
mechanism, 35
Convergence, 207, 277–278, 298
Copyrights, 192, 197
infringement of, 219–220
Cosby Show, The, 119
Counterprogramming, 122–123, 131
Country and western music, 145–146
Creating value, 11, 25
Creative
abrasion, 54
artists, 42
conflicts, 28, 30–32
control, 27–28, 30–32
role of contracts in, 33–34
decisions, 25
process, 28
resources, 9, 241, 278–279, 283–284, 293
systems, 290, 296–298
Creativity, 5–6, 18–19, 27
Credence goods, 290
Critics, 181, 256, 290, 296, 300
of corporate radio, 162
of deregulation, 155, 172
music, 58
television, 29
Crossing Jordan, 124
CSI, 125, 131
Cultural goods
defining, 17
Cultural imprinting, 199
Cultural industries, 4–5
control vs. autonomy in, 52–54
creating value in, 24
defining, 6–7, 17–19
mass production feature of, 27
reasons for studying, 8–10
rise of, 42
search for success in, 290–293
Cultural institutions, 58–60, 62
hybridized identity of, 67
question of identity in, 57
Cultural products, 5
value of, 23
Cultural spaces, 277, 281
Cultural tastes
between countries, 277
shifts in, 293
uniform, 276
Culture, 6
Australian, 268
business of, 5, 276, 289–290
exposure to, 280
monolithic, 283
and politics, 259
societal, 237
via the medium, 227
Culver City, 50

D

Decca, 208, 211
Decision making, 12, 137–138, 184–187, 266, 294
programmer, 171–172
reducing the risk of, 181
Demand analysis, 290, 295
de Mille, Cecil, B., 47
Depth of identification, 37
Deregulation, 155–156, 172, 174
Designing Women, 24–25, 28–38
origins of, 28–30
Dickson, W. K. L., 198
Differentiation, 180–181
Digital audiotape (DAT), 218–219
Digital Compact Cassette, 218
Digital media, 193, 228
Director unit system, 48, 50
Director's cut, 41
Dish, The, 265
Disney, 182–183, 202, 265, 275–276, 296–297
Distinctive identity, 228, 231, 234, 236–237, 268
Distribution, 9
Diversity,135–136, 138, 156, 168–170, 240, 277–278, 280, 282, 284, 296, 307
Division of labor, 243–244, 282, 284
Dominant
logic, 195
players, 195–196
Don Juan, 209
Donaldson, William, 142
Doubleday, 278
Dramaturgical approach, 17
Driving-markets approach, 272
Dyadic trust, 258

E

Economics
of cultural goods, 108

marketplace, 63
neoclassical, 206
of television production, 250
utilitarian, 59, 64
Economies of scale, 284
Ed Sullivan Show, The, 123
Edison, Thomas, 198–201
Electronic Arts, 81
Embedded depictions, 205–206
Emerging industries, 228–229
Emerging industry segments, 105–106
EMI, 215, 218
Entertainment, 6
Environmental
imprinting, 196
scanning, 196
E.R., 119
Essex County Newspapers, 114
Everybody Loves Raymond, 123–124
Evolutionary Scenarios, 242, 277, 281–284
Exhibitors, 47, 192, 200, 267, 270–272
Experience
economy, 9–10
goods, 290–291
Experts, 48, 173, 194, 290, 292, 300
music, 173

F

Familiarity, 19, 83, 161, 169, 243, 292
Fanning, Shawn, 219
Fear Factor, 131
Feature film, 47, 49, 200
Australian, 265
first, 46
rise and dominance of, 201–202
FEED, 115
Fees, 216
Festivals, 290, 301
Fight Club, 188
Film industry, 195, 294
American (from 1895 to 1920), 197–202
Australian, 241
evolution of, 192
executives, 180, 183
local, 263–264, 268, 271–272
poststudio era of, 53–54
Film previews, 45, 51
Financial risk, 42
Financing, 187, 267
private, 241, 265, 272
Fine, Mike, 149
First-order linkages, 245, 247, 257
First-order partners, 248
Fleishman, Debi, 146
Flexible specialization, 290, 296, 298
Florida Care Giver, 115
Folk music, 145–146
Foolish Wives, 49
Formal vs. informal power, 28
45-rpm disc, 215–216
Forum Shops, 9–10
Franchises, 180–181
Friends, 119
Funspot, 142

G

Genesis, 78
Genius of the system, 45
Genre groupings, 144
Globalization, 12–13, 240–242, 258, 276–277, 284, 306
in cultural industries, 277–280
impact of, 281
scenarios of, 281*t*
Goldman, William, 177–178
Government subsidization, 271
Great Train Robbery, The, 46
Greed, 49
Griffith, D. W., 47, 201

H

Hawkins, Trip, 79
Hayes, Wade, 146
Henson, Jim, 249
Hercules, 275
Hollywood
executives, 178–179, 185–186, 189
studios, 10, 42, 45–46, 178, 181, 188, 263, 265, 273, 279, 292
Holographic organizations, 59
Home Recording Act, 218
Homogenization, 13, 156, 172, 240, 280–283
“Hot 100”, 140, 146

Hub organizations, 244–248, 256
Hughes, Kevin, 151
Hugo, Victor, 275–276
Hunchback of Notre Dame, The, 275
Hybridized organizational identity, 26, 57–62
Hybrids, 59, 169, 280, 282, 284
Hypercompetition, 132

I

Identity, 12, 30 (*see also* Organizational identity)
  conflict, 57–59, 61–62, 66
  of show, 30, 34–38
  of writer, 30
Ideographic organizations, 59–60
Incumbent inertia, 197–199
Incumbents, 61, 85, 94, 100, 106, 195–197 (*see also* Video games *and* Web-based periodicals *and* Webzines)
  in film industry, 196
  inertia, 197–202
Independence Day, 188
Individual inspiration, 290, 296–298
Industry, 6–7
  evolution, 196
  macroculture, 196
  recipes, 292
  wisdom, 136, 181–182
Information
  ambiguous nature of, 179–184
  categorization, 229
Innovation, 18, 180–181
  need to balance, 19
Innovations
  in film technique and narrative, 47
Innovative products, 18
Institutional
  convergence, 207–208
  fields, 196
Institutionalist approach, 17
Intellectual development, 5
Intuitive insight, 137, 181–182
Investors, 231, 264–265, 270, 274
Israel–Palestine conflict, 241
Israel—Palestine joint venture with CTW, 250–256
Israelis, 240–241, 251–256, 258

J

Jackson, James, A., 142
Jackson, Peter, 4
Jaguar, 80–81
Jazz Singer, The, 209
Jesse L. Lasky Feature Film Company, 48
Judith of Bethulia, 47
Jukeboxes, 210–212

K

Kazaa, 219
King of Queens, The, 124
Knowledge
  acquired by motion picture executives, 178–179
  ambiguity, 179–184
  creation, 186–187
  explicit forms of, 184–185
  implicit, 188
  tacit, 179, 185, 189
    lack of, 186–187
Kuttab, Daoud, 251, 253–255, 257

L

L.A. Law, 119
Laemmle, Carl, 47–49, 200*tn*, 201
Las Vegas, 131
Law and Order, 124, 130
Lawsuits, 198, 220
Lead-in effect, 124, 127–128, 131
Levi, Yoel, 26, 64–66
Lion King, The, 183, 297
Litigation, 197, 197*t*, 198, 202
Little Mermaid, The, 275
Logics of action, 196, 199, 202
Lord of the Rings, The, 3–4
Lott, Senator Trent, 171
Lubin Company, 48

M

Magnetic-tape recording, 215
Managerial
  attention, 196
  hierarchies, 45–46
  lack of vision, 187–189

perspectives, 11
problems, 19
Market
activity, 148–149
atomized depictions in, 205–208, 221
contextual factors in, 206–207, 221
embedded depictions in, 205–206
attention, 150
categorization, 150–151
construction, 290, 295
demand, 11
demographics, 83, 156, 162, 165, 168–169
dominance, 202, 273
innovation, 151, 290, 295
psychology, 12
transformation, 205
trends, 179–180
Marketplace
ambiguous, 207–208
competitive, 264, 267
economics, 63
leader, 233
succeeding in, 291
Market Development Fund, 80
Market information regime, 136, 143–152
Mass production, 7, 27
Mayer, Louis, B., 47, 49, 51, 188
McCain, Senator John, 172
McCarthy, Senator Joseph, R., 145
Mercer, Johnny, 213
Mercury, 214, 217
Merry-Go-Round, 49
Merry Widow, The, 49
MGM, 25, 42, 47, 49–51, 53–54, 289
MGM (records), 214
Micro vs macro analysis, 15–16
Microsoft, 83–84, 86, 96, 99
Halo, 93
Xbox, 83–85, 94, 98
Middle East, 244, 265
childhood environment of, 257
peace in, 256
Sesame Street in, 250–252
Mike O'Malley, 127
Mobilizing resources, 279, 283
Moguls, 46–47
Motion picture industry, 8, 42, 119, 121, 132, 137–138, 177, 241, 279, 294, 300
ambiguous knowledge in, 186
developments within, 179, 185
executives, 178–179, 181, 185–186, 189–190
Motown, 217
MP3, 219
Mulitmedia technology, 109–110
Muppets, 249, 254
Muriel's Wedding, 265, 268
Music
chart, 136–137, 140, 143, 148
director, 58
at the symphony orchestra, 60–66
formats (managing), 157–158
industry, 136–137, 139, 143, 148, 195, 285
online, 220
programming, 156–158, 159*n*1, 160–162, 165, 169, 172–174
recorded, 156
videos, 218
Music Television (MTV), 217
"Must See TV," 119

N

Napster, 219
Narratives, 8, 50, 199–201
Neilson rating, 127–128
Network rents, 246
New
archival tradition, 17
media, 144, 174, 227–231, 233–234, 236–237
Newcomers, 195–196, 202
strategies of, 108–109
Nintendo, 77–81, 81*n*1, 82, 85–86, 93
Gameboy, 93
Gamecube, 83–85
Super Nintendo, 78
Nintendo 64, 82, 93, 98
Normative–utilitarian identity, 59–61, 63–64, 66
Notre-Dame de Paris, 275
NPD Funworld, 75

O

Odyssey game system, 76–77
128-bit systems, 82–85
Operation TNT, 215

Opportunism, 247, 255
Organization sets, 16–17
Organizational
  contracts, 33
  fields, 143, 148, 153, 305
  forms, 284, 290, 302
  identity, 37, 59, 67
  ideologies, 59–60, 64
  relationships, 28
  structures, 19, 58–59, 66, 306–307
Ownership concentration, 155–157, 162, 170–171, 173–174

P

Pairwise comparisons of webzines, 114
Palestinian Territories, 244
Palestinians, 240–241, 244, 251–256, 258
Parallelism, 35, 38
Patent rights, 192, 198, 200
  infringement, 198
  litigation over, 197
Payola, 171–173
Peer-to-peer systems, 219
Philips, 217–218
Pickford, Mary, 201
Picnic at Hanging Rock, 265
Planning, 182–183
Playlist(s), 158–159, 159*n*1, 161–162, 167–168, 170, 172–173
Polarity, 138, 179, 189, 294, 297–298
Pong, 77–78
Positioning of cultural products (*see also* Scheduling), 120–122
  competitive, 129
  concept of, 132
Postproduction, 43
Poststudio era, 46
Power, 28
  asymmetries, 35
  conflict, 31–32, 35
  dependencies, 28
  shifts, 27–28, 36
  struggles, 35–36
  symmetries, 35
Praise Bob, 114
Preproduction, 43
Prerecorded music market, 207
  broadcasting of, 211–214, 221
  developments in production of, 212–221
  digital copies in, 219–220
  dominance in, 208
  epochal shifts in, 207
  product conceptions in, 208
  superior advances in, 209–210
Prestudio era, 46
Principal photography, 43, 45
Priscilla, 268
Product differentiation, 290, 295, 298
Production, 43
  clusters, 281*t*, 290, 301–302
Professional boundaries, 231
Programming
  categories, 127
  homogenization, 156
  practices, 158, 160, 168–171, 173
  repertoires, 160–171
    analytical, 162–164
    collaborative, 166–168
    and music formats, 168–171
    populist, 164–166
    standardization, 162
    subjective, 160–162
    in the 21st century, 171–174
  selection criteria, 156, 158, 160
Project-based
  management, 267
  organizations, 43
Publishing industry, 106, 108–109
  incumbents in, 108
  linkages in, 109

Q

Queen of the Desert, 265

R

Rabbit-Proof Fence, 265
Radio airplay, 140, 158, 163, 167, 170, 173, 193, 221
  acceptance of, 212–214
  opposition to, 210–212
Radio Control Soaring, 114–115
Radio industry, 209
Radio programmers, 143, 157–158, 160
  autonomy of, 173
  as gatekeepers, 158
Radio station clusters, 156
Radio stations

contemporary commercial, 157–158
homogenization of programming on, 156
and promotional payments, 170
and record transformation, 170
and threat of corporate radio, 173
Rationalization, 152, 154
RCA Victor, 208, 210–211, 215
*Rechov Sumsum/**Shara'a Sumsum***, 241, 254
Recognizability, 19
Record
album, 209
business, 139
companies, 136–137, 140, 149, 157–173, 193, 292, 306
firms, 208–221
promoter, 151, 163, 167
sales, 148
Record-selection, 157, 160, 168
Recording
companies, 136–137, 149, 157–168, 170–173, 193, 292, 306
industry, 206
Red Queen effect, 300
Relational contracts, 34–35
Repository of knowledge, 196
Resource
endowments, 196
holders, 227–228, 231, 236
Rights
of authorship, 54
of ownership, 54
Rhythm and blues, 144–145
Rivalry, 196
Rough cut, 43, 45
Royalties, 79–80, 88, 95, 211, 215–216, 239, 256
Rules of competition, 196
Rushes, 43, 50–51

S

Scheduling (of television shows), 120–126
competitive positioning, 125–127
complimentary positioning, 124–125, 127
stable positioning, 123–124, 127
Schenck, Nick, 51
Script(s), 24 (*see also* Continuity scripts)
conferences, 25
as communication device, 29–30
development, 45
Search goods, 290
Second-order linkages, 245, 247, 258
Second-order relationships, 245–246
Sega, 77–81
Dreamcast, 82
Saturn, 81–82, 97
Seinfeld, 119, 123
Selznick, David, 51
Sequels, 181, 187
Sesame Street, 240–241, 244, 248–250, 254, 255*f*, 257
78 rpm discs, 208–209, 215
Shallet, Mike, 149
Shine, 265, 268
Simple rules, 184, 187
Situation comedy, 29
16-bit video game industry, 78–79, 81
U.S. sales of, 80*f*
64-bit system, 80
Small firm networks (SFNs), 243, 245, 259
Social interaction, 229–231
Sony, 86, 93, 218
Sony MiniDisc, 218
Sony Playstation, 81–82
PS2, 82–83, 94
SoundScan, 149
Standardized tastes, 280, 281*t*, 282
Star system, 46–47
Stein, Bruce, 81
Strategic organization, 42
Strategy
of counterprogramming, 125, 131
of positioning, 121, 132
of timing, 123
Strictly Ballroom, 265, 268
Structural-cultural analysis, 307–308
Structural
dynamics, 58, 62, 66
features, 16, 306
Structuralist approach, 16–17
Studio era, 44*f*, 46
Studio system, 45–46
disintegration of, 187
Subjective vs objective conceptions, 16–17
Success
first-time, 71
repeated, 72

Successful products, 11
Survivor, 125, 131
Symbolic products, 18
Symphony orchestra
  conflictual identity elements in, 57–58
  defined, 60
  hybrid identity of, 62
  musicians' strike at, 60
  role of music director, 60–66
  specialization of identities in, 61
  structure of, 60–61, 61*f*

T

Technology, 72–73
  adoption of, 206, 208
  changes in, 293, 307
  development of, 7
  diffusion, 206, 208, 214, 221
  firms, 195–197, 199, 201
  impact of, 299
  innovations in, 12
  and market transformation, 205–206
  modern, 301
  new, 7, 12, 206–207, 216, 242, 281*t*, 298
  role of, 290
Techno-rational industry logic, 158
Telecommunications Act of 1996, 155–156
Television
  broadcasting industry, 120
  networks, 122, 132
  programming, 122, 127
  series, 24, 28, 33
  shows, 30, 120–122, 130–132
    scheduling of, 122–126
Thalberg, Irving, 25, 42, 47–54
There's Something About Mary, 188
33 1/3 rpm disks, 209
33 1/3 rpm long-playing (LP) disc, 215–217
32-bit Playstation, 81
32-bit Saturn system, 81
32/64-bit systems, 79–82
  U.S. sales of, 80*f*
3DO Interactive Multiplayer, 79–80
Thriller, 216
Timing
  of new video game technology, 101
  of radio programs, 167
  of successful cultural products, 119–122
  of television programs, 120, 131–132
  of web-based publishing, 106
Titan A. E., 188
Titanic, 188
Tolkien, J. R. R., 3–4
"Top 100" singles chart, 139
Touched by an Angel, 126
Trade, 283
  barriers, 241
  charts, 158
  growth of, 277–278
  magazines, 158–159, 165
  publications, 31, 47, 136, 152–153
Transactional contracts, 28, 33–34
Transnational corporations, 243
Triadic networks, 246, 248, 248*f*, 256
Trust, 198, 200–202
trust, 243–245, 247–246, 258
Turbo Technologies' Duo, 79
Twentieth-Century Fox, 278

U

Ulitsa Sezam, 249
Uncertainty, 18–19, 97, 98*n*5, 105, 107, 158, 178, 182, 185, 189, 192, 207, 220, 229, 290, 293–294, 302
Uniformity, 277, 283
United Nations Educational and Social and Cultural Organization (UNESCO), 250
Universal Pictures, 42, 47–48, 50
URLs, 110
Utilitarian identity, 57–64, 66

V

Value, 11 (*see also* Creating value)
  of cultural products, 23
Value chain, 9
Values, 8, 16
Vaporware, 98
Variety, 212
Vertical integration, 46, 290, 296, 298
Victor Talking Music Machine, 210
Video game
  console producers, 87, 96–97

development strategies, 88*t*
industry, 72, 279
advertising in, 77, 84–86, 98–100
brand equity, 85, 99–100
competitive dimensions of, 85–89
complementary goods, 79, 82, 84, 87, 95–97, 99–100
credible commitments, 85, 99–100
generations of competition in, 101
history of, 76–85
incumbents in, 85, 94–100
leapfrogging, 83
licensing, 78–80, 84, 87–88, 95, 100
network externalities, 72, 75–76, 85, 94, 99–100
reputation, 85, 99–100
switching costs, 85, 94–95, 97
technological functionality of, 85
third party developers, 76, 78, 82, 84, 87–89, 93–94, 97, 100
systems, 75, 100
backward compatibility of, 83, 85, 95, 95*t*, 96
compatibility of, 75, 83
dominant design of, 98–99
installed base, 79, 81–85, 94–96, 98–100
platforms, 96–97, 100
pricing of, 95*t*
Video games
availability and quality of,
top selling, 89*t*–92*t*
Viewing habits, 123–124
Vitaphone, 209
Vivendi Universal, 218
Von Stroheim, Erich, 49

W

Waiting to Exhale, 188
Warner Communications, 217–218
Weavers, The, 145
Web-based periodicals, 110–111, 114–115
comparison between newcomers and incumbents, 113–115
emergence of, 106–108
strategies of incumbents and newcomers, 108–110
Webzines, 73, 106–111, 113–115
advertising in, 108–112, 114
content generating capabilities of, 111
as a cultural form, 107–108
incumbent producers of, 108–112
West Bank, 244, 251
Western Electric, 209
Wexler, Jerry, 144
Winner-take-all effect, 290, 300
Wolbrun, Dolly, 251

X

Xbox (*see* Microsoft Xbox)

Z

Zanuck, Darryl, 188
Zima Jie, 249

The Business of Culture

Strategic Perspectives on Entertainment and Media